CONTENTS

Foreword by Frederick B. Adams	9
Editor's Preface	11
NICOLAS BARKER: Anthony Robert Alwyn Hobson (written in 1991 for *The Book Collector*)	13
MANFRED VON ARNIM: Grolier bindings in the Otto Schäfer Library	21
GILES BARBER: From Baroque to Neoclassicism: French eighteenth-century bindings at Oxford	33
ELLY COCKX-INDESTEGE: On the history of bookbinding in the Low Countries: a glimpse of Prosper Verheyden and his correspondents, c. 1900-1947	65
GEORGES COLIN: Marques de libraires et d'éditeurs dorées sur des reliures	77
MIRJAM M. FOOT: 'Un grand Duc, immortel à la posterité': some bindings for Anne de Montmorency	117
LOTTE HELLINGA: Peter Schoeffer and the book-trade in Mainz: evidence for the organization	131
BENT JUEL-JENSEN: Three Ethiopic bindings	185
PICCARDA QUILICI: Legature del Piccolpasso e legature Viscontee nella Biblioteca Ambrosiana di Milano	193
DENNIS E. RHODES: Some English, Scottish, Welsh and Irish book-collectors in Italy, 1465-1800	247
DAVID J. SHAW: Books belonging to William Warham, Archdeacon of Canterbury, c. 1504-1532	277
JAN STORM VAN LEEUWEN: Some observations on Dutch publishers' bindings up till 1800	287
JEANNE VEYRIN-FORRER: Notes sur Thomas Mahieu	321
Bibliography of A.R.A. Hobson (to the end of July 1993)	351
Tabula Gratulatoria	364

BOOKBINDINGS AND OTHER BIBLIOPHILY

Anthony R. A. Hobson

BOOKBINDINGS
&
OTHER BIBLIOPHILY

Essays in honour of
ANTHONY HOBSON
edited by Dennis E. Rhodes
Foreword by Frederick B. Adams

EDIZIONI VALDONEGA · VERONA

All rights reserved. No part of this book may be used or reproduced in any manner whatsoever without written permission, except in the case of brief quotations embodied in critical articles and reviews.

© Edizioni Valdonega, Verona · Printed in Italy
ISBN 88-85033-26-1

DISTRIBUTION

North and South America: OAK KNOLL BOOKS, fax 302-328 7274
414 Delaware Street, New Castle, DE 19720

Great Britain: THE BRITISH LIBRARY, fax 071-323 7768
41 Russell Square, London WC1B 3DG

France, Belgium, Luxembourg: LIBRERIE GIRAUD BADIN, fax 0031-4284 0587
22 Rue Guynemer, 75006 Paris

all other countries: EDIZIONI VALDONEGA, fax 003945-834 8876
Via Marsala 71, 37128 Verona, Italy

FOREWORD

It is uncommon, to say the least, for the son of an expert in a certain discipline to follow in his father's footsteps and to succeed with equal brilliance in the same discipline. G. D. Hobson was renowned during the first half of our century for his researches into the history of bookbindings, binders, and their patrons. Now in the second half it is his son Anthony who has made brilliant discoveries in the same field.

His prowess has already been recognized by a special issue of *The Book Collector* compiled in his honour, and I would regard as essential to an appreciation of the man the introductory memoir by Anthony's close friend and fellow biblio-scientist, Nicolas Barker. There he is revealed not only as an auctioneer and scholar, but as a prominent public figure in the book world, with many awards and responsibilities, and also as a collector, connoisseur, paterfamilias, linguist, and seemingly indefatigable traveller (mostly in his own automobile), witness his 1970 *Great Libraries*, published also in French and German.

On his father's death early in 1949, Anthony, then only 27, but mature and knowledgeable beyond his years, became head of Sotheby's book department. Earlier G. D. had produced for Major Abbey a catalogue of his *English Bindings 1490-1940*. Now the collector, desiring to present a second catalogue to his fellow members of the Roxburghe Club, turned to Anthony to compile *French and Italian Collectors and their Bindings*, which appeared in 1953, and has since soared to unpredictable heights in the reference book market. This catalogue was my eminently favourable introduction to Anthony the scholar. Anthony the respected friend had to wait until 1965, which was marked by the Fourth Congress of the Association Internationale de Bibliophilie, which he organized in London, and by the first sale at Sotheby's of a part of Major Abbey's collection of bindings, including a large number not previously catalogued. I attended this sale, with successful results for the Morgan Library.

The Bibliography, which is so usefully included in the present volume, does not list the valuable catalogue of this sale, which was written by Anthony, nor any other of his Sotheby sale catalogues of bookbindings and medieval and Renaissance manuscripts. Essential reference works though they have become, they are omitted at the express request of their author, who regards them as professional work in the line of duty and not as personal writing.

Anthony, who inherited his father's "archive", has never failed to pay due respect to the parental achievements. He edited G. D.'s notes on German Renaissance Patrons of Bookbinding; he added to and corrected

Les Reliures à la Fanfare, which was originally published in 1935; he majestically solved once and for all the ownership problem of the "Canevari" Apollo and Pegasus medallion bindings, first discussed and listed in G. D.'s *Maioli, Canevari and others*; and in his latest and most complex study to date, *Humanists and Bookbinders*, 1989, he reverts to a subject of great interest to G. D., in providing a census of historiated plaquette and medallion bindings of the Renaissance.

As the Bibliography demonstrates, Anthony has reviewed most of the significant books on bookbinding produced in the past forty years. But his reviews and occasional articles have not been limited to his chosen subject; they range over contemporary authors, great houses of Europe, the city and cathedral of Salisbury, notable booksellers, and biographical sketches for the D.N.B. Which only goes to show that he is a humanist of his own century.

After serving for seventeen years on its Council, Anthony succeeded me in 1985 as President of the Association internationale de Bibliophilie. This is far from being a simply honorary post, as the organisation holds a Congress every two years in a host country, and a colloquium or mini-congress in the intermediate years. These require careful planning, diplomacy, patience, and conviviality. In all of this he could have been warmly seconded by his lovable wife Tanya, whose premature death in 1988 was a sad blow. He has nevertheless carried on, with the consistent help of the Executive Secretary, Antoine Coron.

At the close of his review of Dr. Malaguzzi's excellent study of eighteenth century binding activity in Piedmont, Anthony saluted the author of "this exemplary work with fellow feeling and admiration." These words could express the sentiments of the contributors to this festschrift, so conscientiously and selflessly edited by Dennis Rhodes, to whom we are all grateful.

Chisseaux (Indre et Loire)　　　　　　　　　　FREDERICK B. ADAMS
October 1993

EDITOR'S PREFACE

At the end of his introduction to the special number of *The Book Collector* in honour of Anthony Hobson's seventieth birthday (Autumn 1991, p. 314), Nicolas Barker wrote: "A more extended tribute, in which articles by other friends will be printed together with these, is being edited by Dennis Rhodes, who is compiling a bibliography of his [Hobson's] writings".

For various reasons it has been decided not to reprint in the present volume those articles which appeared in *The Book Collector*, with the sole exception of the short piece by Manfred von Arnim, which now contains a number of corrections and has been brought up to date where necessary. The other articles published here are therefore all new; and while they do not comprise in number as many as I had originally hoped for, several of them are of considerable length, and make a substantial contribution to our knowledge of their particular aspects of bibliographical history.

I have tried to choose a title for the book which will emphasize that while the history of bookbinding is the principal branch of bibliography in which Anthony Hobson has specialized over the years, it is by no means in bookbinding alone that he is interested and on which he has written with authority. If the majority of the essays in this volume deal with aspects of bookbinding history, there are also some others which reflect Anthony's deep concern for private book-collectors, the history of great libraries, and questions of provenance, as well as the identification of printers and publishers. In all these subjects he has made, and continues to make, many notable discoveries.

Anthony Hobson is a splendid example of the all-round bibliographer, well travelled and conversant with several languages. As the *Book Collector* pointed out, he has won distinguished honours on both sides of the Atlantic, two of the most recent being his Senior Fellowship of the British Academy and the Gold Medal of the Bibliographical Society of London.

All those concerned in the writing and production of this book hope that Anthony will enjoy it, and even learn something new from it. The editor has no doubts that the contents will live up to the very high standards that Anthony would expect of them; and the editor is also particularly delighted that the volume has found as its publisher Mr Mardersteig, at Verona, which is at the same time one of the editor's own favourite cities, and (more importantly) the city in which Anthony Hobson himself won the Felice Feliciano prize for his book *Humanists and*

Bookbinders in 1991. It was for the eightieth birthday on 8 January 1972 of the most distinguished printer in Europe, the late Giovanni (Hans) Mardersteig, that Nicolas Barker selected, and Will and Sebastian Carter printed at the Rampant Lions Press, that enchanting anthology of English writing *In Fair Verona. English travellers in Italy and their accounts of the city from the Middle Ages to modern times*. One might almost say that the compliment is here returned as Martino, son of Giovanni, publishes this Festschrift in celebration of a fine English scholar. For this we are all indeed most grateful.

One of Anthony Hobson's most demanding activities of recent years has been his influential participation in the events of the Association Internationale de Bibliophilie, which has necessitated much foreign travel and brought him into contact, indeed into friendship, with many booklovers in many countries. I trust that this 'spirit of international bibliophily' (if I may call it so) is amply reflected in the diverse nationalities of the contributors to this volume as well as in the Tabula Gratulatoria which is printed at the end.

London, July 1993

DENNIS E. RHODES

Nicolas Barker

ANTHONY ROBERT ALWYN HOBSON
(written in 1991 for *The Book Collector*)

On 5 September this year Anthony Hobson will be seventy. This takes some believing, on at least two counts: first, he does not look it – his spare figure, upright military bearing and hair only recently touched with grey suggest at least twenty years less; more seriously, the passage of time seems not so much implausible as irrelevant in a career which, if distinguished in many individual ways, is part of still longer traditions. He is essentially a traditionalist. In an age when forenames predominate, he prefers the older custom of initials: 'A. R. A.' is very much the son of 'G. D.'. But like all traditionalists he is alive not merely to the past, which is so vivid to him and to which he gives a new vitality by his own sense of communion with it; he sees the present also with a clarity heightened by a sense for the roots from which it has sprung; the same clarity infuses his vision of the future, whose needs are never by him forgotten.

An important part of all this is family tradition. Geoffrey Hobson was the major partner in Sotheby's and the author of those splendidly printed and still valuable books on the history of bookbinding. Anthony would be the first to acknowledge the debt he owes to the example of his father, an independent but commanding figure at Sotheby's, and a scholar who was one of the first to look beyond the outside of decorative bookbindings, and to consider and compare all the other processes involved in binding a book, and also the sources, in other branches of the decorative arts, from which their decoration was drawn. Geoffrey married late, after the war, and was 39 when Anthony was born at Rhyl, while his parents were staying in North Wales, where his maternal grandfather had been Rector of Rhuddlan. He grew up in his father's lovely house at 1 Bedford Square, but when he was 12, the BM intemperately commandeered the back gardens on the east side of the square to build the Duveen Gallery. The Hobsons moved reluctantly to a new house, 11 Chelsea Park Gardens.

Anthony's school days were spent at Eton, where he was an Oppidan Scholar. They passed without major incident, except that he was able to penetrate to College Library, then only open for one hour on Sundays, under the grudging supervision of the Provost, Henry Marten. Anthony's principal interest was medieval manuscripts, and he asked to see the Eton Apocalypse, and see it he did. Provost Marten held it open (at one opening only) as far away from him as he could.

Holidays added other gifts and tastes. Many visits to France and Switzerland gave him fluent French and made him an expert skier. He also went to Austria, Germany and Italy: his father liked to take a cure and his mother was not well, so the choice of place was determined by this, hence an early familiarity with Carlsbad. His last year at Eton was clouded by his mother's illness and death in November 1938. In the following summer he persuaded his father to come with him on a long holiday to the Dalmatian coast, and as far inland as Sarajevo. This was the last of his continental explorations. On 3 September war was declared and in January 1940 Anthony went up to New College, where he read Modern Languages, in particular French literature. After only four terms, he took his war-shortened B.A. and joined up on 6 June 1941.

He went first to Sandhurst, from which he was posted with an emergency commission to the Scots Guards. The next two years were spent in England, mainly with the 4th Battalion and at the Intelligence School, Matlock; in November 1943 he was posted abroad to the 2nd Battalion, and promoted captain. He landed at Naples and served throughout the Italian campaign with 201 and 24 Guards Brigades, and lastly 6 Armoured Division; he was mentioned in despatches. After the end of the war he became G.S.O. III (Intelligence) with 6 Armoured Division, and was not released until October 1946. Sotheby's beckoned, but he demanded a year off to travel and make up for what he had missed through the war. He went back to Italy, to Greece and Turkey, to Spain and Portugal. He came back with a wide experience of the monuments, the art and architecture of the Mediterranean; and he had added fluent Italian and some Spanish to already excellent French and respectable German.

It was, then, in September 1947 that Anthony joined Sotheby's. Although the firm itself had survived the war unscathed, he found his father, on whom, with Felix Warre, the burden of keeping it going had fallen, worn out. He had hoped to retire before the war, but it was not to be. He remained to superintend the Landau-Finaly sale in 1948, achieved in the teeth of the Board of Trade restrictions on the import (as well as export) of works of art. On 4 January 1949 he died, aged 66, to be succeeded as chairman and head of the book department by Charles des Graz. Owing to the elder Hobson's deafness, he had never been able to take a sale as auctioneer. Des Graz fulfilled this role with rare distinction. As Tim Munby wrote in THE BOOK COLLECTOR, he had no rival. 'The real test of this most exacting of roles is not in the selling of works of the very first importance. Long practice had made des Graz perfect in the more difficult art of selling secondary material fast without missing a bid.'

If, then, Anthony had had the ideal mentor in his father in scholarship, in cataloguing and all the interior business of Sotheby's, des Graz was the perfect model of the outward face of the business, to which Anthony now succeeded. To a schoolboy wandering into the saleroom soon afterwards, he seemed to have a self-assurance and authority beyond his years. He looked older than he was, as he now looks younger. Those were more relaxed days in the sale-room: there were fewer bidders, most of whom knew each other; the auctioneer had to cope with a continuous low buzz of conversation and the occasional interjection of criticism or joke out loud. If Anthony felt any uncertainty, it did not show. When des Graz died untimely in March 1953, he inherited his mantle and something of his manner. He saw to it that the double loss of two such senior figures to what had always been Sotheby's main department was at least outwardly invisible.

Both Geoffrey Hobson and des Graz had maintained the view that London was the international centre of the market for all works of art, besides books, and Sotheby's the best venue for it. This view was now put to the test not just of the Board of Trade's regulations but of the staggering superfluity of ex-King Farouk's collections, released on the market in 1953. Anthony was among those who went out to Egypt to negotiate sales, which inevitably spread beyond Sotheby's then resources.

This highlighted the need for an active presence in America, and in 1955 John Carter joined Sotheby's; he was the ideal choice, after his years with Scribner's and latterly the British Embassy at Washington. Sotheby's, with territorial expansion in and around Bond Street far in the future, was cramped for space, and for many years Anthony and Jake shared adjacent offices, an arrangement which (rather to their surprise) worked remarkably well. The book-rooms over which Anthony presided with Patch at the desk and Frank and Jock in attendance worked with quiet efficiency. Week in, week out, books came and went. Occasionally, there were excitements, such as the sales of Richard Jennings and C. H. Wilkinson, but it was the three Dyson Perrins sales of medieval manuscripts in 1958-60 that projected the book department (and the price of books generally) into the spotlight of big money and publicity. Other sales, notably those from the Tollemache and Brudenell collections, followed, but yet another new era opened with the release of the Phillipps collection in 1965.

By now Anthony knew all there was to know about the sale of such material, and such was his authority that the Robinson brothers, no mean judges of the market, were disconcerted to find that they had almost a back seat. Anthony swiftly set up the annual pre-Christmas sales of medieval manuscripts, alternating with those of more modern manuscripts. He had catalogued the Dyson Perrins manuscripts himself, but for the vast uncharted mass of Phillipps manuscripts he needed help; Andreas

Mayor, an old acquaintance, and formerly a bored Assistant Keeper at the British Museum Department of Manuscripts, came to help. Already, in 1965, Lord John Kerr had joined Sotheby's from Sanders of Oxford to share the burden of auctioneering, and then to take over the day-to-day running of the department. H. A. Feisenberger, with long experience of the book trade from the other side, provided expertise in continental books, especially those on the history of science. With three reliable and congenial colleagues, Anthony could see the book department in good hands. Besides the Phillipps manuscripts, the scientific books of C. E. Kenney, the fine bindings and manuscripts of his father's old friend and his own, Major Abbey, a last clearance from Britwell Court, the Chester Beatty manuscripts, the duplicates from the Pierpont Morgan Library (a presage of the future), came and went. Halcyon years they were, both for collectors and the trade.

Anthony was now able to detach himself a little from the business that had demanded his attention since 1953. He had also become disenchanted with the new and predatory direction of Sotheby's. The acquisition of Hodgson's had its logic, but the acquisition of Parke Bernet and expansion overseas cut at the principle of maintaining London as the world centre of the art-market. The *émeute* over the 'Sotheby' cigarette, though short-lived, was a further divisive factor. Anthony gave up his directorship in 1971, but remained responsible for the continuing Phillipps sales. He slipped away after the last sale in the summer of 1977, and in 1978 H. P. Kraus purchased the rest of the collection. But the long family link has not been broken, since he has been consultant to the Book Department since 1985.

But if Sotheby's held the foreground of his life for a quarter of a century, it was never to the exclusion of other, more personal, business. He was an early contributor to THE BOOK COLLECTOR, with notable articles on the Pillone Library, that at Waddesdon Manor, and (with Tim Munby) a portrait of Major Abbey in the 'Contemporary Collectors' series. *French and Italian Collectors and their Bindings*, which came out in 1953, presented by Major Abbey to the Roxburghe Club and based on books in his collection, was a work of astonishing maturity for one just turned 30. It revealed a familiarity not merely with the subject matter, but also with many related books, as well as a great wealth of bibliographic and historic references. The introduction, written in spare but elegant prose, was at pains not only to list and describe the bindings, but to set them against the general history of their time, the characters and careers of the principal commissioners of fine bindings, and, generally, to organize the topic of the book into a notable piece of cultural history. All these gifts, so early displayed, have characterized all his subsequent work. He would be the first to acknowledge the debt that he owed to the example of his father, and the hereditary possession of a large and comprehensive library on the history of bookbinding. All this may explain his early maturity, but he brought to the subject talents and ideas of his own.

French and Italian Collectors and their Bindings, if revolutionary in approach, was in other respects a conventional book. That is to say, it used a series of examples as a peg on which to hang a study of similar examples of work by the same binders all done for the same collectors. The introduction, however, is not so restricted, but deals with collectors and bookbindings not represented in the Abbey collection. The appendices, similarly, are used to provide valuable lists of the work of different workshops (a practice inherited from his father). If it has a fault, it is rather too great a degree of certainty; for example, Anthony has come to swallow the doubts, forcefully expressed, about the early date of gold-tooled European bindings. But, these trifles apart, it is amazing how substantial the body of work that he published is, and how well it has stood up to the passage of the intervening years.

Great Libraries (1970) was superficially a coffee table book, a collection of illustrations with a linking text which, it might be thought, had no other purpose than to fill the gaps between the pictures. This however would not be an altogether fair assessment. In the first place, there is no adequate history of libraries, and the text is no mere compilation, but the product of wide reading and, much more important, personal exploration on the site. The illustrations, thus, are not merely a collection of pretty pictures, but exceptionally well chosen to display not only the exterior, but the interior fittings and decor of libraries, as well as some of their principal treasures. This makes it an invaluable companion to Masson's *Le Décor des Bibliothèques* (1972), and, when someone gets down to the task of writing the history of libraries, the visual images here will be of considerable value, and the text far from negligible.

A very considerable intellectual divide separates *Great Libraries* from *Apollo and Pegasus* (1975). In the latter, Anthony established an individual style, a type of book, it may be called, that is uniquely his. Again, his starting point was one of his father's books, *Maioli, Canevari and Others* (1926). In essence, his study consists of a re-attribution of the patronage and execution of a group of very beautiful Roman bindings executed in the sixteenth century with a distinctive plaquette of Apollo and Pegasus. Probably more speculative nonsense has been written about this particular group of bindings than any other. It was his primary achievement to have discovered who the original owner was (a figure unknown to previous students of the subject), and to identify the three binders whom he employed. His approach was at once novel and traditional. In the first place, he studied the device, and its literary and iconographic relations. This led him to study the personality of Claudio Tolomei and his works, from which he derived the literary evidence for a collection of books produced by Tolomei for a Genoese, a wealthy young man called Giovanni Battista Grimaldi. The equation of Grimaldi as the owner of the bindings was convincing, and his further work, the identification of the three binders, was based on equally convincing research in the Roman archives. However, all this was backed by careful, and by now very experienced, comparison of the actual books, with lists of all the work attributable to the three binders, whether for Grimaldi or others. The whole story was effectively set against a background of the literary and economic revival in Rome after the Sack in 1527, and a thorough familiarity with the booktrade there, printers and booksellers as well as bookbinders. The study concluded with an account of the dispersal of the library, which brought it down to the year 1861, when the mythistory, with which the book began, commenced. A long series of appendices enlarge the literary context and reinforce the archaeological evidence for the attribution. The whole book, like any original piece of research, makes a very good detective story.

Humanists and Bookbinders (1989) followed a very similar formula. The starting point was a subject touched on in his first book, the origin of gold-stamped bookbinding in Europe. However, his approach to the subject was not limited, like the Apollo and Pegasus bindings, to a particular group of books, united by common patronage or craftsmen. Instead, he sought to demonstrate that bookbindings, like script and decoration, was an integral part of the presentation of a text, in this case the texts of the new humanist movement in Italy. These were traced back to their sources, both Islamic and Classical, and forward to their spread outside Italy, notably France. The book concluded with a new assessment of the authorship of the bindings for the Royal Library at Fontainebleau. Once again, on an even more magisterial scale, the surviving bindings were listed and grouped; a large part of the book is devoted to what must be a definitive list of plaquettes (again a subject that had first caught the attention of G. D. Hobson). Once again, too, the bindings were grouped not merely on the basis of comparable tools or designs but a much wider concatenation of texts and scribes and early owners. The picture thus built up was both generous and original, an unfamiliar but convincing view of the first century of humanism. It can, without exaggeration, be called a contribution to cultural history. Perhaps its most impressive achievement was the relationship of the decorative equipment and style of bookbinders to the ornamental sources from which it came and uses to which similar ornamental motifs were put in other branches of the decorative arts. As noted elsewhere, it was properly awarded the Premio Felice Feliciano in the spring of this year.

All these, reviews and articles in this journal, *The Library, T. L. S.* and elsewhere, make up a formidable and distinguished body of work. Over the years, Anthony has been able to indulge his genius to the very considerable benefit not only of others learned in the history of bookbinding, but of a much larger constituency of those whose field lies in the history of humanism. The captious might call this self-indulgence, but Anthony is too good a disciplinarian to allow himself to escape the rigorous interrogation of sources and conclusions that he applies to others. It is true that he has always preferred only to write about subjects which he likes, and he has been enviably lucky in having the means to do so, and the good taste that has led him among so many beautiful books, such various and delightful libraries.

But besides the auctioneer and the scholar, there are other aspects of Anthony's life and work that require celebration. First, there is the public figure. Anthony has been Sandars Reader in Bibliography at the University of Cambridge, and Lyell Reader at Oxford; Walls Lecturer and Honorary Fellow of the Pierpont Morgan Library; Rosenbach Fellow, University of Pennsylvania; and a Visiting Fellow of All Souls College, Oxford. He has been President of the Bibliographical Society, and is Honorary President of the Edinburgh Bibliographical Society. He has been a Trustee of the Eton College Collections Trust and of Lambeth Palace Library. He has been a member of the Conseil of the Association Internationale de Bibliophilie since 1968, and its hardworking and deservedly popular President since 1985. His long connections with and affection for Italy has been properly recognized in his appointment as Cavaliere Ufficiale Al Merito della Repubblica Italiana, and he is also a Foreign Associate of the Ateneo Veneto. All this represents honour, and honour properly bestowed; it also represents a lot of time and energy, freely given and without thought of return.

Then there is the collector. Anthony, no doubt, would modestly deny himself this title, impeded as he has been by the belief that gamekeepers make bad poachers. But within his self-imposed limitations he has been a discerning and far-sighted amasser of things not always highly valued today. The collection of seventeenth- and eighteenth-century illustrated books has been dispersed now, but it was begun at a time when such things were unfashionable. If you collect modern literature, you have to be not so much rich as adroit in catching what you want before it reaches the waste-paper basket; posterity will live to be grateful for what Anthony has rescued from our own time. In both fields, he has shown a tenacity as well as discrimination worthy of the greatest collectors of the past.

Then there is Anthony in his family, a subject still tender. Like his father, he married late in life, but, like a good *spätlese*, marriage when it came had an uncloyed sweetness. No one who knew Tanya could fail to recognize the qualities that a usually acid critic of human nature saw in the wife of another great book man: 'she was beautiful in face and mind, and never wearied of doing acts of kindness'. So Vicary Gibbs wrote of Margaret, wife of the 25th Earl of Crawford. It was equally true of Tanya, and her death in 1988 was loss to us all, but how much more to Anthony. Happy may he be, nonetheless, in their family, a son and daughters who know and share their father's tastes and sympathies.

We have left till last Anthony the traveller. Anthony is a great traveller: that is, he enjoys visiting strange and new places, takes the pleasures and perils, the excitement and *longueurs* of travel in his stride, and is a resourceful and energetic enjoyer of what he finds en route and when he arrives at his destination. 'Travel, opera, and visiting libraries founded before 1800' are his listed recreations. All of them involve travel, and those who have been lucky enough to go with him on such excursions know that not merely the object, but the incidents of the voyage, will be enhanced by his expertise and enjoyment.

Looking back over a life of such variety and achievement, we can see it all as a journey, a pilgrimage in space and time, in the mind as well as on foot or wheels. In peace or war, Anthony has brought his courage and learning to bear on whatever has come his way. There is no compromise, no going the long way round to avoid confrontation: difficulties have been met head on, and usually vanquished. Yet his is no conventional success story, although his life has been a success by all normal standards. There is, in all this, a stronger sense of commitment and loyalty: to faith, to institutions and, of course, to books and libraries and the long paths and landscapes to which they are the door. To the committed, integrity is all-important. It is a quality that Anthony values in others; his own colours are nailed to the mast. We can only admire this, as we admire the more tangible achievements of a life which has given us so much, and which (we hope and trust) will give us so much more.

MANFRED VON ARNIM

GROLIER BINDINGS IN THE OTTO SCHÄFER LIBRARY

In March 1961 the Schweinfurt bibliophile Otto Schäfer had first choice amongst the seven Grolier bindings from the collection of Maître Loncle[1] and decided to buy four of them. Three years later – and also via H. P. Kraus – came the CASTIGLIONE of 1528 from the Langlois collection,[2] one of the favourite books of Jean Grolier. Not only did he hold five further copies of the *editio princeps*, but also five copies of the 1533 edition (not to speak of the manuscript now in the Laurenziana).

So far as Grolier bindings are concerned all of a sudden Otto Schäfer's library had become the richest in Germany. It still is, on the razor's edge though: Gabriel Austin's census of 1971[3] gives only one specimen for the *Niedersächsische Staats- und Universitätsbibliothek* in Göttingen, but in the meantime three more Groliers have turned up there.[4]

The most distinguished of Mr Schäfer's Groliers is the CRINITUS (see no. III, below), bound by Nixon's "Cupid's Bow" binder and reproduced in *The Book Collector* in 1960.[5] Its front cover has the author's name and the title tooled on a circular onlay of red morocco. Nixon called it "a fine and characteristic example" of the Cupid's bow group.[6]

The four other books were bound by Grolier's "main binder" (recte: binders) of the years after 1538. For a long time this was believed to have been Claude de Picques, allegedly the royal binder of Henry II. But recent research by Mme Annie Charon in Paris archives, her and Anthony Hobsons's deductions,[7] revealed two workshops as the true binders: one was that of Jean Picard, *marchand libraire*, and Aldus' representative in

---

1. ARTHUR RAU, *Maurice Loncle* (= Contemporary Collectors XXIII), in *The Book Collector* 9, no 1 (Spring 1960), pp. 38-44.
2. ARTHUR RAU, *André Langlois* (= Contemporary Collectors XIII), in *The Book Collector* 6, no 2 (Summer 1957), pp. 129-43.
3. GABRIEL AUSTIN, *The Library of Jean Grolier. A Preliminary Catalogue* (New York, 1971). – Supplement: G. AUSTIN, *The Library of Jean Grolier: a Few Additions*, in *Festschrift Otto Schäfer zum 75. Geburtstag am 29. Juni 1987* (Stuttgart, 1987), pp. 437-50.
4. REIMER ECK, *Vier Grolier-Einbände in Göttingen*, in *Imprimatur*, N. F. 12 (1987), pp. 195-208: no. II-IV (no. II = Austin, *op. cit.*, no. 233).
5. A. RAU, *Maurice Loncle* (op. cit.), pl. VI; cf. also p. 40: 'outstanding'.
6. HOWARD M. NIXON, *Grolier's Binders. Notes on the Paris Exhibition* (cf. note 8), in *The Book Collector* (9, 1960, nos. 1 and 2, pp. 45-51 and 165-70), pp. 167-8.
7. ANTHONY R.A. HOBSON, *Humanists and Bookbinders* (Cambridge, 1989), Appendix 7: *Jean Grolier's binders*, pp. 267-71.

Paris from 1540 until 1547. He bound our numbers I, II and IV, and stamped them with solid tools only (I, IV), or also with open tools (no. II). When Picard fled in September 1547, his successor as Aldus' representative and as bookbinder became a Gommar Estienne, who first had to bind Henry II's library in Fontainebleau. So only from 1552 onwards could he work for other bibliophiles, such as Jean Grolier (vide our no. V, stamped with hatched tools).

All Groliers now in the Otto Schäfer Library had been exhibited in 1959 in the *Bibliothèque nationale*, but none of them was reproduced in the catalogue.[1]

The CRINITUS (no. III) was reproduced in 1960 (see above).

When the Grolier Club of New York on its *Iter Germanico-Helveticum* 1970 visited the collection of Mr Otto Schäfer in Schweinfurt[2] all its Groliers were on display and the LUCRETIUS (no. IV) was even reproduced on the covers of the small catalogue,[3] printed in 250 copies only.

Of the remaining three Groliers now in Schweinfurt only the CATULLUS (no. II) has ever been reproduced, – albeit in the Lignerolles album of 1894, also not in reach of too many.

Therefore, the *Festschrift* for Anthony Hobson seemed to be the most proper place to describe and reproduce all together the five Groliers in the Otto Schäfer Library.[4]

The order of descriptions is alphabetical, arranged by author. The technical descriptions of the bindings try to follow the style of H. Nixon's London catalogue,[5] also the numbering of tools is taken from there. As for the provenances I almost fully relied on Gabriel Austin's painstaking monograph[6] (but they are given in a slightly different way here, such as handwritten names and notes printed in italics, dealers' names not in italics).

---

1. *Exposition de La Société de la Reliure Originale, accompagnée d'une présentation de reliures ayant appartenu à Jean Grolier* (Paris: Bibliothèque nationale, 1959).

2. ROBERT NIKIRK, *The Grolier Club Iter Germanico-Helveticum* (New York, 1973), pp. 71-88.

3. MANFRED V. ARNIM / ADALBERT LAUTER, *A Selection of Illuminated Manuscripts, Printed Books, and Bindings in The Otto Schäfer Collection Schweinfurt. Exhibited on the Occasion of the Visit of The Grolier Club of New York, 29 May 1970.* – Out of print.

4. Since the first appearance of this essay in *The Book Collector* in 1991 all five bindings have been dealt with in *Europäische Einbandkunst* (see note 5, p. 23). The few corrections there were taken into account for this second edition of the essay.

5. HOWARD M. NIXON. *Bookbindings from the Library of Jean Grolier. A Loan Exhibition, 23 September-31 October 1965.* London, British Museum. To the description of Grolier bindings in Schweinfurt remarks on the state of edges and endpapers have been added (following the kind advice of Gabriel Austin).

6. See note 3, p. 33.

1. CASTIGLIONE, Baldassare. *Il Cortegiano*. Venice: Aldo & Andrea d'Asola, April 1528. 2°. – Initials in gold; Aldine anchors in blue, silver and gold. (Fig. 1)
Olive brown morocco (322:210:24 mm), gold-tooled. Within frames of gold and blind lines a complex mainly rectangular interlace forms three horizontal circles with strapwork above and below. Solid tool C. de P. 10. Title and ownership inscription on upper cover; motto on lower. Original back, six raised bands; empty panels outlined by a single gold line. Turn-ins and edges of boards with single gold line. Standard Grolier end-leaves at each end: vellum paste-down – two conjugate paper leaves – free vellum leaf conjugate with paste-down – two conjugate paper leaves.
Provenance: [ ]. – *Ex libris* [Jean-Puget de] *La Serre* [1600-1665]. – [ ]. – *Blanien*. – [ ]. – Ex libris André Langlois [Paris; cf. A. Rau, *André Langlois*,[1] p. 131]. – [Arthur Rau, Paris]. – *H. P. K*[raus] *1/64*; sold to Otto Schäfer in 1964 (shelf mark: OS 350).
Austin[2] 89,1; BN[3] 73; Schweinfurt[4] 174; Arnim[5] 36. Not in Le Roux de Lincy[6] and Shipman.[7]

2. CATULLUS, Caius Valerius / Albius TIBULLUS / Sextus PROPERTIUS. / [*Opera*]. Edited by H. Avantius. Venice: in aedibus Aldi et Andreæ soceri, March 1515. 8°. – Initials in gold; Aldine anchors in blue, silver and gold. (Fig. 2)
Dark brown morocco (173:103:23 mm), gold-tooled; hexagram, in middle of rectangular panel and of solid and open tools C. de P. 1, 2, 3, 8*a* & *b*, 11, 16, 41*a* & *b*. Title and ownership inscription on upper cover, motto on lower. Original back, five raised bands; panels outlined by gold line and each filled with a single impression of tool C. de P. 12**. Turn-ins, edges of boards, and standard Grolier end-leaves as on the CASTIGLIONE (no. 1).
Provenance: [16th century owner with his Latin notes on second fly leaf and p. 41]. – [Guglielmo Libri; sale: Paris, 28 June 1847, 315 (935 ffr)].

1. See note 2, p. 21.
2. See note 3, p. 21.
3. See note 1, p. 22.
4. See note 3, p. 22.
5. Manfred v. Arnim, *Europäische Einbandkunst aus sechs Jahrunderten. [219] Beispiele aus der Bibliothek Otto Schäfer*. Schweinfurt 1992.
6. Adrien-Jean-Vincent Le Roux de Lincy, *Recherches sur Jean Grolier, sur sa vie et sa bibliothèque* (Paris, 1866).
7. Carolyn Shipman, *Researches concerning Jean Grolier, his life and his library with a partial catalogue of his books by A. J. V. Le Roux de Lincy*. Edited by Baron Roger Portalis. Translated and revised by Carolyn Shipman (New York, 1907).

Fig. 1. Castiglione. *Il Cortegiano*. Venice 1528. 2°. 322:210 mm.
Front cover

Fig. 2. Catullus et alii. [*Opera*]. Venice 1515. 8°. 173:103 mm.
Back cover

Blue stamp: J. L. H[ebbelynck; Helbelinck?; Heblelinck?; sale: Paris, 17 March 1856, lot 954 (2500 ffr)]. – [Raoul, comte de Lignerolles; sale II: Paris, 5 March 1894, lot 792 with reproduction, (10.000 ffr); bought by Damascène Morgand (no stock number)]. – [Albert, comte de Naurois [†1905]. – [Adolphe Bordes; with his note on acquisition: 10.000 fr, *1898*]. – [Maurice Loncle; ticket numbered *85*; cf. A. Rau, *Maurice Loncle*,[1] p. 40]. – [H. P. Kraus]; sold to Otto Schäfer in March 1961 (shelf mark: OS *236*).

LE ROUX DE LINCY 60; GROUCHY[2] p. 303; SHIPMAN 96; AUSTIN 96; BN 56; SCHWEINFURT 171; Arnim 38.

3. CRINITUS, Petrus. *De poetis latinis*. Florence: Giunta, 31 January 1505. 2°. Initials in blue or red, larger ones outlined in gold (painted in 1801/02 in Renaissance style). (Fig. 3)

Brown morocco (278:194:17 mm), gold-tooled; elaborate design of curving scrolls and tools WB 5 and CB 1, 8, 17, 26, 45*a* & *b*, 46*a* & *b*, 47*a* & *b*, also (not in Nixon): five-pointed star and two (three) hatched tools (a pair similar to C. de P. 65*a* & *b*). Front cover with title (on central circular onlay of red morocco) and ownership inscription; lower cover with motto. Original back, six raised bands; re-tooled (seventeenth century) with semis of small fleur-de-lis.[3] Edges of covers have panels of diagonal gold lines alternating with single gold lines. Vellum paste-downs at each end; at the beginning one pair (formerly two pairs?) of paper end-leaves, at the end two pairs.

Provenance: [ ]. [Claude Gros de Boze; *Catalogue des livres du cabinet de M. de Boze*, Paris 1745, p. 322?; sale: Paris 1753, 2578, (15 l.); December 1754, 1224 (26 l.)]. *Ex Bibliotheca Parisiana Londini 1791* [Pâris d'Illins sale: London, 28 March 1791, lot 186 (£ 1/9); bought by Strange]. [William Fowle; sale: Sotheby, 28 November 1801, (£ 1/11/6)]. M[ichael] *Wodhull* (1740-1816) with his acquisition note and price for colouring of the initials [Wodhull sale: Sotheby, 11 January 1886, lot 854 (£ 156); sold to Quaritch]. – [P(aulin?) Caperon; sold to Damascène Morgand; *Bulletin Morgand* V (1890), 17972 (7000 fr); *Répertoire méthodique* (1893), 2597 (5000 fr); in 1893 sold for 2500 fr to Paul Brenot (his label PB numbered *3,202*); in 1897 bought back by Damascène Morgand (stock number *24292* on inner front cover); in 1899 sold for 7500 fr to Adolphe Bordes]. [Maurice Loncle, ticket

---

1. See note 1, p. 21.
2. E. H. VICOMTE DE GROUCHY, *A propos d'un livre de Jean Grolier*, in *Bulletin du bibliophile* (1894), pp. 283-303, 379-95.
3. Same re-tooling as on the MARLIANI of 1544 in London/BL; see Nixon (as note 11), no. 112 with reproduction.

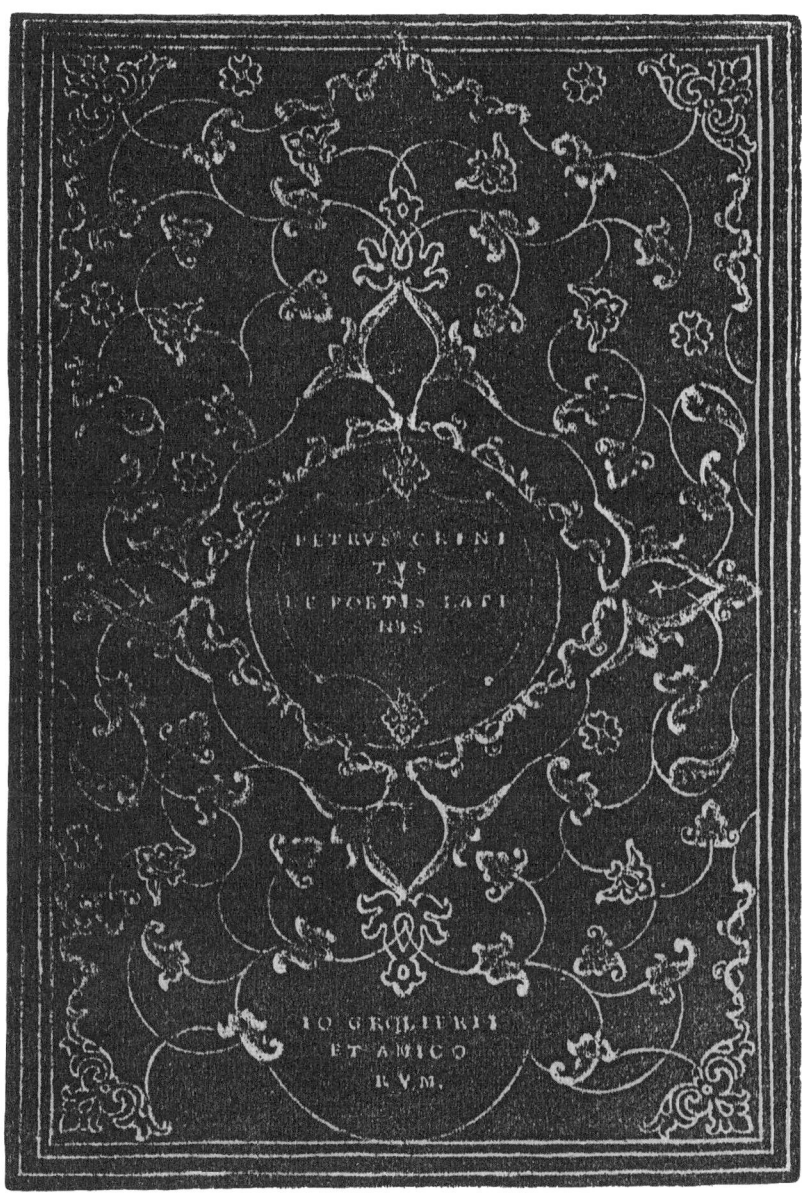

Fig. 3. Crinitus. *De poetis latinis*. Florence 1505. 2°. 278:194 mm

numbered *83*; cf. A. Rau, *Maurice Loncle (op. cit.)*, p. 40 and reproduction on pl. VI]. [H. P. Kraus]; sold to Otto Schäfer in March 1961 (shelf mark: OS *220*).

LE ROUX DE LINCY 90; GROUCHY p. 301; SHIPMAN 150; AUSTIN 150; BN 124; SCHWEINFURT 175; Arnim 39; NIXON, *Grolier's Binders*,[1] p. 167.

4. LUCRETIUS, Titus. *De rerum natura, libri VI*. Edited by A. Navagero. Venice: in aedibus Aldi et Andreæ soceri, January 1515. 8°. – Initials in gold; Aldine anchors in blue, silver and gold. (Fig. 4)

Dark brown morocco (173:102:24 mm), gold-tooled; complex mainly rectangular interlace with solid tools C. de P. 1, 2, 3, 8*a* & *b*, 12. Title and ownership inscription on front cover, motto on lower. Original back, five raised bands; panels outlined by a single gold line and each filled with a single impression of tool C. de P. 12**. Turn-ins, edges of boards, and standard Grolier end-leaves as on the CASTIGLIONE (no. 1).

Provenance: [16th century owner with his Latin notes inside back cover]. – Shelf mark *D 8:71* [of Charles Spencer, 3rd Earl of Sunderland (1674-1722); *Catalogue of books in the library at Blenheim Palace*, Oxford 1872, 94b; Sunderland sale III: Puttick & Simpson, 17 July 1882, 7690 (£ 300); sold to Léon Techener, sale I: Paris, 4 May 1886, 240 (6050 fr)]. – [Comte de Sauvage; sale: Paris, 9 March 1898, lot 47 (11.500 fr)]. – [Comte Albert de Naurois (†1905)]. – Adolphe Bordes (with his book-plate, and note on acquisition: *10.000* fr, *1898*). – [Maurice Loncle, ticket numbered *88*; cf A. Rau, *Maurice Loncle (op. cit.)*, p. 40]. – [H. P. Kraus]; sold to Otto Schäfer in March 1961 (shelf mark: OS *221*).

GROUCHY p. 300; SHIPMAN 308; AUSTIN 308; BN 59; SCHWEINFURT 172 (with reproduction on covers of catalogue); Arnim 37. Not in Le Roux de Lincy.

5. ZANTANI, Antonio. *Le imagini...degli imperatori*. [Engravings by Enea Vico.] Parma: Enea Vico, 1548. 4°. (Fig. 5)

Brownish-red morocco (234:161:16 mm), gold-tooled; elaborate curving interlace and hatched tools C. de P. 47, 66*a* & *b*. Title and ownership inscription on upper cover, motto on lower. Smooth back with panelling in double gold lines. Edges of boards as on the CRINITUS (no. III). At the beginning now one pair of paper end-leaves (formerly two pairs), at the end two pairs; at each end one leaf used as paste-down. The paper has watermark Crowned Eagle with letter F on its breast (type Briquet[2] 146).

1. See note 6, p. 21.
2. C[HARLES]-M[OÏSE] BRIQUET, *Les Filigranes. Dictionnaire historique des marques du papier dès leur apparition vers 1282 jusqu'en 1600*. 4 vols (Leipzig, 1923).

Fig. 4. Lucretius. *De rerum natura*. Venice 1515. 8°. 173:102 mm.
Front cover

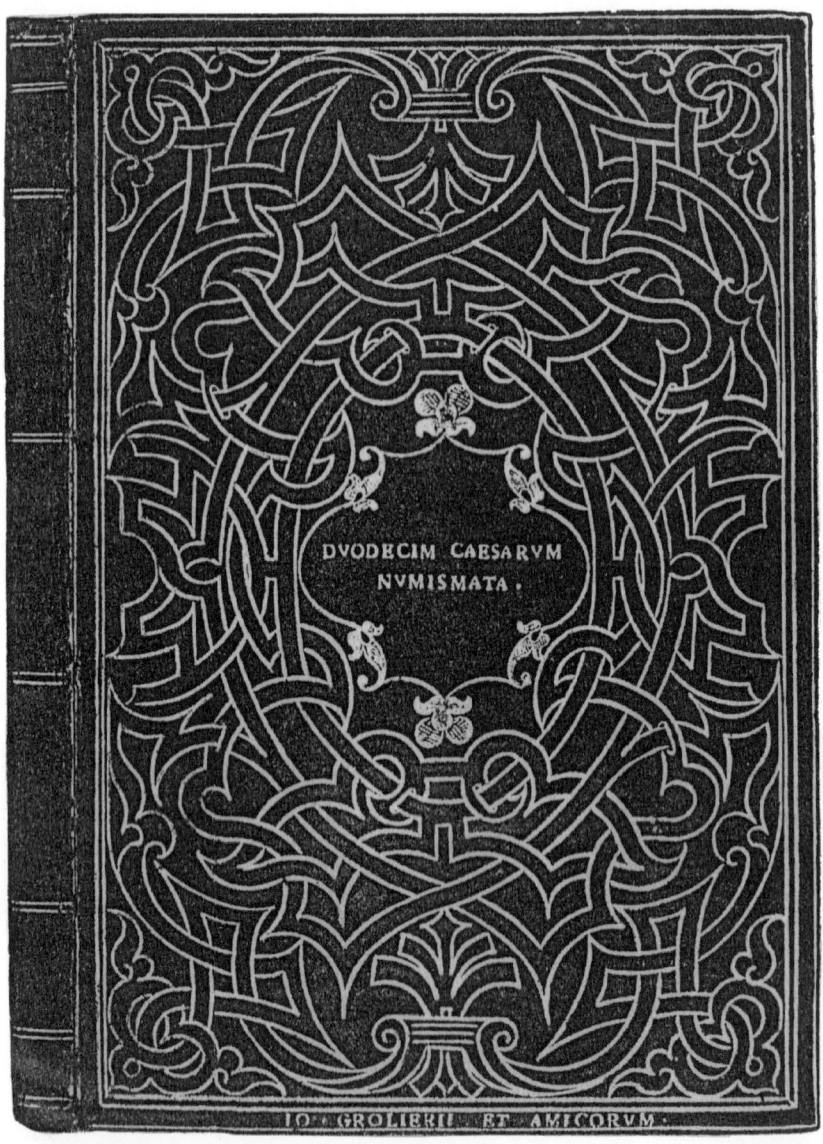

Fig. 5. Zantani. *Le imagini degli imperatori*. Parma 1548. 4°. 234:161 mm.
Front cover

Provenance: [ ]. – *La Bourdaizière*. – [ ]. – [Léon Cailhava; sale: Paris, 21 October 1845, lot 863 (500 fr.).] – [Pierre-Adolphe marquis de Coislin; sale: Paris, 29 November 1847, lot 544 (400 fr)]. – [Guglielmo Libri; shown in the Art Exposition, Manchester 1857; Libri sale: Sotheby, 1 August 1859, 932 (£ 15/10); sold to John T. Payne]. – [George Nicholson]. – [Felix Slade; sale: Sotheby, 3 August 1868; lot 1100]. – [Earl of Orford; with ticket "A.I.E., 1874, Exhibitor's name", filled in *Lord Orford*; sale: Sotheby, 14 March 1902, lot 203 (£ 162); sold to Quaritch]. – [Damascène Morgand, with stock no. *26865* of 1902 on inner front cover; sold for 10.000 fr to Adolphe Bordes.] – [Maurice Loncle, ticket numbered *84*; cf A. Rau, *Maurice Loncle (op. cit.)*, p. 40]. – [H. P. Kraus]; sold to Otto Schäfer in March 1961 (shelf mark: OS *235*).

LE ROUX DE LINCY 325; SHIPMAN 528 (identical with 530); AUSTIN 528; BN 130; Schweinfurt 173; Arnim 40.

GILES BARBER

FROM BAROQUE TO NEOCLASSICISM: FRENCH EIGHTEENTH-CENTURY BINDINGS AT OXFORD

Most great libraries are the result of a combination of slow and deliberate institutional acquisition, sometimes enlightened and sometimes less so, and of personal benefactions, each of the latter reflecting the nature of the donor, his interests and his times. Each influence often complements the other. Thus when looking at the holdings of a library or, in the case of Oxford University and its colleges, a group of libraries, one must consider how their holdings were built up and at what date acquisitions were made and why. This is perhaps especially true in the field of bookbindings, the study of which the Hobson family have made particularly their own, and will come as no surprise to the author, inter alia, of *French and Italian collectors and their bindings illustrated from examples in the library of J. R. Abbey* (1953) and of *Great libraries* (1970). The recording of Oxford's gold-tooled bindings started with W. Salt Brassington's *Historic bindings in the Bodleian* (1891) and was continued by Strickland Gibson's *Some notable Bodleian bindings* (1901-4). G.D. Hobson's *Bindings in Cambridge libraries* (1929) set new standards and revealed new wealths which, at Oxford and under the leadership of Ian Philip, Howard Nixon and Graham Pollard, inspired the Bodleian to take a lead in the nineteen sixties in organising, under the aegis of the Standing Conference of National and University Libraries, a series of research and instructional courses. Anthony Hobson naturally shared with Nixon the role of lecturer for the Renaissance period and was thus one of the advisors of the 1968 Bodleian exhibition "Fine bindings, 1500 to 1700, from Oxford libraries", the contents of which were recorded in an illustrated catalogue.

The exhibition aimed to show Oxford's strength in the early periods of gold-tooled bookbinding, ending with the colleges' support of Oxford and other English Restoration bookbinders. It was also felt that Oxford holdings for later periods were not at the same level and that what was already a large exhibition would trail off if the period of time were to be extended. This situation was radically altered within a few years by first the deposit in, and then gift to, the Bodleian of the Broxbourne Library, collected by the late Albert Ehrman. This magnificent collection, only partly revealed by Howard Nixon's 1956 *Broxbourne Library: styles and designs of bookbindings from the twelfth to the twentieth century*, and which was still being added to, not only greatly strengthened Oxford's earlier period holdings but covered much, if not all, of the more modern periods in which hitherto the libraries had been distinctly weak.

The present survey, resulting in part from the study of the remarkable collection of French eighteenth-century bindings formed by Baron Ferdinand Rothschild at Waddesdon Manor, close to Oxford and now under the National Trust (and of which Anthony Hobson published the first, if brief, description), aims to see what more important decorated bindings of that period can now be found in Oxford. The Bodleian with the collections of Francis Douce, and more recently with the Shackleton collection of the works of Montesquieu, is not short of French books of that period, nor is the Taylorian, the university's library for modern continental literature, with its strong Voltaire and Enlightenment collection. The colleges too contain much material of the Ancien Régime, not least a number of copies, in almost as many states, of the *Encyclopédie*, that at the Queen's College being one of the rare ones in contemporary red morocco and with the cancels. The bindings of such working copies of books have much to teach the bibliographer and the book trade historian as a recent analysis of the Ralph Leigh Rousseau Collection now at Cambridge University Library (which could be duplicated by a similar one of the recent bequest of the Vivienne Mylne Collection of eighteenth-century French novels to the Taylor Institution) aims to show. The present study is however concerned with the complementary field of more self-conscious and deliberately more decorative binding, one which, it is hoped to show, was equally typical of that very ornamentally aware time.

The list which follows does not claim to be exhaustive. Bodleian examples come from many different collections and others are spread around in different places in the many college libraries. Knowledge of these, as that of so much of the holdings of college libraries, is largely due to Mr Paul Morgan. It is however hoped that the list contains both the majority of the finest bindings and a fair representation of the good quality work, often signed by known binders, to be found in Oxford. The survey took as its basis the semi-official index of bindings in the Bodleian, started by the late Ian Philip and continued by Paul Morgan (who also indexed the Broxbourne Collection) and the present writer, together with similar indexes to the manuscript collections. All listed bindings thought to be of the period were seen and studied in detail. The resulting list is divided into five sections since this allows the material to be presented not only chronologically but also in style groupings. The five sections are: 1 Early; 2 Mosaics of all dates; 3 Frame designs using composite stamps; 4 Dentelles; 5 Later eighteenth century, mainly more Neo-Classical style, bindings. Within each group any signed bindings have been put first (in alphabetical order of binders if required), all sequences being put in chronological order by date of imprint. This latter order is not significant for works published before the eighteenth century but for items of the period does at least provide a date before which they can not have been bound. A number being almanacks the date of their publication is of course also likely to be the actual date of their binding. All items are in the Bodleian Library unless otherwise stated.

Before embarking on the list it may be helpful to recall the names and dates of the binders mentioned and also the origin and date of accession of the main Bodleian collections involved. Brief notes are appended to each entry but more general comment is given at the end of the article.

French Binders:

Atelier à la Tulipe. Michon identified three groups of bindings using such a tool in the period 1740 to 1785. One uses compass-based designs, another floral ones and the third was associated with Count Tessin. See L. - M. MICHON, *Les reliures mosaïquées du XVIIIe siècle*, Paris, 1956, pp. 51-52.

Atelier avant 1715. Characterised by the use of morocco doublures and filigree tools with a mosaic frame and central motif. See Michon pp. 19-20 who mentions the names of Luc-Antoine Boyet and Louis-Joseph Dubois.

Boyet, Luc-Antoine, fl. 1648-1733.
  Relieur du Roi 1698-1733.

Bradel, Alexis-Pierre, fl. 1772-1821. Successor to his uncle, N.-D. Derome.

Courteval, Christian name unknown. fl. 1796-1836. Rue des Carmes. An established binder in the classical style.

Derome, Jacques-Antoine. 1696-1760. A member of the famous Derome family and the father of Nicolas-Denis.

Derome, Nicolas-Denis, 1731-88. Called "Derome le Jeune". Often considered as the greatest binder of his day.

Dubois, Louis-Joseph, fl. 1698-1728.
  Relieur du Roi 1689-1728.

Dubuisson, Pierre-Paul, fl. 1746-62.
  Relieur du Roi 1758-62.

Du Seuil, Augustin 1673-1746.
  Relieur du Roi 1717-46.

Lemonnier, Jean-Charles-Henri, fl. 1757-?80.
  Relieur du duc d'Orléans.

Marchal, [Pierre?]. Metz, probably 1770s or 1780s, formerly rue Pierre-Hardie, then rue des Petites-Tapes. Pierre Marchal was admitted to the Metz *confrairie* in 1758, having married the widow of Joseph Nafteur and the 1764 trade census lists him as both bookseller and binder. See A. RONSIN, "La communauté des imprimeurs et relieurs de Metz (1615-1791)", *Annales de l'Est*, 5 ser., vol. 11 (1960), pp. 211, 222.

Mouillie, Christian name unknown. Late XVIIIth century-1803. Same address as Derome le Jeune.

Padeloup, Antoine-Michel, 1685-1758.
  Relieur du Roi 1733-58.

Bodleian Collections:

Auct. The Anatomy School lecture rooms at the south west corner of the first floor in the Schools Quadrangle were transferred to the library around 1789 and from at least 1825 important early printed books were given shelfmarks in this "Auctarium".

Broxbourne. The library formed by the late Albert Ehrman (1890-1969), deposited in the Bodleian in 1971 and given to the library in 1978. For an account of Ehrman as a bibliophile see N. J. BARKER, "Albert Ehrman", *The Book Collector* 19, (1970), pp. 455-64.

B[ibliotheca] S[eldeniana]. The BS shelfmark was instituted around 1668 as an extension of the general classification and covered books housed in Selden End, the part of the Bodleian built in 1634-36 and used to house the library of the jurist John Selden (1584-1654) which came in 1659.

Buchanan. The books of Thomas Ryburn Buchanan (1864-1911), lawyer, politician and sometime Librarian of All Souls, were received, as a gift from his widow, in 1941. See S. GIBSON, "Bookbindings in the Buchanan Collection", *Bodleian Library Record*, II (1941) pp. 6-12.

Bywater. The bequest of Ingram Bywater (1840-1914), a noted Classical bibliophile, sometime Sub-Librarian of the Bodleian and later Regius Professor of Greek, was received in 1914.

Gibson. Strickland Gibson (1877-1958) was a member of the Bodleian staff from 1891 to 1945, being the first Keeper of Printed Books. He was an active force in bibliographical studies, a Gold Medallist of the Bibliographical Society, and his collection, received in 1959, was largely intended to exemplify book history points to students. See H. J. DAVIS, "The Strickland Gibson Collection", *Bodleian Library Record*, 6 (1961) pp. 645-54.

Douce. The collections of Francis Douce (1757-1834), received by bequest, were possibly the most important single donation ever received by the library.

Vet. This is a general shelfmark for books of the period 1501 to 1850 and was introduced around 1937.

French bindings of the eighteenth century

Section 1: Early bindings

1. *Psalterium Davidicum*, 1555, Paris, G. Estienne, 12°.
Blue morocco; triple fillet to the boards with a circle at the intersections. At the centre the arms of Count Hoym (1694-1736). A crowned Polish eagle features on each panel of the spine. An olive morocco doublure has a wide border of Polish eagles. Shelfmark: Broxb. 14.5.
Hoym sale (1738, no. 96); Thomas Brooke (bookplate); Ingham Brooke (1908 ms note); Mortimer Schiff (label, sale 6 July 1938 item 868).
Bound during Hoym's stay in Paris 1720 to 1729. According to A. Ehrman's note Padeloup's label, present at the foot of the titlepage, was inadvertently removed during cleaning. S. de Ricci records it as present (*French signed bindings in the Mortimer L. Schiff Collection*, New York, 1935, 1, 6).

2. [Senault, L.], *Heures nouvelles tirées de la Sainte Ecriture*, [1680?], Paris, l'autheur et C. de Hansy, 8°.
Red morocco, with two thin decorative rolls, the panels are decorated by a semé of a tool of flowers in a vase. Broxb. 38.12.
No further details available. The volume is late seventeenth century in feel and may date from then, although copies of this work were bound up over quite a long period and the present volume has therefore been included as an example of the early work of the period under review.

3. [Anon] *La Confrairie de la Très-Sainte Trinité et rédemption des captifs*

[running title: Instruction familière], Lyon, [no publisher or date but the Permission is dated 1706], 12°.

Green morocco. Within a small roll and a fillet are the arms of Marie Leczinska (1703-68), Queen of France (Olivier 2507 stamp 4). Large fleurs de lis in the corners. Similar fleurs de lis are found in the spine panels. 8° H 277 BS.

The arms indicate that the binding must be after 1725, the date when the queen married Louis XV, and provide a good example of the traditional seventeenth century armorial style.

4. BEGAULT, G. *Panegyriques et sermons*, 1711, Paris, Simart, 2 volumes, 8°.

Red morocco; roll border, arms in the centre. 8° A 333 BS.

Provenance: Louis Auguste de Bourbon, duc du Maine (1670-1736), the son of Louis XIV and Madame de Montespan (Olivier 2603, stamp 6).

5. *Office de la Semaine Sainte en latin et en françois, à l'usage de Rome et de Paris*, 1728 [Privilège 1738], Paris, Veuve Mazières, 8°.

Red morocco, small exterior roll, fanfare style plaque (panel stamp) with central oval filled with stamp bearing the arms of Marie Leczinska (Olivier 2507 stamp 1 version, with the side branches in groups of two). The spine decorated with the pallet block of an interlace design with a central fleur de lis. Coloured floral endleaves. Vet. E 4 e. 74.

Bought 1993. From the Convent of the Visitation of Mary, Rouen. Bound with one of the two fanfare style "plaques" in use from this date to the mid seventeen forties and which precede the more baroque plaques in use from then until the end of the century (See G. D. HOBSON, *Les reliures à la fanfare*, 1935, plate XXIII right, equally with the arms of Marie Leczinska). These interesting bindings, which link sixteenth and late eighteenth century styles, are particularly associated with the queen, her circle and such Books of Hours published by this firm. For a later plaque binding see no. 51.

Section 2: Mosaic bindings

6. *Officium parvum beatae Mariae* (Use of Rome), [Manuscript, French, early XVIth century], 12. (SC 21593).

Light brown morocco; wide blue morocco border with rectangular interlaced shapes containing fleurs de lis, stars and filigree curl ornaments. In the centre a blue lozenge and, within it, a red one bearing a fleur de lis (on the lower cover a star). The spine panels bear a series of circular and lozenge shaped onlays in brown, blue, red and tan, the foot hatched. No lettering. A blue morocco doublure with an interlace frame bears a shield with the French royal arms and has around it fronds and a seme of dots. (Fig. 1) MS Douce 19.

The decoration of the boards, with interlace mosaic, and of the spine, with characteristic circles and lozenges, suggests the work of Padeloup.

7. [Anon] *Instruction sur les dispositions qu'un doit apporter aux Sacremens de Pénitence et d'Eucharistie*, 1709, Paris, G. Desprez, 8°.

Light brown morocco; dark green morocco border with gold tooling, a similar central lozenge having, within it, a smaller red one. The spine features black and red onlays as well as other panels without onlays, all decorated with the same ornament (a double line square with semicircular side, made by the use of a bracket tool) featuring on the cover panel. Doublure of red morocco with broad gold-tooled border. Broxb. 43.18.

R. Hoe (bookplate, *Historic and artistic bookbindings*, no. 98, plate; 1911 sale lot 1796); M. Schiff (sale 24 March 1938 lot 246); J. R. Abbey (sale 1965 lot 402, plate 73, "of ravishing quality"). Michon p. 70, no 133, "Avant 1715" group, mentioning the names of Luc-Antoine Boyet and Louis-Joseph Dubois.

8. [Anon] *Exercices sur les Sacremens de Pénitence et de la Sainte Eucharistie* [with] *Réflexions des Saints Peres sur la sainte Eucharistie*, 1712, Paris, L. Josse & C. Robustel (1712, Paris, Roulland), 8°.

Olive morocco; deep border tooled in two rows; mosaic shapes inset from each corner, also a large green morocco mosaic pomegranate with stem and stamens in the centre. A flame tool, possibly Padeloup's, occurs on the corner mosaic pieces. Buchanan f. 61.

Provenance: Aubry 1836 (ms signature). A manuscript note ascribes to either Padeloup or Lemonnier. See *Bodleian Library Quarterly*, II, p. 10.

9. *Almanach royal pour l'année 1726*, 1726, Paris, veuve d'Houry et C.M. d'Houry, 8°.

Red morocco; with oval, lobed and heart-shaped onlays of olive and citron leather, featuring numerous small tools and, in the centre the arms of a member of the Pâris family whose apple also occurs on the spine panels. Gold and white pastedowns. Broxb. 45.5.

Provenance: Antoine Pâris the elder (or a brother such as Claude Pâris de la Montagne, Joseph Pâris de Verney or Jean Pâris de Monmartel). Hector Le Fuel (bookplate, early twentieth century). Michon no. 179,

Fig. 1. *Officium parvum beatae Mariae* (Use of Rome), [Manuscript, French, early XVIth century], 12. (SC 21593).

attributed to the second Atelier à la Tulipe. Nixon, *Broxbourne Library*, no. 84 with plate and recognising Dr Hobson's help with the Pâris provenance.

10. *Almanach royal pour l'année 1737*, 1737, Paris, veuve d'Houry, 8°.
Olive morocco with onlays of red morocco, all-over design of a tile-shaped pattern ("a répétition"), one series with a stylised cross, the other with a U-shaped tool. The spine as the covers. Doublure of black morocco, with a roll-tooled border and central arms (a lion alone), the latter made up and not an armorial block. Dutch gilt floral endleaves. Broxb. 46.17.
Formerly attributed to Angelique-Victoire de Bournonville, duchesse de Duras (1686-1764). F. Cortland Bishop (sale 1938 lot 76), J.R Abbey (A.R.A. HOBSON, *French and Italian Collectors*, no. 41, plate, sale 1965 lot 17). Michon, p. 74, no. 202. Dr Hobson records that this and the succeeding lot in the Abbey sale (18 *Almanach royal* 1743, now in the British Library) belong to a series of almanacks in mosaic bindings with the arms of Bournonville or Bournonville/Duras. Eight of the series, dating between 1731 and 1746, are in the municipal library at Dijon; two are reproduced by Michon as plates 18 and 19. This is the only known series of almanacks in mosaic bindings. The present arms are not recorded in Olivier, Hermal and de Roton and could apply to a number of families. A pencil note in the volume attributes to the Saulx-Tavannes family but the most distinguished contemporary member was a cardinal (Olivier 1790).

11. *Heures présentées à Madame la Dauphine* [Marie Thérèse Raphaele de Bourbon, Infanta of Spain, 1727-1747, first wife of the Dauphin Louis, [1745-46], Paris, T. de Hansy, 8°.
Red morocco; border of semicircles, a large central flower with four smaller ones, two above and two below, all with onlays of light brown, green and red. The spine also has mosaic panels, each with a small bulbous vase tool. Gilt starred endpapers. (Fig. 2) Broxb. 90.2.
C.P.J.B. de Bourgevin de Vialart de Moligny (bookplate. Sale 1795), M. Schiff (sale 23 March 1938 lot 218), J.R. Abbey (1965 lot 378). Guigard II p. 81. Michon p. 81, no. 322, attributed to the second Atelier à la tulipe.

12. *Nouvelles étrennes spirituelles dédiées à Monseigneur le Dauphin* [the future Louis XVI], 1769, Paris, L.G. de Hansy, 12°.
Red morocco; a border of simple fronds and flower heads. Green onlay

Fig. 2. *Heures présentées à Madame la Dauphine* [Marie Thérèse Raphaele de Bourbon, Infanta of Spain, 1727-1747, first wife of the Dauphin Louis, [1745-46], Paris, T. de Hansy, 8°.

tulips in the corners and a larger onlaid pomegranate in the centre. Small flowers on the spine. Gold and white star and dot pastedowns. Broxb. 1.35.

Provenance: Lambert 1770 (ms note), M. Schiff (sale 1938 lot 449), J. R. Abbey (sale 1965 lot 510). Michon p.79, no.291, attributed to the second Atelier à la Tulipe.

13. *Heures royales dédiées à la Reine*, 1778, Paris, de Hansy, 12°.

Dark red morocco, plain fillet border, large tulips in each corner, large made-up pomegranate in centre, both tulips and pomegranate being, in part, on an onlay of green leather. Gibson 25.

No evident provenance. The queen was Marie Antoinette.

14. *Eucologe, ou Livre d'église*, 1789, Paris, Libraires associés, 8°.

Red morocco; three outer rolls, within four green flowers in corners and central wreath with, in the middle, an altar and birds, inscribed around "Unissons nous". The spine has circles, diamonds, and hearts held by birds. Marbled endleaves. Buchanan e. 114.

No provenance. Despite the date and motto the binding seems to be more amatory than revolutionary in intent.

15. *Calendrier de la Cour*, 1789, Paris, Veuve Herissant, 18°.

White calf; frame of green morocco with three gilt rolls. An interior panel under mica has a plain red ground, four decorative roundels and a metallic oval frame to the centre where there is a watercolour sketch of a couple sitting on a bank near trees. The spine appears to be of paper and has red and gold markings. Blue silk pastedowns, the front one having a silvered mirror held in by gold braid and the back one a concertina pocket. Endleaves of blue paper with a gold speckle. The whole kept in a contemporary red morocco box decorated with a feather, oval and star roll. Broxb. 1.28.

No provenance. Clearly a luxury production. The only mica binding in Oxford.

Section 3: Folio border element bindings: i Signed

16. [Padeloup] *Représentation des fêtes données par la Ville de Strasbourg pour la convalescence du roi* [Louis XV. The whole "inventé par J. M. Weiss"], [1745], Paris, L. Aubert, outsize folio.

Red morocco; large gilt floral frame made up by the use of four repeated elements. The corner cartouches bear the arms of Bourbon-Maine.

The ten-panel spine bears the crowned cypher in a frame with fleur de lis. Pink silk pastedowns. Douce Prints a. 6.

A ticket reading: "Relié par Padeloup Relieur du Roy, place Sorbonne à Paris", features at the bottom of the titlepage. Padeloup bound virtually all the copies of this work, all of which are signed in this manner. Here the right hand centre ornament on both upper and lower covers is of the wrong sort and should be the other version of this block, facing the other way up. The copy was presumably intended for Louis Auguste de Bourbon, Prince de Dombes (1700-1755), the second son of the Duc du Maine who had died in 1736. The prince died without issue.

Another copy of this work, in a similar binding, is to be found in Oriel College. This is bound in dark green morocco and bears the arms of Louis XV (Olivier 2495 stamp 10) in the centre. It came with the Lord Leigh (1742-1786) bequest. Oriel College: o. a. 12.

17. [Padeloup] LE BRUN, Charles, *La Grande galerie de Versailles et les deux salons qui l'accompagnent*, 1752, Paris, Imprimerie royale, outsize folio.

Dark blue/green morocco; border of four different frame elements, one resembling a series of waves and coming in both left and right facing versions. Ten bands on the spine, the panels having a central lozenge-shaped ornament centred on a bird with a leaf in its beak. Pink watered silk pastedowns, endleaves watermarked Dupuy Fin Auvergne 1742. Eight flower roll on turn-ins. (Fig. 3) Oriel College: o. a. 6.

Padeloup ticket in its usual place at the foot of the titlepage. Monsieur Paul Culot reports that Padeloup's accounts for binding all copies of this book exist. Lord Leigh bequest. This design is very uncommon.

A royal decree introduced the necessity of dating paper in that year but due to an error in drafting the date 1742 was used for several decades afterwards.

Section 3: Folio border element bindings: ii Unsigned

18. SANTI BARTOLI, P., *Recueil des peintures antiques imitées fidèlement*, (explication des peintures par P. J. Mariette & le comte de Caylus), 1757, 60, Paris, Guerin, folio.

Red morocco; outer drawer-handle roll, then a six-flower roll and, within, a frame of four tree-branch elements (a large corner, a midpoint cartouche, and both left and right linking pieces). A bulbous vase and flowers tool occurs in the corner cartouches and a flat basket of flowers

Fig. 3. [Padeloup] Le Brun, Charles, *La Grande galerie de Versailles et les deux salons qui l'accompagnent*, 1752, Paris, Imprimerie royale, outsize folio.

in the midpoint ones. A heavy silver lock bears Lord Leigh's arms. Flat spine with false bands marked by a vine-leaf roll. Leaf-combed marbled pastedowns, fly leaves bear the watermark MGIS 1742. See note re date 1742 under no. 17. Oriel College: Cedar Room.

Acquired for Lord Leigh by the London bookseller Paul Vaillant; owner's bequest. A very rare work with thirty-three extraordinary coloured plates which, according to Brunet, was only printed in thirty copies. The copy in the Bibliothèque nationale, Paris, is also in red morocco and has the arms of Marie Antoinette. Brunet refers to four other copies in three different coloured leathers. The same frame elements are found on a copy of the Strasbourg "fêtes" bearing Padeloup's ticket (Sotheby 20 Oct., 1964, lot 363). Not in Cohen.

Section 4: Dentelle bindings: i Signed bindings

19. [N.D. Derome] Bartholomaeus of Pisa, *Liber conformitatum (vite beati Francisci)* [Ed by F. Zeno], 1510, Milan, G. Pontius, folio.

Red morocco; wide outer dentelle incorporating corner shells, palmettes, thistles, leaves and sprays of curling dots in a traditional eight point undulating movement. Lettered in the second panel of the spine and with the date in the third. Blue silk pastedowns. Vet. F 1 c.25 (formerly Arch. Bod. D. subt. 81 then Arch.Bod. D. c. 11).

Derome's ticket (1780-85 Ract-Madou F 1) is in the usual place, top left of the verso of the flyleaf facing the titlepage.

20. [N.D. Derome] Carthusians, Order of, *Statuta ordinis Cartusiensis a doṁno Guigone priore Cartusie edita*, 1510, Basle, J. Amerbach, folio.

Red morocco; deep dentelle border, shell corners, open lattice ornament, branching fronds. Spine with flower tool in lozenge, lettered directly and with the date in the third panel. Blue silk paste-downs, alternating eight-flower turn-in roll. Thick boards with double fillet. Blue silk marker, red, white and green headbands. (Fig. 4) Queen's College: Sel. d. 35.

Derome's ticket (1780-85 Ract-Madou F1) in the usual place, top left of the verso of the first flyleaf. Also label of C.I. Stewart, a London bookseller.

Section 4: Dentelle bindings: ii Unsigned bindings

21. [Book of Hours in French and Latin, XV? century]

Green morocco: deep dentelle border with frond work, ovals in corners

Fig. 4. [N.D. Derome] Carthusians, Order of, *Statuta ordinis Cartusiensis a domno Guigone priore Cartusie edita*, 1510, Basle, J. Amerbach, folio.

bearing an angel with sword and shield, also quadrilobes at the midpoints containing the letters IHS. Other tools include an open tulip head. At the corners the interior side of the innermost tool is closely dotted. The ground to the dentelle area is similarly criblé. Flat spine. Unusual turn-in roll. Pink watered silk pastedowns. Keble College: MS 39.

W. Tite 1875 - C. E. Brooke bequest 1911. This volume has striking resemblances (the two types of cartouche, the *criblé* ground, a woody frond, the same green morocco) with a 1745 *Daphnis et Chloe* in the Bibliothèque municipale at Rouen (Leber 1977), listed by Michon as no. 225.

22. *Speculum humanae salvationis*, [c.1474/75, Utrecht], folio. (Proctor 8822; BMC IX.2; IB 47001)

Red morocco; double fillet, dentelle with shell corner, open lattice and interlace tools, also thistle and bird (head turned to left) in frame. Flat back lettered down spine SPECULUM HUMANAE SALVATIONIS EDITIO PRINCEPS CIRCA ANNO 1440. Leaf-combed marble endleaves with watermark 1742. (Fig. 5) Douce 205 = Arch. G d. 56.

No provenance. A book Douce was much interested in, as can be seen from his numerous notes on the flyleaves. The framed bird tool is often automatically associated with Derome le jeune but the ownership of the several close, but different, versions has not yet been sorted out. See note concerning date 1742 under no. 17.

23. *Cest le mistère de la passion Jesu crist iouée à Paris et Angers*, 1499, Paris, A. Verard, folio. (Proctor 8368)

Red morocco; outer roll and double fillet, fine dentelle border with shell corners, large fronds and floral and other tools producing a fine movement. Lettered in the second and third panels with the date. Combed marble endleaves. Douce 150.

No provenance. The dating of bindings with only general decorative tools and no particular ones remains difficult and this one could be any time between 1750 and 1780 although the inclusion of the date on the spine, a collector's reaction, suggests a later rather than an earlier one.

24. OUDRY, J. B., *Réflexions sur la manière d'étudier la couleur en comparant les objets les uns aux autres*, [Manuscript, 1749], 4°.

Red morocco; drawer handle border, dentelle border with shell corner and fan, separate tools including cock, stag, lozenges. Dark red silk pastedowns. Broxb. 83.22.

Fig. 5. *Speculum humanae salvationis*, [c.1474/75, Utrecht], folio.
(Proctor 8822; BMC IX.2; IB 47001)

No provenance. Nixon, *Broxbourne Library*, no. 87 with plate, points out that the unlinked use of separate tools to form the dentelle is unusual. He also suggests that the presence of animals may contain an allusion to the author's reputation as an animal painter.

25. LUCRETIUS, *Della natura delle cose*, 1754, Amsterdam, 2 vols, 8°.
Olive morocco; double fillet etc, deep dentelle border, open lattice corners with fronds, other areas bounded by swags and the inside space semé with small flowers. Flower in spine panels. Combed marble endleaves. Buchanan d. 62, 63.
No provenance. This free-thinking work rejecting divine interference in world history was popular with liberal-minded Enlightenment collectors and is often found in fine bindings.

26. MASENIUS, J. *Sarcotis carmen, cura et studio J. Dinouart*,1757, Lyons et Paris, J. Barbou, 12°.
Red morocco; unusual dentelle with calligraphic style corner piece (used, the other way up, at the midpoints) and snail-like curl. Flat spine with pomegranate ornament. Peacock tail marbled endleaves. Broxb. 43.23.
Described by Rahir (*Livres dans de riches reliures*, 1910, no. 239) as by Derome.

27. *Office propre de Saint Charles Borromée*, 1758, Paris, Herissant, 12°.
Red morocco, thin dentelle border, plain fronds at corners. Flat spine, combed marble endleaves. Keble College: Brooke 100.
Bookplate of Thomas Brooke FSA.

28. FOURNIER, P. S. *Manuel typographique*,1764, Paris, l'auteur et chez Barbou, 2 vols, 8°.
Red morocco; dentelle of generalised frond tools. Spine with three flower tool, combed marble pastedowns. Douce F 315, 316.
No provenance. The most important French typographic manual of the eighteenth century, this text is usually found in a good binding but because of its technical nature rarely in a fine one.

29. [Louis Philippe, duc d'Orléans], *Chasses du cerf faites par l'Equipage de Monseigneur le Duc d'Orléans pendant l'année 1768*. [Manuscript, c. 1769], 12°.
Red morocco; dentelle border with stags and bounding dogs in the corners. Framed bird tool at midpoints. Arms of the duke of Orleans (not in Olivier) in the centre. Flat spine with tooled bands and decorated with fleurs de lis. Broxb. 90.23

Louis Philippe, duc d'Orleans (father of Philippe Egalité, 1725-85, sale 1787), Edouard Kann (sale Paris November 1930), C.F.G.R. Schwerdt (his catalogue *Hunting, Hawking and Shooting*, vol. iv, p. 116 and plate 34). Nixon (*Broxbourne Library* no. 90, p. 181, plate) suggests that the bird tool was common to several Paris binders and refers to Dr Hobson's link with a group the latter attributes to Dubuisson (*French and Italian Collectors*, p. 93) while considering that the tools here are different. This was clearly part of a series since an almost identical volume covering 1762, featured in the R. von Gutmann sale at Sotheby's on 2 April 1993, lot 49.

Section 5: Late bindings: i Signed bindings

30. [Courteval] EPICTETUS, *Enchiridion, curante J. B. Lefebvre de Villebrune*, 1782, Paris, P.D. Pierres, 12°.
Red morocco; single ropework fillet with circles at the intersections. Flat spine, gilt bands and circles. Green silk pastedown. Buchanan g. 34.
Ticket (COURTEVAL RELIEUR, RUE DES CARMES, no. 5) top left of verso of first flyleaf.

31. [Derome, N.D.] [BIBLE in Latin, manuscript, French, late 13th century, size. SC 21687].
Light brown calf; triple exterior fillet with rosette at the intersections. Six-panel spine, each with broken wavy diagonal lines. Olive label, marbled endleaves. MS Douce 113.
Derome ticket (1785-89 Ract-Madou K 1) on first vellum leaf, verso top left facing the start of the text.

32. [Derome, N.D.] (LORRIS, GUILLAUME DE & MEUNG, JEAN DE), *Le roman de la rose*, [Manuscript, French, 15th century], size. (SC 21946).
Green calf; triple fillet with rosettes at the intersections. Ribbon-type roll on spine, pink silk pastedowns, flyleaves watermarked 1742. MS Douce 371.
Derome ticket (1785-89 Ract-Madou L 2) at the centre foot of the first page.

33. [Derome, N.D.] [BIBLE in Latin. c. 1454/55, Mainz, J. Gutenberg and P. Schoeffer], 2 volumes, folio. (GW 4201)
Blue morocco; double panel of fleur de lis and similar type rolls with five petalled flower at the corners. Bodleian gilt stamp in center. (Fig. 6) Auct. M.1.11,12 = Arch. B b.10,11.

Fig. 6. [Derome, N.D.] [BIBLE in Latin. c. 1454/55, Mainz, J. Gutenberg and P. Schoeffer], 2 volumes, folio. (GW 4201)

Derome ticket (1785-89 Ract-Madou K 3) top left on verso of first flyleaf, opposite the titlepage. Given by Erhard Neninger, burgermaster of Heilbron, to the Carmelites of Heilbron before 1475 and used by them up to the eighteenth century. Cardinal Lomenie de Brienne (sale 1724, lot 1). The Bodleian stamp was presumably added shortly after the acquisition of the book in 1793 at a cost of £ 100 (Macray pp. 275, 465). Only two other copies of the Gutenberg or "42-line" Bible are known in eighteenth century French bindings (Paris, Bibliothèque nationale and Bibliothèque Mazarine), four being in eighteenth century English bindings, the remaining forty or so copies being largely in other bindings.

34. [Derome, N.D.] [BIBLE in Latin, before 1471, Strassburg, A. Rusch], 2 volumes, folio. (GW 4209)
Red calf; panel of three rolls. Bodleian gilt stamp. Seven panel spine, corner decoration, flower centres with dotted lozenge. Marbled pastedowns, endleaves watermarked 1782. Auct. M. 1. 12,13.
Derome ticket (1785-89 Ract-Madou K 4) top left verso of flyleaf facing the text.

35. [Derome, N.D.] HERODOTUS, *Historiarum liber novem, interprete Laurentio Valla*, 1474, Venice, I. Rubeus, folio. (IB 20067)
Red morocco; eight rolls in three panels with spike tool or star at intersections. Bodleian gilt stamp. Six-pointed star in spine panels. Blue silk pastedown. Auct. K. 2.17.
Derome ticket (1785-89 Ract-Madou K 4) verso top left of flyleaf facing text.

36. [Derome, N.D.] BOETHIUS, A.M.T.S., (*De consolatione philosophiae*), 1479, Pinerolo, I. Rubeus, folio. (GW 4517)
Green morocco; triple fillet with rose stamp at the intersections. Bodleian gilt stamp in the centre. Six panel spine with small classical ornament. Date on spine. Pink silk pastedown, endleaf watermarked 1789? Auct. N. 1.16.
Derome ticket (1785-89 Ract-Madou L 3) top left verso of last flyleaf facing text. Bought in 1817. See also no. 34.

37. [Derome, N.D.] PIUS II POPE (Aeneas Silvius Piccolomini), *De parvis mulieribus*, (?1507), [?Paris], 8°. (Pellechet 172)
Red morocco; triple fillet panel with eight-pointed star at the intersections. Flat spine, star top and bottom, lettered up long central panel. Marbled endleaves. Douce A 337.

Derome ticket (1785-89 Ract-Madou K 4) top left verso of second flyleaf. Douce's note suggests that this may be the copy which one Nowell bought at the Pâris sale.

38. [Marchal] CORNELIUS NEPOS, *De vita excellentium imperatorum*, 1767, Paris, Barbou, 12°.
Red morocco; triple fillet panel with circles at intersections. Spine panels with sunflower ornaments, marbled pastedowns. Broxb. 70.30.
Label bottom left of upper pastedown reads: Se vend à Metz, chez MARCHAL, Libraire & Relieur, ci-devant rue Pierre-Hardie, présentement rue des Petites-Tapes, entre la Place S. Jacques & le café Moreau, No. 2971. A gift from Lord Kenyon to Albert Ehrman.

39. [Mouille] VALERIUS MAXIMUS, GAIUS, *Factorum: ac dictorum memorialium liber* (ed. by B. Accursius), 1475, Milan, Zarotus, folio. (IB 25959)
Mottled and speckled calf; triple fillet panel. Bodleian gilt stamp in the centre. Seven-panelled spine featuring framed bird tool. Title in the second panel, imprint and date at the foot. Marbled pastedowns. Auct. N. 4.1.
A label reading: "Relié par MOUILLE Rue S. Jacques, Hôtel de la Couture, No. 65" [the 5 is in pen and the original engraved figure was probably 69] is to be found top left of the verso of the lined free marbled endleaf.

40. [Mouille] [SCRIPTORES REI MILITARIS: Frontinus, Vegetius, Aelianus, Modestus], *De re militari*. 1496, Bologna, Plato de Benedictis, folio.
Plain mottled calf with equal triple fillet. Red title label, green date and place label. Neo-classical roll at foot. Dark purple, blue and white spot-marble endleaves. Queen's College: Sel. a. 263.
Similar label to previous item but the last number is clearly a nine. At the end of the text is an early inscription "ex libris Sti Euurtii Aureliensis" and on the titlepage are two of the red stamps of the Bibliothèque royale. The reference below, R. 564 A, is probably the old Paris royal library shelfmark. Rhodes 1598.

Section 5: Late bindings: ii Unsigned

41. VIRGIL, [*Opera*], 1473, Rome, V. Gallus & S. de Luca, folio. (Proctor 3358)

Brown calf; triple fillet border with rosette at intersections, Bodleian gilt stamp in centre. Spine covered with left and right hand grotesque curls, each in rows. Green label with author, title and date. Auct. N.4.26.

A note by E. G. Duff, 1885, says "Bound by Du Seuil from internal evidence". The reason for this is not obvious. The sections making up the volume appear to have come from a number of different sources, only those in the second half being in good condition and having much unity.

42. SENECA, L. A., *Ad Lucillium epistole*, [c. 1474, Strassburg, A. Rusch], folio. (BMC I.32 IB 650)

Green morocco; triple fillet with rose stamp at the intersections. Spine with floral swag and ornamented rolls, lettered directly. Auct. N. 3.27.

The textblock at least formerly belonged to the Jesuit College at Porentruy, Switzerland. Bought 1802. The binding has many features in common with that of no. 31.

43. AMMONIUS, son of Hermias, *In quinque voces Porphyrii commentarius*, 1499, Venice, Z. Callierges, folio. (Proctor 5645,46; GW 1618)

Red patterned morocco; triple fillet panel with rosettes at intersections. Seven-panel spine, each with lozenge and bird tool. Nineteenth-century style curled marble endleaves. Byw. A. 3.16.

No provenance but old catalogue entry ascribes to Derome.

44. ERASMUS, *Exomologesis* [and other works], 1524 [and up to 1538], Lyons, 8°.

Dark green morocco; triple fillet with rosette corners. Flat spine, triple fillets for bands, pomegranate ornament. Byw. I. 3.2.

No provenance.

45. PORZIO, S. *De coloribus libellus*, 1548, Florence, L. Torrentini, 4°.

Red morocco; triple fillet, no rosettes. Small flower on spine panels. Byw. K. 1.17.

Gomez de la Cortina, marquis de Morante, *Catalogus*, IV, Madrid, 1857; no. 6853 ("Padeloup"), Van Bellengen (sale Brussels 1883, lot 444).

46. FOLENGO, T. *Poemata* (Merlin Cocaius), 1554, Venice, heirs of Petrus Ravani, 16°.

Green morocco; simple panel made from roll with ovals and dashes in ovals. Flat spine with thistle-type ornament. Stone marble pastedown. Douce C 385.

Douce's note suggests that this item might have featured in a La Vallière sale.

47. AESCHYLUS, *Tragoediae* VII, 1557, [Geneva], H. Stephanus, 4°.

Green morocco, triple fillet, the centre one being notably wide. Six-point star at the intersections. Five-petal flower to panels, combed marble endleaves. Byw A. 1.9.

Textblock signature of Jacques Poisse (16th century). Ellis & Elvey bill (£5. 5s) 1890 saying the binding was by Padeloup.

48. BELON, P. *Portraits d'oyseaux, animaux, serpens...d'Arabie & Egypte*, 1557, Paris, C. Cavellat, 4°.

Red morocco; triple fillet, rosette corners. Prominent spine bands, acorn decoration. Combed marble endleaves. Don. d. 20.

Priest 1820, Beckford (sale 30 June 1882, lot 777), J. H. Burn, his gift to the Bodleian 1933.

49. SUETONIUS TRANQUILLUS, GAIUS. [*De Caesarum vitis. De Illustribus grammaticis. De Claris rhetoribus. Horatii vita. Plinii vita. Lucani vita*], 1644, Paris, Imprimerie royale, 12°.

Red morocco with equally spaced triple fillet. Flat gilt spine lettered directly. Curled marble endleaves. Gibson 22.

H. T. Liddell (MS inscription "from my father 1810 [possibly 1816]"). Liddell (1797-1878, second Baron and first Earl Ravensworth) would have been at either Eton or Cambridge dependent on how the date is read. His father was the patron of George Stephenson and he himself a cousin of H. G. Liddell, the Dean of Christ Church and father of Lewis Carroll's friend Alice Liddell.

50. HOMER, *Ilias & Odyssea. Cum Latine versione C. Schrevelio*, 1665, Leyden, F. Hackius, 2 volumes, 4°.

Red morocco; triple fillet, rosette corners. Arms of Madame de Pompadour (Olivier 2399 stamp 5 middle size although the stamp appears to be 2 mm larger). A pink on the spine panels. Combed marble endleaves. Broxb. 36.10.

Madame de Pompadour (not in the 1765 sale catalogue), William Morris, his gift to Sir E. Burne Jones, Viscount Birkenhead. Since the work is not in the Pompadour sale catalogue it is likely that, as in a certain number of other cases, the arms are a forgery, added in the nineteenth century. Although they were doubtless not unique in this, Madame de Pompadour's books seem to be a particularly favourite subject for such treatment.

51. *Almanach royal pour l'année 1751*, 1751, Paris, Le Breton, Red morocco; overall panel stamp or "plaque" (Rahir 1910 no. 184a). Such stamps were used, particularly for almanachs, from the mid 1740s to the 1790s. For an early example see no. 5. Standard interlaced spine panels. Ivory and gold floral endleaves bearing the inscription: Georg Christoph Stoy exc: Aug: Vin: cum. Privilegio. Sac: Caes: Mai:. (Fig. 7) Broxb. 46.18.

52. [Diderot, D. & D'Alembert, J. Le R., eds] *Encyclopédie, ou Dictionnaire raisonné des arts et des sciences*, 1751-1765, Paris [& Neufchatel = Paris], 17 vols, folio.
Red morocco; triple (equally spaced) fillet to boards with rosette at intersections. Covers otherwise plain. Spine with hexagonal central panels containing flowers, lettered directly. Classical wave scroll at head and foot. Leaf-combed marble pastedown. Queen's College: 42 E 12-F 17.
Bought in 1840s through the R. Mason bequest. Copies in contemporary French red morocco are rare and the fact that this is on "grand papier", that it has the frontispiece in both states, that the first three volumes are all of the first issue and that it contains a number of cancels, makes it of great interest. Since all the volumes are bound identically it is however not clear exactly when, or over what period, the set was bound.
There are six other copies of the early printings of the *Encyclopédie* in Oxford (All Souls, Bodleian, Christ Church, Lady Margaret Hall, Magdalen, and the Taylorian) but all have English calf bindings. Since the weight of the book was already considerable it would only have been reasonable for it to have been imported in sheets and bound up locally.

53. SENTEUIL, Jean de. *Hymnes* traduites en François par J[ean] P[oupin] C[ure] P[rieur] D['Auxon]. 1760, Paris, J. Barbou, 8°.
Blue morocco; triple fillet with small ornament at the corners. Large central ornament probably from one block and comprising fan sides and lobed and fronded base. Broxb. 46.20.
Dedicated to Madame la Dauphine (then Marie Josephe de Saxe, wife of the Dauphin Louis and mother of Louis XVI). J. R. Abbey (sale 1965 lot 599). A very unusual binding.

54. LA FONTAINE, J. *Contes et nouvelles en vers*, 1762, Amsterdam [Paris, Barbou], 2 volumes, 8°.
Olive green morocco; the usual "de présent" fillet and tool decoration (apparently designed by Gravelot) framing the boards and the flat

Fig. 7. *Almanach royal pour l'année 1751*, 1751, Paris, Le Breton, Red morocco; overall panel stamp or "plaque" (Rahir 1910 no. 184a).

spine, the latter having at the foot "ANNEE/1762". Pink silk pastedowns. Broxb. 40.16-17.
Provenance: R. Hoe (sale, pt. 1, 1911, lot 1965), Schiff (sale 1938, lot 928), J. R. Abbey (sale 1965 lot 427). Kept loose with the volume is a manuscript receipt signed by La Fontaine and dated 1661. One of the most famous illustrated French books of the century, the "Fermiers Generaux" La Fontaine *Contes* was described by the Goncourt brothers as one of the finest disbursements of witty and sensual money of Louis XV's reign. The result of open-ended funding was the triumph of Eisen's vignettes and Choffard's tailpieces. This is the standard binding.

55. *Etrennes dediées aux prince*, Nouvelle édition, 1762, Paris, Dufour, 16°.
Gauze over pasteboard; embroidered with white beads as a ground and also with dark and light blue beads to provide a central pattern of a heart with fronds and other decoration. The flat spine is decorated in a similar manner, dark and light blue panels alternating. Blue silk flyleaves. The whole is kept in a contemporary red morocco slip box decorated with an ornamental roll and lettered "ANNE NOUV". Broxb. 2.6.
Inside the upper half of the box is inscribed: Donné par Victor Simon Oeillet de Trasimene le premier Janvier 1762". Albert Ehrman's note reads: "The finest bead binding I have seen".

56. *Exercices spirituels pour les Confrères et Soeurs de la Confrairie du trèssaint Sacrement, première érigée à Paris, en l'église paroissiale de Saint Jacques de la Boucherie*, nouvelle édition, 1774, Paris, Prault, 8°.
Red/brown morocco; outer border of various ornaments, central wreath enclosing a pilgrim kneeling before the Host. Flat spine. Dark blue paper pastedown. Broxb. 44.23.
No provenance. Albert Ehrman suggested that the central medallion might be the badge of the relevant confraternity. Dark blue, often shiny, endleaves became popular in the 1770s.

57. [LOUIS XVIII (Louis, comte de Provence)], *Catalogue des livres de la bibliothèque de Monsieur au Chateau* [de Brunoy], [manuscript, after 1786], folio.
Brown calf; triple fillet with rosettes, arms of Charles Ferdinand, duc de Berry (Olivier 2548 stamp 9) in centre. Flat spine, lettered up. Shiny blue endleaves. Broxb. 84.26.
Charles Ferdinand, duc de Berry; C. F. Bishop (sale 1938, lot 1377); W. Loring Andrews. The comte de Provence became "Monsieur" in 1777.

The duc de Berry (1778- assassinated in the Paris Opera 1820) was the second son of the comte d'Artois (later Charles X) and thus the nephew of the owner of the library. Brunoy, of which Louis XVIII made the Duke of Wellington marquis, lies to the south east of Paris.

As was mentioned at the beginning, these books represent the collecting both of academic private collectors interested in either the text of the book or in its aesthetic appeal. The result is a selection which may or may not be fully representative of the binding styles of the period, fine or more general, although, as it happens, it does here appear to be fairly correct for the former. The books were not collected contemporaneously although both Douce's buying and the Bodleian's was carried out right at the end of the century and within a few years of the binding being done. Many items were however acquired much later by the libraries in question or by the immediate donors to them, and notably so at the end of the nineteenth century or in the twentieth. Bearing these caveats in mind one can nevertheless consider what these fine and interesting books, containing many major bibliographical items, show us of French eighteenth century book binding.

Two different conclusions can be drawn from such a review of holdings: firstly there are the statistical, listing covering materials, kinds of books, sources of ownership and the like, and secondly there are the aesthetic and technical aspects, looking at the styles chosen for the material at various dates and seeing how these may have been affected by general artistic fashions or by advancing technical expertise, the latter of course often driven by economic imperatives. It is clear, for instance, that red morocco was by far the most popular covering material, being used in just over half the cases. Green, brown and olive, in that order, all come as virtually equal second but even all together they are notably less popular than the red. A survey of the nature of books bound shows that about eight per cent were manuscripts, some older, some contemporary, but just under half the items were printed books appearing before the eighteenth century and one third of these were incunables. About ten per cent of the sample were works such as *Almanachs royaux* which can be dated with some assurance to the year of their publication but the big subject division is clearly between religious books and works which can be termed literary classics, these groups being of roughly the same size and making up two thirds of the list. From this one might hazard that two particular markets could be identified, the one being a social one for almanacks and religious works, while the other was a more bibliophile one concentrating on important and "collectable" books of which, in the later years of the eighteenth century at least, incunables played a notable role.

Any consideration of the social standing of the commissioners or recipients of these bindings must start with the fact that only seven items, some fourteen per cent, bear armorial stamps. One of these, however, that with the arms of Madame de Pompadour (no. 50), is suspect since the work does not feature in her catalogue and a trade in adding her arms to well-bound eighteenth-century books is known to have existed. Four more, however, have respectable contemporary provenances and may well have been bound for these owners or libraries. There is, perhaps surprisingly, only one item with the straight royal French arms, those of Louis XV (no. 16 bis) although one must also add another with those of his queen, Marie Leczinska (no. 3). One work (no. 40) however apparently comes from the royal library. Three nevertheless belong to members of "the blood", namely those for the prince de Dombes (no. 16), the duc d'Orleans (no. 29) and the comte de Provence (no. 57). Other members of the French aristocracy represented include the Duras-Bournonville family (no. 10) and that of Bourgevin Moligny (no. 11). Another proper representative of this eighteenth-century world is the book (no. 9) bound for a member of the Pâris family, long the financiers of the Ancien Régime. The count Hoym (no. 1) was the Polish ambassador in Paris and among other noble owners one should mention Lord Leigh (1742-1786), the benefactor of Oriel College, by whom it seems likely that nos 16 bis and 17 were owned. These provenances therefore give a good cross-section idea of the top bibliophile world of the period in France.

Equally, looked at from the point of view of the historical evolution of styles, the bindings at Oxford afford an excellent over-view of those of the French eighteenth century. Here both aesthetic and technical considerations come into play. The bindings listed above illustrate how, with *de luxe* books, the fashion of the early years for highly tooled works moved on, through the colourful mosaics and the equally highly tooled dentelles (which nevertheless rely on contrasting their design with an untouched expanse of fine leather), to impressive but more easily produced works. These were of different sizes, at first large items but later also to small ones, for which, as in earlier times panel stamps (meaning here large border stamps applied by presses) were used. Later, under the purifying influence of Neo-Classicism, there was a reversion to the simpler "fillet and fine leather" style at the end of the century, the rolls and tools involved being new in design and finely worked but in an austere and elegant fashion.

The first three items in the list above, with their simple exterior fillets or rolls and their owners' arms in the centre, represent well the standard style of the late seventeenth and early eighteenth centuries. The mosaics, which follow, contain both items related to the "Avant 1715" group (associated with Luc-Antoine Boyet and Louis-Joseph Dubois) and a number of which closely recall proven early Padeloup styles. Here one has items with mosaic frames, with flowers and with general colour patterns, some realistic, some naive, but all bringing some new verve and colour as a reaction to the more austere late years of Louis XIV. The "Sacre", or coronation, of Louis XV in 1722 was a notably stage-managed affair and special arrangements were made for binding the large number of copies of the engraved record. Padeloup was again concerned and for the large volumes of plates more industrial techniques had to be employed, hence the return to the use of larger engraved stamps, usable in combinations, and applied by a press. Later smaller format panel stamps were again used for almanacks and standard prayer books.

The third style of the century was the dentelle where a "lacy" border, at first fairly rectangular but later with more movement and curves, was made up by the use of numerous flowing frond tools, bursting out of shell-like corners and culminating in sprays and dots, sometimes with this decorated area underlined by having a highly dotted ground, all of which contrasted with the blank fine leather left in the centre. The dentelle recalls the magnificent metal work of the period and closely resembles the ornate plaster ceilings in the Dauphin's apartment at Versailles. The sheer boisterous complexity of the mosaic and the dentelle were evidently likely to bring out a reaction in decorative style and this was heralded both by Padeloup's return to straight-lined frames and by the special design, usually attributed to Gravelot (one of the first times a famous named contemporary designer is associated with a binding decoration), where carefully calculated and relatively sparse neo-classical patterns are brought in. A return to sobriety follows with a meticulous use of rolls and lines. This was evidently felt to be suitable by the more serious and academically minded book-collecting world of the late eighteenth century and thus both contents such as incunabula and binding were an attraction to a Bodleian which at last had some funds for purchase. One may now regret their, to our view, desacration of such bindings with a heavy Bodleian armorial stamp but perhaps this can be taken as a sign of their times when ownership was still marked in this traditional manner.

In general, then, Oxford today can display good examples of virtually all the styles of decorative bookbinding current in eighteenth century France, one of that country's many fine periods in this art. These holdings are, as fine bindings usually are, due largely to library benefactors: to start with, as ever, the inimitable and inspired Francis Douce, but more recently and, in this field, outstandingly, to Albert Ehrman and his family. Others too have shared these enthusiasms, collectors, librarians, and, one should add particularly, booksellers and auctioneers who, like the Hobson family, have done so much to rescue, to identify and to recognise such bindings. These works brought pleasure in their time and, identified and understood, can now be preserved for the appreciation and joy of future generations.

Note: The plates illustrating this article have largely been provided by the Bodleian Library which is glad thus to be honoured by being associated with this tribute to Dr A. R. A. Hobson. The others are reproduced by kind permission of the authorities of Keble, Oriel and The Queen's Colleges. The author wishes to recognise the friendly and invaluable assistance of Mr Paul Morgan and of Mr M. Dudley, Mr C. Harrison, Mr W. G. Hodges, Mrs M. Kirwan, Dr W. E. Parry, Miss H. Powell, Dr J. S. G. Simmons, Mrs M. Szurko, Mr M. L. Turner, and Dr D. G. Vaisey, Bodley's Librarian.

Bibliographical note:

The following are the principal works referred to or used for this article:

BARBER, G. G. "Brochure, cartonage, reliure: the provisional protection of print in the late eighteenth century", *Rousseau and the eighteenth century: essays in memory of R. A. Leigh*, edited by M. Hobson, J. T. A. Leigh and R. Wokler, Oxford 1992, pp. 43-58.

Bodleian Library, Oxford, *Fine bindings 1500-1700 from Oxford libraries*, [exhibition catalogue], Oxford, 1968.

HOBSON, A. R. A. *French and Italian Collectors and their bindings, illustrated from examples in the library of J. R. Abbey*, Oxford, 1953.

HOBSON, A. R. A. "Waddesdon Manor", *The Book Collector*, 8 (1959), pp. 131-139 [also in *Gazette des Beaux Arts*, 54 (1959), pp. 87-94].

MICHON, L.- M. *Les reliures mosaïquées du XVIIIe siècle*, Paris, 1956.

MORGAN, P. *Oxford libraries outside the Bodleian*, 2nd edition, Oxford, 1980.

NIXON, H. M. *Broxbourne Library. Styles and designs of bookbindings from the twelfth to the twentieth century*, London, 1956.

OLIVIER, E., Hermal, G., de Roton, R. *Manuel de l'amateur de reliures armoriées françaises*, 29 vols, Paris, 1924-1925.

Philip, I. G. *Gold-tooled bookbindings* [in the Bodleian], Oxford, 1951.

Rhodes, D. E. A *Catalogue of incunabula in all the libraries of Oxford University outside the Bodleian*, Oxford, 1982.

Thoinan, E. *Les relieurs français 1500-1800*, Paris, 1893.

Elly Cockx-Indestege

ON THE HISTORY OF BOOKBINDING IN THE LOW COUNTRIES: A GLIMPSE OF PROSPER VERHEYDEN AND HIS CORRESPONDENTS
(c. 1900-1947)

On the 26th of July 1932, the Flemish expert on bookbinding in the Low Countries at the time, Prosper Verheyden, wrote a long letter from Antwerp to the Dutch expert on bibliography in The Hague, Miss M. E. Kronenberg. He reported on his visit to London a few weeks before. I single out the following passage: "Dus, ik ben te Londen geweest; op bezoek bij Geoffrey D. Hobson, die mij al zijne wrijfsels heeft laten doorwerken: die van Gottlieb, van Gibson, van Husung, van Weale, en mij bracht bij Col. Moss te Sonning on Thames, waar de Thames al zo breed is als de Nethe te Lier en de Dijle te Mechelen; en bij Alb. Ehrman te Londen, en bij Quaritch, waar de heer Ferguson één dienstvaardigheid is. Maar Hobson is veel meer dan die bibliofielen en groote verzamelaars; hij is een schat van een vent, zoó aandachtig om U voort te helpen. Na een dag hindert U zijn hardhoorigheid niet meer bij het gesprek: gij kent de juiste maat, en die hoeft niet eens groot te zijn, maar juist. Ook bij den hr Goldschmidt ben ik op bezoek geweest tot diep in den nacht: wat een geestig mensch, en wat een geheugen! Hebt gij zijn opstel over Gottlieb gelezen? – Dan heb ik ook gewerkt bij de dochter van James Weale, in dezes huis, in het huis dat ook een toevlucht was voor Guido Gezelle. En in de Art Library, South Kensington. En in British Museum...".[1] [Then, I have been in London, invited by Geoffrey D. Hobson who let me go through all his rubbings: those from Gottlieb, Gibson, Husung and Weale. He took me to Col. Moss at Sonning on Thames, where the Thames is nearly as wide as the Nethe in Lier and the Dijle in Mechelen.[2] And I was with Alb. Ehrman in London, and visited Quaritch where Mr. Ferguson is most obliging. But Hobson is much more than those bibliophiles and great collectors; he is a man worth his weight in gold, who cannot do too much for you. After one day you are no longer troubled by his hard hearing: one knows the exact measure which doesn't even have to be loud, but exact. I paid also a visit to Mr.

---

1. The Hague, Royal Library, Special Collections, Correspondence M. E. Kronenberg.
2. In the small old town of Lier, 15 km. southeast of Antwerp, where the two rivers Nethe meet.

Goldschmidt until deep into the night: what a witty man and what a memory! Did you read his article on Gottlieb? – And I went to Weale's house where his daughter is living; it is the house where Guido Gezelle found a refuge.[1] And I was in the Art Library, South Kensington, [now the Victoria and Albert Museum] and in the British Museum".] Back home, Verheyden was exhausted, but blissfully happy.

Hobson and Verheyden knew each other for barely two years. They started writing each other letters from about 1930 on; it came to an end with Verheyden's death in 1948. Born in 1873 in the beautiful, historic town of Mechelen, midway between Antwerp and Brussels, Prosper Verheyden was a self-made man who developed very early a broad interest in and deep knowledge of the book in the Low Countries, particularly during the fifteenth and sixteenth centuries. The decoration of bindings became finally his preferred field. He had a very personal style of writing; the reading of his letters, articles and essays is for his countrymen a real pleasure – which makes it difficult to translate them.

A year or so before his death, he asked my father, Luc Indestege, if he would agree to receive his whole documentation on bookbinding, expressing the hope that the history of bookbinding in the Low Countries could be completed. Alas, at the time my father died, in 1974, this history was still unwritten: too much field-work remained to be done and neither could devote himself exclusively to this task. Nevertheless, the documentation had grown considerably and a whole series of articles had been published. This documentation contains substantial archives of rubbings, photographs and old slides, annotations and comments, a reference library, and last but not least correspondence.

Among the over one hundred and fifty correspondents whose letters,

1. Guido Gezelle (1830-1899), famous poet-priest from Bruges, was known also as an 'Anglophile'. He had been teaching English at the St. Lodewijkscollege, was appointed rector of the Seminarium Anglo-Belgicum (1861-1865) and by the end of his life rector of the English convent of nuns (reg. canons of St. Augustin). Gezelle had indeed many English friends and went several times to England. James Weale (1832-1917), a convert to the Roman Catholic Church, settled in Bruges in 1857, where he found abundant sources for his study of Christian art in Flanders. In 1858 both men met for the first time. Back in England, Weale was living in Clapham from 1878 until his death. There he was visited by Gezelle in September 1888 and 1899, who there met with understanding and friendship, which cannot be said he always got from his superiors in Bruges. Cf. on this topic CHRISTINE D'HAEN, *De wonde in 't hert: Guido Gezelle, een dichtersbiografie* (Tielt s. d.) and MICHEL VAN DER PLAS, *Mijnheer Gezelle: biografie van een priester-dichter, 1830-1899* (Tielt & Baarn 1991). The correspondence with his English friends has recently been published: *De briefwisseling van Guido Gezelle met de Engelsen 1854-1899*. Ed. Boudewijn de Leeuw, Patrick De Wilde, Kris Verbeke, onder leiding van Ada Deprez (Gent 1991), 3 vols. [= Koninklijke Academie voor Nederlandse taal- en letterkunde, Reeks V: Publikaties van de Commissie voor Moderne Letteren; 25].

postcards and scrawls have been preserved, the larger part are from institutions or individuals, answering Verheyden on standard questions on the whereabouts of a binding or providing him with rubbings or photographs. The other, smaller part, exceeds the former in its quality: here we find the experts on bookbindings, the book historians and bibliographers, the bibliophiles.

The most important of them all is undoubtedly Geoffrey D. Hobson (1882-1949). About eighty, often long letters, often with a P. S., between 5 December 1930 and 27 October 1947, with an interruption of five years during World War II. There are, further, letters from Albert Ehrman (1890-1969) in London and Beaulieu, Hants., from Ernst Philip Goldschmidt (1887-1954) in London, from Max Joseph Husung (1882-1944) in Berlin, from M. E. Kronenberg (1881-1970) in The Hague, from Ernst Kyriss (1881-1974) in Stuttgart, from Col. William E. Moss (1875-1953) in Sonning on Thames and West Byfleet, from J. Basil Oldham (1882-1962) in Shrewsbury, from Rena Pennink (1885-1985) in The Hague, from Berthe van Regemorter (1879-1964) in Antwerp, from Willem de Vreese (1869-1938) in Ghent, later Rotterdam and Voorschoten, to cite the most important.

Although some letters are dated from the very beginning of this century, it is not until 1930 that the correspondence becomes abundant. The reason is obvious: Verheyden was responsible for the contribution on bookbinding at the World Exhibition in Antwerp in 1930. Nearly 300 items, from public and private collections mainly in Belgium, were on exhibition from June to September, described and published as part v in the section Old-Flemish Art.[1] Verheyden preferred his native tongue, Dutch, when writing his articles, but this did not prevent him from managing French or English with his foreign correspondents. Probably all his letters were handwritten. In very few cases a minute is kept in the archives. What happened in the meanwhile to all his letters, dispersed over Europe, is not yet entirely known to me. In any case, his letters to G.D. Hobson, M.E. Kronenberg and R. Pennink are preserved.[2] Husung had been active for a number of years in the Gesamtkatalog der Wiegendrucke in Berlin, but no letters of Verheyden were found.[3] Ernst Kyriss, a well-organized man, surely kept all his correspondence; his widow died in 1981 and we may suppose that she left it to the children.[4] As for Berthe

---

1. *Wereldtentoonstelling voor koloniën, zeevaart en Oud-Vlaamsche kunst, Antwerpen 1930. Afdeeling der Oud-Vlaamsche kunst, deel V Boekbanden: Catalogus* (Brussel 1930), 208 pp., 18 cm.

2. Those to the last two in the Royal Library in The Hague, Special Collections.

3. Letter from the GW to the present writer, December 1979.

4. Peter Amelung was so kind as to answer my questions about the intellectual heritage of Kyriss: the Württembergische Landesbibliothek in Stuttgart has his collec-

van Regemorter, her estate came into the hands of her nephew who informed me that no letters have been found.[1]

Among the letters Prosper Verheyden received during the thirties up to c. 1945/46, those of Hobson and Kronenberg are among the most interesting and captivating. Yet I will not present those here. I leave it to Anthony Hobson to deal with his father's correspondence. As to Miss Kronenberg's letters to Verheyden, I may refer to a first, very modest booklet recently published.[2] For the time being I will concentrate here on three other persons: Ernst Kyriss, Col. Moss and Emile Dacier.

On the 24th of July 1932 Ernst Kyriss answers what is apparently Verheyden's first letter to him. "Für Jhre ausführlichen Mitteilungen über den Brüsseler Einband mit dem Aufdruck 'Johes de Dutche me fecit' und vor allem die Uebersendung des sehr interessanten Kataloges mit seinem reichem Material danke ich Jhnen bestens". The 'Brussels binding', decorated with a panelstamp with two rows of five animals in circles and divided by the inscription as cited above, is described in the Antwerp catalogue of 1930, n. 2, among the Antwerp bindings. Very soon Verheyden corrected the provenance to Brussels, as is evident from this letter and from Verheyden's working copy of his Catalogue.[3] The Antwerp catalogue in hand, Kyriss checked in the library where at the time he was gathering material for his own research, the Municipal Library in Augsburg where he found another copy of a Johannes De Dutche binding, on an incunable.[4] "Genügt Jhnen für Jhre Zwecke, eine Vervielfältigung,[5] wie Sie solche bei Mr. Hobson gesehen haben? Selbstverständlich bekommen Sie von mir alles, was Sie interessiert. Denn nur durch Zusammenarbeiten lassen sich brauchbare Ergebnisse erzielen. Sie müssen Sich nur einige Tage gedulden, bis ich mein Material in dieser Hinsicht durchgegangen habe." It took Kyriss however a few years before he could inform Verheyden on more Flemish panelstamps

---

tion of rubbings, his scientific reference library, but no letters. (Letter to the present writer dated 11.5.1992).

1. Letter from P. Van Regemorter dated 12 June 1992.
2. The present writer, *Over Bossche banden, Esopus en een prognosticatie: een greep uit de correspondentie tussen M. E. Kronenberg en Prosper Verheyden uit 1932* (Wildert 1992). [On bindings of 's-Hertogenbosch, Aesopus and a prognostication: selected correspondence between M. E. Kronenberg and Prosper Verheyden from 1932]. This is a private press publication of the Carbolineumpers in Wildert (prov. Antwerp).
3. See note 4. Cf. also his "La reliure en Brabant" in *Le livre, l'estampe, l'édition en Brabant du XVe au XIXe siècle* (Gembloux 1935) pp. 166-7 [Mémorial de l'exposition d'art ancien à Bruxelles].
4. Hain 109; GW 7219; I. Hubay, *Incunabula der Staats- und Stadtbibliothek Augsburg* (Wiesbaden 1974) [= Inkunabelkataloge Bayerischer Bibliotheken], n. 612.
5. Consequently it concerns copies or reproductions of rubbings.

in the German libraries he was visiting. In his letter of 20 March 1937 Kyriss informs Verheyden about the "Niederländische Einbände" he could find, but "Ich glaube jedoch kaum, dass für Sie etwas Neues dabei ist. Der von Jhnen verfasste Katalog von Antwerpen, auf den mich seinerzeit Herr Hobson aufmerksam machte, hat mir dabei vorzügliche Dienste geleistet".

Verheyden and Kyriss regularly sent each other offprints of their articles. On the 15th March 1937 Kyriss writes to Verheyden: "Für die Zusendung Jhres Aufsatzes in Het Boek über Godefridus Bloc sage ich Jhnen meinen verbindlichsten Dank.[1] Ich habe mich darüber sehr gefreut und habe Jhre ausführliche Abhandlung mit grossem Interesse durchgearbeitet. Ich darf Sie bei dieser Gelegenheit darauf aufmerksam machen, dass A. Rhein im "Allgemeinen Anzeiger für Buchbindereien" Jahrgang 1936, Seite 353/4 über "Einband Pressendruck 100 Jahre vor Gutenberg" unter Beigabe von 3 Abbildungen schreibt. Wenn Sie diesen Aufsatz nicht kennen und sich dafür interessieren, kann ich Jhnen gerne die Nummer der hier erscheinenden Zeitschrift zusenden.[2]

Vor kurzem habe ich endlich auch Jhre grosse Arbeit über "La reliure en Brabant" erhalten. Ich habe sie zwar noch nicht gelesen, aber schon die erste Tafel zeigt zwei ganz ungewöhnlich interessante Einbände, so dass die Lektüre, zumal bei der sehr übersichtlichen Anordnung des ganzen Stoffes ein sehr grosser Genuss zu werden verspricht. Sie erschliessen hier zusammenfassend viel Neuland, das zum grossen Teil bisher unbearbeitet war oder nur in weit zerstreuten und schwer erreichbaren Abhandlungen beschrieben worden ist..." and a few days later: "Ihre neue Arbeit scheint ja ausserordentlich Interessantes und Neues an den Tag zu bringen. Solche Funde glücken einem nur in den allerseltensten Fällen".[3]

At the time when Verheyden was in London with Hobson, he came across a rubbing which Husung (or was it Gottlieb?) had made in Salzburg[4] of an intriguing panel. It shows two rows of four animals – deer,

---

1. P. VERHEYDEN, "Huis en have van Godevaert De Bloc, scriptor en boekbinder te Brussel, 1364-1384" in *Het Boek*, XXIV, 1937, pp. 129-45.

2. This issue must evidently have been sent to Verheyden, although I am unable to find it. The title runs "Einband-und Pressendruck hundert Jahre vor Gutenberg"; it concerns the Henricus Walram-Platte: two rows of five animals in circles, divided by an inscription. Rhein published another article with the title "Wann und wie begann der Pressenblinddruck" in *Archiv für Büchbinderei*, 31, 1931, fasc. 10, pp. 69-72, which deals with the same topic. Adolf Rhein, from Erfurt, bookbinder and teacher in a 'Gewerbeschule', was obviously interested in the technique of bookbinding.

3. Letter to Verheyden dated 20 March 1927.

4. V. 7. F. 88 in the Oeffentliche Studienbibliothek (now Universitätsbibliothek); it contains two incunabula printed in Venice and Treviso (HC 10328, Goff L-302; HCR 13661, Goff Q-21).

dog, dragon, boar – divided by two coats of arms – fleur de lys, rampant lion –, surrounded by the inscription "Non possum prohibere / canem quin latrat vbique nec queo / mendaci claudere / labra viro iheronimus papal me lighauit". Verheyden made a sketch of the rubbing and wrote to Ernst von Frisch, director of the library in Salzburg. He learned incidentally that four other bindings with the Papal panel were the property of St. Nicholas' church in Isny (Württemberg).[1] The Salzburg binding has in addition small tools in the border – rosette, heraldic lion, griffin – and a contemporary provenance mark.[2] Otto Leuze, the former librarian of the Württembergische Landesbibliothek, who in his above cited article mentions a similar binding containing an Antwerp and a Nuremberg imprint, was inclined to localize the Papal panel in the Netherlandish or Lower Rhine area. Kyriss, who had them inspected again, was unable to find any information on Papal or the origin of the bindings, but "dabei liegt doch zweifellos, allgemein gesprochen, ein niederländischer Einband vor".[3] At the time the contemporary owner of the Salzburg binding, Johannes Gaisser, was not yet identified. G.D. Hobson however was able to identify him as a citizen of Augsburg and trace him in Paris in 1493 and 1500, where he bought Parisian panels, afterwards used by a German binder.[4] Yet the binder Papal remains unidentified. Victor van der Haeghen mentions him, in 1485, without comment (according to a note by Verheyden; no source is given).

Kyriss' last letter to Verheyden, dated 5 April 1947, remained unanswered; Hobson informed him of Verheyden's illness. Soon after his death, Kyriss and my father started writing letters, a correspondence which lasted for about twenty five years.

One of the main collectors of books and bindings emerging from Verheyden's letters is Colonel Moss. We have seen already that Verheyden made his acquaintance thanks to G. D. Hobson. As a collector, Moss concentrated mainly on bindings, printing and William Blake.[5] In fact, his old panel stamp bindings were limited to Godfrey, Spierinck or

1. O. LEUZE, "Die Bibliothek der Nikolauskirche in Isny" in *Zeitschrift für Bücherfreunde*, N. F. 15 (Leipzig 1923) pp. 60-63. Letter dated 19 October 1932 from Husung to Verheyden. The Isny bindings are 'Sammelbände' of mainly Parisian imprints (1. H 1648; 2. HC 10458; 3. GW 4824, C 1686, HC 10220; 4. GW 3917, 4037, 4049, 3909); an old provenance mark refers to Paris.
2. Letter dated 4 August 1932 from E. von Frish to Verheyden.
3. Letter dated 11 February 1941 from Kyriss to Verheyden.
4. G. D. HOBSON, "Parisian bindings, 1500-1525" in *The Library*, Fourth Ser., IX, 1931, pp. 393-434, pp. 410-11 n. 7.
5. See S. GIBSON, "Colonel William E. Moss" in *Bodleian Library Record*, 5, 1955, pp. 155-66.

Reynes.[1] Nevertheless the five letters Verheyden received from Moss between 1933 and 1938 manifest mutual sympathy and esteem; even unexpected common interests came to the surface. Let a few quotations from the letters speak for themselves.[2]

"As you know, I do not know very much about the old stamped bindings, although I like them. I have however one small note for you. You will know our friend Goldschmidt's No. 129... English panel of two saints one with name 'S. Katerine' the other with no name. Goldschmidt says 'S. Roch (?)' with a 'leper's rattle'. I have records of three more examples of this, all at Cambridge college libraries, besides the 'Dynus' which Dunn had.[3]

"Now there turns up a book, MS Statutes of the Austin Canons, with one of these stamps, St Katherine, on one cover, and the other on the lower cover: and this is entitled 'S. Thomas'. It is not a 'leper's rattle' which he holds but a 'builder's rule' that is, a 24-inch measuring-rod with a hinge, doubled so as to look like a pair of compasses!

"It is very interesting to me, as I supposed that this representation of S. Thomas was quite local and Italian (Raffaello &c.): but it may help to explain why some of the very oldest Lodges of Freemasons called themselves Lodges of S. Thomas. The emblem was supposed to be a Compass, that is all![4]

"Mr Hobson wants me to send you photographs of the Goltzius binding presented to Philip of Austria, King of Spain, 1563, which is in the Bodleian Library. I am happy to do so. I add to these, photographs of a volume I have, Goltzius' presentation copy of the same book to Balthasar Schetz, Baron of Hoboken, which you will see is just the same thing, with Goltzius' own motto 'HVBERTAS AVREA SECLI'. What is very odd is that my book went into the possession of an owner at Constantinople, whose name I cannot be sure of, he writes so very large! Perhaps Ioannes Zlatouitas?[5]

"I have not been idle about the Van den Ghein Bell. I thought I would

---

1. Letter dated 24 July 1932 from Moss to Hobson.
2. The frequent use of new paragraphs here has not been systematically respected.
3. On St. Roch panels see G. COLIN, "L'image de saint Roch estampée sur des reliures" in *Le Livre et l'Estampe*, 37, 1991, n. 135, pp. 7-69.
4. Moss also collected works on freemasonry.
5. Moss' copy of Goltzius *Julius Caesar sive Historiae imperatorum Caesarumque Romanorum* (Bruges 1562 [altered to 1563]), is lot 741, with reproduction, in Sotheby's Catalogue of the sale of the 2nd of March 1937. C. E. DEKESEL in his *Hubertus Goltzius, the father of ancient numismatics, Venlo-Weertsburg 30.10.1526 - Bruges 24.10.1583: an annotated and illustrated bibliography* (Gandavum Flandrorum 1988), a privately distributed publication in draftform, does not mention, at least not explicitly, the Moss copy. According to Dekesel, there are two issues of this edition.

verify the few in England which Dr van Doerslaer mentions. I am afraid that three of them turn into one. I have had a long letter from the Vicar of Whalley in Lancashire where one is, and he has told me much which supplements Dr Doerslaer. My Bell, I find, has the same 'frise' as the 1593 bell at Dannenberg-Elbe, by Jean Van den Ghein I: also the angels' heads with cartouches are the same as those on the bell of 1585 of Peter II, at Malines, S. Jean. This Malines bell is 50 cm. high and 60 cm. diameter. Mine is the same. The Whalley bell has three medallions (I) Vierge et Enfant (II) Fuite en Egypte...Riposo (III) St George et Dragon.

"May I keep your book by Dr van Doerslaer a little longer? I am writing to the publisher to enquire whether it is possible to buy it now, as the Vicar of Whalley wants to buy one if he can?

"I have not found the armorial on the Bell. I do not think it is English. I do not think an English order for a Bell would have been accompanied by a drawing of an armorial! I think it must be the armorial of some small convent in Flanders!

"Further, I believe I have found by an accident, the Cambridge Bell of 1548. The description given by Dr van Doerslaer,... "Hall Bell"...tells us nothing. I believe it belongs to Peterhouse College, one of the oldest at Camb., and hangs over the Dining-Hall of that College, and is used to ring the hour of Dinner! It means, that it is a small Bell only. I shall hear presently about it.

"My correspondent, the Vicar of Whalley, tells me that he is sure that Van den Ghein Bells are to be found also in Mexico, and not improbably in Peru, and perhaps elsewhere in South America. Dr van Doerslaer never contemplated this, I think. There is a book on Mexican bells, which may be in Bodley,...accent on 'may'...written by an Irish monk, and printed 'sub umbra montis Popocatepetl' which means quite a number of places![1]

From this letter it appears that Moss had a more than superficial knowledge of old bells. This undoubtedly added something to the sympathy between Moss and Verheyden.

---

1. Letter dated 12 March 1933 from Moss to Verheyden. This long passage shows the common interest of both men in bells and carillons. Verheyden was for many years the secretary of the "Mechelse Beiaardschool" [the Mechlin School of Carillon], now "Koninklijke Beiaardschool Jef Denijn, Internationaal Hoger Instituut voor Beiaardkunst", the friend of Jef Denyn (1862-1941), famous carilloneur of his native town of Mechelen, and of William Gorham Rice of Albany, N. Y. (†1945), member of the Civil Service Commission of the State of New York and author of several books on the art of carillon. GEORGES VAN DOORSLAER, a medical doctor in Mechelen, is the author of *Les Van den Ghein, fondeurs de cloches, Canons, sonnettes et mortiers à Malines*, (Antwerp 1910). Of the Van den Gheyns Mathias (1721-1785) is the most famous, well known as carilloneur in Louvain.

Illustrating their interest in books and bibliography in general is the story of "a mysterious book by Van Praet". On 24 December 1934 Moss wrote to Verheyden as follows: "Quite long ago I was 'intrigued' (horrible English!) by a reference made by Le Roux de Lincy, 'Jean Grolier' to a mysterious book by Van Praet, being a first and uncompleted edition of his 'Catalogue des livres imprimés sur vélin', which contained notes about bindings for Grolier, Maioli Lauwrin and others...Dr Thomas found it for me at the British Museum...very dusty und uncared-for, minus back, and one cover fallen off. You will find a lot about it in Brunet, Manuel, sub VAN PRAET. Also in the Sale Catalogue of J.C. Brunet, Partie 1. no 705. There are only seven copies on paper and two on vellum existing. All the rest was destroyed. Yet it is a huge folio of 544 pages. It describes 73 books on vellum only...and about 400 on paper, bindings, libraries, book-collectors &c. Brunet says that one paper copy was given to the Library of Bruges. Will you find out for me if it is still there? [...] The British Museum copy of Van Praet was J.J. de Bure's. I shall try to 'locate the other copies! [added by hand] for my reprint'.

The next letter, dated 27 January 1935, proves that Verheyden did go to the Municipal Library in Bruges: "Many thanks for your enquiries at the Library of Bruges!

"Still...je reste un peu incrédule...I cannot forget that I could not find this big Van Praet at the British Museum myself! I hunted in the great long catalogue under VAN PRAET...found the well-known octavo edition, and other things: tried PRAET, VAN, and found more things but not my book: then I gave it up and handed it over to Dr Thomas, who turned on some poor young man to apply methods of seriousness. It was there...sub. CATALOGUE...Horrible!

"Now it seems that Van Praet printed in 1805, chez Crapelet aîné, 20 pages as specimen. This he sent to Bruges, as you have found. Then in 1813 the big book came out, in two parts both dated 1813, but he had to reprint the first 20 pages again, and there were so many additions to these that there are 13 leaves, or 26 pages additional, all numbered page 20, before one comes to page 21. [added by hand] (printed by Crapelet fils).

"I hazard a guess that Bruges received a copy lightly bound in thin boards (like the British Museum copy [added by hand] was!) without the first 20 pages, but with the new 26 pages numbered 20, [...] and therefore, no title-page at all! It was intended that they should bind it up with the 1805 piece they had. Which...about 1814-15, was a work not done! And if some poor young assistant librarian came across a book without a title-page, how would he put it in the Catalogue of the Library? You must look for a big folio about 32 to 33 centimetres high, or even more than this, as it may be 'uncut and unopened'...and about 8 centimetres in thickness:

probably in thin boards covered with 'percaline' of dull rose colour.

"But what a commentary on bibliographical labour! If you have no title page, or a very wrong title-page (because 'vélins' are only a small part of the book) you have made your work 'inabordable' to the very persons who might use it!"[1]

To be fair to the 'poor young assistant librarian' or whoever, it should be explained that the *Catalogue* was published anonymously – hence the entry sub CATALOGUE in the British Museum Catalogue!

When visiting the old library of the British and Foreign Bible Society in London, Col. Moss looked for bindings which might be of some interest to Verheyden. Alas, "They have some bindings on show, but most are on the shelves, and as there is no catalogue of them the librarians do not know what there is. [...]

"In the show-cases I saw a nice 'Spes' binding and thought of you at once. And your notion that the original design of these was Protestant... 'propagandisme par reliure'..."[2]

Moss tells in the same letter, written from Rivey Lodge in West Byfleet, Surrey, that he has been seriously ill, that he moved from The Manor House in Sonning-on-Thames nearer to London and that he sold most of his 'library of rare bindings and books, and big books of reference', keeping all his portfolios of photographs and notes, 'and am just as happy, with less anxiety for safety of valuable objects all round me'.[3]

In the last letter Verheyden received, Moss tells that Hobson wrote him about "another book of rubbings, mostly of books at the 'Sunderland' sale" which he wants to see.[4]

The last of the three persons of whom I propose to evoke the relationship with Prosper Verheyden, is Emile Dacier.

---

1. *Catalogue des livres imprimés sur vélin, avec date, depuis 1458 jusqu'en 1472. Première partie 1457-1470*. Paris: De Bure Frères libraires, janvier 1813, 20 p., [*]2 A-E2, followed by pp. 20(1)-20(26), E_1-E_6[2] E_7[1]; pp. 21-543, [1], F-6T2. On the verso of the half-title is printed "Ce Catalogue n'a point été continué sur ce plan, et n'a jamais été publié. Il n'en a été conservé que six exemplaires sur papier et deux sur VELIN, pour lesquels ce titre a été imprimé". One of the seven paper copies is kept at the Royal Library in Brussels, uncut, in boards covered with yellow brown treemarble (II 52. 994 C LP). The copy was bought from the bookseller Bluff in September 1888.

2. Letter dated 20 December 1937 from Moss to Verheyden.

3. Sotheby's Catalogue, sale 2-9 March 1937; parts of his collection in Sotheby's Catalogue, sale 10-11 May 1937 (nos 470-476), 19-20 December 1938, and Quaritch Catalogue no 534 (1937).

4. Letter dated 27 February 1938. In the sale catalogue of his collection two lots, 1222 and 1223, are rubbings from bookbindings, the first a collection made by J. J. Howard, the other one by Henry S. Richardson, respectively 9 and 7 vols. In Quaritch's Catalogue lot 39 are rubbings of armorial stamps.

'Chartiste' and art historian, Emile Dacier (1876-1952) was 'inspecteur général des bibliothèques et archives de France' from 1936 until 1941.[1] Shortly after World War II he was asked by the Parisian publishing house Rombaldi on the Boulevard St Germain to cooperate in an ambitious project called "Encyclopédie du livre"; paper, typography, illustration and bookbinding were to be treated. Dacier was to be the director of the volume devoted to bookbinding. It would concentrate on technique as well as decoration and what he calls "la reliure courante". The volume is scheduled at over 300 pages, 350 reproductions in the text and 20 colour plates. French bindings will be treated by Robert Brun, Louis-Marie Michon, Jacques Guignard and Dacier himself. "Reste la reliure étrangère. Mon ami G. D. Hobson vient de m'écrire qu'il accepte de traiter la reliure anglaise, et j'ai l'espoir que T. de Marinis fera la reliure italienne. Pour la reliure des Pays-Bas, l'opinion unanime est qu'*il n'y a que vous* qui puissiez la traiter. Il s'agit d'écrire environ 20 pp. du livre, soit la valeur de 40 à 45 pp. de dactylographie à grand interligne. On illustrera cela d'une vingtaine de reproductions de reliure, avec des figures au trait dans le texte, si vous le jugez bon (marques, signatures, étiquette, fers caractéristiques, etc.). Rétribution: 300 fr. la page imprimée, payables à la remise du manuscrit, le 1er avril 1946.

"Ce n'est pas tout. Je souhaiterais vivement que vous vous chargiez aussi d'écrire un court chapitre concernant les toutes premières reliures sans décoration, dont l'histoire et la technique peuvent être présentées d'ensemble, sans distinction de pays. Une dizaine de pages du livre, avec quelques illustrations, seraient sans doute suffisantes."[2] Verheyden was not conceited enough even to consider this second request: he wrote at the bottom of Dacier's letter "Répondu le 17 Sept. '45. Accepté. Quant aux reliures primitives non décorées, parlons-en à Hobson". From a draft of Verheyden's answer to Dacier, it is clear that Verheyden enjoyed this invitation but "Quant au chapitre relatif aux toutes premières reliures sans décoration, dont l'histoire et la technique seraient présentées sans distinction de nationalité, ne vous semble-t-il pas que c'est précisément M. Hobson qui est tout indiqué pour l'écrire? L'historien principale des reliures romanesques pour ne citer que ces oeuvres-là des 'primitifs' de la reliure, n'est-il pas qualifié mieux que personne pour s'occuper des

---

1. A. MARTIN in *Dictionnaire de biographie française*, IX (Paris 1961) col. 1465.
2. Letter dated 20 August 1945 from Dacier in La Lézardière, Nazelles (Indre-et-Loire) to Verheyden. Later, in his letter dated 16 November 1945, Dacier thinks "que l'on avait fait la part de la reliure flamande un peu trop serrée, en comparaison de certains des autres chapitres. En conséquence, et pour vous mettre à l'aise si besoin, il a été convenu que vous pourriez aller jusqu'à 30 à 35 pages, de sorte que vous ne soyez pas gêné dans votre exposé".

reliures les plus anciennes? […]" Dacier is happy with Verheyden's answer to point one. As to point two, he will risk asking G. D. Hobson, but "je ne vous tiens pas encore quitté…"[1] In the same letter he informs Verheyden that Hobson and De Marinis accepted, and: "J'attends une réponse pour l'Espagne, et je n'ai pas encore pris de décision pour l'Allemagne, ce qui n'est pas sans me préoccuper, car il ne me déplairait pas de me passer des Allemands. Voilà le problème." And further "Il faut faire quelque chose de beau, mais surtout de sérieux, de sûr, de complet autant que possible, avec de bonnes et nombreuses images, bref, un livre sur la reliure comme il n'en existe pas d'autre pendant longtemps. Je vous suis bien reconnaissant de m'y aider".

In April 1946 Dacier was still expecting the various contributions.[2] Verheyden's contribution was probably never completed, even if it was begun: not only did his health deteriorate, but the last quoted paragraph of Dacier's letter may have given him cause to think about the scientific objective of the project! The "Encyclopédie du livre" – a "monument" as Dacier saw it – seems never to have been published.[3]

---

1. Letter dated 23 September 1945 from Dacier to Verheyden.
2. Four people were to contribute on bookbinding in France (see above), Verheyden for the Netherlands, Tammaro de Marinis for Italy, Hueso Rolland for Spain.
3. J. VALLERY-RADOT, "Discours prononcé aux obsèques", and R.-A. WEIGERT, "Bibliographie de ses travaux (1898-1952)", in *Bulletin de la Société de l'histoire de l'art français*, 1952, pp. 113-5, 116-53.

Georges Colin

LES MARQUES DE LIBRAIRES ET D'ÉDITEURS DORÉES SUR DES RELIURES

La présente contribution à l'hommage rendu aujourd'hui à A.R.A. Hobson, au savant et à l'ami, porte sur un sujet qu'il lui est arrivé plus d'une fois de traiter, comme en témoignent, dans les notes de bas de page, les références à ses articles ou à ses livres. Elle lui doit beaucoup, car, il y a quelques années déjà, il m'a fourni très libéralement ses notes sur les reliures attribuées à John Norton, notes copieuses qu'il retrouvera maintenant, s'il veut bien lire les pages qui suivent.[1]

Les marques, dites parfois typographiques, dorées sur des reliures font l'objet, depuis plus de cent ans, d'une attention particulière.[2] Tant sur leur rareté que sur leur signification, l'accord s'est fait depuis longtemps et, dans les publications historiques comme dans les catalogues de ventes, on répète que les reliures ornées de telles marques sont extrêmement rares et que cette rareté, selon l'hypothèse de Goldschmidt, vient de ce qu'elles étaient destinées aux seuls exemplaires que les clients pouvaient examiner dans la boutique, à une époque où les livres se vendaient en feuilles.[3]

Il reste cependant un point obscur. Avant l'introduction de la dorure sur cuir, des libraires ont mis leur nom sur des reliures, généralement à l'aide de plaques estampées à froid. Selon Goldschmidt encore, la plupart des noms que l'on trouve sur les reliures anciennes ne sont pas des noms de relieurs, mais de libraires.[4] Robert Brun va plus loin et, non sans exagération, voit dans presque toutes les reliures à plaques, signées ou non, des reliures faites pour des libraires; puis, passant aux reliures à marques dorées, il n'y voit que la continuation toute naturelle d'une pratique courante en librairie.[5] Or dans une autre étude, à propos de l'introduction de

---

1. D'autres collègues m'ont aimablement aidé, que je suis heureux de remercier ici: Mesdames Mirjam Foot, A.M. Frachon, Geneviève Glorieux, Geneviève Guilleminot, Knospe, Philippa Marks, Hélène Richard, Stein, et Messieurs Ch. Alschner, Giles Barber, Bernard H. Breslauer, Pierre Campagne, Dominique Courvoisier, Paul Culot, Armin Hetzer, Manfred Mühlner, P.R. Quarrie, David W. Riley, Eric Speeckaert, Jan Storm van Leeuwen, Jean Toulet, Rowan Watson, John Wing.
2. Pour alléger le texte, on dira «marques dorées» même quand le décor est en argent ou qu'il a été obtenu «à sec», mais à l'aide d'un fer ou d'une plaque à dorer.
3. E. Ph. Goldschmidt, *Gothic and Renaissance bookbindings*, Londres, 1928, p. 40.
4. Goldschmidt, *op. cit.*, pp. 33-34.
5. Robert Brun, *Guide de l'amateur de reliures anciennes*, Bulletin du bibliophile et du bibliothécaire, 1935, p. 449.

la dorure dans la reliure commerciale, il écrit: «Les reliures ne sont plus jamais signées; leur marque distinctive, lorsqu'elle existe, n'est plus qu'un fleuron doré au centre du plat, mais alors ce fleuron reproduit toujours, en la simplifiant parfois, la marque typographique de celui qui en fait usage. A cette époque il devient impossible de dresser des listes de reliures offrant des marques de libraires ou d'imprimeurs. Elles deviennent en effet tout à fait exceptionnelles.»[1] Comment concilier ce caractère exceptionnel soudain avec la continuation toute naturelle d'une pratique courante en librairie?

Il convient donc de vérifier d'abord si les reliures à marques dorées sont réellement exceptionnelles. Or, en voulant faire le compte des spécimens connus, on s'aperçoit qu'il est parfois difficile de décider si un emblème doré au centre d'un plat de reliure est bien une marque d'imprimeur ou de libraire, alors même qu'il ressemble à une marque notoire. Il se peut en effet qu'il n'ait, sur la reliure, qu'une fonction allégorique, voire décorative. Ainsi il ne faut pas, comme Marius Michel et Léon Gruel, prendre pour des reliures aldines celles où figure une ancre autour de laquelle s'enroule un dauphin, car elles sont viennoises et non vénitiennes.[2] Des différents phénix attribués au libraire Gabriele Giolito, seul celui qui est accompagné des initiales GG est réellement sa marque.[3] Il convient de n'attribuer à Sébastien Gryphe et à ses successeurs que le griffon, symbole de la Diligence, tenant dans ses griffes un cube, symbole de la Constance, auquel est rattaché un globe ailé, emblème de la Fortune; un griffon sans cube ni globe ailé est un emblème assez répandu, étranger à l'officine lyonnaise; c'est le cas entre autres d'un griffon signalé par Ilse Schunke.[4] Une main tenant un bouquet désigne plusieurs imprimeurs français du XVIe siècle; cet emblème a cependant joui d'une telle vogue comme ornement de reliure, qu'il faut le considérer comme un symbole général, de fidélité ou de puissance et de vigilance.[5] Les armes de l'Uni-

---

1. ROBERT BRUN, *Les reliures d'éditeurs et les premières reliures commerciales en France*, Arts et métiers graphiques, 49, 1935, pp. 30-34.
2. MARIUS MICHEL, *La reliure française*, Paris, 1880, p. 25; LÉON GRUEL, *Manuel historique et bibliographique de l'amateur de reliures*, I, Paris, 1887, p. 40. ILSE SCHUNKE, *Signet-Einbände*, Otto Glauning zum 60. Geburtstag, II, Leipzig, 1938, pp. 107-108. ILSE SCHUNKE, *Ein Wiener Renaissance-Einband aus der Palatina in der Vatikanischen Bibliothek*, Gutenberg-Jahrbuch, 1960, pp. 388-396, fig. 3. PAVLINA HAMANOVA, *Aus der Werkstatt des Wiener Aldus Buchbinders*, Gutenberg-Jahrbuch, 1967, pp. 272-277 (avec nombreuses références bibliographiques).
3. A.R.A. HOBSON, *Apollo and Pegasus*, Amsterdam, 1975, pp. 97-100.
4. Bremen, Staats und Universitätsbibliothek, BS 0512, olim III. 1. b. 3: JACOBUS ZIEGLER, *Sphaerae atque astrorum coelestium ratio, natura et motus*, Bâle, Johann Walder, 1536. Un frottis de ce griffon, exécuté par le restaurateur de la Bibliothèque de Brême, m'a été fourni par le Dr. Armin Hetzer, Conservateur de la Section des livres précieux.
5. Brun, *Guide...*, 1938, p. 11.

versité de Cambridge, qui ornent plusieurs reliures, sont peut-être copiées de la marque de Thomas Thomas, imprimeur de l'Université; il serait néanmoins téméraire de lui attribuer ces reliures.[1] Bien qu'il soit entouré de la devise «LOVE KEEPETH THE LAWE, OBEIETH THE KING, AND IS GOOD TO THE COMENTE»[2] qui semble l'identifier aux marques de plusieurs imprimeurs et libraires anglais et écossais, le fer ovale au pélican nourrissant ses petits, est probablement le super-ex-libris d'un collectionneur privé.[3] La marque d'Etienne Groulleau est, écrit avec raison Mme Guilleminot, un pied de chardon abondamment fourni; mais la reliure qu'elle attribue à cet imprimeur est ornée d'une fleur et non d'un pied abondamment fourni.[4] Une ancre figure sur une reliure qui contient un livre imprimé par Thomas Vautrollier, or plusieurs des marques typographiques de celui-ci représentent une ancre; mais la devise de ces marques est Anchora Spei, tandis que celle de la reliure est Animae anchora spes viva Hebr. 6. VS 18-19.[5]

L'atelier d'imprimerie que Hans Kilian avait fondé à Neuburg à la demande du Palatin Ottheinrich, avait pour marque une femme semant des lettres de l'alphabet. Pareille représentation figure aussi sur des reliures. Ilse Schunke a montré qu'elles ont été faites pour Ottheinrich, à Heidelberg et non à Neuburg, et qu'elles ne sont pas des reliures de librairie ou d'édition. Peut-être la femme semant des lettres était-elle un emblème favori du prince, décorant, pour cette raison, et des reliures de sa bibliothèque et des livres sortis de l'imprimerie qu'il avait voulue.[6]

Il est d'autres emblèmes devant lesquels on hésite à trancher; il en est ainsi de Samuel Selfisch, le seul Allemand qui, selon Ilse Schunke, aurait fait dorer sa marque sur des reliures. Or les reliures qu'elle cite sont, dans une certaine mesure, comparables à celles que l'on attribuait à Hans Kilian. Elles couvrent des livres scolaires du prince Christian de Saxe et portent les armes de Saxe au premier plat, la marque de Selfisch

---

1. A. N. L. MUNBY, *Query no. 2. Early trade bindings*, The book collector, 1952, pp. 128-129.

2. Sur la signification de cette devise, voir C.B.L. BARR, *Note 291. Bindings with the device of a pelican in its piety*, The Book Collector, 1968, p. 351.

3. A.R.A. HOBSON, *Note 291. Bindings with the device of a pelican in its piety*, The Book Collector, 1967, pp. 509-510. Mentionnons ici pour mémoire une plaque ovale, haute de 4 pouces, représentant un berger en vêtements de l'époque Stuart, accompagné d'un chien et assis au pied d'un phare. A.R.A. Hobson, qui l'a signalée, n'a jamais cru que ce fût une marque commerciale, en dépit du titre donné à sa note: *Early trade bindings* (The Book Collector, 1953, pp. 221-222).

4. G. GUILLEMINOT, *Une reliure à la marque d'Etienne Groulleau*, Revue française d'histoire du livre, 5, 1982, n° 36, pp. 441-444.

5. GOLDSCHMIDT, *Gothic...*, n° 246, pl. XCVII.

6. SCHUNKE, *art. cité*, pp. 104-112, plus spécialement p. 108.

n'apparaissant qu'au second.[1] On peut donc se demander s'il s'agit bien de reliures commerciales.

Pour l'Angleterre, on est tenté, dans une première approche, d'étudier ensemble les plaques au faucon couronné[2] et celles qui représentent un arbre accompagné de la devise «Noli altum sapere». Les reliures qu'elles ornent ont en effet des traits communs, à commencer par celui d'être sorties, en tout ou en partie, des mains de Williamson, relieur à Eton.[3] On connaît même une reliure ornées du faucon au premier plat et de l'arbre au second, curiosité qui rappelle une reliure ornée simultanément des marques, estampées à froid, de Denis Roce et Hémon Lefèvre. Aucune relation d'affaires entre Roce et Lefèvre n'étant connue, G. D. Hobson expliquait cette rencontre exceptionnelle par la négligence d'un relieur travaillant pour ces deux libraires.[4]

Parmi les livres marqués de l'arbre ou du faucon, on trouve plusieurs éditions anciennes et même un manuscrit du XVe siècle; on n'y rencontre pas de titres doublés; des oeuvres différentes sont reliées ensemble. Bref on pourrait être tenté de prendre le faucon et l'arbre pour les marques de deux bibliothèques. Ce n'est pourtant pas le fait, car des reliures à la devise «Noli altum sapere» appartenaient, à la même époque, à des propriétaires différents.[5]

Comme d'autre part on ne connaît pas de libraire ayant pour marque un faucon couronné, l'hypothèse d'un simple ornement de dorure, qui fut employé pour plusieurs clients, convient pour cet emblème.[6] On ne peut en dire autant de l'arbre, que l'on imagine difficilement comme simple ornement de dorure, et que, surtout, on peut rapprocher de la marque d'éditeur de John Norton, elle-même copiée de celle des Estienne.[7] Sur les onze livres imprimés en Angleterre que l'on a conser-

---

1. Schunke, art. cité, p. 111 et note 2; H. Zimmermann, *Samuel Selfisch, seine Signete und ihre Zeichner*, Zeitschrift für Bücherfreunde, N.F., 17, 1925, pp. 129-137.
2. Robert Birley signale six reliures au faucon couronné, dans *The history of Eton College Library*, article publié dans The Library, Fifth Series, vol. XI, 1956, p. 247, note 2. Dans la monographie portant le même titre, qu'il a publiée à Eton en 1970, il déclare en connaître neuf, mais il n'en donne pas la liste (p. 72, note 24, 1).
3. Birley, op. cit., pp. 23-24.
4. G.D. Hobson, *Parisian binding 1500-1525*, The Library, 11, 1931, p. 411. Robert Brun (Guide..., 1935, p. 501, note 5) a mal compris le texte de Hobson.
5. R. Birley, *The history of Eton College Library*, Cambridge, 1970, p. 24.
6. G. D. Hobson a démontré que le faucon couronné n'est pas la marque de propriété de la reine Elizabeth (*Bindings in Cambridge libraries*, Cambridge, 1929, p. 106).
7. Dans *Bindings with the device of a pelican in its piety*, (The Book Collector, 1967, pp. 509-510) A.R.A. Hobson doute qu'un seul exemple de reliure commerciale dorée anglaise survive. Tant pour *Noli altum* que pour le faucon couronné, il penche pour des ornements de relieurs.

vés dans des reliures ornées de l'arbre, deux ont été publiés par Norton, qui a joué un rôle actif dans l'imprimerie d'Eton, a fourni de nombreux livres au Collège et a été payé par celui-ci pour la fourniture de reliures.[1] Reste cependant que la présence de livres anciens et de manuscrits dans la liste des reliures à l'arbre est inhabituelle pour une marque de librairie.

Ces réserves m'ont conduit à dresser un relevé dont sont exclus, de manière peut-être trop subjective, les exemples qui me semblent douteux (voir annexe). J'ai tenté d'y classer les marques chronologiquement, mais cet ordre est aléatoire, car le commencement d'une carrière de libraire ou la date d'édition d'un livre relié ne sont que des terminus post quem. Néanmoins, dans l'état actuel de nos connaissances, il apparaît clairement que les plus anciennes reliures à marque dorée ont été faites à Paris pour Conrad Resch en 1523. Pour faire admettre une précision si stricte, il est utile de revenir sur une controverse ancienne dont le sujet, dépassant celui des marques proprement dites, touche à la manière dont les livres étaient vendus autrefois.

En 1887 Léon Gruel écrivait, à propos de la marque de Charles Langelier: «les imprimeurs et les libraires avaient chez eux des ateliers de reliures. Le plus souvent, lorsqu'un livre venait d'être imprimé, les exemplaires passaient en bloc dans ces ateliers et en sortaient habillés d'une manière uniforme, avec la marque distinctive de la maison.»[2] Cette théorie fut aisément combattue par Jérôme Pichon et Georges Vicaire qui, dès 1894, lui opposent l'argument de l'extrême rareté des spécimens connus.[3] Mais leur propre hypothèse, selon laquelle les reliures à marques recouvriraient les exemplaires personnels des imprimeurs-libraires-éditeurs, ne résiste pas non plus à l'examen. Il arrive en effet que la même marque figure sur les reliures de plusieurs exemplaires d'un même ouvrage. En outre certains livres conservés dans des reliures à marques contiennent des noms de possesseurs de l'époque, étrangers à la profession. Enfin si les libraires mettaient leur marque commerciale sur les volumes de leur bibliothèque personnelle, pourquoi d'autres marchands n'en faisaient-ils pas autant?

Si l'on prend l'exemple de Christophe Plantin, dont la bibliothèque est conservée à Anvers, au Museum Plantin Moretus, on constate que sur onze reliures frappées du compas d'or, quatre appartiennent aujourd'hui à cette institution, dont deux seulement proviennent de l'officine achetée

---

1. BIRLEY, *op. cit.*, p. 24.
2. GRUEL, *Manuel...*, p. 41.
3. J. PICHON & G. VICAIRE, *Documents pour servir à l'histoire des libraires de Paris*, Bulletin du bibliophile et du bibliothécaire, 1894, p. 29.

en 1876 par la Ville d'Anvers. Ces deux derniers volumes eux-mêmes faisaient probablement partie des invendus.[1]

Il n'y a pas non plus de raison de croire que les reliures à marques ont été faites pour des exemplaires de présent.[2] Au XVIe siècle, la manière habituelle d'offrir un livre est d'y apposer une dédicace, soit à l'encre dans le volume, soit en lettres d'or sur la reliure: rien de tel dans les exemplaires connus.

Le théorie proposée par Goldschmidt est plus large que ne pourraient faire croire les citations qui en sont faites fréquemment. L'hypothèse selon laquelle les reliures à marques auraient été commandées par le libraire pour que les livres exposés dans la boutique puissent être examinés par les clients, s'inscrit en effet dans une vision générale de la vente des livres aux XVe et XVIe siècles. Pour Goldschmidt, les imprimeurs et les éditeurs fournissaient aux libraires des livres en feuilles. C'était à l'acquéreur final de porter son livre à un relieur de son choix, à moins qu'il préférât laisser ce soin à son libraire. En resumé, la reliure d'édition, qui est de pratique courante aujourd'hui, était inconnue autrefois. Si un nom, une marque, un indice semble associer une reliure ancienne à un imprimeur, c'est que ce dernier avait aussi sa boutique de librairie. En faisant relier, soit dans son atelier, soit chez un relieur indépendant, un ou plusieurs exemplaires d'une de ses propres éditions, il agissait en libraire, non en éditeur.[3]

Certains érudits, dans les années trente, semblent n'avoir pas admis cette distinction, tels Adolf Schmidt, Hellmut Helwig et Hermann Knaus.[4] Récemment encore, Jos Hermans estimait même qu'il suffit de trouver deux reliures («meer dan één»: plus d'une) commandées par un imprimeur pour que l'on puisse parler de reliures d'éditeur.[5] Mais il semble bien qu'aujourd'hui la tendance générale soit de penser «reliures de libraires», même lorsque l'on écrit «publishers' bindings» ou «Verle-

---

1. G. COLIN, *Le compas d'or sur des reliures*, Ex Officina Plantiniana, Antverpiae, 1989, pp. 325-336.
2. P. HÖGBERG, *Reliures belges à l'Université d'Upsal*, De Gulden Passer-Le Compas d'or, 5, 1927, p. 2. Jos HERMANS, *Oude banden: aantekeningen over vroege uitgeversbanden uit Parijs en Keulen*, Codex in context, Nijmegen, 1985, pp. 175-197, spécialement p. 178.
3. E.P. GOLDSCHMIDT, *Prinzipien zur Lokalisierung und Datierung alter Einbände*, Jahrbuch der Einbandkunst, 2, 1928, pp. 3-13.
4. HELLMUTH HELWIG, *Neue Beiträge zu dem Stempelmaterial des «Meisters der sogenannten Koberger-Einbände»*, Archiv für Buchbinderei, 35, 1935, pp. 81-84. ADOLF SCHMIDT, *Zur Geschichte deutscher Buchbinder im sechzehnten Jahrhundert*, Beiträge zum Rollen- und Platteneinband im 16. Jahrhundert, Konrad Haebler (...) gewidmet, Leipzig, 1937, pp. 1-109, spécialement pp. 87-88. HERMANN KNAUS, *Über Verlegereinbände bei Schöffer*, Gutenberg-Jahrbuch, 1938, pp. 97-108.
5. HERMANS, *art. cité*, p. 177.

gereinband». A cet égard, l'expression choisie par Vera Sack est caractéristique: «die sog. Verlegereinband», ce qui correspond à peu près à «ce qu'il est convenu d'appeler la reliure d'éditeur».[1] Herman de la Fontaine Verwey pensait probablement de même lorsqu'il employait l'expression «Printer's or publisher's own shop», alors que son premier exemple était celui d'une reliure au nom d'un imprimeur, contenant un livre imprimé par un autre.[2]

Contre la notion de reliure d'édition, Goldschmidt faisait valoir entre autres un argument de poids: «If the bindings with publishers' names or marks are original publishers' bindings in the sense that all copies of their books would be issued in uniform bindings with their mark on it, then surely all such bindings must contain books published by the man who signed the binding. Is this actually the case? Certainly not.»[3] La liste publiée ici en annexe lui donne largement raison. Seuls Resch, Plantin (mais non les Moretus), Barbou et Lecoq y apparaissent avec des livres exclusivement édités par eux. Mais pour chacun des deux derniers, on ne connaît qu'un seul spécimen, de sorte que cette observation n'est pas significative. Et pour Plantin, l'unicité de chaque titre rend peu probable l'hypothèse de reliures d'édition.

Pourtant la reliure d'édition, bien que rare, n'était pas absolument inconnue. Les archives révèlent des exemples d'éditions commandées à l'Officine plantinienne par des autorités religieuses et dont un nombre important d'exemplaires (par exemple 600 sur 1050) devaient être fournis reliés aux commanditaires et l'ont été effectivement.[4]

Mais si les reliures commandées d'avance par les éditeurs existaient donc, par contre il ne semble pas que l'on en connaisse portant la marque distinctive de l'un d'eux. L'exemple que nous fournit Conrad Resch n'en est que plus intéressant. Les reliures à sa marque contiennent divers textes bibliques érasmiens, imprimés en 1523 à Paris par Pierre Vidoue pour Conrad Resch, dans un format inhabituel, très petit et allongé (environ 100 mm. de haut sur 45 de large). Exemple précoce de l'appropriation du décor au texte, sur le premier plat des reliures sont représentés soit l'apôtre Paul, soit l'apôtre Mathieu, soit les armes du Christ, selon le contenu du livre. Avec la marque de Resch, pressée sur le second plat, cela fait quatre plaques, qui ont les mêmes dimensions, adaptées au format

---

1. V. SACK, *Verlegereinbände und Buchhandel Peter Schöffers*, Archiv für Geschichte des Buchwesens, 13, 1972, col. 249-287.
2. H. DE LA FONTAINE VERWEY, *Amsterdam publishers' bindings from about 1600*, Quaerendo, 5, 1975, pp. 283-302.
3. GOLDSCHMIDT, *Gothic...*, p. 35.
4. G. COLIN, *La fourniture de livres reliés par l'Officine plantinienne*, Gutenberg Jahrbuch, 1990, p. 356.

très particulier des volumes. Il est clair qu'elles ont été conçues spécialement pour eux. Il s'agit donc bien de reliures d'édition.

On objectera peut-être que nous ne savons pas combien d'exemplaires Resch a fait relier à sa marque, alors qu'une quantité importante est souvent considérée comme une des caractéristiques de la reliure d'édition, non seulement pour la technique industrielle du XIXe siècle, mais même pour les procédés manuels d'autrefois.[1] Il est vrai qu'en pratique les reliures commandées par un éditeur pour la vente d'une édition, même partielle, sont presque toujours nombreuses. Mais pour définir l'essence même de la reliure d'édition, ce critère est contestable. Ce qui compte, c'est l'intention, dans le chef de l'éditeur, de faire relier tout ou partie de son édition. La décision qu'a prise Resch de faire confectionner spécialement des plaques à dorer pour certaines de ses éditions, garantit cette intention.

Il n'est pas absolument certain que toutes les reliures à la marque de Resch aient été faites la même année : pour des raisons d'économie, même au XIXe siècle, à l'époque de la reliure industrielle, on ne reliait pas en une seule fois tous les exemplaires d'une édition.[2] Mais on peut supposer que Conrad Resch a fait relier au moins une partie de son édition tout de suite. C'est pourquoi on peut dater de 1523 l'apparition, sur le marché, de livres reliés à sa marque. À cette époque, aucun de ses confrères n'a encore fait appel à la technique nouvelle de la dorure : c'est ce qui ressort de la liste publiée en annexe.

Dans l'une de ses plaques, l'apôtre Paul est placé dans une niche d'un dessin encore gothique. Mais Mathieu, les armes du Christ et la marque de Resch elle-même sont disposés dans un décor architectural de la Renaissance. Si donc on peut voir en Conrad Resch l'un des représentants peu nombreux du style néo-gothique, il est surtout le premier représentant de la Renaissance dans la reliure commerciale française.

Mais s'il est le premier en date, Geofroy Tory est le premier par la perfection. La célébrité de cet artiste ne doit pas faire oublier qu'il était aussi marchand[3] et que le dessin superbe du pot cassé, qui orne ses éditions et ses reliures, est en définitive une marque commerciale. De loin supérieures, du point de vue ornemental, à toutes les reliures à marques du XVIe siècle, les siennes sont l'exemple le plus raffiné de ce que doit être une bonne reliure commerciale qui, pour favoriser la vente du livre, doit faire beaucoup d'effet à moindres frais.

1. H. HELWIG, *Verlegereinbände im 15. und 16. Jahrhundert*, Archiv für Buchbinderei, 38, 1938, pp. 81-85, 93-95. S. MALAVIEILLE, *Reliures et cartonnages d'éditeur en France au XIXe siècle*, Paris, 1985, p. 14.
2. S. MALAVIEILLE, *op. cit.*, Paris, 1985, p. 15.
3. AUGUSTE BERNARD, *Geofroy Tory*, 2e éd., Paris 1865, p. 76 et *passim*.

La plus grande des deux plaques au pot cassé a probablement été conçue pour les *Heures* de 1531.[1] On pourrait peut-être donc, ici aussi, parler de reliures d'édition. Cependant trois des spécimens connus ornés de la petite plaque contiennent des livres qui n'ont pas été édités par lui. Il s'agit donc bien de reliures de librairie.

Comme si elles assuraient la transition avec les amples plaques estampées à froid qui les ont précédées, les plaques à dorer de Resch et de Tory couvrent presque entièrement les plats. Après eux, les marques distinctives des libraires ne sont plus que des fleurons dorés au centre des plats. C'est alors qu'elles deviennent tout à fait exceptionnelles, dit Robert Brun,[2] s'inscrivant ainsi dans une longue suite de bibliographes unanimes. Un seul cependant a laissé entendre que les reliures à marques de libraires étaient communes. Ce n'est pas Léon Gruel, que sa théorie sur les éditions entières reliées de manière uniforme aurait pu mener pourtant à pareille déclaration; mais il ne s'est pas exprimé sur le sujet.[3] Cet esprit rare, c'est G.D. Hobson: «This [Norton's] stamp is found on the following bindings [...] and no doubt, being a trade-mark, on many other bindings unknown to me».[4] Or c'est le bon sens: une marque commerciale n'est pas faite pour rester confidentielle. Certains libraires se sont procuré plusieurs fers ou plaques: Tory, 2; Langelier, 2 ou 3; Gryphe, 3; Merlin, 3; Plantin, 6 (dont quatre achetées en même temps);[5] Marnef, 2; Bogard, 3; Velpius Anthoine, 2; Norton, 3. Pourquoi commander plusieurs fers, si c'est pour dorer quelques exemplaires exposés dans la boutique? Mais d'autre part si les libraires d'autrefois vendaient en grand nombre des livres reliés à leur marque, comment se fait-il qu'il s'en soit conservé si peu?

Au fait, combien en reste-t-il? La liste publiée en annexe est-elle, sinon exhaustive, du moins à peu près complète? Nous n'en savons rien. Il y cent ans, Gruel connaissait une reliure à la marque du compas d'or; on en recense onze aujourd'hui. En 1981 on a pu dresser une liste de huit reliures à la marque de Langelier; on en connaît vingt et une maintenant.

---

1. A.R.A. Hobson, *Humanists and bookbinders*, Cambridge, 1989, p. 176.
2. Robert Brun, *Les reliures d'éditeurs et les premières reliures commerciales en France*, Arts et métiers graphiques, 49, 1935, pp. 30-34.
3. Contrairement à ce qu'a compris Goldschmidt (*Gothic...*, 1, pp. 34-35) Gruel n'a pas dit non plus qu'elles étaient «excessivement rares». Ce n'est pas à leur sujet, mais à propos des reliures signées par les relieurs, qu'il a employé cette expression, dans un passage que Goldschmidt a fait passer à la postérité en en dénonçant l'obscurité et l'étrange logique. Le passage est obscur en effet, mais la logique de Gruel n'est pas étrange. Ce qu'il prétend, c'est que les noms estampés sur les reliures anciennes sont généralement ceux de libraires, rarement ceux de relieurs. C'est exactement la thèse de Goldschmidt.
4. G.D. Hobson, *Bindings in Cambridge libraries*, Cambridge, 1929, p. 106.
5. Museum Plantin Moretus, Arch. 36, f° 69.

Mais est-il correct de dire «on en connaît»? Bien que le *je* passe pour haïssable, «j'en connais» serait plus modeste, car nul ne sait ce que d'autres connaissent.

Pour les noms, emblèmes, rébus, estampés à froid, à l'aide de fers, de plaques ou de roulettes, Robert Brun cite de nombreux libraires, mais pour chacun d'eux un petit nombre d'exemplaires. Toutefois Michon avait recensé 53 reliures d'André Boule, mais il déclarait que toutes les autres plaques sont rares.[1] Ici aussi nous sommes tributaires d'expériences isolées. Car si, par exemple, aux cinq reliures portant la roulette de Claude Chevallon signalées par Brun, on ajoute celles que révèlent diverses sources, on arrive, provisoirement, à un total de onze.[2] Une enquête systématique dans les bibliothèques révéleraient peut-être davantage de spécimens. Mais quoi qu'il en soit, dans l'état actuel de nos connaissances, les reliures de librairies estampées à froid n'apparaissent déjà ni plus ni moins nombreuses que celles à marques dorées.

La rareté relative des unes et des autres doit être mise en parallèle avec la rareté des éditions anciennes elles-mêmes. Nous connaissons une seule reliure à la marque de Barbou. Elle recouvre un exemplaire des *Heures de la Vierge à l'usage de Limoges*, qui est, lui aussi, le seul connu. Frappés de ce que cette reliure est unique, nous sommes prêts à supposer qu'elle a été faite, seule, pour qu'un seul exemplaire de l'ouvrage pût être feuilleté dans la boutique. Mais trouvons-nous étrange qu'un seul exemplaire des *Heures de Limoges* soit connu et allons-nous imaginer que Barbou n'a imprimé que celui-là? Si tant de livres anciens ont disparu, malgré la protection que constitue une reliure, comment les reliures elles-mêmes, non protégées, auraient-elles subsisté?

Des reliures à marques dorées, Robert Brun pensait: «leur aspect, d'ordinaire peu soigné, les a fait négliger des amateurs. Beaucoup ont disparu, remplacées au cours des âges par des reliures plus luxueuses».[3] Ce jugement est trop sévère, car elles sont en général très correctement soignées. Par exemple souvent leurs tranches sont dorées. Mais il est vrai que les décors importants sont rares (Hugues Barbou, Madeleine Boursette, Jacques Dupuys) et cette relative modestie explique peut-être leur disparition. Même à notre époque, où la reliure est pourtant considérée

1. L.-M. MICHON, *La reliure française*, Paris, 1951, p. 34.
2. GOLDSCHMIDT, *Gothic...*, p. 189. P. FAIDER, *Exposition documentaire de reliures anciennes*, Mons, 1929, n° 79 (une reliure exposée, une autre citée). BRUN, *Guide...*, 1937, p. 215 (il signale quatre ouvrages, mais omet de préciser que l'un d'entre eux comporte deux volumes; il connaissait donc cinq reliures à la marque de Chevallon). HERMANS, *art. cité*, pp. 178-185. E. K. SCHREIBER, *Catalogue twenty-five*, New York [1991], n° 82.
3. ROBERT BRUN, *Les reliures d'éditeurs et les premières reliures commerciales en France*, Arts et métiers graphiques, 49, 1935, pp. 30-34.

au moins comme un témoin archéologique digne d'être conservé, un spécimen à la marque de Guillaume Merlin a été détruit, dans la bibliothèque même qui l'avait signalé avec fierté, et il n'a même pas été remplacé par une reliure plus luxueuse.[1] Ces considérations valent aussi pour les reliures estampées à froid, car si, bien conservées, elles font parfois beaucoup d'effet, frustes, elles sont les victimes toutes désignées des soi-disant restaurateurs.

Peu communes de nos jours, peut-être à cause de ces destructions, les reliures de librairie, à froid ou dorées, nous apparaissent toutefois moins exceptionnellement rares à mesure que le temps passe, nous révélant des spécimens auparavant ignorés. De leur temps, elles ont dû être plus nombreuses encore. L'étaient-elles suffisamment pour que, nous passant de l'hypothèse étroite des exemplaires montrés aux clients dans la boutique du libraire, nous puissions imaginer la vente en grande quantité de livres reliés à sa marque? Dans les spécimens qui nous restent, on lit parfois des mentions de propriétaires anciens, qui prouvent que les livres ne sont pas restés dans la boutique, mais qu'ils ont été vendus. On hésite cependant à tirer de ces exemples une règle générale, car ces mentions de propriétaires anciens ne sont pas très nombreuses. En outre, si les exemplaires reliés à l'emblème d'un libraire avaient été vendus par lui en grand nombre, nous trouverions probablement de nos jours des doubles, reliés de même. Certes la liste publiée en annexe en montre quelques cas, mais peu nombreux.

L'examen de ces doubles amène de nouvelles observations. On les trouve chez Conrad Resch, Geofroy Tory, Charles Langelier et Jean Bogard. Nous avons vu que les spécimens à la marque de Resch sont des reliures d'édition et que ceux de Tory pour les *Heures* de 1531 en sont peut-être aussi. Or pour les reliures de Langelier et de Bogard, les ouvrages en deux exemplaires ont été édités par eux-mêmes. Est-ce hasard ou s'agit-il aussi de reliures d'éditions?

L'étude des reliures à marques dorées nous invite à des conclusions diverses, tantôt tranchées, tantôt prudentes. Toutes n'étaient pas destinées uniquement à permettre l'examen des livres en vente dans les boutiques des libraires. Les reliures d'édition, quoique exceptionnelles, étaient connues au XVIe siècle. Celles de Conrad Resch, au moins, se rapprochent le plus de ce que recouvre aujourd'hui le concept de reliure d'édition: spécialement conçues pour des éditions bien déterminées, elles portaient la marque de l'éditeur.

---

1. Voir la liste publiée en annexe, *s.v.* Merlin, C. 2. Sur la destruction, de nos jours, de reliures du plus haut intérêt, voyez: J. A. Szirmai, *Stop destroying ancient bindings*, Gazette du livre médiéval, n. 13, automne 1988, pp. 7-9.

Les autres reliures à marques nous apparaissent comme des reliures de librairie. Du spécimen unique de Jean Bailleur aux vingt et un spécimens de Charles Langelier, leur rareté connaît des degrés si divers qu'il est malaisé d'en tirer des conclusions. Les titres doublés sont peu nombreux, de sorte qu'il est difficile de supposer que les libraires faisaient relier à leur marque un grand nombre de livres destinés à la vente. Mais certains exemplaires portent des indications manuscrites de propriétaires de l'époque. Si donc l'hypothèse étroite des exemplaires à examiner dans la boutique peut encore être utile, du moins citons Goldschmidt entièrement : «A publisher would probably bind a few copies in his own bindings, or have them bound with his distinctive mark, to keep them on view in his shop *and also to sell* to purchasers who did not prefer to see to the binding themselves». Les archives démontrent amplement que l'on pouvait en effet acheter des livres reliés.[1]

Telles sont les réflexions qu'inspirent et les sources d'archives et les exemplaires conservés. Bien que ces derniers soient plus nombreux qu'on ne le laisse souvent entendre, il faudrait en connaître davantage pour mieux comprendre leur fonction. En 1935 Robert Brun pensait qu'un certain nombre se cachent encore sur les rayons de bibliothèques publiques.[2] Cette supposition vaut probablement encore aujourd'hui.

LISTE DE RELIURES À MARQUES DE LIBRAIRES DORÉES

Les adresses bibliographiques des livres cités ci-dessous ont été données dans la langue de l'ouvrage, sauf quand elles ne me sont connues que par des citations qui ne respectent pas ce principe et que, faute de bibliographie aisément disponible, je n'ai pu les rétablir.

CONRAD RESCH

Libraire-juré, à Paris de 1516 à 1526, et à Bâle.

La plaque à dorer qui représente la marque de Conrad Resch est proche de l'une des gravures sur bois dont il s'est servi dans ses éditions,

---

1. R.B. McKerrow, *An introduction to bibliography for literary students*, Oxford, 1927, pp. 121-127. G. Colin, *La fourniture...*, pp. 356-357. J. M. Noailly, *Le catalogue de l'imprimeur Antoine Cellier, Charenton-Paris, 1665*, Psaume, 6, 1991, pp. 131-148.
2. Robert Brun, *Les reliures d'éditeurs...*, pp. 30-34.

à savoir celle reproduite par Renouard sous le n° 966.[1] Tout comme cette gravure, elle montre l'écu de Bâle tenu par un seul dragon, placé derrière l'écu. Mais le dessin de la plaque à dorer est inversé, y compris l'étui de crosse, ce qui est incorrect du point de vue héraldique.

Une des reliures appartenant à la Bibliothèque nationale de Paris est reproduite, ouverte, dans: ROBERT BRUN, «Les reliures d'éditeurs», *Arts et métiers graphiques*, 49, 1935, p. 34; l'article ne précise pas laquelle. Les trois reliures appartenant au Musée Condé sont décrites dans: L. DELISLE, *Chantilly: le cabinet des livres*, Paris, 1905, pp. 144-145, nos 701-703.

1. *Testamentum Novum*, Luteciae, industria Petri Vidovaei, in aedibus Conradi Resch, 1523, in-24.
Wolfenbüttel, Herzog August Bibliothek, 1330. 6 Theol.
Au premier plat, plaque aux armes du Christ, portant dans le bas l'inscription REDEMPTORIS // MV(N)DI ARMA. Tranches dorées et ciselées.

2. *Epistolae apostolicae...*, Luteciae, industria Petri Vidouaei, in aedibus Conradi Resch, 1523, in-24.
Paris, Bibliothèque Nationale, Rés. A. 6350 (olim A+518).[2]
Au premier plat, plaque à l'image de saint Paul, sous un arc gothique; au bas, l'inscription SANCTE PAVLE // ORA PRO NOBIS. Tranches dorées et ciselées.

3. D. ERASMUS, *Paraphrases in omnes epistolas Pauli apostoli germanas...*, Luteciae, typis Petri Vidouaei, impendio Conradi Resch, 1523, in-24.
Chantilly, Musée Condé, VIII c 1.
Premier plat comme le n° 2. Tranches dorées et ciselées.

4. *Même ouvrage.*
La Haye, Bibliothèque Royale, 229 J 46.
Premier plat comme le n° 2. Tranches dorées et ciselées.

5. *Même ouvrage.*
Paris, Bibliothèque Nationale, Rés. A 7143 (1).
Premier plat comme le n° 2. Tranches dorées et ciselées.

6. D. ERASMUS, *Paraphrasis in epitsolas* (sic) *Pauli*. Lutetiae, typis Petri Vidovaei, impendio Conradi Resch, 1523, in-24.
Chantilly, Musée Condé, VIII c 2.
Premier plat comme le n° 2. Tranches dorées et ciselées.

---

1. PH. RENOUARD, *Les marques typographiques parisiennes des XVe et XVIe siècles*, Paris, 1926-1928.
2. Une des trois reliures de la Bibliothèque Nationale est reproduite, ouverte, dans ROBERT BRUN, *Les reliures d'éditeurs...*, p. 34.

7. *Même ouvrage*.
Paris, Bibliothèque Nationale, Rés A 7143 (2).
Premier plat comme le n° 2. Tranches dorées et ciselées.

8. D. ERASMUS, *Paraphrasis in Evangelium Matthei*. Luteciae, typis Petri Vedouaei, impendio Conradi Resch, 1523, in-24.
Chantilly, Musée Condé, VIII c 5.
Au premier plat, plaque à l'image de saint Mathieu auquel un ange présente un livre. Tranches dorées et ciselées.

GEOFROY TORY

Imprimeur, libraire, relieur, graveur. Installé en 1525 «au Pot cassé en la rue Sainct Jacques», à Paris, mort en 1533.

A. PETITE PLAQUE, SANS LE TORET

1. HIERONYMO BENIVIENI, *Opere*, Florence, Heredi di Philippo di Giunta, 1519, in-8°.
New York, Pierpont Morgan Library, 1182.
Provenance: James Toovey. Cf. HOWARD M. NIXON, *Pierpont Morgan Library*, n° 5, avec reproduction; PAUL NEEDHAM, *Twelve centuries of bookbindings*, New-York-London, 1979, n° 44, avec reproduction.
Le cuir d'origine a été remonté dans une reliure moderne.

2. PETRARCHA, *Le volgari opere del Petrarcha*, Vinegia, per Giovanniantonio & Fratelli da Sabbio, 1525, in-4°.
Londres, British Library, c. 47. g. 20.
Reliure soignée: le cuir est du maroquin; la plaque est entourée de fers divers; les tranches sont dorées et ciselées.
Reproduite dans: W. Y. FLETCHER, *Bookbinding in France*, London, 1895, p. 11, et dans: W. Y. FLETCHER, *Foreign bookbindings in the British Museum*, London, 1896, pl XVI.

3. *Horae in laudem Beatiss. Virg. Mariae ad usum Romanum*. Parrhisijs, à praelo Colinaeo, pro... Gotofredo Torino, 1527, in-8°.
Propriétaire actuel inconnu.
Provenance: Estelle Doheny Collection; acheté par la librairie Maggs à la vente citée ci-dessous.
Exemplaire sur vélin. Reliure reproduite dans L. MILLER, *Edward L. Doheny Memorial Library; Catalogue of books and manuscripts in the Estelle Doheny Collection*, Los Angeles, 1940 [-1955], pl. XVIII; et dans *The*

Estelle Doheny Collection, IV, New York, Christie, Manson & Woods International Inc., 17-18 oct. 1988, n° 1106 (repr. en couleurs, p. 78).

4. *Hore beate marie virginis secundum usum Romanum*, Parisius, per Germanum Hardouyn, s.d., (vers 1527), in-8°.
Paris, Bibliothèque Nationale, Vélins 1531.
Exemplaire sur vélin, miniaturé. Sur la doublure du premier plat: MD XIXe febr. 1514 (date qui se rapporte, ça va de soi, à un événement antérieur à l'édition, mais qui est d'une écriture du XVIe siècle). Tranches dorées.

5. *Cebes*, Paris, Tory, 1529 in-12.
Londres, Victoria & Albert Museum.
Provenance: Corby Castle, Cumberland; acquis en 1933.
Le cuir d'origine a été remonté dans une reliure qui porte l'étiquette: «Bound by H. Scott, 11 English St. Carlisle». La dorure des tranches est peut-être moderne.

6. G. B. EGNAZIO, *Summaire de chroniques*...translate...en langaige francoys, par Maistre Geofroy Tory de Bourges, Paris, Geofroy Tory, 1529, in-8°.
Oxford, Broxbourne Library.
Provenance: vente Firmin Didot, 1878, n° 688; acheté par Hetzberger en 1950.
La plaque a été frappée sans or. Au premier plat, seule la partie centrale est préservée. Les tranches ont probablement été dorées ou redorées au XIXe siècle. Reproduction du second plat: H. M. Nixon, *Broxbourne Library*, London, 1956, n° 20.

7. GEOFROY TORY, *Champ fleury*, Paris, Geofroy Tory et Giles Gourmont, 1529, in-folio.
Copenhague, Bibliothèque Royale, 10-323.
La plaque a été frappée sans or. Cette reliure, qui n'était pas connue, a été découverte en 1987 par M. Paul Culot, qui publiera prochainement une note à ce sujet.

8. GOTOFREDUS TORINUS (Geofroy Tory), *Aediloquium*, Parisiis, apud Simonem Colinaeum, 1530, in-8°.
Paris, Bibliothèque Nationale, pYc 1284.
Tranches dorées. Reproductions dans: H. BOUCHOT, *Les reliures d'art à la Bibliothèque nationale*, Paris, 1888, pl. XXXII; H. LOUBIER, *Der Bucheinband von seinen Anfängen bis zum Ende des 18. Jahrhunderts*, 2.Aufl., Leipzig, 1926, p. 182; J. MÉGRET, *Geofroy Tory*, Arts et métiers graphiques, 1932, n° 28, p. 13.

B. GRANDE PLAQUE, AVEC LE TORET.

1. *Horae in laudem beatiss. virginis Mariae ad usum Romanum*, Parrhisiis, Gotofredus Torinus, 1531, in-4°.
Londres, Victoria & Albert Museum, L. 1402-1931.
Description et reproduction dans: John P. Harthan, *Bookbindings*, London 1961, p. 27, n° 20, pl. 20.

2. *Même ouvrage.*
Mariemont, Musée, 46.
Provenance: ex-libris d'Ambroise-Firmin Didot (vente II, Paris, 1879, n° 129), d'Henri Bordes et de Robert Hoe (vente II n° 1690). Cf. *Reliures du Moyen Age au Ier Empire*, Bruxelles 1955, n° 27, pl. III; *Prestige de la Bibliothèque [du] Musée de Mariemont*, Mariemont 1967, n° 28, pl. XI.
Tranches dorées et ciselées (candélabres, motifs floraux). Dos refait au XIXe siècle, avec adjonction de l'initiale de François Ier.

3. *Même ouvrage.*
Melbourne, Public Library of Victoria.
Provenance: E. Ph. Goldschmidt (*Gothic and Renaissance bookbindings*, n° 159, pl. LIX).
La plaque est frappée sans or. Au titre et au dernier feuillet: «Appartient à Guillaume Dannes, bourgeois, marchand de Paris»; dans le calendrier, une note de sa main nous apprend qu'il était né en 1487. Cf. HOWARD M. NIXON, *Broxbourne Library*, p. 46, note 2.

4. *Même ouvrage.*
New York, Pierpont Morgan Library, 15432.
Provenance: Léon Gruel (cf. son Manuel, II, pp. 167-168, avec reproduction). Cf. HOWARD M. NIXON, *Pierpont Morgan Library*, n° 5b, avec reproduction; A.R.A. HOBSON, *Humanists and bookbinders*, Cambridge, 1989, reproduction p. 176.
Tranches dorées.

5. DIODORE DE SICILE, *Les Troys premiers livres de l'histoire*, Paris, à l'enseigne du Pot cassé, 1535, in-4°.
Chantilly, Musée Condé.
Provenance: Ambroise Firmin-Didot (vente à Paris, Librairie Firmin-Didot et Cie, 1881, n° 492).
La plaque a été pressée sans or. Geofroy Tory étant mort en 1533, on attribue à sa veuve l'édition du Diodore de Sicile et l'emploi de la plaque au Pot cassé sur l'exemplaire de Chantilly.

6. Reliure vide.
Paris, Bibliothèque Nationale, Rés. v 1948.

CHARLES LANGELIER

Libraire à Paris, 1536-1563.

Il n'y a pas de raison d'attribuer conjointement aux deux frères, Arnoul (1536-1557) et Charles (1535-1563), l'emploi, sur des reliures, de la marque aux anges liés. Sur tous les exemplaires connus figurent en effet les seules initiales C.L. Goldschmidt tente d'expliquer ce fait par un partage des responsabilités entre les deux frères associés, Charles s'occupant de la reliure, Arnoul veillant à l'impression des textes.[1] Or en matière de reliures de librairies, ce qui était important du point de vue commercial et sur quoi il fallait attirer l'attention, ce n'était pas les reliures ni les relieurs, mais les livres à vendre et les libraires qui les vendaient. Les initiales dorées sur les reliures aux anges liés désignent donc Charles Langelier seul, en tant que libraire.

Eugénie Droz, probablement avec raison, désigne comme auteur des «belles reliures ornées de la marque aux anges liés» Léon Vertault, qui demeurait dans la maison de Charles Langelier et à qui celui-ci fit un legs.[2] L'original de ce testament, sur lequel M. Paul Culot a attiré mon attention il y a bien longtemps, devrait être comparé aux actes cités par Philippe Renouard,[3] car ce qu'en a dit Eugénie Droz n'est pas très clair: Vertault s'appelait en réalité Verton ou même Berton, «à condition que ce soit bien le même personnage que Loys Verton».

Dans son catalogue 104, part II, [1981], M. Bernard H. Breslauer a relevé huit reliures portant l'une ou l'autre marque de Charles Langelier. Elles sont signalées ci-dessous par la mention 'Breslauer', suivie du numéro qu'il a donné.

A. GRANDE MARQUE

1. THUCYDIDE, *L'historie de la guerre qui fut entre les Péloponnésiens et les Athéniens*, Lyon, François Juste, 1534, in-4°.
Roanne, Bibliothèque Municipale, R 4/175.
Provient des Frères Minimes de Roanne.

2. F. LE ROY, *Le dialogue de consolation entre lame et raison*, Arnoul et Charles les Angeliers frères, 1537, in-8°.
Cambridge (Mass.), Harvard College Library (R. MORTIMER, *Catalogue of books and manuscripts, Harvard College Library*, 1, Cambridge, Mass., 1964, n° 174).

---

1. GOLDSCHMIDT, *Gothic...*, n. 186, p. 264.
2. E. DROZ, *Les chemins de l'hérésie*, I, Genève, 1970, p. 359.
3. PH. RENOUARD, *Documents sur les imprimeurs...*, Paris 1901, pp. 47 et 261.

Provenance: baron Jérôme Pichon (ex-libris et note autographe dans la reliure); GOLDSCHMIDT (*Gothic...*, n° 186).
Breslauer 6.

3. DESIDERIUS ERASMUS, *Lingua*, Lugduni, S. Gryphius, 1538, in-8°.
Propriétaire actuel inconnu.
Provenance: E. Ph. Goldschmidt (vente à Londres, Sotheby, 5 avril 1955, n° 266, avec reproduction au catalogue); acheté par Mc Leish.

4. AUSONIUS, *Opuscula varia*, Lyon, Sébastien Gryphe, 1540, in-8°.
Bruxelles, Bibliothèque Royale, II 13. 440 A LP.
Provenance: ex-libris manuscrit de Nicolas Penot, 1629, et de Pierre Mesnayer, XVIIIe siècle; acquis à la vente de la bibliothèque du Dr Alexandre-Louis-Simon Lejeune, Bruxelles, F. Heussner, 20-28 novembre 1862.
Breslauer 8.

5. SUÉTONE, *Des faictz et gestes des douze Caesars*, Paris, Arnoul Langelier, 1540, in-8°.
Propriétaire actuel inconnu.
Provenance: vente de la bibliothèque du comte A. W[erlé], Paris, Henri Leclerc, février 1908, n° 172; [Léon Gruel]; vente à Paris, Pierre Chrétien, 27-28 novembre 1967, n° 238.
La reliure n'est pas reproduite aux catalogues des ventes Werlé et Gruel, mais Breslauer, qui l'a probablement vue, la classe parmi celles qui ont la grande marque.
Breslauer 5.

6. PHILIPPE DE COMMINES, *Cronicque & Histoire*, Paris, Jacques Regnault, 1563 (=1543), in-8°. Relié avec, du même auteur, *Cronicques du Roy Charles Huytiesme*, Paris, Maurice de La Porte, in-8°.
Leeuw-Saint-Pierre (Belgique), Librairie Voltaire, *Catalogue périodique de livres anciens et modernes*, [1992], n° 4.

7. JEAN-BAPTISTE EGNACE, *Sommaire de chroniques*, traduction de Geofroy Tory, Paris, Charles Langelier, 1543, in-8°.
Besançon, Bibliothèque Municipale, Rés. Rel. XVIe, 59.
Provenance: D. Billerez 1579, Francisci Billerez, Est. Billerez 1693.
Tranches dorées, avec un décor grossier ciselé; ciselés également les mots SAM (? tranche de tête) VARIER (tranche de gouttière) POINSOT (tranche de queue).

8. FRANCESCO PATRIZZI, *Le livre de police humaine*, extraict... par... Gilles d'Aurigny, Paris, Charles L'Angelier, 1544, in-8°.
Collection privée.

Provenance: J. R. Abbey, vente Sotheby, 21 juin 1965, n° 106. Martin Breslauer, Londres, List. XXXVIII, 1966, n° 47.
L'exemplaire Abbey a appartenu aux franciscains de Dijon.
Breslauer 7.

9. [MARTIAL D'AUVERGNE], *Aresta amorum*, Parisiis, Renatus Houdouyn, Iohannes David & Paschasius Le Tellier Carolo Langelier, 1544 (1545 n.s.), in-8°.
Collection privée.
Provenance: baron Jérôme Pichon? (vente à paris, H. Leclerc et P. Cornuau, 3-14 mai 1897, n° 1079); F[auchier]-D[elavigne] (vente à Paris, L. Giraud-Badin, 4 novembre 1938, n° 75, pl. IX); Georges Heilbrun (catalogue 37 [1972], n° 104).
Tranches dorées. L'exemplaire provient certainement de Fauchier-Delavigne, peut-être du baron Pichon; faute de reproduction au catalogue de la vente de ce dernier, on ne peut en décider.

10. PAULUS AEMILIUS, *Les cinq premiers livres de l'histoire française*, Paris, Michel Fezandat, 1556, in-folio.
Oxford, Taylor Institution, Arch. Fol. F. 1556.
La marque est poussée en argent.

B. PETITE MARQUE

1. RAYMOND JORDAN, *Les contemplations du simple devot*, Paris, Arnoul & Charles les Angeliers, frères, 1538, in-8°.
Paris, Bibliothèque Nationale, Rés. D 80. 359.
Provenance: ex-libris gravés de van der Heule et de Merlin d'Estreux de Beaugrenier.

2. DIODORE DE SICILE, *Les trois premiers livres de l'histoire*, Paris, Arnoul & Charles les Angeliers, frères, 1541, in-8°.
Paris, Bibliothèque Nationale, Rés. 2024.

3. *Même ouvrage.*
Cambridge (Mass.), Harvard College Library.
Description et reproduction: RUTH MORTIMER, *Harvard College Library: Catalogue of books and manuscripts*, Part I, vol. 1, n° 174.
Breslauer 3.

4. JOANNES FERRARIUS, *Commentarius de appellationibus*, Lugduni, apud Sebastianum Gryphium, 1542, in-8°.
Paris, Bibliothèque Nationale, Rés. p. F 17.
Acquis à la vente Lyon, 10 novembre 1968, n° 25.

5. ALARD, *Selectae similitudines*, Parisiis, apud Arnoldum Angelier, 1543, in-8°.
Propriétaire actuel inconnu.
Provenance: Léon Gruel (*Manuel*, I, pp. 41-42, reproduction hors-texte); vente à Paris, Pierre Chrétien, 27-28 novembre 1967, n° 239.
Breslauer 2.

6. NICOLLE DE LESCUT, *Les institutions imperialles*, Paris, (René Houdouyn, JeanDavid & Pasquier Le Tellier pour) Charles Langelier (& Vivant Gaultherot), 1544, in-8°.
Propriétaire actuel inconnu.
Provenance: Martin Breslauer, *Catalogue 104*, Part II, New York, s.d., n° 155 (avec reproduction); avait figuré dans les catalogues 91, 1959 (n° 53, pl. III), 92, 1960 (n° 105, pl. IX) et 94, 1961 (n° 93, avec reproduction), de la même firme, quand elle était établie à Londres.
Breslauer 1.

7. FRANCESCO PATRIZZI, *Le livre de police humaine...extraict... par...Gilles d'Aurigny*, Paris, Charles l'Angelié, 1546, in-8°.
Paris, Bibliothèque Nationale, Rés. *E 637.
Provenance: Malieveni (? écriture gothique de transition); ex-libris manuscrit des Célestins de Paris, XVIIIe siècle.

8. *Même ouvrage*.
La Haye, Koninklijke Bibliotheek.

9. *Les costumes des duchez, contez & chastellenies du bailliage de Sens*, Paris, Charles Langelier, (pas avant 1558), in-8°.
Laon, Bibliothèque Municipale.
Provenance: abbaye de Vaucler, XVIIIe siècle.
A la fin du volume figure un portrait de François Ier, gravé en [15]58.

C. FER INDÉTERMINÉ

1. JOANNES MILLAEUS, *Praxis criminis persequendi*, Paris, 1541.
Brème, Staats- und Universitätsbibliothek, XIII. 8. a. 11; exemplaire disparu pendant la seconde guerre mondiale.
Cette reliure a été signalée en 1936 par Ilse Schunke, qui ne l'a pas reproduite. Rappelant l'exemplaire de Goldschmidt (qui est à la grande marque), elle dit qu'il y en a un autre exemplaire à Brème, mais avec une autre disposition de la devise «Les Anges liés».

2. *Les treselegantes et copieuses annales des trespreux tresnobles treschrestiens et excellens moderateurs des belliqueuses Gaulles*, Paris, 1544.
Propriétaire actuel inconnu.

Volume cité par Gruel (*Manuel*, I, p. 42: collection particulière), qui reproduit la marque, non par photographie, mais par dessin. Ce dessin ressemble à celui de la grande marque, mais il y a tant de différences entre eux que Jos Hermans[1] n'hésite pas à y voir une troisième variante. Au contraire, Breslauer classe ce volume parmi ceux qui portent la grande marque (n° 4 de sa liste). Le commentaire du numéro précédent rend plausible l'existence d'une troisième variante, existence affirmée d'autre part sans réserve par Léon Gruel dans son compte rendu de l'exposition de 1894.[2]

SÉBASTIEN GRYPHIUS

Imprimeur-libraire à Lyon, 1524-1556; Françoise Miraillet et Antoine Gryphius, successeurs, 1556-1564; puis Antoine seul, 1565-1599.

A. FER À LA PIERRE PLATE, AUX PETITS CÔTÉS ÉGAUX

1. *Exposition de l'histoire des dix lépreux*, [Genève, Jean Gérard], 1539, in-8°. Relié avec NOËL BEDA, *La confession & raison de la foy*, [Neuchâtel, Pierre de Vingle, ±1533], in-8°.
Paris, Bibliothèque Nationale, Rés. D² 15. 956-15. 957.
La marque a été frappée probablement en argent. Les plats anciens, en chèvre, sont remontés dans une reliure neuve.

2. BALDESSAR CASTIGLIONE, [*Il Cortegiano*?], Lyone, [Guglielmo Rouillio?], 1562, [in-16?].
Propriétaire actuel inconnu.
Provenance: Léon Gruel.
La marque de cette reliure est reproduite dans le *Manuel* de Gruel (II p. 89) par un dessin assez négligé. Il n'est pas certain qu'elle soit identique à celle de l'exemplaire précédent.

B. FER À LA PIERRE MOINS PLATE, LE PETIT CÔTÉ À DROITE

1. DIODORUS SICULUS, *Bibliothecae historicae libri XVII*, latine, Lugduni, Sebastianus Gryphius, 1552, in-12.
Propriétaire actuel inconnu.
Provenance: Joseph Baer, Frankfurt a. M., catalogue 750, n° 252, pl. 26.

---

1. HERMANS, *art. cité*, note 43.
2. L. GRUEL, *Quelques mots sur l'exposition rétrospective de la reliure au Palais de l'Industrie en 1894*, Bulletin du bibliophile et du bibliothécaire, 1894, pp. 633-649.

C. FER À LA PIERRE PLATE, LE PETIT CÔTÉ À GAUCHE

1. Léon Gruel, dans son *Manuel*, reproduit par dessin cette marque qui ressemble à celle, gravée sur bois, répertoriée par Silvestre (486). Il dit que la reliure sur laquelle elle est frappée lui appartient, mais il omet d'en préciser le contenu. Il se pourrait qu'il s'agisse de l'album vendu à Paris par Pierre Chrétien, 27-28 novembre 1967, n° 242; la notice du catalogue dit: «La marque qui figure sur la présente reliure est reproduite au *Manuel*, II, page 89», malheureusement le *Manuel* reproduit deux marques et le catalogue ne précise pas laquelle figure sur l'album.

GUILLAUME MERLIN

Libraire à Paris, 1538-1574.

A. INSCRIPTION: IN HOC CYGNO VINSES (*sic*)

1. *Breviarium Romanum*, Parisiis, Gulielmus Merlin, 1546, in-8°.
Paris, Bibliothèque Sainte-Geneviève, BB 643 Rés.
Provenance: sur la doublure du premier plat, ex-libris imprimé du legs de la bibliothèque du cardinal Maurice Le Tellier à l'abbaye Sainte-Geneviève.
Tranches dorées.

2. *Horae ad usum Romanum*, Parisiis, Apud Guillelmum Merlin, 1552, in-16. Lyon, Bibliothèque du Musée des Tissus, R 56.

B. INSCRIPTION: IN HOC CYGNO VINCES

1. *Haebraea, Chaldaea, Graeca et Latina nomina*, Paris, Robert Estienne, 1537, in-8°.
Etait autrefois relié avec un autre ouvrage, qui a été enlevé et remplacé par des feuilles blanches.
Propriétaire actuel inconnu.
Provenance: Claude Dalbanne?[1]

2. *Hortulus animae*, Parisiis, in aedibus Henrici Coipel pro Guillelmo Merlin, 1569-1570, in-8°.
Paris, Bibliothèque Mazarine, Rés. 23. 889.[2]
Provenance: *Guilielmus van Welda(m)me Bruxelle(nsis) 8ª Aprilis 1573*

---

1. Brun, *Guide…*, 1938, p. 65. C. Dalbanne, *Notes sur Guillaume I Merlin libraire parisien*, Gutenberg Jahrbuch, 1958, pp. 143-148.
2. La cote donnée par Brun est erronée.

(...) *Romae x Augusti 1575; io ai comprata aquista officio de m. guilelmus Weldame [Brux]ellensis. Andrian Husman Gandencis* (XVIIe siècle).
Tranches dorées. Fleuron dans les entrenerfs. Seul le premier plat porte le fer B; le second porte le fer C.

3. L. MIRE, *Vie de Jésus-Christ*, Paris, 1533.
Tournai, Bibliothèque de la Ville. Exemplaire détruit dans les bombardements de mai 1940, avec la presque totalité de l'institution. Décrit dans: E.-J. Soil de Moriamé & Adolphe Hocquet, *Exposition des arts décoratifs anciens et du livre*, Tournai, 1930, p. 182. n° 91.

C. INSCRIPTION: IN HOC SUGNO VINCES

1. L'*Hortulus animae* qui porte le fer B au premier plat, porte le fer C au second.

2. *Heures a lusaige de Rome*, Paris, Jehan Amazeur pour Guillaume Merlin, 1553, in-8°.
Olim: Amsterdam, Universiteitsbibliotheek, 2508 H 22.
Reproduction: C. P. BURGER, *Het Abecedarium als algemeen verbreid leerboekje*, Het boek, 16, 1927, pp. 28-32, pl.
Cette reliure a été détruite entre 1927 et 1975, et remplacée par un demi-parchemin (communication de M. Kees Gnirrep, actuel Conservateur des Livres rares et précieux).

PONCET LE PREUX

Libraire à Paris, 1498-1559.

1. DESIDERIUS ERASMUS, *Familiarium colloquiorum opus*, Coloniae, H. Alopecius, 1542, in-8°.
Londres, Victoria & Albert Museum, Binding Drawer 42, Al. 148-1865. Cf. JOHN P. HARTHAN, *Early trade bindings*, The Book Collector, 1, 1952, p. 266.

2. *Coustumes générales et particulières du Royaume de France*, Paris, Poncet Le Preu, 1552, 2 t./1 vol. in-folio.
Laon, Bibliothèque Municipale, 247 inq.
Provenance: Louis Despinois ou d'Espinoys, licencié ès droits, 1552.
La marque n'est pas seulement dorée, elle est rehaussée de cire noire, tout comme les fleurons d'angles. Reliure reproduite dans: G. Colin, *A binding with the mark of Poncet Le Preux*, The Book Collector, 23, 1974, p. 213-214.

GABRIELE GIOLITO DE' FERRARI

Imprimeur-libraire à Venise, 1538-1578.

1. Suetonius, manuscrit sur parchemin, 1433, in-4°.
New York, Collection Grenville Kane.
Cf. TAMMARO DE MARINIS, *La legatura artistica in Italia*, II, Firenze 1960, pp. 16-117, n° 2155, pl. C43.
Maroquin marron; décor doré aux petits fers.

JEAN BAILLEUR

Libraire et relieur à Paris, 1544-1581, sa présence à Genève est attestée en 1559.

1. PLATO, *Opera*, Lugduni, I. Tornaesius, 1550, in-16.
Paris, collection particulière.
Provenance: Librairie Éric Speeckaert (*Cent livres, reliures, autographes & manuscrits de 1484 à 1956*, Bruxelles, [1991], n. 11, avec reproduction de la reliure ouverte).
Entrelacs mosaïqués au dos.
La marque dorée au centre des plats peut être reproduite ici grâce à l'aide aimable de M. Speeckaert. L'échelle de reproduction est approximative.

2. PIERRE LAGNER, *Ex M. T. Cicerone insignium sententiarum elegans & perutile compendium*, Lugduni, Apud Ioan. Tornesium & Gulielmum Gazerum, 1551, in-16.
Paris, collection de M. Dominique Courvoisier.
Entrelacs mosaïqués au dos.

L'OFFICINE PLANTINIENNE

Imprimerie, maison d'édition, librairie à Anvers, 1555-1867.

A. CADRE OVALE À ARABESQUES

1. *Le livre de l'institution chrétienne*, Anvers, Christofle Plantin, 1557, in-12.
Anvers, Museum Plantin-Moretus, O. B. 1. 5. (olim R 277).
Tranches dorées.

B. CARRÉ POSÉ SUR POINTE

1. HENRICUS JOLLIFUS & ROBERTUS JONSON, *Responsio ad illos articulos…Joannis Hoperi.* Antverpiae, Christophorus Plantinus, 1564, in-8°.
Anvers, Museum Plantin Moretus, R 21. 14 (olim R 531).

2. ALDUS MANUTIUS, *Orthographiae ratio*, Antverpiae, Christophorus Plantinus, 1564, in-16.
Propriétaire actuel inconnu.
Provenance: Pringault; Léon Gruel (*Manuel*, II, p. 132).
Maroquin rouge.

C. RUBAN CROISÉ ACCOMPAGNÉ DE FLEURS

1. M. ANNAEUS LUCANUS, *Opera*, Antverpiae, Christophorus Plantinus, 1564, in-16.
Propriétaire actuel inconnu.
Provenance: ex-libris manuscrit de Wolfgang Iöchlinger von Pfanberg, 1600; vente Starhemberg, Cologne, Venator, Versteigerung XV/XVI, 15-18 septembre 1956, n° 254; acheté par feu le libraire Menno Hertzberger pour sa bibliothèque privée.
Tranches dorées.

2. C. VALERIUS FLACCUS, *Argonauticon lib. VIII*, Antverpiae, Christoph. Plantinus, 1566, in-16.
Anvers, Museum Plantin-Moretus, O. B. 1. 9.
Provenance: signature d'Abraham Ortelius sur le titre; mention anonyme, en allemand, de l'achat de cet exemplaire à Anvers en 1598 (Ortelius était mort le 4 juillet de cette année); ex-libris de Gustave Van Havre, (vente à Amsterdam, F. Müller, 3-5 avril 1906).
Tranches dorées.

3. NICOLAUS ESCHIUS, *Exercitia quaedam pia*, Antverpiae, Christophorus Plantinus, 1569, in-16.
Upsal, Bibliothèque de l'Université, Bokband 1500-1. Nederland 5.
Provenance: au verso du 3e feuillet de garde du 1er plat, entrelacs dessinés à la plume et inscription: A N // α n° D(omi)ni // 1574; sur le titre: Col. Brauns.

D. FER OVALE

1. HORATIUS, *Ars poetica*, Antverpiae, Christophorus Plantinus, 1564, in-8°.
Anvers, Museum Plantin-Moretus, O. B. 2. 21.

Provenance : jésuites de Louvain, 1602 ; ex-libris du marquis de Granges de Surgères (vente de sa bibliothèque, Bruxelles, J. De Winter, 28 janvier-5 février 1927, n. 572 ; avec reproduction).
Maroquin rouge. Tranches dorées.

E. RUBAN RECOURBÉ ACCOMPAGNÉ DE FLEURS

1. T. LUCRETIUS CARUS, *De rerum natura*, Antverpiae, Christophorus Plantinus, 1565, in-8°.
Copenhague, Bibliothèque Royale, 170, 119.
Provenance : Hartmann Sebacher 1659 ; Georgius Francus, D. P. Argentorati 1666.

F. CADRE À VOLUTES

1. ADOLPHUS OCCUS, *Impp. Romanorum numismata a Pompeio Magno ad Heraclium*, Antverpiae, Christophorus Plantinus, 1579, in-4°.
Leyde, Bibliothèque de l'Université, 1371 D 24.
Provenance : selon le catalogue de l'exposition *Schatten uit de Leidse Bibliotheek*, 2-25 juin [1967?], n° 44, cet exemplaire a appartenu à Juste Lipse. Contrairement à ce que prétend ce catalogue, la devise du fer à dorer n'est pas en espagnol, mais en latin. Elle ne se lit pas *Constancia et labores*, mais bien *Labore et Constancia*.

2. JUSTUS LIPSIUS, *Electorum liber I*, Antverpiae, Christophorus Plantinus, 1580, in-8°.
La Haye, Bibliothèque Royale, 145 G 24.
Provenance : Joannes Basius (avec la devise *Sustine et abstine*, le tout en gothique soignée, qui semble de l'époque du livre) ; collection Mensing (acheté en 1909).
Tranches dorées.

G. AVEC LAURIER ET PALME

1. *Novum Testamentum*, [Graece], Lugduni Batavorum, Ex Officina Elzeviriorum, 1633, in-12.
Oxford, Broxbourne Library, R 168.
Provenance : John Dixon Book 1696 (ex-libris manuscrit).

MADELEINE BOURSETTE

Libraire et imprimeur à Paris, 1541-1556.

1. *Biblia*, Lutetiae, Robertus Stephanus, 1545, in-8°.
Paris, Bibliothèque Nationale, Rés. p. A. 17.

L'exemplaire provient de la collection de Léon Gruel; il est reproduit en hors texte dans son *Manuel*, II, à l'article Boursette.

Sur cette belle reliure, en veau écaille, des filets dorés et à froid forment un cadre contenant, en haut et en bas des rinceaux dorés, à gauche et à droite une longue invocation religieuse. L'effet global est assez décoratif, d'un esprit différent de la plupart des reliures à marques dorées.

JÉRÔME DE MARNEF

Libraire à Paris, 1546-1595.

A. PÉLICAN TOURNÉ À DROITE, DANS UN OVALE

1. POLYBIUS MEGALOPOLITANUS, *Historiarum libri priores quinque*, Lugduni, Seb. Gryphius, 1554, in-16.
Propriétaire actuel inconnu.
Provenance: *Bibliothèque de M. B.ˣˣˣ et autres provenances*, Genève, Nicolas Rauch, vente des 29-30 mars 1954, n° 198, pl. 11.
Tranches dorées.

2. AULUS GELLIUS, *Noctes Atticae*, Parisiis, Hieronymus de Marnef, 1564, in-16.
Propriétaire actuel inconnu.
Provenance: Léon Gruel (décrit à la même page du *Manuel* et vendu en 1967 sous le même numéro que la marque B, 3).
Tranches dorées.

3. M. T. CICERO, *Orationes*, Lugduni, Antonius Gryphius, 1567, in-8° (tome III seul).
Paris, collection de M. Dominique Courvoisier.

4. M. T. CICERO, *Epistolae familiares*, Lugduni, Antonius Gryphius, 1560 (corrigé à la main: 1569), in-16.
Bruxelles, Bibliothèque royale, LP 9294 A.
Provenance: Librairie Jörg Schäfer, Zurich, catalogue n° 37, lot 2.

5. M. T. CICERO, *De philosophia*, Lugduni, Antonius Gryphius, 1570, in-8°.
Oxford, Broxbourne Library, 11. 1.

B. PÉLICAN TOURNÉ À GAUCHE

Dans toutes les marques de Marnef gravées sur bois pour orner ses éditions, le pélican est tourné à droite.

1. JUVENALIS & PERSIUS, *Satyrae*, Paris, Jérôme de Marnef, 1561, in-16.
New York, Martin Breslauer, Catalogue 104 II, n° 173.
Tranches dorées.

2. LACTANTIUS FIRMIANUS, *Opera*, Paris, Hier. de Marnef, 1561, in-12.
Propriétaire actuel inconnu.
Provenance: E. Ph. Goldschmidt (*Gothic & Renaissance bookbindings*, n° 230, pl. CVIII).

3. CICERO & DEMOSTHENES, *Sententiae selectae*, Parisiis, Hieronymus de Marnef, 1566, in-16.
Propriétaire actuel inconnu.
Provenance: Léon Gruel (*Manuel*, II p. 119; vente à Paris, Pierre Chrétien, 27-28 novembre 1967, n° 247).
Tranches dorées.

JEAN BOGARD

Imprimeur, libraire, éditeur à Louvain, 1562-1597, et à Douai, 1574-1627.

A. CADRE OVALE GRAS

1. FRANCISCUS TITELMANNUS, *Elucidatio paraphrastica in librum D. Job*, Lugduni, Gulielmus Rovillius, 1554, in-16.

B. Jean Bogard   C. Jean Bogard

Louvain, Faculteit der Godgeleerdheid, Fonds Groot Seminarie 3205 A 23.
Provenance: cachet du Séminaire archiépiscopal de Malines.

2. L.A. SENECA, *Sententiae in locos communes*, Antverpiae, typis Gerardi Smits, apud Lucam Bellerum, 1576, in-12.
Anvers, Museum Plantin-Moretus, A 2582.
Provenance: ex-libris manuscrit de J. Gevartius (XVIe siècle?).
Ce livre a été utilisé dès le XVIe siècle, car une main de l'époque a écrit des proverbes ou des devises sur la doublure du premier plat et sur le premier feuillet de garde.

3. SIMON DE VALLAMBERT, *Cinq livres, de la manière de nourrir et gouverner les enfans des leur naissance*, Poitiers, De Marnef & Bouchetz, 1565, in-4°.
Sur la page de titre, ex-libris manuscrit de l'époque: "A Jacques Suijs D.F.P.N."
Acheté par M. François Chamonal, libraire à Paris, qui a bien voulu me le signaler en mai 1993.

B. CADRE RECTANGULAIRE

1. PROSPER AQUITANICUS, *Opera*, Lovanii, Ioannes Bogardus, 1565, in-4°.
Anvers, Bibliothèque de la Ville, 4357 R 44 d.
Provenance: ex-libris manuscrit de la bibliothèque des frères mineurs d'Anvers (XVIIIe siècle).
L'exemplaire contient de nombreuses notes de lecture du temps. Au second plat, le fer est poussé de travers, et sur les deux plats, le bas de la marque n'est pas doré.

2. *Même ouvrage.*
Bruxelles, Bibliothèque Royale Albert Ier, LP 63 A. Acheté en 1958.

3. *Même ouvrage*, 1566.
Bergues-Saint-Winoc, Bibliothèque Municipale, 1 40.
Provenance: capucins de Bourbourg.

4. ARISTOTELES, *De natura aut rerum principiis libri VIII*, Duaci, Joannes Bogardus, 1576, in-4°. Relié avec les oeuvres suivantes du même auteur, sorties des mêmes presses: *De coelo libri*, 1575; *Liber de mundo*, 1575; *Meteorologicorum libri*... (le titre manque); *De animo libri III*, 1575; *Libelli qui parva naturalia vulgo appellantur*, 1575.
Bruxelles, Bibliothèque Royale Albert Ier, LP 8397 A.
Provenance: note de lecture de M. Phylippus, 23 février 1581, à la fin du

De coelo; Léon Gruel (son *Manuel* 1 p. 57 indique «collection particulière», mais on retrouve le volume à la vente Pierre Chrétien des 27-28 novembre 1967, n. 250, où se sont vendus plusieurs reliures provenant de la collection Gruel); ex-libris Charles Vander Elst (vente anonyme, Monaco, Claude Guérin, 13 mai 1985, n° 15).
Nombreuses notes de lecture du XVIe siècle.

C. CADRE OVALE MAIGRE

La différence avec le cadre ovale gras se perçoit entre autres par les volutes, plus larges dans celui-ci.

1. JOANNES HESSELS, *Declaratio quod sumptio Eucharistiae...*, Lovanii, Ioannes Bogardus, 1566, in-8°. Relié avec: ejusdem, *Tractatus pro invocatione sanctorum*, ibidem, 1564, in-8°.
Mons, Bibliothèque de l'Université, 1000/40.
Provenance: deux ex-libris manuscrits biffés et par suite peu lisibles: Claudius (?) behaste (?); Ad usum fratris (...?) Bosque (?) Montensis 1591; monastère de Saint-Denis-en-Broqueroie.

2. *Catechismus ex Decreto Concilii Tridentini*, Lovanii, Ioannes Bogardus, 1567, in-8°.
Bruxelles, Bibliothèque Royale Albert Ier, VB 1809 A LP.
Provenance: les gardes ayant été renouvelées, il est possible que des notes de propriété aient disparu. Le fonds VB de la Bibliothèque royale Albert Ier contient presque exclusivement des livres provenant de la bibliothèque de Philippe II et de ses successeurs, ainsi que des couvents brabançons.

D. MARQUE NON DÉTERMINÉE

Selon Henri Stein, Gruel possédait une reliure à la marque de Bogard sur un livre de 1566 (H. STEIN, *L'Exposition du Livre à Paris*, Centralblatt für Bibliothekswesen, 12, 1895, p. 35).

SAMUEL SELFISCH

Libraire, 1564-, imprimeur et papetier, 1596-1615, à Wittenberg.

1. AESOPUS, *Fabulae*, Francofurti ad M., 1566.
Dresde, Landesbibliothek, Litt. Graec. B 2702 (Kurf. Bibl. 4 a).
Tranche rouge avec fers dorés, pas particulièrement raffinée, selon Ilse Schunke.

2. HORATIUS, *Poemata*, s.l.n.d.
Dresde, Landesbibliothek (disparu pendant la deuxième guerre mondiale).[1]

BARTHOLOMAEUS GRAVIUS

Imprimeur, libraire, éditeur à Louvain, 1530-1578.

1. *Psalterium Davidicum*, Antverpiae, Gulielmus Silvius, 1568, in-8°.
Louvain, Faculteit der Godgeleerdheid, Fonds S. J., 15L1 1568 L.
Provenance: ex-libris manuscrits, du XVIe siècle, de Jacques Lescornet, chanoine de N.-D. de Bruges, et d'Arnold van Mechelen.

JACQUES KERVER

Libraire et imprimeur à Paris, 1535-1583.

1. *Heures de Nostre Dame*, Paris, Jean le Blanc pour Jacques Kerver, 1569, in-8°.
Londres, British Library, C. 64. c. 11.
Provenance: ex-libris manuscrit, du XVIe siècle, d'une religieuse, «seur mari le blan».

HUGUES BARBOU

Libraire à Lyon, 1558-1566; imprimeur et éditeur à Limoges, 1573-1600.

1. *Heures de la Vierge à l'usage de Limoges*, Limoges, Hugues Barbou, 1573, in-8°.
Limoges, Bibliothèque Municipale, Rés. Lim. T. 53.
Dans l'ensemble des reliures à marques de libraires, celle de Barbou se distingue par son important décor doré: plaques de centre et coins à arabesques en relief, semé d'étoiles.[2]

JACQUES DU PUYS

Libraire à Paris, 1540-1589 (?)

1. *Les coutumes générales de France*, 1581, in-folio.
Propriétaire actuel inconnu.

---

1. Communication de Mmes Knospe et Stein.
2. J. CONDAMIN, *Heures à l'usage de Limoges, Hugues Barbou (1573)*, Bulletin de la Société archéologique et historique du Limousin, 89, 1962, pp. 115-116.

Provenance: Léon Gruel.
La plaque de Du Puys ne m'est connue que par le dessin qu'en a donné Gruel dans son *Manuel*, où il a omis d'indiquer le titre du livre ainsi relié. En revanche il donne ce titre dans son compte rendu de l'exposition de 1894.[1]

JEAN II LECOQ

Imprimeur à Troyes, 1550-1588.

1. *Heures à l'usage de Rome*, Troyes, Jean Le Coq, s.d., in-8°.
Troyes, Bibliothèque Municipale.
Le calendrier de ces Heures commence en 1585.

GIUNTI

Famille d'imprimeurs et éditeurs à Venise, Florence, Lyon, Burgos, Salamanque et Madrid, XV\ua75b-XVII\ua75b siècles.

1. ARISTOTELES, *Organum, sive logica*, Basileae, ex officina Oporiniana, 1585, in-8°.
Propriétaire actuel inconnu.
Provenance: ex-libris de Léon Gruel; vente à Paris, Pierre Chrétien, 27-28 Novembre 1967, n. 251.
Cette reliure n'est connue que par la description du catalogue de la vente signalée ci-dessus. Le premier plat est orné d'un médaillon central doré portant la marque des Giunti, qui est répétée à froid tout autour; le second présente une bordure de feuillages et de têtes de guerriers encadrant quatre portraits.

L'OFFICINE VELPIUS ANTHOINE

Velpius, Rutgerus: imprimeur, libraire, éditeur à Louvain, 1565-1580; à Mons, 1580-1585, à Bruxelles, 1585-1614. Son gendre Hubert Anthoine (ou Antoine-Velpius) travaille avec lui à partir de 1598; il meurt en 1630. L'officine continue sous la direction de sa veuve, de 1630 à 1635, puis de son fils, Hubert II, jusqu'en 1670.

---

1. GRUEL, *Manuel...*, II, p. 74, et *Quelques mots sur l'exposition rétrospective de la reliure au Palais de l'Industrie en 1894*, Bulletin du bibliophile et du bibliothécaire, 1894, pp. 633-649, spécialement p. 640.

A. PETITE MARQUE

1. AMBROSIUS PARAEUS, *Opera chirurgica*, Francofurti ad Moenum, Ioannes Feyrabend, 1594, in-folio.
Bruxelles, Bibliothèque royale Albert Ier, VB 4650 C LP.
Provenance: ex-libris manuscrit de l'abbaye de Dielegem-lez-Bruxelles (XVIIIe siècle?).
La marque de l'officine apparaît à l'intérieur d'une grande plaque décorative dont le centre est évidé.

A. Velpius Anthoine

B. GRANDE MARQUE

1. IASPAR GELLIUS, *Poemata sacra*, Lovanii, Io. Baptista Zangrius, 1599, in-4°.
Bruxelles, Bibliothèque royale Albert Ier, II 10. 825 A LP.
Provenance: ex-libris manuscrit du couvent des carmes déchaux de Termonde, 1676; ex-libris gravé de Th. de Jonghe.

2. *Recueil des traittez de paix, trèves et neutralité entre les couronnes d'Espagne et de France*, Anvers, Balthasar Moretus, 1643, in-4°.
New York, Lathrop C. Harper, Catalogue 239, n. 98 (avec reproduction de la reliure).
Provenance: ex-libris manuscrits du comte Wolfgang Engelbrecht von Auersperg, 1655, et de son frère le prince Johann Weichardt.

B. Velpius Anthoine

JOHN NORTON

Libraire et éditeur à Londres, à Eton et en Ecosse, 1586-1612. Son successeur: Roger Norton.

AI. BASE DU TERTRE À CINQ FESTONS

1. EURIPIDES, *Tragoediae septendecim*, Venetiis, apud Aldum, 1503, in-8°.
Collection particulière.

2. TERENTIUS, *Comoediae*, Lugduni, Mathias Bonhome, 1560, in-8°.
Oxford, Christ Church, A. D. 7. 16.
Provenance: ex-libris manuscrit de William Creed, Fellow of Corpus Christi College, mort en 1711.

3. *Biblia*, Lugduni, Ioannes Frellonius, 1566, in-8°.
Manchester, John Rylands University Library, R 77477.

4. JOHN JEWEL, *A Defense of the Apologie of the Churche of Englande*, London, Henry Wykes, 1571, in-folio.
Washington, *Folger Shakespeare Library*, STC 14602 copy 4.
Provenance: W. J. Leighton (vente à Londres, Sotheby, 27 octobre 1919, n° 2390); Sir R. Leicester Harmsworth.
Description et reproduction: F. A. BEARMAN, N. H. KRIVATSY, J. F. MOWERY, *Fine and historic bookbindings from the Folger Shakespeare Library*, Washington, 1992, pp. 42-43.

5. THEMISTIUS, *Orationes XIIII*, [Genevae], Henricus Stephanus, 1562, in-8°. Relié avec Aeschines, *Epistolae Graecae*, Rostochii, Jacobus Lucius, 1578, in-8°.
Propriétaire actuel inconnu.
Provenance: Edward Gordon Duff (vente à Londres, Sotheby, 16 mars 1925, n. 166); E. P. Goldschmidt, Catalogue 87, n° 148.

6. *Biblia Sacra, Hebraice, Graece, et Latine*, [Heidelberg], ex Officina Sanctandreana, 1587, 2 vol. in-folio.
York, Minster Library, XII. D. 1-2.
Les plats anciens sont incrustés dans une reliure du XVIIIe siècle.

7. NICOLAUS CLENARDUS, *Institutiones ac mediationes in graecam linguam*, Francofurdi, Andreae Wecheli haeredes, Claudius Marnius, & Ioannes Aubrius, 1590, in-4°.
Propriétaire actuel inconnu.
C'est probablement le n. XXXIII de la liste de G. D. Hobson[1] e le n° 236 de la vente de W. H. Corfield (Sotheby, Wilkinson & Hodge, 21 novembre 1904). La date de 1610 donnée par le catalogue de la vente Corfield est douteuse, car la *Bibliographie des oeuvres de Nicolas Clénard* par Louis Bakelants et René Hoven (Verviers, 1981) ne relève aucune édition cette année.

8. ISOCRATES, *Orationes et epistolae*, Genevae, Henricus Stephanus, 1593, in-folio.

---

1. G. D. HOBSON, *Bindings in Cambridge Libraries*, Cambridge, 1929, p. 106.

Londres, British Library, G 8532.
Provenance: Thomas Grenville.

9. DIOGENES LAERTIUS, *De vitis…clarorum philosophorum libri X*, Genevae, Henricus Stephanus, 1593, in-8°.
Londres, British Library, C. 108. b. 8.
Provenance: Israel Huitt (XVIIe siècle, peut-être XVIe); Rev. Stockton (XVIIIe-XIXe siècle.).

10. JOHANNES OPSOPAEUS, *Sibyllina oracula*, Parisiis, [Abel L'Angelier], 1599, in-8°.
Oxford, Broxbourne Library, 29. 4.

11. HORATIUS, *Poemata*, Genevae, Paulus Stephanus, 1600, in-8°.
Windsor, Eton College Collections.
Provenance: Maggs, Catalogue 1075, I, n° 18.

12. *Bible*, London, 1601, in-4°.
Propriétaire actuel inconnu.
Provenance: Dr. Ginsburg (Burlington Fine Arts Club, *Exhibition of bookbindings*, London, 1891, n° 42, pl. LXXIX).

13. WILLIAM LILY, *A short introduction to grammar*, London, J. Norton, 1607, in-8°.
Windsor, Eton College Collections, An. 7. 9.
Acquis en 1731.

14. NICOLAUS MULERIUS, *Tabulae Frisicae Lunae-Solares*, Alkmaar, (I. Meesterus), 1611, in-4°.
Londres, British Library, 532. g. 9.
Provenance: ex-libris manuscrit de J. Nobles, 1698.
Reliure neuve dans laquelle on a inséré un plat de la reliure ancienne.

15. XENOPHON, *De Cyri institutione libri VIII*, Eton, in Collegio Regali, 1613, gr. in-4°.
Londres, British Library, 294. f. 29.
Exemplaire interfolié; pas de marque de propriété.

16. WILLIAM BROWNE, *Britannia's Pastorals*, London, George Norton, 1616, in-folio.
Salisbury, Cathedral Library, T. 2. 45.

A2. MÊME PLAQUE, MAIS CASSÉE

1. ARISTOTELES, *De Rei P. beneadministrandae ratione*, Paris, 1567. Relié avec *Organon*, Francfort, 1597.

Propriétaire actuel inconnu.
Provenance: sur le premier plat, le nom de Charles Somerset; au second, sa devise; vente Colonel Joseph W. Weld, Londres, Christie, Manson & Woods, 24 juillet 1970, n° 32.

2. *The Genealogies recorded in the Sacred Scriptures* [and] *The Whole Books of Psalms*, London, Stationers' Company, 1611, in-8°.
Londres, British Library, C. 108. c. 21.
Provenance: ex-libris manuscrit de John Wiles, 7 juin 1766.

B. BASE DU TERTRE RECTILIGNE

1. MARCUS TULLIUS CICERO, *Orationum volumen III*, Londini, Ioh. Iacsonus & Edm. Bollifantus, 1585, in-8°.
Oxford, Broxbourne Library, 10. 22.
La plaque a été employée sans or.

C. BASE DU TERTRE COURBE

1. WILLIAM LILY, *[Grammar]*, London, assignes of J. Battersbie, 1597, in-8°.
Cambridge, King's College, A 9. 12.

2. HORATIUS, *Poëmata*, [Genevae], Paulus Stephanus, 1600, in-8°.
Oxford, Christ Church, A. D. 7. 17. Ex-libris manuscrits de William Gardiner et d'Audly Cory.

3. CLAUDIUS PTOLEMAEUS, *Hypothesis stellarum errantium*, et six autres opuscules de divers auteurs, manuscrit, vers 1600.
Oxford, Bodleain Library, Auct. F. 1. 2.
Provenance: offert en 1609 à la Bodleian Library par Henry Savile (1549-1622).

4. ARISTOXENUS, *Elementorum harmonicorum libri tres*, et six autres opuscules de divers auteurs, manuscrit, vers 1600.
Oxford, Bodleian Library, Auct. F. 1. 3.
Provenance: offert à la Bodleian Library par Henry Savile.
Reliure ornée de grandes plaques de centre et coins.

5. GREGORIUS NAZIANZENUS, *In Julianum Invectivae duae*, Etonae, J. Norton, In Collegio Regali, 1610, gr. in-4°.
Windsor, Eton College Collections, Gut. B. 2. 11.

D. RELIURES DONT LA PLAQUE N'A PU ÊTRE DÉTERMINÉE

1. *Psautier*, manuscrit, Angleterre méridionale, vers 1425-1535.

Propriétaire actuel inconnu.
Provenance: vente Sotheby, du 6 décembre 1983, n° 62; acheté par Laurence Witten, libraire à Southport, Connecticut.

2. JEAN CRESPIN, *Lexicon Graeco-Latinum*, [Genevae], Haeredes Eustathii Vignon, 1595, in-4°.
Propriétaire actuel inconnu.
Provenance: vente Ilchester, Sotheby, 14 mai 1962, n° 152; acheté par Maggs, libraire à Londres.

3. *The Bible*, London, Deputies of Christopher Barker, 1597, in-folio.
Propriétaire actuel inconnu.
Provenance: vente George Goyder, Londres, Sotheby, 23 juin 1958, n° 20; acheté par Sawyer.
La marque de l'arbre au second plat seulement; au premier, faucon couronné.

4. JOHANNES KEPLER, *Ad Vitellionem paralipomena quibus astronomiae pars optica traditur*, Francoforti, 1604, in-4°. Relié avec cinq autres opuscules du même auteur, publiés de 1609 à 1614, notamment à Prague et à Leipzig.
Propriétaire actuel inconnu.
Provenance: vente Bute, Londres, Sotheby, 3 juillet 1961; acheté par Kraus.

5. EDMUND SPENSER, *The Faerie Queene*, London, Mathew Lownes, 1609, in-folio.
Propriétaire actuel inconnu.
Provenance: vente Sotheby du 24 juillet 1922, lot 598.
C'est le n. xxxvi de la liste de G. D. Hobson.

LOUIS & DANIEL ELZEVIER

Libraires, éditeurs et imprimeurs à Amsterdam, en association de 1655 à 1665; après le retrait de Louis, Daniel dirige seul l'officine, jusqu'en 1680.

A. GRANDE MARQUE

1. HENRICUS REGIUS, *Philosophia naturalis*, Amstelaedami, apud Ludovicum et Danielem Elzevirios, 1661, in-4°.
Cambridge, St. John's College, Aa. 2. 54.
Veau marbré. La marque est dorée quatre fois au dos du volume, mais non sur les plats (dos reproduit dans Burlington Fine Arts Club, *Exhibition*

of bookbindings, London, 1891, pl. LXIX). Le livre contient de nombreuses annotations prouvant qu'il se trouvait en Angleterre peu de temps après la date de son édition.

2. Titre inconnu
Propriétaire actuel inconnu.
Exemplaire orné sur les plats de la marque des Elzevier (reproduite par gravure dans le *Manuel* de Gruel, I, p. 95).

3. MOLIERE, *[Oeuvres]*, lieu et date inconnus, 5 vol. (reliés en un volume?).
Propriétaire actuel inconnu.
Exemplaire cité par Gruel (I, p. 95) comme étant orné au dos de «ce même motif remplissant chaque entre-nefs».

B. PETITE MARQUE

1. TERENTIUS, *In quem triplex edita est P. Antesignani*, Lugduni, Apud Mathiam Bonhomme, 1560, in-4°.
Paris, Institut Néerlandais, Fondation Custodia.

Mirjam M. Foot

UN GRAND DUC, IMMORTEL
À LA POSTERITÉ

Anne de Montmorency was born on 15 March 1493, the second son of Guillaume, Baron of Montmorency and Anne Pot.[1] From the age of about ten, he shared the education of the future King Francis I. His childhood came to an abrupt end with the death of his mother in 1510; Anne volunteered for the army of Louis XII, the beginning of a most distinguished military career. In 1514 he entered the service of the crown, spending much of his time at court. With the death of his elder brother in 1516 he became heir to the extensive Montmorency property. Six years later he became marshal of France and received the order of St Michel. He was imprisoned, together with his king, after the battle of Pavia in 1525 and in the following year Francis I made him grandmaster of France and governor of the Languedoc. In 1527 he married Madeleine de Savoie, who bore him five sons and seven daughters. The death of his father in 1531 made him Baron of Montmorency. In 1538 he was created Constable of France.

As well as being a soldier, courtier and statesman, Anne de Montmorency had great taste in art and architecture. He had a passion for ceramics and collected innumerable works of art which he displayed in his castles and other residences. Best known of these are the castle of Chantilly (built between 1524 and 1530), that of Ecouen (constructed from 1538 to c. 1555, although it may not have been finished until 1559), and his 'hotel Neuf de Montmorency' in the rue Sainte-Avoye in Paris. He was fond of hunting, hawking and shooting, a connoisseur of fine wines and a gourmet, partial to exotic fruit. On one occasion Jean Grolier sent him eight bergamot pears and two melons, at that time a little-known luxury.

He fell out of grace with Francis I and retired to Chantilly in 1542, but when Henry II ascended to the throne five years later, Anne came back in favour. He maintained a close friendship with the king, who called him his 'compère' and created him Duke in 1551. During Francis II's brief reign he was in disgrace and again returned to Chantilly, to be called back to the court at the accession of Charles IX.

He remained all his life a patron of the arts, building and extending his

---

1. B. Bedos Rezak, *Anne de Montmorency, Seigneur de la Renaissance*, Paris, 1990 (and for information below).

residences and enlarging his collections of sculpture, paintings, ceramics, tapestries, enamels, medals and, of course, books and manuscripts. There were libraries at Chantilly, Ecouen and in his house in Paris, containing reference books, military and historical works, science, literature, and books on religion. These libraries have largely been dispersed and de Montmorency's books can now be found in collections in France and elsewhere.

His excellent taste is reflected in the illumination of his manuscripts and in his choice of bindings. It is likely that his close proximity to the courts of Francis I and Henry II, as well as his friendship with Jean Grolier, introduced him to the best Parisian ateliers, and the bindings he owned bear witness to the artistry and craftsmanship of a fair number of binderies. Whether this was due entirely to his own catholic taste or to the habits of his friends and dependants, is not so easy to determine. Nor is it all that easy to be sure whether, when ordering his books to be bound, he specified the style of the decoration himself, or whether he left this to his binders. He may also have acquired some of his books already bound.

Of the twenty-four bindings that once belonged to Anne de Montmorency that I have seen,[1] I have been able to identify nineteen and I have attributed these to eight different binders' shops. This is only a fraction of de Montmorency's library. According to the inventories published by Mirot,[2] de Montmorency had, in his house in Paris alone where the smaller part of his collection was kept, 174 books, bound either in velvet or in white, black or red calf. Blue and green morocco and vellum bindings are also mentioned. The library where these books were kept was simply furnished with two leather chairs, one red one black, a table, and glass-fronted, lockable bookcases with red serge curtains fringed in red, white and yellow, to keep the sunlight off the bindings.

Many, but not all, of de Montmorency's bindings display his coat of arms (or, a cross gules between 16 allerions or eaglets azure). Those that do, show it surmounted by either a baron's coronet or by one that was meant to serve de Montmorency after he had become a duke.

Three examples, without coats of arms, come from the shop that Ilse Schunke called the 'Fontainebleau Meister'.[3] There is in the literature a

1. I am grateful to Monsieur Antoine Coron and to Monsieur Thiérry Crepin-Leblond for references to a number of these bindings. T. CREPIN-LEBLOND, *Livres du Connétable. La bibliothèque d'Anne de Montmorency*, Clamecy, 1991 lists 49 items. Not all bindings in this catalogue have been identified correctly.

2. LÉON MIROT, *L'Hôtel et les collections du Connétable de Montmorency*, Paris, 1920, especially pp. 57-58, 70-73, 103-105, 161-162. I am grateful to Madame Annie Charon for drawing these inventories to my attention.

3. ILSE SCHUNKE, 'Der klassische Grolier-Buchbinder in Paris', *Gutenberg Jahrbuch* 1953, p. 164.

certain amount of confusion as to whether or not this shop belonged to Étienne Roffet, the royal binder, but Howard Nixon[1] was firmly convinced that it did not and I share his conviction. The tools used by the Fontainebleau binder are closely similar to those employed by Étienne Roffet, but they are not identical. The binding on Appian's *Histoire romaine* (vol. II) translated by Claude de Seyssel, a manuscript on vellum written in 1510 (Chantilly, Musée Condé, MS 763), comes from the Fontainebleau binder's shop. It is of brown goatskin, tooled in gold with solid tools. The border shows the eaglets from the Montmorency arms, and in the centre, in a cartouche that is derived from the 'tabula ansata', is his motto, APLANOS. On the lower cover this motto appears in Greek. The binding has four pairs of ties, an Italianate feature, and the solid tools used by the Fontainebleau binder and by several other Parisian binders during the 1520s and 1530s derive their design from Italian, especially Venetian, models. The 'tabula ansata' also shows Italian inspiration. This tablet with handles, used as a frame for inscriptions on classical sarcophagi, can be found as a frontispiece in Paduan manuscripts of *c*. 1460 and it appears on Venetian, Neapolitan and Florentine bindings of the first two decades of the sixteenth century. Anthony Hobson, in *Humanists and Bookbinders* (Cambridge, 1989) gives several examples of this decorative device derived from classical sources. It shows more clearly and in a purer form on another binding from de Montmorency's library that I have not been able to identify. This covers a manuscript of François Habert, *Les deux paraphrases chrétiennes*, a poem written on vellum and dedicated to Anne de Montmorency, whose name is on the lower cover, while the upper cover has the motto VERTU AU CIEL VOLE (Chantilly, Musée Condé, MS 528). Two fairly similar bindings of black goatskin from the Fontainebleau bindery show on the upper cover the motto APLANOS in Greek in a rectangular frame (whose connection with the 'tabula ansata' has become rather faint), with above and below it arabesque ornaments built up of the same solid Italian-inspired tools, surrounded by a field strewn with eaglets. One of these bindings, on a manuscript of Guerry d'Igny's *Sermons*, translated by Jean de Ganay, is at Montpellier (Fig. 1), and the other covers a vellum copy of *Les Coutumes...du bailliage de Senlis*, Paris 1540, now in the Bibliothèque Nationale (Rés. Vélins 457).[2] It has the arms of Anne de Montmorency, his motto and his constable's sword painted on the first page. The lower cover has the motto in Latin.

1. H. M. NIXON, *Sixteenth-century gold-tooled bookbindings in the Pierpont Morgan Library*, New York, 1971, pp. 27, 34.
2. ILSE SCHUNKE, 'Der Meister der Estiennebibel und die Renaissance-Buchbinder in Paris', *Bibliothèque d'Humanisme et Renaissance* 1959, pl. 6.

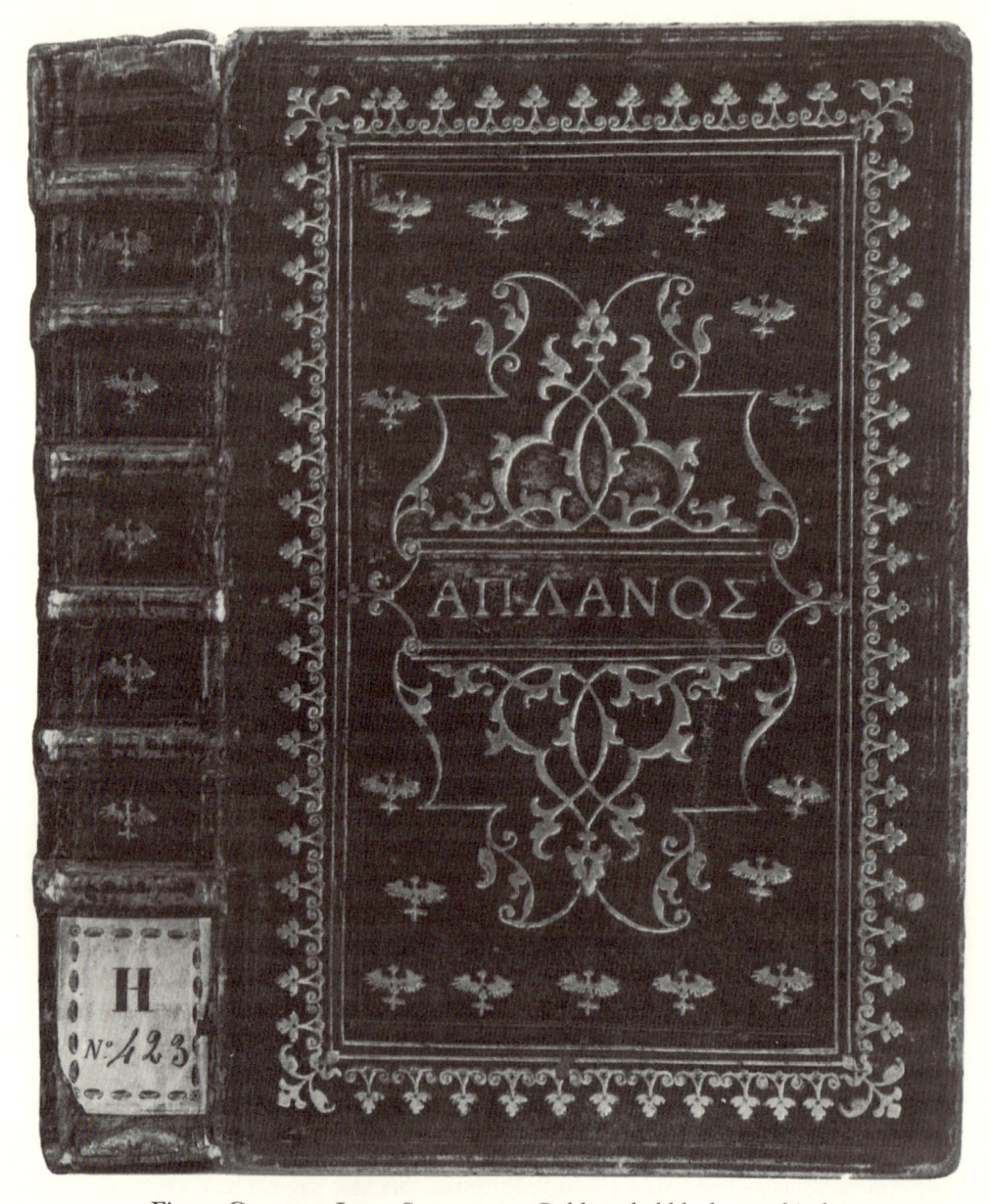

Fig. 1. Guerry d'Igny, *Sermons*, ms. Gold-tooled black goatskin by the Fontainebleau binder. Montpellier, Bibliothèque interuniversitaire, MS. H423.

A shop that was active in Paris during the 1530s and 1540s was that of the Pecking Crow binder. He worked for a number of distinguished patrons (including two kings, Francis I and Henry II – although he was not a royal binder). King James V of Scotland owned a binding from this shop and Cardinal de Granvelle and Thomas Wotton both patronised it.[1] The binding for de Montmorency that was made in this shop covers a manuscript on vellum of Paulus Paradisus, *La vie et naissance du prophète Moyse*, 1539 with the arms of de Montmorency and his constable's sword painted on the title-page (Bibliothèque de l'Arsenal, MS 5093 Rés). It is made of brown goatskin, tooled in gold, with on the upper cover the French royal arms on a semis of fleurs-de-lis, while the lower cover has the generous statement: QUOD HABEO HOC TIBI DO on a semis of eagles. The Pecking Crow binder possessed an eagle tool, which he also used on a 1533 Venice Castiglione in a private collection. Monsieur Crepin-Leblond suggests in his catalogue, *Livres du Connétable. La bibliothèque d'Anne de Montmorency* (no. 5) that this (and no. 39 in an almost identical binding) were presented by Anne de Montmorency to Francis I. If this is so, the manuscript must have been bound fairly soon after it was written in 1539, as Anne fell out of favour with the king late in 1540 and withdrew from the court.

The next binder to be discussed, in whose workshop the manuscript of Valerius Maximus, *Les neuf livres*, in 3 volumes, 1544 (Chantilly, Musée Condé, MS 835-837),[2] may have been bound, also worked for Thomas Wotton. The tools with which volume one of this manuscript has been decorated can also be found on bindings made by Wotton's binder A. He was active during the 1540s and there may have been a connection between him and the Pecking Crow binder.[3] All three volumes of the Valerius Maximus manuscript are bound in calf decorated with black paint, and every one has been tooled in gold to a different design. Volume I shows a design of interlacing strapwork, familiar from bindings made for Jean Grolier; volume II has interlaced strapwork borders but a quite different effect is produced by the large elaborate central cartouche on a dotted ground, containing Anne de Montmorency's name on the upper cover and his title on the lower; while the covers of volume III are almost entirely taken up by an even more elaborate cartouche built up of gouges (curved and straight lines), surrounding the word APLANOS. This motto was also tooled in the border of the binding of volume II. All three volumes have gilt and gauffered edges. It is possible that the open tool at

---

1. M. M. FOOT, *The Henry Davis Gift*, vol. 1, London, 1978, pp. 129-138.
2. G. D. HOBSON, *Maioli, Canevari and Others*, London, 1926, pl. 49.
3. M.M. FOOT, *op. cit.*, pp. 133-134, 143.

the corners of the covers of volume 1 is identical with a tool used by Grolier's Cuspinianus binder. This shop certainly produced the binding of Polybius, *Histoires*, a manuscript on vellum *c.* 1543-45, now at the Walters Art Gallery in Baltimore (Fig. 2).[1] It is made of white calf, tooled in gold and decorated with paint and it has the constable's motto (in Greek) in the centre. As will be obvious from his name, this binder worked for Jean Grolier; he was also patronised by Thomas Mahieu in the early-to-mid-1550s.[2]

Another binder who worked for Mahieu, his so-called 'Aesop' binder, produced at least one binding for de Montmorency. The manuscript of Nicolas Berthereau, *Payement des gentilshommes et officiers de la maison du Roy*, 1550 (Bibliothèque Nationale, MS Clairambault 813) appears to have been bound in this shop, as the rather distinctive hatched curving tools that appear in blind on the lower cover have been found in combination with a number of other tools that can be firmly ascribed to Mahieu's Aesop binder.[3] The black calf binding has on the upper cover the royal arms of France and HD monograms, as used by Henri II. The coat near the bottom of the upper cover has been overpainted and altered to show the Montmorency arms. The constable's sword with a banderole with his motto decorates both covers, while the lower cover has the full title of the manuscript tooled in the centre. Monsieur Crepin-Leblond has suggested in his catalogue (no. 17) that this may have been taken from Henry II's library and given to Anne de Montmorency by the author, who was secretary to the king and a close friend of the constable.

It is just possible that the binding of P. Godefroy [*De hereticis*] Paris 1555[4] was bound by the shop that worked for Peter Ernst Count Mansfeld. It is in light brown calf, tooled in gold and decorated with white paint, and the ducal arms of de Montmorency have been painted in the centre. The word APLANOS appears near the top and the bottom of the covers and the pair of curved hatched tools on either side of this motto may have belonged to the Mansfeld binder.[5]

The two ateliers that produced the majority of the bindings that belonged to de Montmorency are those of Gommar Estienne and the Cupid's Bow binder. Gommar Estienne was discovered by Madame Annie

---

1. D. MINER, *The History of Bookbinding, 525-1950 AD. An Exhibition held at the Baltimore Museum of Art*, Baltimore, 1957, no. 275.

2. H. M. NIXON, *op. cit.*, pp. 80-84.

3. *Ibid.*, pp. 115-118.

4. Langlois collection, see A. RAU, 'Contemporary Collectors XIII, André Langlois', *The Book Collector* VI (1957), p. 132, pl. 2.

5. H. M. NIXON, *op. cit.*, pp. 119-126. E. VAN DER VEKENE, *Les reliures aux armoiries de P.E. de Mansfeld*, Luxembourg, 1978.

Fig. 2. POLYBIUS, *Histoires*, ms. Gold-tooled white calf by Grolier's Cuspinianus binder (lower cover). Walters Art Gallery, Baltimore.

Charon. In 1555 he published for Anne de Montmorency a Prayer book and Psalter. The title-page[1] is decorated with a wide border containing de Montmorency's arms (with a duke's coronet) his constable's sword, his motto, his monogram and the staff of 'Grand Maistre'. The dedication copy – now at Chantilly (Musée Condé) – is bound in black goatskin and tooled in gold to an arabesque design with eaglets and the initials of Anne and his wife, Madeleine de Savoie. Gommar Estienne is mentioned in a number of documents which have been published by Madame Charon.[2] From 1548 he was bookseller to the king and in 1550 he is mentioned as bookbinder to the king. It seems probable that Gommar Estienne took over as 'relieur du roy' in 1549, when Étienne Roffet died, and that he filled this post until 1559 when Claude Picques obtained the position.

Both Annie Charon and Anthony Hobson[3] have written about Gommar Estienne and his relationship with Jean Grolier, for whom he also appears to have worked. I will not repeat their conclusions (nor argue their differences) here. Tools that occur on royal bindings when Estienne was 'relieur du roy' turn up later when Claude Picques held the office. It seems to me perfectly possible that both Estienne and Picques, once they had become royal binders, were too grand to work at the bench themselves and that they instead used the best Paris finisher available at the time. After all, in France, binding and finishing were as a rule carried out by separate craftsmen. This would account for the apparent continuation of the tools, while it could also explain why these tools were used to such different effects during the reigns of successive kings, if one assumes that the 'relieur du roy', the man responsible for the binding of the king's books, was the man who specified the designs. It is, however, highly likely that Gommar Estienne was responsible for the binding of the dedication copy of his own and only publication. The same atelier made three *à la Greca* bindings for de Montmorency, all three on books printed in Paris by Robert Estienne. Dionysius Alexandrinus (or Denys le Périégète), *De situ orbis libellus*, Paris 1547 (Bibliothèque Nationale, Rés. J.1831), is in very dark brown goatskin over wooden boards, tooled in gold and silver. It has the raised headcaps that are characteristic of *à la Greca* bindings and there are traces of four pairs of clasps on plaited thongs. The painted arms of de Montmorency have his baron's coronet and his motto is lettered in gold and silver. The flat spine has a semis of eaglets. The binding of Dion Cassius, *Romanarum historiarum libri XXIII*,

---

1. A. R. A. HOBSON, *Humanists and Bookbinders*, Cambridge, 1989, fig. 176.
2. ANNIE PARENT, *Les métiers du livre à Paris au XVIe siècle (1535-1560)*, Geneva, 1974; ANNIE PARENT-CHARON, 'Nouveaux documents sur les relieurs parisiens du XVIe siècle', *Revue française de l'histoire du livre*, XXXVI (1982), pp. 389-408.
3. A. R. A. HOBSON, *op. cit.*, pp. 209-13, 271.

Paris 1548 (Bibliothèque Nationale, Rés. J.192 bis)[1] is in a very similar binding, and so is that of Alexander Trallianus, *Medici libri*, Paris 1548 (Bibliothèque de la Sorbonne). All three have been decorated to the same design and with the same tools, all three have brass bosses, all three show the features typical of *à la Greca* bindings and all three were made before 1551. The fifth binding from this shop was made well after de Montmorency had become a duke. It was probably made *c.* 1560 or soon thereafter and it covers Pierre de Paschal, *Henrici II Galliarum Regis elogium*, Paris 1560 (Fig. 3). Two other copies of this book were bound by the same atelier, one for Henry II, the other for François, Duc de Guise. By this date, they must have been the responsibility of Claude Picques.

Four bindings come from the shop that Howard Nixon christened the Cupid's Bow binder.[2] Like a number of binderies already mentioned, this shop also worked for Jean Grolier who patronised it from *c.* 1547 to 1555. A number of other distinguished collectors, such as Cathérine de Medici, Marc Laurin, Louis Sainte-Maure (Marquis de Nesle), Pope Paul IV, and Alfonso II d'Este, duke of Ferrara, owned bindings from this shop. One of the bindings made there for Anne de Montmorency dates from before 1551. It covers a fine Portolan *Atlas* on vellum, drawn by Freducci in 1528, which is now at the Royal Library in the Hague.[3] De Montmorency's arms are surmounted by a baron's coronet, and the lower cover displays the constable's sword with his motto. The Cupid's Bow binder continued to work for de Montmorency after he had become a Duke. A copy of G.B. Susio, *I Tre libri della ingiustitia del duello*, Venice 1555 (Chantilly, Musée Condé) was bound by him in brown calf, tooled in gold and decorated with paint. The lower cover has the constable's sword in the centre. The coronet that surmounts the painted arms on the upper cover differs from that normally used for the Duke of Montmorency in that it shows fleurons and a fleur-de-lis instead of the more familiar strawberry leaves. Brunet[4] concluded that it must have been meant as a marquis's coronet and he therefore thought that the binding belonged to Anne's son, François. No herald would wholeheartedly approve of this coronet (not even for a marquis), but binders were notoriously sloppy heralds. The Cupid's Bow binder could do better, though, and the copy of Jean Le Gendre, *Tiers livre de la fleur et mer des hystoires*, Paris 1550, bound in light brown calf, tooled in gold and decorated with coloured

---

1. H. BOUCHOT, *Les Reliures d'art à la Bibliothèque Nationale*, Paris, 1888, pl. XXXVI.
2. H. M. NIXON, 'Grolier's binders', *The Book Collector*, IX (1960), p. 49.
3. E. DE LA FONTAINE VERWEY, 'Une reliure pour le Connétable Anne de Montmorency dans la Bibliothèque Royale à la Haye', in *Studia Bibliographica in honorem Herman de la Fontaine Verwey*, Amsterdam, 1966, pp. 375-388, pls. 1-2.
4. G. BRUNET, *La Reliure ancienne et moderne*, Paris, 1878, pl. 62.

Fig. 3. Pierre de Paschal, *Henrici II Galliarum Regis elogium*, Paris, 1560. Gold-tooled brown calf by Claude Picques. Paris, Musée du Petit-Palais, Dutuit B 673.

Fig. 4. PEDRO DE MEDINA, *L'Art de naviguer*, Lyons, 1554. Gold-tooled brown calf by the Cupid's Bow binder. Glasgow University Library, Hunterian Collection, Dp. 2.11.

Fig. 5. Jean Le Gendre, *Tiers livre de la fleur et mer des hystoires*, Paris, 1550. Gold-tooled brown calf by the Cupid's Bow binder. Bibliothèque Mazarine.

paint shows a more conventional ducal coronet (Fig. 5). The same binder used the ducal coronet on Pedro de Medina, *L'Art de naviguer*, Lyons 1554, now in the Hunterian library at Glasgow (Fig. 4). This book, 'en veaù rouge doré, avec les armoiries du connétable', is listed among the 'Livres trouvez audict cabinet du Roy' (no. 329) in an inventory of the contents of de Montmorency's house in the rue Sainte-Avoye made in 1556.[1]

Anne de Montmorency died at the age of 75, on 12 November 1567 as a result of wounds received in the battle of Saint Denis. Ronsard in his *Epitaphe* calls him 'un grand Duc...immortel à la posterité,[2] an immortality to which his books and bindings have certainly contributed.

---

1. LÉON MIROT, *op. cit.*, pp. 58, 72, 104. To a twentieth-century observer the binding appears to be of brown calf.
2. P. DE RONSARD, *Oeuvres complètes*, Paris, 1923-24, vol. 4, p. 322.

Lotte Hellinga

PETER SCHOEFFER AND THE BOOK-TRADE IN MAINZ: EVIDENCE FOR THE ORGANIZATION

Peter Schoeffer is one of those early printers whose work is not at all rare, for it survives in very many copies, preserved in many great libraries. His work shares this happy fate with that of some of the other outstanding entrepreneurs of the period, for example Anton Koberger and Aldus Manutius. Their dominant role in the book production of their time remains tangible, and is most conveniently demonstrated in printers' indexes to incunable catalogues, since most of the work of their printers' shops can be identified beyond doubt. Only gradually has it been understood, however, that the impact of Schoeffer (and some other printers) on the dissemination of printed books extended well beyond the books he produced himself. There is some, but not much documentary evidence for this aspect of Schoeffer's business, and this is far exceeded by what can be inferred from the mass of evidence surviving in many copies of books with which he can be connected. As copies of books printed by Schoeffer came to be examined, it was gradually established that the work of certain binders was often found on them. Significantly, the work of one of these binders was found not only on books printed by Schoeffer, but also and in much greater numbers on books printed by others, especially printers in Strasbourg, Basel, Cologne and Venice. Thus fresh evidence came to light that showed that Schoeffer acted as importer and retailer of books printed elsewhere, sometimes as formal agent for a colleague printer, on other occasions probably in a less formal arrangement. Books bound by this binder, whether printed by Schoeffer himself or by others, could be linked to Schoeffer's printing house by the frequent occurrence of printers' waste of Schoeffer imprints used as paste-downs. This warranted the conclusion that Schoeffer had regularly commissioned work from this binder.

As early as 1908 Adolph Tronnier discussed the significance of such a link between some of Schoeffer's books and a binder,[1] while even a few years earlier, in 1905, Gottfried Zedler had made an observation to the same effect.[2] Since in these publications there was only a question of

---

1. ADOLPH TRONNIER, *Die Missaldrucke Peter Schöffers und seines Sohnes Johann.* Mainz 1908, pp. 28-220. [Veröffentlichungen der Gutenberg Gesellschaft 5-7]. See also his 'Von Einbandspiegeln / Mainzer Rechnungsbüchern und Gülten der Gensfleisch Familie' in: *Gutenberg Jahrbuch 1936*, pp. 30-47.
2. GOTTFRIED ZEDLER, *Das Mainzer Catholicon*, Mainz 1905, p. 46. [Veröffentlichungen der Gutenberg-Geselllschaft 4].

either Schoeffer's own imprints bound with his printers' waste, or a book to which he was thought to be closely related, the term 'Verlegereinband', or 'Publisher's binding' was used. This turns out to be somewhat misleading, since by now more books *not* printed in Mainz than Schoeffer imprints are known to be bound by Mainz binders, arguably in connection with Schoeffer. In 1938 H. Knaus discussed these binders extensively,[1] with much new supporting evidence in the form of printer's waste, but the link between printer, binder, location and book-trade was definitely established by Dr Vera Sack in 1971 with a magisterial command of the relevant material.[2] The reason for me to return to the matter after Dr Sack's authoritative article is that I think it is possible to perceive yet another dimension to Schoeffer activity. Since the rate of survival allows us to examine a large number of copies of books printed in Schoeffer's printing house between 1467 and c. 1480 it becomes possible to recognize the work of a very limited number of rubricators, flourishers and illuminators. It becomes clear that, although part of Schoeffer's production was sold to other destinations blank and unadorned, just as it had come off the press, a sizable proportion was 'finished by hand' in conjunction with the printing house, and therefore presumably in or near Mainz. There can be great similarity in the decoration of copies of the same edition, but it also becomes clear that there was variation in the levels of luxury in which this handwork was to be executed. Only a relatively small number of the decorated copies survive in their original bindings, but conversely, the copies of Schoeffer editions still in original Mainz bindings are all decorated or illuminated in Mainz. It begins therefore to be possible to establish a link between the work of binders (and that of one in particular) and that of the flourishers/illuminators. In other words, it becomes clear that Peter Schoeffer commissioned the 'finishing by hand' of books printed at his press by decoration and by binding. On a different occasion I have already shown that this could be preceded by a final manual correction of all copies of a printed text after it had left his press.[3]

1. HERMANN KNAUS, 'Über Verlegereinbände bei Schöffer', in: *Gutenberg Jahrbuch 1938*, pp. 97-108. Knaus supplemented this later with: 'Schöffers Handel mit Zell-Drucken' in: *Gutenberg Jahrbuch 1944/49*, pp. 91-2.
2. VERA SACK, 'Über Verlegereinbände und Buchhandel Peter Schöffers', in: *Börsenblatt für den Deutschen Buchhandel - Frankfurter Ausgabe* 27, 1971, pp. 2775-2794. Also in: *Archiv für Geschichte des Buchwesens* 13, 1972-3, cols. 249-288. Dr Sack gave me permission to make use of her work as I have done in the present article and in particular in the Appendix. I am most indebted to her generosity.
3. LOTTE HELLINGA, 'Editing Texts in the First Fifteen Years of Printing', in: Dave Oliphant, Robin Bradford (eds.), *New Directions in Textual Studies*, Harry Ransom Humanities Research Center, The University of Texas at Austin 1990, pp. 127-149.

Having established this link it can come as no great surprise that decoration by the same recognizable hands can be found in some of the imported books bound by Mainz binders, although this has not yet been investigated quite so extensively. Thus the analysis and documentation of the 'handwork' in individual copies of printed books can contribute at least a few brush-strokes to an emerging tableau: that of the many connections and contacts, personal and impersonal, which constituted the trade in printed books and their wide dissemination in Western Europe in the first decades of printing. It is a picture of great complexity. As we begin to perceive its outlines and salient points we also begin to grasp that the cultural history of the printing trade cannot remain content with the reasonable knowledge of early book-production that has been built up in several centuries of bibliographical recording. On this solid basis it is now possible to study and compare individual copies and perceive features not produced by the press (such as annotation, binding and illumination) which, although not mechanical, they may have in common. The result can be a perception of influences, dependencies and connections in book-production that a mere bibliographical record will not reveal. The present paper sets out to explore some of these features further, and since this is an account of work still in progress, it seeks more to point to a programme for further work rather than to establish definitive results.

THE BINDER 'KYRISS 160'

Since Dr Sack listed in 1971 a substantial part of the material and used this as the basis for some important conclusions, it seems best to begin with summarizing the valuable conclusions of her article. She concentrated on one of the binders who can be connected with Peter Schoeffer. He was designated by Ernst Kyriss[1] as the workshop 'M mit Krone I', after one of his decorative tools, but failing any form of name that can be attached to him it is easiest to name him after the place he occupies in Kyriss's repertorium and call him 'Kyriss 160'. He must have been a prolific worker, and many of his bindings still survive. Dr Sack identified some 60 distinctive tools by which his bindings can be recognized, but unfortunately she could not illustrate her article. Kyriss provided rubbings of 11 tools, and a far larger number (28) can be found in the rubbings collected by Paul Schwenke.[2] I illustrate here a selection of the tools that I have found most useful for identification (see Fig. 1).

1. ERNST KYRISS, *Verzierte gotische Einbände im alten deutschen Sprachgebiet.* Vol. 1, Textband, and three volumes with plates. Stuttgart 1951-58. Vol. 1, pp. 128-9, with a list of bindings, Plates 321-2.
2. ILSE SCHUNKE, *Die Schwenke-Sammlung gotischer Stempel und Einbanddurchrei-*

Taking into account that a large proportion of this binder's work is found on books which (in other copies) have been much sought-after collectors' items from the eighteenth century on, it becomes likely that what is still extant can only be a part of what he once must have produced. Much of his work was probably replaced by collectors' bindings. Some of his bindings I have seen are now in such condition that they cannot be expected to survive much longer. As it is, the figures for still extant bindings are impressive. Whereas Kyriss had listed only one manuscript and 33 printed books with bindings of this workshop, Dr Sack listed and discussed 94 copies of printed books (some found together in one volume, others in multi-volume works) and four manuscripts, all in libraries in Germany. There are at least four items listed by Kyriss not covered by Dr Sack (at Prague and Tübingen, Wilhelmsstift). By examining copies in other collections I have been able to add 22 items to Dr Sack's list, mainly of books printed by Schoeffer himself. We can confidently expect more copies to come to light. Dr Sack's main observations and conclusions can be summed up as follows:

1. There is abundant evidence that the workshop was active in Mainz itself.
2. There are several instances of bindings with binders' waste from Schoeffer editions. This points to a close relationship with Schoeffer.
3. Schoeffer must have sold a part of his publications after they were bound, for early owners of volumes in these bindings can be found far from the Mainz area.
4. The binder must also have worked for other clients in Mainz, e.g. when binding manuscripts.
5. A second Mainz binder, Hanns Oisterreicher, must also have worked for Schoeffer.
6. The number of texts in the list is limited and several texts are represented in many editions. A large proportion belongs to the *Corpus iuris civilis* and other legal texts, and many of the texts had been printed by Schoeffer himself as well as by others at a later date.

bungen 1: Einzelstempel, Berlin, 1979. [Beiträge zur Inkunabelkunde 3. Folge 7], the binder 'Kyriss 160' illustrated on p. 2, no. 35 = p. 309, no. 2 (Kyriss Plate 321 no. 4); p. 5, nos. 134, 135; p. 8, no. 210-211 (Kyriss 2); p. 11, no. 271 = p. 15, no. 366a (Kyriss 8); p. 19, no. 456 (Kyriss 11); p. 21, no. 1; p. 25, no. 82a (Kyriss 9); p. 38, no. 125; p. 44, no. 256; p. 87, no. 20; p. 90, no. 8 (Kyriss 5); p. 125, no. 34; p. 140, no. 42; p. 143, no. 15; p. 165, no. 199; p. 191, no. 152; p. 192, no. 165; p. 196, no. 270; p. 203, no. 38; p. 204, no. 60, 60a; p. 235, no. 73; p. 261, no. 318; p. 262, no. 336; p. 265, no. 443; p. 286, no. 210 (Kyriss 1); p. 291, no. 348; p. 298, no. 37 (Kyriss 7). Schwenke-Schunke did not reproduce Kyriss nos. 3; 6, 10.

7. The list of books in Kyriss 160 bindings can be seen as a stock catalogue of a specialized scholarly bookshop ('Verkaufskatalog einer wissenschaftlichen Fachbuchhandlung').

8. Some printers occur with remarkable frequency and can be identified as Schoeffer's trade-contacts: as can be expected from other sources, Peter Drach, Anton Koberger, Ulrich Zell, and Heinrich Quentell. On a much larger scale are the contacts with several printers in Strasbourg and with Michael Wenssler in Basel. Everything is surpassed, however, by the frequency with which Venetian printers are found; Dr Sack surmises that the merchant Peter Ugelnheimer played a part as intermediary.

9. Schoeffer did not take up competition with other printers when they started to produce the same texts he had printed.

10. Early ownership notes show that Schoeffer's clients were not only found locally but also in Franconia, Bavaria and Cologne.

Dr Sack stressed in particular the implication her evidence had for an understanding of Schoeffer's specialism: first as a publisher, then as a bookseller, of texts meeting particular requirements: both kinds of law, philosophical theology (Thomas Aquinas, Antoninus Florentinus, Petrus Lombardus), bibles, patristic texts, and to a much lesser extent classical authors. To support her point she arranged her list in alphabetical order, thus emphasizing the authors Schoeffer the publisher had in common with Schoeffer the bookseller. Re-arranged chronologically, as presented in an Appendix to this article, it is possible to stress another aspect: the development of Schoeffer's business that can thus be perceived. On the basis of this rearrangement (which incorporates the items I have been able to add to Dr Sack's list) it is possible to abstract some telling figures. The peak of activity becomes evident when we divide the material chronologically, in the first instance into decades according to the dates of printing of the books. The earliest book listed is a copy of the Boniface, printed by Fust and Schoeffer in 1465, the last item was printed in 1510 in Strasbourg (and is bound in a volume with the binding date 1511), but the greatest activity clearly took place in the decade between 1470 and 1480.

	COPIES	VOLUMES
1465-1469	7	7
1470-1479	56	54
1480-1489	25	20
1490-1499	34 (and 15 incunabula not specified)	18
1500-1510	6	4

It is revealing to distinguish Peter Schoeffer's share in these books.

	PETER SCHOEFFER	OTHERS
1465-1469	7 copies (2 eds., 2 titles)	0 copies
1470-1475	15 copies (8 eds., 7 titles)	5 copies (5 eds., 5 titles)
1476-1479	3 copies (2 eds., 2 titles)	33 copies (30 eds., 26 titles)
1480-1489	0 copies	25 copies (24 eds., 21 titles)
1490-1499	0 copies	34 copies (34 eds., 31 titles)
1500-1510	0 copies	6 copies (6 eds., 6 titles)

We can conclude these initial statistics by indicating in which cities these book were printed:

1465-1469	Mainz	7 copies
1470-1479	Mainz	18 copies
	Basel	11 copies
	Venice	10 copies
	Padua	4 copies
	Strasbourg	4 copies
	Marienthal	2 copies

1 book each: Cologne, Lyon, Nuremberg, Speyer, Reutlingen, Rostock, and J. Numeister (Mainz?).

1480-1489	Venice	10 copies
	Basel	3 copies
	Strasbourg	2 copies
	Speyer	2 copies
	Vienne	2 copies

1 book each: Treviso, Milan, Parma, Lyon, Cologne, Nuremberg.

1490-1499	Venice	8 copies
	Strasbourg	5 copies
	Mainz	4 copies
	Freiburg	4 copies
	Basel	3 copies
	Cologne	3 copies

1 book each: Lyon, Pavia, Pescia, Leipzig, Nuremberg, Heidelberg, Speyer.

1500-1510	Cologne	2 copies
	Basel	2 copies
	Leipzig	1 copy
	Strasbourg	1 copy

For the early years it is unlikely that these figures are an entirely accurate representation of Schoeffer's activities as importer of books, but they indicate quite clearly that in the mid-1470s he started to shift the emphasis from printing books to importing the same works produced by other printers. The books he imported were to be retailed after binding by a binder (or binders) in Mainz and, as we shall see, after some embellishment by local rubricators, flourishers and painters where appropriate. They received therefore much the same kind of treatment that had given many copies of his own publications an unmistakable stamp of the traditions of the booktrade in Mainz. There is, however, no reason to think why the binder Kyriss 160 would have had no other clients in Mainz. Dr Sack herself gives as example the Mainz collector Balthasar Geyer to whom the collection of eleven quarto imprints bound in 1511 had belonged. This volume provides no obvious connection with Peter Schoeffer. Two volumes with manuscripts, not listed here, which had belonged to Archbishop Diether von Isenburg may also have been bound without any connection with Peter Schoeffer. The suggestion of Peter Schoeffer's role as importer and retailer begins to lose force of conviction when the multiple copies of editions printed by other printers cease to appear in the list. In so far as recorded at present the last such instance is found on a book printed in 1482, the two copies of Gregorius IX, *Decretales* printed by Michael Wenssler in Basel (GW 11463). There is much to suggest in the material now available that Schoeffer had a regular arrangement with Wenssler. By implication it is also likely that there were trade agreements with other printers who occur frequently in the list, e.g. Jacobus Rubeus, Nicolas Jenson, the firm of Johannes de Colonia and Johannes Manthen, and later Johannes de Gregoriis and Baptista de Tortis, all in Venice, Johann Herbort in Padua, Heinrich Eggestein in Strasbourg, Peter Drach in Speyer. For later years there is less evidence, but some speculation is especially justified for the titles that are so strongly represented in the list in earlier years: Bonifacius VIII, *Liber sextus Decretalium*, Gregorius IX, *Decretales*, Gratianus, *Decretum* and the *Epistolare* of Hieronymus.

TWO OTHER BINDERS

Before considering the rubricating and decorating of copies in conjunction with the work of binder Kyriss 160 we must briefly consider the work of two other binders who can be connected with printing in Mainz. One of them signed his bindings with his name, Hanns Oisterreicher, on a banderolle tool. The connection with Schoeffer had been recognized by A. Tronnier, but his work was most extensively studied and discussed by H. Knaus in 1938.[1] Dr Sack listed the eight volumes (containing nine works) known to have been bound by him, all but one in the Stadt-

---

1. Tools used by this binder are illustrated in ADOLF SCHMIDT, 'Albert Hus und Hanns Oesterrich, zwei Buchbinder des 15. Jahrhunderts', in: *Jahrbuch der Einbandkunst* 1, 1927, p. 36 sqq., and his work was further discussed by H. Knaus (1938) quoted in note 3, pp. 103-5. Also illustrated in ILSE SCHUNKE, *Die Schwenke-Sammlung* (see p. 133, note 2), p. 84, no. 32; p. 214, no. 22; p. 295, no. 429.

bibliothek in Trier and with early Trier provenance. His activities seem to have been mainly confined to the years 1472-1475. His work can be summarized as follows:

Books printed in:

1468	1 copy (printed in Strasbourg, Printer of Henricus Ariminensis
1472-1475	8 copies (7 volumes)

Printed by

Mainz (P. Schoeffer)	3
Strasbourg (Pr. Henr. Ariminensis)	3
Cologne (Zell, Winters)	2
Rome (A. Rot)	1

Since these bindings can be linked to Schoeffer's workshop by printer's waste found in them we can consider them as further evidence for Schoeffer's trade relations. With six additional books this more than doubles the evidence for imports before 1476.

Lastly, there is another binder who has at times been connected with Mainz, elsewhere with Butzbach. This is a binder whose activities are earlier than those of the others, and whose work is to date found only on books printed in Mainz and on one undated manuscript. The printed books are:

1459, GUILL. DURANTI, *Rationale Divinorum Officiorum*.
    GW 9101, München BSB-Ink D-324. (binder's waste: ms Hebrew Pentateuch)
1462, *Biblia latina*, vol. 2, GW 4204. Mainz, Gutenberg Museum Ink. 32
1465, BONIFACIUS VIII, *Liber vi Decretalium*, GW 4848. Trier, Priesterseminar
1470, HIERONYMUS, *Epistolare*, Hain 8553, Strasbourg BU
1470, HIERONYMUS, *Epistolare*, Hain 8553, Wolfenbüttel HAB

The timespan 1459-1470 suggested by the dates of publication of these books may in fact not apply to the bindings and the period over which they were produced began later probably. The Munich copy of the Duranti is, as has been explained elsewhere, a copy made up of vellum sheets in the final state of the book and some paper sheets marked up with proof corrections.[1] It is a copy that had belonged to the library of the St Martin cathedral in Mainz, and its make-up gives the impression that in this case the presence of proofsheets indicates that the very last sheets still available in the printer's shop were used to put it together. Proofsheets on paper, serviceable although somewhat short of perfection, were used

---

1. LOTTE HELLINGA, 'Proof-reading in 1459: The Munich copy of Guillelmus Duranti, Rationale', in: Hans Limburg, Hartwig Lohse, Wolfgang Schmitz, eds.), *Ars impressoria, Entstehung und Entwicklung des Buchdrucks*. München etc. 1986, pp. 183-202.

where the vellum sheets of the proper print-run had run out. The date of binding may therefore be a good deal later than that of publication. The catalogue of the incunabula in Munich (BSB D-324) identifies the binding as 'Butzbach', with reference to the Schwenke-Schunke collection of rubbings of bindings where some of the tools found on these bindings are illustrated.[1] There is no obvious connection with Butzbach in the Duranti nor in any other of the printed books. The bindings indicated as 'Butzbach-style' in the collection from the Butzbach church library now in the University Library in Giessen have no resemblance to these bindings at all. There is, however, one manuscript in this collection with Butzbach provenance in a blind-stamped binding decorated with one of the tools used by the Duranti binder. A rubbing of this binding is in the Schwenke-Schunke collection in the Staatsbibliothek, Berlin, and this binding must have given rise to the designation 'Butzbach'.[2] The four other bindings are positively linked with Mainz printing. The binding on the Bible of 1462 has pastedowns of printer's waste from the same edition. The Trier copy of the Boniface is famous for having harboured as pastedowns two leaves from the 42-line Bible.[3] It is curious that it is a paper copy (one of two known of this edition), but it has no markings of proofreading, and its textual status has not been investigated. The two bindings on Hieronymus are both on copies with Mainz decoration. They are a remarkable complement to the six copies of this book bound by the binder Kyriss 160, all with Mainz rubrication and decoration. The activity of the binder of the Duranti may perhaps have started a few years earlier, but for some years both binders must have been working at the same time, and it is very likely that both worked in Mainz. I illustrate a few of his tools (Fig. 2).

1. Tools found on this group of bindings were illustrated in ILSE SCHUNKE, *Die Schwenke-Sammlung* (see p. 133, note 2) p. 4, no. 99a, 105; p. 8, no. 201; p. 32, no. 91a; p. 160, no. 74a; p. 162, no. 127; p. 194, mo. 222a.

2. Examples of bindings 'Butzbacher Art' can be found using the catalogue of the manuscripts in this collection: WOLFGANG GEORG BAYERER, *Die Handschriften des ehem. Fraterherrenstifts St. Markus zu Butzbach*, Teil 1. Wiesbaden, 1980 [Handschriftenkataloge der Universitätsbibliothek Giessen 4]. I am most grateful to Dr. Anneliese Schmidt, Staatsbibliothek in Berlin, who sent me copies of the documentation compiled by Schwenke and Schunke. This showed that Handschrift 742 in Giessen UB, with fifteenth-century owners, first in Frankfurt, then in Butzbach, belongs indubitably to the Duranti group of bindings.

3. The two leaves were discovered in 1892 by Heinrich Volbert Sauerland and their identification was confirmed in the following year by Karl Dziatzko. They were also discussed by H. Knaus (1938), p. 107. More recently they were extensively described by Gunther Franz, who recognized that at least one page was a proof page with variants. See his 'Die Schicksale der Trierer Gutenbergbibeln: Zwei Makulaturblätter mit Druckvarianten', in *Gutenberg Jahrbuch 1988*, pp. 22-42.

EVIDENCE FOR THE 'HAND-FINISH' OF PRINTED BOOKS: PROBLEMS OF DATING

Rubrication, flourishing and illumination of copies offer a different kind of evidence. It is perhaps useful to reflect for a moment on the decreasing scale of certainty in identification with which we have to deal. Compared with other means of identification where books are concerned, typography offers a sophisticated system as an instrument for establishing printers and at least approximate, often fairly accurate dating. For hardly any of the editions listed in the Appendix is the printer or approximate date of printing in dispute. (The collection of legal texts now thought to have been printed c. 1494 by Kilian Fischer in Freiburg, formerly assigned to J. Amerbach in Basel is an exception). Decorative tools on bindings bring together the work of specific workshops, with the assumption that, as in typographic material, binding tools or a combination of tools, are particular to individual workshops. The grounds for dating, however, are more insecure than for typography, because generally there is much less dated material that can serve as a frame of reference. The list of bindings in the Appendix is primarily arranged in the chronological order of completion of printing of the books on which they are found, on the grounds that a book cannot be bound before it is printed. The considerable gaps in date of printing of several works bound together (see, for example, the last two items in the list) demonstrate the extent to which this scheme may deviate from the reality of the order in which these books passed through the binder's hands. The printer's waste used as paste-downs in some of the bindings can give a similar indication. The first book on the list, the Thomas Aquinas, *Summa* P.II.2 of 1467 (Hain *1459) offers the most extreme example. The copy in the Germanisches National Museum in Nuremberg has printer's waste of the Justinian of 1468; the copy in the Bibliotheca Philosophica Hermetica in Amsterdam contains two paste-downs, one a leaf of the same book, the other from the Aquinas edition of 1469 which proves that the book was not bound before 1469. The copy at the Frankfurt Stadt-und Universitätsbibliothek has printer's waste of a Boniface, either the edition of 1473 or that of 1476, and was therefore bound at least six years after the printing of the book. Further study of these bindings, for which this list may provide the basic material, is bound to add refinement to this initial attempt.

The same uncertainty in dating applies to all manual 'finishing' of books once they had left the press: manuscript correction of the text, rubricating, elaborate decoration with penwork flourishes or more ambitious illumination. The date of completion of printing merely offers a *ter-*

minus post quem. When there are reasons to think that this finishing by hand was connected with the printing house, there is also ground for guessing that these operations took place within a 'reasonable' time after completion on the press, but this notion leaves of course a wide margin of uncertainty. A buyer's date can sometimes offer an indication. The Vatican Library copy (Ross. 613) of the Thomas Aquinas *Summa Theologica* P.II.2, printed in 1467, is rubricated in Mainz and begins with an interlocking initial and penwork flourishes typical of the decoration of many copies of this book. It has also buyer's notes by a doctor Georgius Czingel of Schlettstadt who bought the book in 1472. In the light of the many copies known to have been decorated in this style it is likely that the book was already 'finished by hand' when he bought it.

RUBRICATION AND DECORATION OF BOOKS COMMISSIONED BY PETER SCHOEFFER

The chronology of decoration and illumination leaves a very large area of uncertainty, but this is not what has exercised researchers. Their main preoccupation has been to identify workshops and individuals, especially in the case of outstanding artists.

In the last twenty years several major publications have much contributed to the appreciation of Mainz as a centre for the decoration and illumination of books, and in particular printed books. Especially through the study of the earliest books printed in Mainz a great deal of light has been thrown on the illumination of the 42-line Bible (and hence on its distribution over a substantial part of the European reading world North of the Alps) and also on the work of an artist known as the Fust-Master.[1] This illuminator, who had an unmistakable individual style, is thought to have left Mainz around the time of Fust's death in 1466, just when the activities of the binder Kyriss 160 started in earnest. Until now much less has been published about Mainz work after the Fust-Master's departure, although at one level of execution (the highest level) Elgin

---

1. Eberhard König has developed insight into book illumination in Mainz in a sequence of studies which began with a survey of the illumination of the Gutenberg-Bible in the Kommentarband to the Ideon-Verlag facsimile (eds. Wieland Schmidt and Friedrich-Adolf Schmidt-Künsemüller), Munich, 1979. Of his further studies two in particular should be mentioned since they partly correct earlier work: 'Für Johannes Fust', in: Hans Limburg, Hartwig Lohse, Wolfgang Schmitz (eds.), *Ars Impressoria: Entstehung und Entwicklung des Buchdrucks*, München etc., 1986, pp. 285-313. 'New Perspectives on the History of Mainz Printing: A Fresh Look at Illuminated Imprints', in: SANDRA HINDMAN (ed.), *Printing the Written Word: The Social History of Books, circa 1450-1520*, Cornell University Press, Ithaca and London, 1991, pp. 143-173.

Vaassen has listed Mainz illumination of the 1470s and 1480s and provided many illustrations.[1] By a strange irony her study appeared in the same year and in the same periodical as Dr Sack's article about Schoeffer's bindings, but the two studies, although mutually relevant, failed to benefit from one another.

What follows started off as an investigation of the decoration of copies of Hieronymus *Epistolare* (Hain *8553-4), completed (in two issues) by Peter Schoeffer on 7 September 1470, an investigation carried out jointly by Professor Eberhard König and myself and still in progress. The uniformity of flourishing in many of the recorded copies soon convinced us that there must have been a direct link with the publishing house. Our survey is almost comprehensive: of the 90 copies recorded at present we have either seen or received documentation of 82. Of these 33 are decorated or illuminated in Mainz, 44 elsewhere, and five remained blank. I have since extended this work by an orientation into the decoration of other books printed by Peter Schoeffer in the period 1467-1479, to a total of over 300 copies. To this figure can be added six copies of books with painted illumination listed by Elgin Vaassen which I have not seen. Even if I have not been able to be as (almost) comprehensive for the other books printed by Schoeffer as we have been for the Hieronymus edition, what I have seen amounts to a substantive sample.[2] Taken together this

---

1. ELGIN VAASSEN, 'Die Werkstatt der Mainzer Riesenbibel in Würzburg und ihr Umkreis', in: *Archiv für Geschichte des Buchwesens* 13, 1973, cols. 1121-1428.

2. In my survey I have limited myself to the dated editions of Peter Schoeffer. The undated editions are in smaller formats, aimed at a different kind of presentation, and since most are devoid of decoration would unnecessarily complicate the picture. Many copies of the books printed by the Catholicon press have Mainz decoration, but since this press cannot be equalled to Peter Schoeffer's (while he is likely to have had an involvement in it) and since in essence I consider these books as undated, they are not included here although they fit in the pattern. A complete list of the 402 copies which I have surveyed would far exceed the boundaries of this article. I shall confine myself to a list of the collections where I have examined copies of Mainz printing: Augsburg, SStB; SB in Berlin; Braunschweig, StB; Brown University RI, Annmary Brown Memorial Library, John Carter Brown Library; Cambridge, Trinity College, UL; Cambridge (Mass.), Harvard University, Houghton Library, Law Library; Chantilly, Musée Condé; Chatsworth Collection; Copenhagen, KB; Darmstadt, Hessische LHB; Dresden, Sachsische LB, Edinburgh, NLS; Frankfurt-am-Main, StUB; Freiburg-im-Breisgau, UB; Giessen, UB; Glasgow UL (Hunterian Library); Gotha, Forschungsbibliothek; Jena UB; Leipzig, Buchmuseum; London BL; Longleat Collection; München BSB; New Haven (Conn.), Beinecke Library; Nürnberg, GNM; Oxford, Bodleian Library; Paris, BN, Bibliothèque de l'Arsenal, Bibliothèque Sainte-Geneviève; Trier, StB, Priesterseminar; Biblioteca Apostolica Vaticana (partially); Washington LC (partially); Wolfenbüttel HAB; Würzburg UB. Books which have passed through the auction rooms in the years since 1987 have been included. Of the 90 copies recorded on the ISTC database of HIERONYMUS, *Epistolare* (1470), documentation in the form of slides or photographs has been received of all (and 49 have

evidence serves to demonstrate that Schoeffer had organized a large-scale operation for finishing his books by hand, and that in this period he preferred organizational over typographical means for achieving the complicated 'articulation' of the texts he produced. From 1457 onwards Fust and Schoeffer had worked with complex system of initials, various sets each printed in red and blue, and variously applied in individual copies within editions. These attempts to achieve the completion of books entirely by typographical means seems to have been abandoned from 1465 in favour of instructions to rubricators, flourishers and painters. Schoeffer's ambitions for providing differentiation by typographical means were in this period confined to the red printing of titles and colophons, until the introduction of more differentiated typefaces in the mid-1470s began to provide a technical alternative. This could be produced in black on white only, and therefore with one inking and one pull of the press. The earliest example of the application of this alternative resulting in a lively typographical layout is the Joh. de Turrecremata, *Expositio super toto psalterio*, completed on 11 September 1474 (Hain *15698). Hence there is no significant 'handwork' in copies of this book or its reprints of 1476 and 1478.

By multiplying the number of copies examined, the area of uncertainty about links between printer/publisher and book-decorators in Mainz can be diminished, merely by taking evidence out of the isolation that is unavoidably created by singling out one particular book. Unlike bindings, where material proof in the form of printer's waste of Schoeffer editions found in many bindings can be presented as evidence for a connection with the printing house, the decoration of books offers hardly any hard evidence to testify to a link with Schoeffer. Fortunately, in one penwork initial, drawn in a style with many individual features and found in a number of books, Schoeffer's mark (so well known from the two-shielded printer's device) is playfully incorporated in the penwork infill (Fig. 4).

This initial is drawn in one of the hands we can identify with near-certainty as that of an individual. There are several such hands, and when we can recognize their work in copies of a number of editions,

---

been personally examined), with the exception of copies in Alba Julia, Brno UL, Budapest UL, Moscow, Russian State Library (5). My indebtedness to the curators of all these collections is great, but I must single out for particular thanks Mademoiselle Ursula Baurmeister (Paris, BN), Dr E. Hertrich (München BSB), Dr. G. Powitz (Frankfurt-am-Main StUB), and Dr K.-H. Staub (Darmstadt, HLHB) who not only gave me generous access to the collections in his care but also informed me about the copies in the library of the Seminary at Monreale (recorded by G. Schirò, *Le biblioteche di Monreale*. Palermo, 1992, p. 34).

Fig. 1. Some tools used by the binder Kyriss 160 (actual size)

published in a timespan of about a dozen years, their individuality becomes more marked and more convincing. Even so, there remains a substantial amount of material where we may hesitate to ascribe it to an individual – a small group of people, an *atelier*, was in all likelihood working in the same style – but where we can apply with some confidence the generic identification 'Mainz work'.

A BRIEF DESCRIPTION OF THE STYLES FOUND IN SCHOEFFER'S BOOKS

Rubrication.

At the simplest level even the rubrication of copies shows some distinct characteristics. Colours are bright red or bright red and blue, and remained even in quality throughout the period. There are two levels of paragraph marks; the half-round one usually with the top well elongated to the right, and a less important one consisting of one or two dashes elongated into underlining the first word of the paragraph and even more often used for the distinction of overrunning lines. The work of one individual rubricator can be recognized by the elegant loop with which he often ended this line. His hand is encountered in very many copies (Figs. 5, 6). From the uniformity in colour and material used it seems very likely that the rubricators also drew the simple one-colour lombard initials, in red or in red and blue. Occasionally little figures were left white by way of decoration. Several forms (I and in particular A, see Figs. 6 and 7) are very distinct and constant. It is possible that sets of stencils were used, and occasionally an outline in drypoint has remained visible. It has to remain a speculation, but it seems likely, that Schoeffer drew on his experience as a calligrapher (and probably also a designer of types) to determine the form and standard of these and the larger initials found in uniform styles throughout the books.

In a number of copies rubrication was applied but space for more important decoration was left open for the customer to complete according to his own taste. In such copies we encounter therefore a mixture of styles. Examples are the copies in the Bibliothèque nationale of Clemens V, *Constitutiones* of 1467 (vélins 387) and the Thomas Aquinas of 1469 (Rés. D.2615) with Mainz rubrication and French illumination; similarly the Clemens V, *Constitutiones* of 1471 in the same collection (vélins 367-9) has Mainz rubrication and Italian illumination.

Fig. 2. Some tools used by the Duranti binder (actual size)

Fig. 3. Some tools used by the binder Kyriss 160:
Binding of HIERONYMUS, *Epistolare*, Mainz, P. Schoeffer, 1470. Trier,
Stadtbibliothek (detail, enlarged).

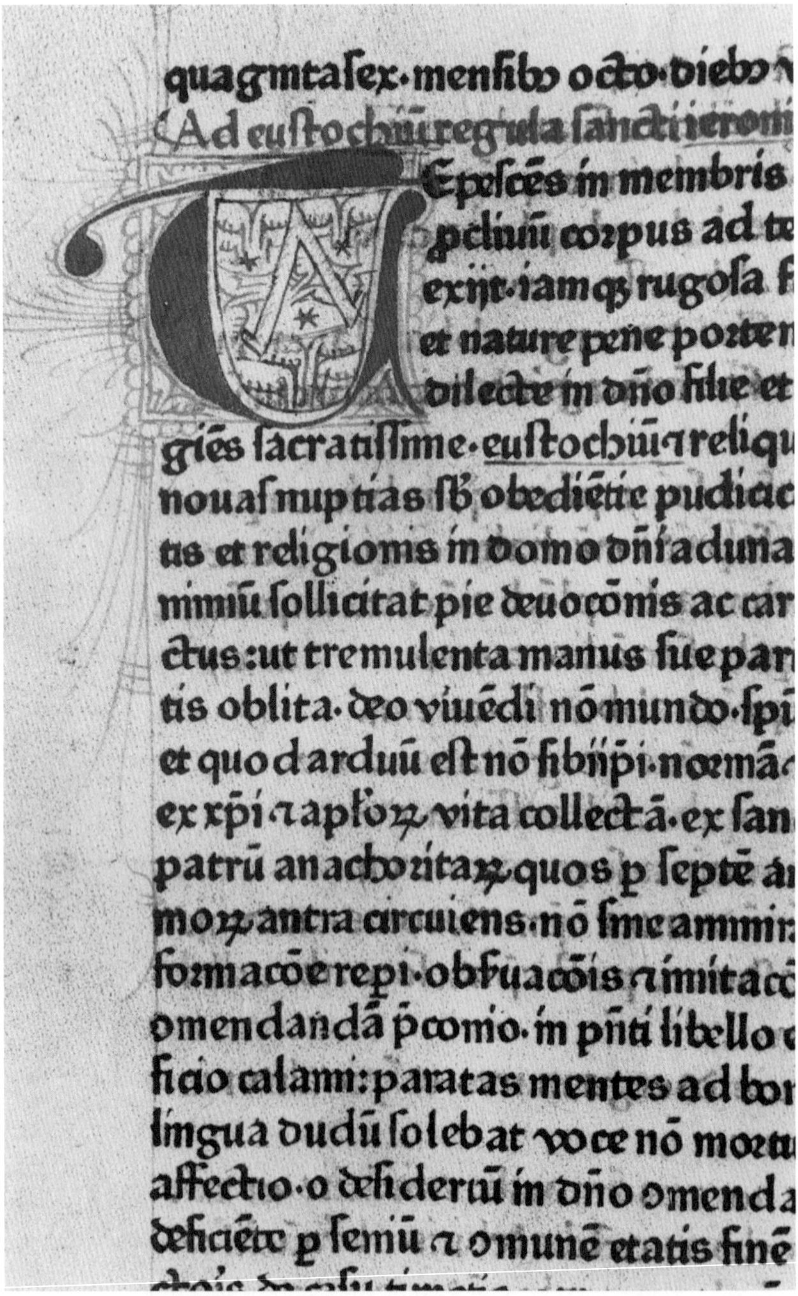

Fig. 4. Schoeffer's device appears as the infill on an initial. HIERONYMUS, *Epistolare*, Mainz, P. Schoeffer, 1470. Private collection (formerly Doheny).

Calligraphic initials with penwork flourishes.

In this category we find large numbers of more important initials, sometimes only one at the beginning of a book, as in the Thomas Aquinas of 1467, in other books at the beginning of each major section, as in the Hieronymus of 1470 or the Latin Bible of 1472. They are often, but not invariably, interlocking red and blue, and occasionally the side-pieces are elaborated to contain human figures, or monsters. The interlocking could be elaborated to contain pomegranate figures. The penwork flourishes, often in a free style and continuing down the entire page, are usually in purple, but sometimes in red and rarely in blue. Infills could be in purple, red and blue, occasionally with green touches (Figs. 8-11). A few hands can be recognized in the penwork, but there could be considerable variation. One flourisher excelled in drawing profiles (Fig. 11). In the initials three hands at least can be recognized, but it is likely that several more individuals were at work, some following with more success than others the models of their masters.

Many copies of the editions of Boniface are decorated with initials in a style of their own, rather heavy in blue with red penwork, or red with blue penwork. Here we apparently encounter a style that was traditional to the book. It is also found in copies of the edition of 1465.

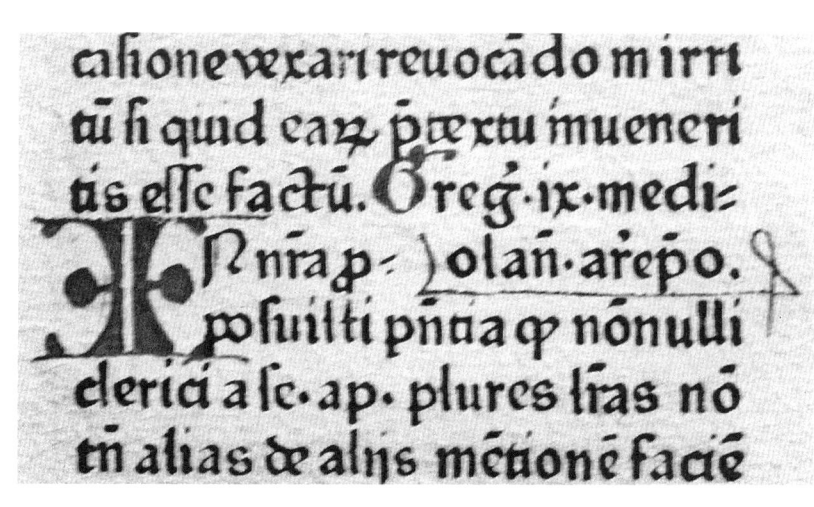

Fig. 5. Rubricator: simple initials, underlining with loop.
From: Gregorius IX, *Decretales*. Mainz, P. Schoeffer, 1473.
Trier, Stadtbibliothek.

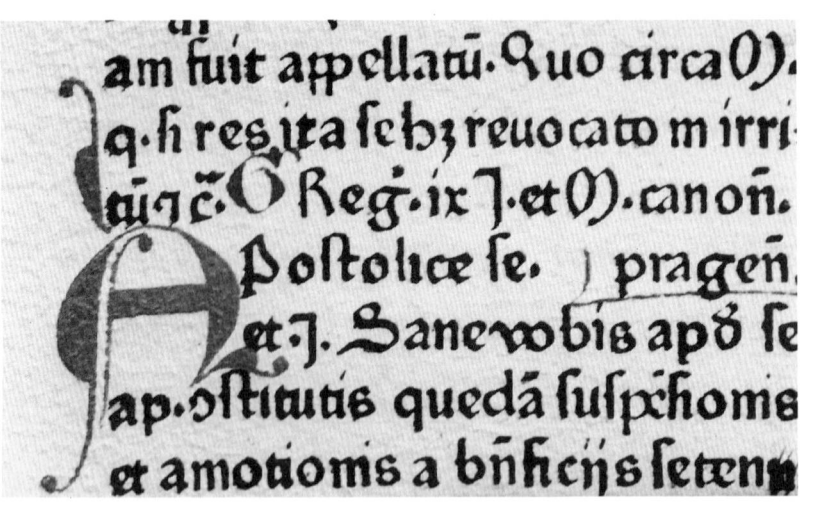

Fig. 6. Rubricator: simple initial. From: Gregorius IX, *Decretales*.
Mainz, P. Schoeffer, 1473. Trier, Stadtbibliothek.

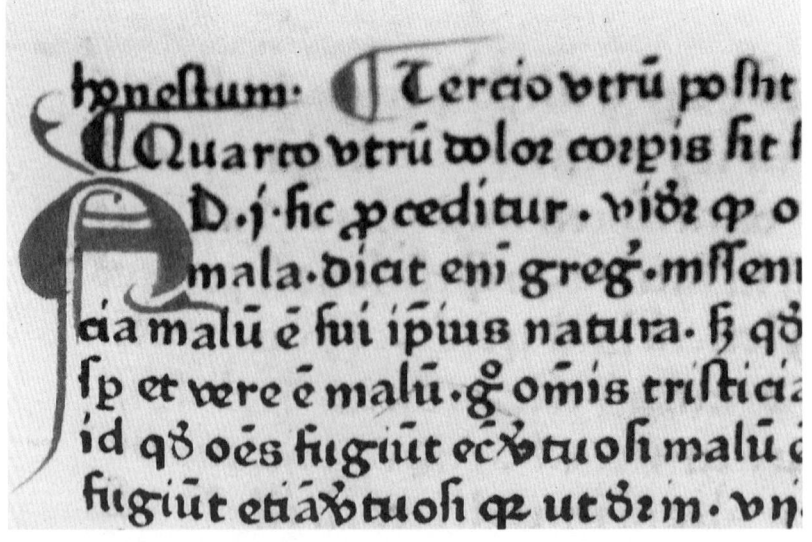

Fig. 7. Rubricator: simple initial in variant form, paragraph marks, heading
letter. From: Thomas Aquinas, *Summa P. II.1*. Mainz, P. Schoeffer, 1471.
Würzburg UB, Hubay 2010/3.

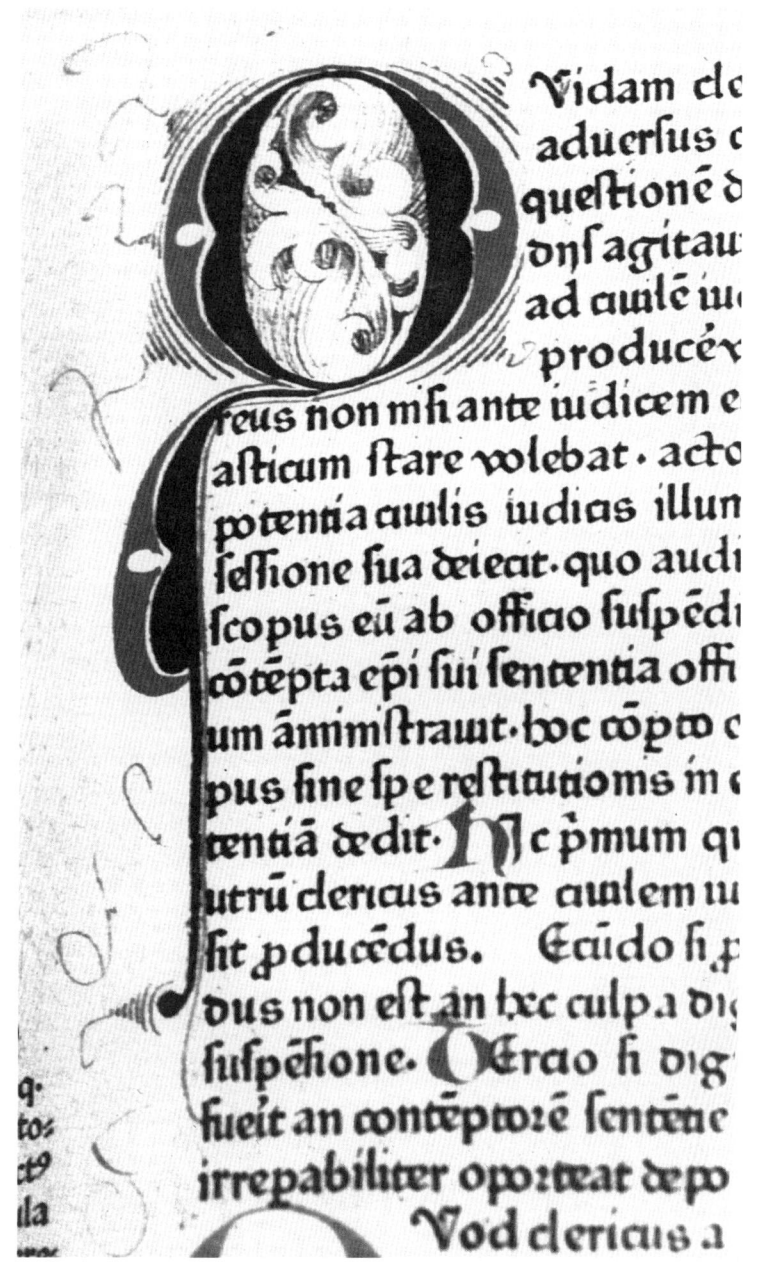

Fig. 8. Flourisher: Interlocking initial, flourish with parallel strokes. From: GRATIANUS, *Decretum*. Mainz, P. Schoeffer, 1472. Frankfurt a. M. StUB.

Painting.

The painted initials and border decoration follow the style set by the Fust Master, and the artist mainly responsible for this decoration must have been a conscious successor to the tradition. Borders, or sections of borders, often sprout from a gold bar dividing the columns of an opening page (Fig. 12). Colours are pale pink, pale green, grey, vivid blue, red and yellow. Motifs are scrolled leaves, very few flowers, and very occasionally animals or birds. An owl solemnly seems to remind the reader of the presence of either the publisher or the artist. Further ornaments are often gold balls surrounded by penwork. The painted initials are usually scrolled, painted on a square background of silver or gold, or, conversely, in silver on a coloured background. The historiated initials and miniatures are of very high quality with vivid, anecdotal scenes (figures set in a landscape or in a room, Figs. 12-16). At least two hands painting miniatures can be recognized: ranging from the fine artist as seen in Figs. 12 and 13, and also in, for example, copies of the Justinianus, *Codex* of 1475 (Fig. 14), to the lesser artist who took over in the Gregorius of 1473 in the British Library (Fig. 15). Impossibly stiff miniatures are found in the Trier copy of Gregorius which in other respects shows all the hallmarks of Mainz work. There are several examples of unfinished miniatures and borders among the books listed; one is illustrated here. (Fig. 16)

A constant motif in almost all the painting is a small triangle formed out of parallel strokes. These can be found surrounding the miniatures or the initials, and are also integrated in some of the flourished initials: see Figs. 8, 9, 12, 13, 14, 15. In work of the late 1470s, when painting had become much scarcer, these pyramids are also found surrounding opening pages in some of the books decorated with penwork only. This motif seems to have the function of a kind of signature of a workshop. It is particularly telling that more than one hand used the parallel stroke pyramids, e.g. in the British Library Gregorius mentioned above, where they are used by both miniaturists working in the same book.[1]

---

1. Similar configurations of parallel lines to form a triangle can be found in some Dutch penwork particular to the Eastern part of the Netherlands. The motif is used in these borders in a different way. See ANNE S. KORTEWEG (ed.), *Kriezels, aubergines en takkenbossen: Randversiering in Noordnederlandse handschriften uit de vijftiende eeuw*. Zutphen [1992], in particular Plate VII and fig. 118 (Utrecht UB Hs. 43, written in 1466 at the Florenshuis in Deventer by Lambertus van Rees).

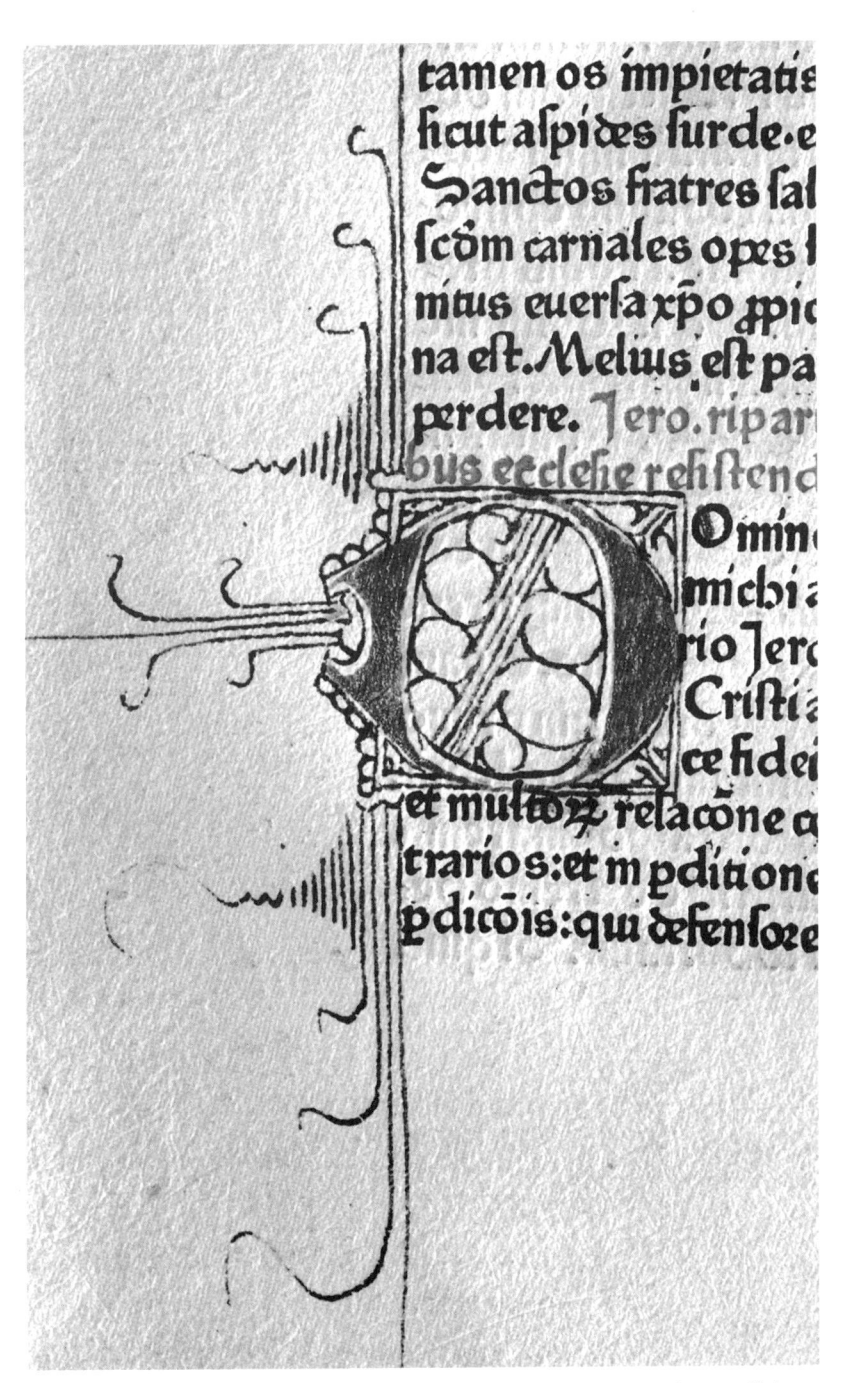

tamen os impietatis
ficut aspides surde. e
Sanctos fratres sal
scōm carnales opes
mtus euersa xpo spi
na est. Melius est pa
perdere. Jero. rip ar
bus ecclesie resistend
Omin
michi
rio Jero
Cristi
ce fidei
et multoȝ relacōne c
trarios: et m pditionc
pdicōis: qui defensore

Fig. 9. Flourisher: Red initials with heavy blue penwork, parallel strokes. From: HIERONYMUS, *Epistolare*, Mainz, P. Schoeffer, 1470, Leipzig, DBM.

Fig. 10. Flourisher: Interlocking initial, red and blue, with purple penwork.

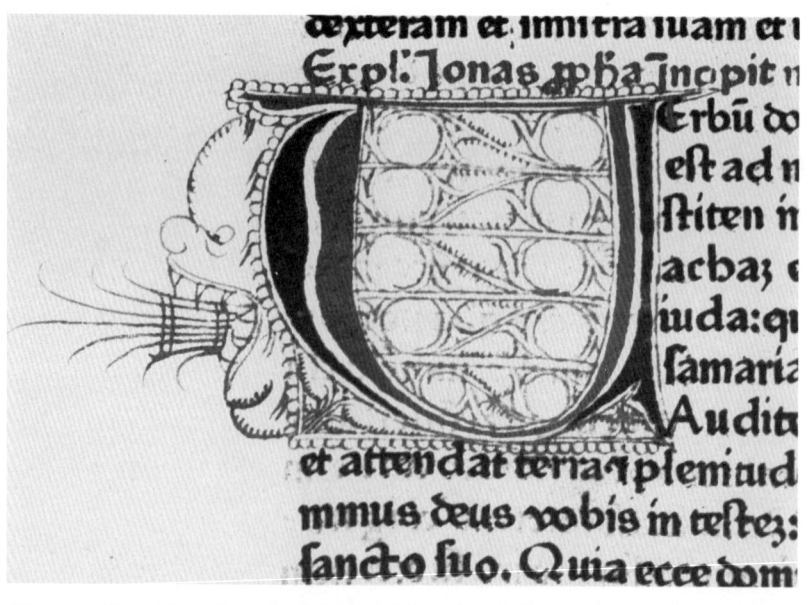

Fig. 11. Flourisher: Interlocking initial, red and blue with purple penwork, profile. Both from: *Biblia latina*, 1472. London BL., IC. 168.

Fig. 12. Painter: Historiated initial with a figure in a landscape. Flourishes with parallel strokes. From: HIERONYMUS, *Epistolare*. Mainz, P. Schoeffer, 1470, London BL, C. 11. e. 13 (detail of leaf [a]1 recto).

A SURVEY OF THE COPIES IN WHICH MAINZ DECORATION IS FOUND

The combinations as found in Schoeffer's books of work of recognisable and not-so-recognisable individuals are subject to seemingly endless permutation and within the large quantity of material available lead to patterns of considerable complexity and hence to increasing uncertainty and areas of speculation. For the present study, which aims to provide an insight into the organization of parts of Schoeffer's business, a different approach presents itself which can be a useful preliminary to mastering a large amount of material. It is useful to leave aside (for the time being)

Fig. 13. Painter: Historiated initial with a figure in an interior setting.
From: Bonifacius VIII, *Liber sextus Decretalium*. Mainz, P. Schoeffer,
1473. Leipzig, DBM. (detail of leaf [a]1 recto).

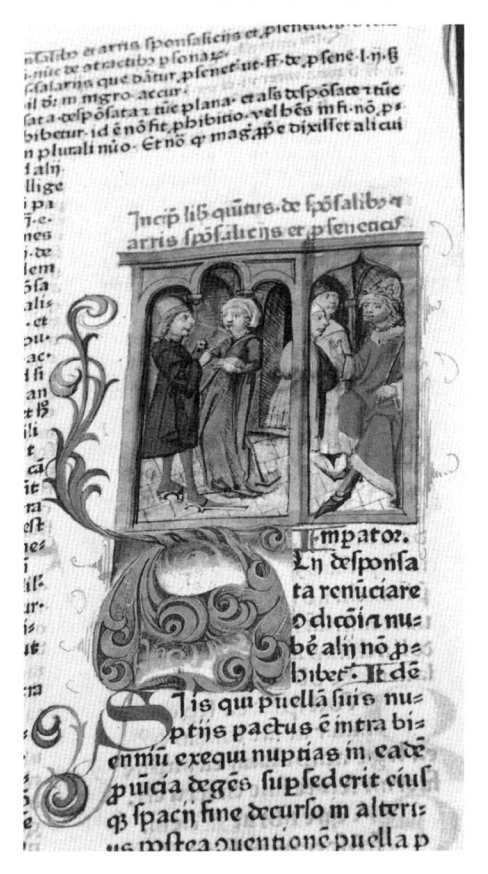

Fig. 14. Painter: Miniature and illuminated initial. From: JUSTINIANUS, *Codex*. Mainz, P. Schoeffer, 1475. London BL, C. 11. e. 5.

Fig. 15. Painter: Miniature and painted initial. From: GREGORIUS, *Decretales*, 1473. London BL, C. 11. e. 4.

the question of the individual identity of the people who worked on these books and refrain from speculation about the relation between *ateliers* and their structures or hierarchy, but consider first what kind of work Schoeffer commissioned. He must have aimed to produce books at several price-levels or levels of luxury, or even at varying stages of completion of the book, apart from the copies that went to customers in a pristine state to be rubricated and painted in styles conforming to their individual wishes. A preliminary sorting of the more than 400 copies examined or about which information is readily available shows the following distinct levels in Schoeffer's commissions:

oſu hoc nomē p interptacōes deriuacōes ul'ebi
tollē nō ē meū · fuſpicois rō pȝ · €ſȝ eč ß refricare
iplatu tñ ß nome ſup cet'a viguit · xxij · e eni ipe q̃
tñ reliqua romanoȝ p̃tificū noia · xi · nō trāſcēde:
que eč ſolus bñdicti nome aſcēdit · Inter canoni
ſtarios ß nome viguit · habuimus eni iohes the
edū nō ex ordie · ſȝ ex fructu · Johes galeñ · vult a
ſpanū ·
Jo. fau:
utō a. Jo·
panū. Jo·
ce ſenate:
cȝ · cardi:
qui minor
eciȝ docto
oñ · me q̃r
nūc inter
es ſolus ·
torios de
forte pa
u occupa
a ,put pȝ
etiā com
vix pñt
tū q̃ ſta
ia multa
cu ſabilis
ōma lecti
oe ſin gu:
mantur ·
rebȝ ex:
turaliter

Incip. cōſtōnes de · ipe · v ·
vna cū apparatu dñi Jo · an ·
Ohannes epus ſuus ſuo:
rū dei dilectis filijs · docto:
ribȝ a ſcolaribȝ vniũſis bo:
nome cōmorātibȝ ſaluteȝ et

Fig. 16. Painter: Unfinished miniature and part of the design for border.
From: CLEMENS V, *Constitutiones*, 1471. London BL, IC. 162.

A: rubrication, including simple lombard initials in red and blue. Further work could be executed elsewhere.
[Examples: Bonifacius, 1473. Frankfurt/Main StUB, Ohly-Sack 662; Thomas Aquinas, 1469. Paris BN Rés. D 2615. Mainz rubrication and a fine French initial.]

B: as A, plus large initials, often interlocking in two colours, with infills and penwork flourishes.
[Example: Biblia latina 1472. London, the British Library, IC. 168]

C: as B, plus painted initials and painted border.
[Example: Bonifacius, 1473. Harvard Law Library, Walsh vol. 1 no. 11]

D: as C, plus historiated initial(s).
[Example: Hieronymus, 1470. London, the British Library, C.11.e.13/14]

E: as D plus painted miniatures.
[Example: Justinianus, Codex, 1475. London, the British Library, C.11.e.5]

It is possible, and I think even necessary, to reduce this even more to define in the simplest terms what skills Peter Schoeffer was seeking for the 'finishing by hand' of his books:

1. for A: Rubricators, for capital strokes in red, paragraph-marks, writing headings, drawing simple, one-colour initials.

2. for B: Flourishers, for two-colour initials with decorative penwork and infills in two or more colours.

3. for C: decorative painting of borders, initials with extended decoration.

4. for D and E: painting of historiated initials, miniatures.

With this simplified scheme it is possible to survey the decoration and illumination of the large dated books produced by Schoeffer in the years 1467-1469, in the period when the activity of the Fust Master had ceased. Even from a survey of this preliminary nature it can be deduced that the peak of this activity coincides with that of the binder Kyriss 160, and tails off from 1476. A further investigation of books imported and sold by Schoeffer could modify this picture, and in particular add evidence for activity in the late 1470s, and later years.

RUBRICATION AND ILLUMINATION IN SCHOEFFER EDITIONS 1467-1479

	Mainz	rubric.+flourishing	+painting	NOT Mainz	TOTAL
1467, Thomas Aquinas Hain *1459		12		11	23
1467, Clemens V GW 7078	2	1		3	6
1468, Justinianus GW 7580	2	7	1	3	13
1469, Thomas Aquinas Hain *1481	1	11		10	22
1470, Bonifacius GW 4850	1	1	2	2	6
1470, Hieronymus Hain *8553, *8554		26	7	44+5 blank	82
1470, Mammotrectus Hain *10554		2		1	3
1471, Valerius Maximus Hain *15774	1	4		10	15
1471, Clemens V GW 7080	6		3	6	15
1471, Thomas Aquinas Hain *1447	4	6		8	18
1472, Biblia latina GW 4211	1	6		9	16
1472, Gratianus GW 11353		2	9	14	25
1472, Justinianus GW 7582	2	5	1	3	11
1473, Bonifacius GW 4853	2	8	4	8	22
1473, Augustinus GW 2884		3	2	9	14
1473, Gregorius GW 11451	4	3	10	12	29
1474, Henr. de Herpf Hain-Cop. *8523	2	3		10	15
1475, Justinianus GW 7722	5	1	3	6	15
1475, Bernardus GW 3940		4		7	11
1476, Bonifacius GW 4857		1		4	5

1476, Justinianus GW 7590	2		4	6
1476, Clemens V GW 7090	3		3	6
1477, Decisiones Rotae Romanae GW 8201	1		1	2
1477, Justinianus GW 7751		1	4	5
1478, Paulus de S. Maria Hain-Cop. 10766	2			2
1478, Barth de Chaimis GW 6544	2			2
1479, Gregorius GW 11457	1	1	1	3
				403

(Not included: The editions of Joh. de Turrecremata, *Expositio super toto Psalterio* of 1474, 1476 and 1478).

CONCLUSIONS

The idea of producing printed copies at various levels of perfection had existed in Mainz from an early stage on. After the Psalters of 1457 and 1459 had been produced with spectacular but complicated initials printed in two colours, the Duranti *Rationale* of 1459 appeared on the market with three levels of execution: with printed initials, with painted decoration provided by one of the great Mainz painters (the Fust Master), and with initials left blank to be commissioned by the buyer. For the Bible of 1462 a similar choice was offered.[1] The sorting and separation of copies to produce consistently the various states must have complicated the work of the press to a great extent. In the large books produced from 1465 onwards (after an interval of three years due to the Mainz Feud) there is no such variation in the use of initials, and this must have been a deliberate decision to simplify procedures in the printing house.

In the analysis of manuscript illumination it has often been pointed out that initials represent a hierarchical system and that their size and their illumination or decoration are an important element in the structuring of text as presented in a particular book. The structure had to be pre-determined by the scribe in order to leave appropriate spaces for the illuminator who would work on the presentation of the text when the manuscript was at a later stage of completion. Precisely the same principle applies to the production of printed books, with the added complica-

---

1. EBERHARD KÖNIG, *The 1462 Fust & Schoeffer Bible...With an original leaf from the 1462 Bible*. Akron & Evanston, 1993.

tion that the work for each book was multiplied in hundreds of copies.

Apparently the printing of coloured initials was thought to be a technically difficult and commercially too simple solution to the problem. The change in practice from 1465 onwards is on the one hand a streamlining of the production process within the printer's workshop, for there was no more need to distinguish issues (or even copies) with variations in the use of typographic initials. Organizing the flourishing and painting by hand would produce an additional advantage in giving much scope for flexibility and variation of price levels. Greater variety could be introduced than was possible by work on the printing press alone, while there remained a lively individual touch to each book, even when executed to specified standards. At one end of the scale there were books with splendid painted borders and miniatures, at the other end were the blank copies. Schoeffer's typography was such that copies sold in a blank state to France or Italy could be decorated without clashing styles offending the tastes of local illuminators or clients. There was also the possibility of offering the book with a certain amount of rubrication, but leaving the most spectacular finishing to the client. The purchaser could obtain the book in a binding, but there are also a substantial number of copies of books illuminated in Mainz, but bound in contemporary bindings of other origin which testify that in this respect too there was flexibility for the buyer. In commercial terms, one could say that by offering a flexible product Schoeffer opened up the largest possible market. For a number of years Schoeffer thus managed to strike a happy balance in the transition from hand-produced to printed book.

As we all know, this could be no more than an intermediate phase; at some point in time, not long after the peak of Schoeffer's own book-production, printers began to use woodcut or even metal-cast initials as a matter of course. To judge from copies examined, Schoeffer's organization of book-decoration was most productive in approximately the same years as the height of activity of the binder Kyriss 160, that is 1470-75. There are a few splendid instances of illumination of works printed after 1475 (the latest one known at present is a Gregorius of 1479 in the Annmary Brown Memorial Library, in a Kyriss 160 binding); there is also simple work to be found in books of the late 1470s with features (the triangle of parallel strokes) suggesting that their penwork comes from the same workshop as some of the most spectacular painting.

My researches have been mainly confined to Schoeffer's own imprints and are still in progress. There are major collections still to be explored, and Schoeffer's imprints are so widely dispersed that an effective completion of a survey such as the present one is not in sight. As to the books imported by Schoeffer, identifying Mainz illumination in them is much a matter of chance, unless an early Mainz binding can point to a connection with Schoeffer and Mainz. Chance led me to an Augustinus *De Civitate Dei*, printed in 1470 by Vindelinus de Spira (GW 2877) in the Hunterian Library, Glasgow (By. 1.3), a copy (in an 18th-century binding) embellished with what are undoubtedly initials drawn in Mainz. Less fortuitous was the find of a Boccaccio printed in Venice 1472-73, GW 4475-82), for it is bound with a copy of the Mainz *Grammatica Rhythmica* (GW 5592), now in the University Library, Jena. It has a fine painted initial. Several of the imported books bound by the binder Kyriss 160 have already been recognized as decorated by Mainz artists (see Appendix 1). I therefore hope that the present study will stimulate further research, and that with systematic investigation of all copies with Mainz bindings, and the exploration of more collections, it will be possible to refine the emerging picture of this side of the business of Peter Schoeffer.

A further question to be addressed is where the books in bindings and with illumination which we now recognize as revealing their Mainz origin were offered for sale: was that only in Mainz, or did they pass on in the trade to be offered by book-dealers elsewhere? There is ample evidence that Schoeffer's books were offered for sale elsewhere: there are his advertisements, there is documentary evidence for his connections with Peter Drach in Speyer, Ulrich Zell in Cologne, with Koberger in Nuremberg, and a solid basis to infer that he had agents in Paris, North and Eastern Germany, and probably Venice.[1] To date no attempt has been made to link this evidence with extant copies. Buyers' notes should now be studied more closely in the light of our new understanding. Nevertheless, a copy like the Hieronymus *Epistolare* of 1470, now in the Bibliothèque Municipale in Saint-Omer, in a Mainz binding and with initials and penwork wholly characteristic for Mainz decoration, was not likely to have been bought by its first owner, Maître Jacques de Houchin, in a bookshop in Paris. Schoeffer's books exported to France usually received French styles of illumination, as can be seen in many copies now in French libraries. Canon de Houchin bequeathed the book to the collegiate church of Saint-Omer in which city it remained – unlike the other books in his considerable collection which were sold by public auction in September 1481 eight months after his death. We may perhaps now indulge in the agreeable picture of this erudite book-lover choosing for

1. For Schoeffer's relations in the book-trade see i.a. HELLMUT LEHMANN-HAUPT, *Peter Schoeffer of Gernsheim and Mainz*, Rochester, New York, 1950, esp. Chapter v, 'Bookseller, Merchant, Citizen', pp. 85-106 with reference to. W. Velke's publication of Schoeffer's advertisements (1908); Vera Sack, see note 4, with particular reference to Ferdinand Geldner's publication of the account book of Peter Drach (1964).

himself this copy of Hieronymus while on a visit to Mainz. His bequest shows the high value he put on this book.

Painting, decoration and binding are manifestations of the direct interest the publisher Peter Schoeffer took in the presentation of his work to the public. In the period when after the death of Johann Fust he began to have sole responsibility for the Mainz publishing firm, he decided that it was better to organize manual labour and artists than to try to arrive at the desired effect on the press alone. Moreover, in particular the bindings reveal that he decided that there was advantage in having books printed by other, perhaps more specialized firms and retail them from Mainz than to produce them himself in print. This development points to specialization in the printing business, and to Schoeffer's shrewd awareness that with mechanization it does not pay to duplicate the work of others. It is a trend that has much wider implications for our understanding of the developing trade of printed books in the fifteenth century, but it can hardly be more manifest than in the influence Peter Schoeffer exerted on the enormous productivity of the Mainz binders and flourishers in the 1470s and the continued work of one binder.

APPENDIX

The Work of the Binder Kyriss 160 in Chronological Order

		printer's waste	Mainz painting	flourishing	rubrication
Bound not before 1465:					
17. xii.1465 Bonifacius VIII, Liber sextus Decretalium GW 4848	Mainz Fust & Schoeffer Frankfurt StUB, *Sack 15*			★	★
Bound not before 1467:					
6.iii.1467 Thomas Aquinas, Summa Theologica II.2 Hain 1459	Mainz P. Schoeffer Augsburg SB, *Sack 84* Frankfurt StUB, *Sack 85* Copenhagen RL *Madsen 3932* Michelstadt, Kirchenbibl. Staub 143 Paris, Bibl. de l'Ars. T. 1316			★	★
Bound not before 1468:					
	Nuremberg GNM, *Sack 86*	Schoeffer 1468			
Bound not before 1469:					
	Amsterdam, Bibl. Phil. Herm (formerly Doheny)	Schoeffer 1467, 1469		★	★
Bound not before 1473 or 1476:					
	Frankfurt StUB, *Sack 85*	Schoeffer 1473 or 1476			

		printer's waste	Mainz painting	flourishing	rubrication
Bound not before c. 1470:					
S.d. (1469/70) Catholican, Bull's Heud paper	Mainz Pr. of Catholican Stuttgart LB, Inc. fol. 2254				
17.iv.1470 Bonifacius VIII, Liber sextus Decretalium GW 4850	Mainz P. Schoeffer München BSB B-699, 2nd copy				
7.ix.1470 Hieronymus, Epistolare Hain 8553/4	Mainz P. Schoeffer				
	Beromünster, Stiftbibl. H. Mattman (1970) No. 62			★	★
	München BSB 2° Inc. c. a. 30a			★	★
	Reutlingen SB, Inc. 20 P. Amelung, Katalog No. 46			★	★
	Saint-Omer BM	Schoeffer 1470		★	★
	Stuttgart LB, *Sack 59*	Schoeffer 1470		★	★
	Trier StB	Schoeffer 1470	★	★	★
Bound not before 1472:					
14.vi.1471 Valerius Maximus Facta et dicta memorabilia Hain-Cop. 15774	Mainz P. Schoeffer Frankfurt StUB *Sack 95A*			★	★

		printer's waste	Mainz painting	flourishing	rubrication
Bound not before 1472:					
13.viii.1472 Gratianus Decretum GW 11353	Mainz P. Schoeffer				
	Frankfurt, StUB *Sack 42*		★	★	★
	Göttingen SUB gr 2° Ius Canon. 24/2 Inc.				
	Wolfenbüttel HAB, Borm 1169		★	★	★
	Würzburg UB, Hubay 941/3	Schoeffer 1470	★	★	★
c. 1471-72 Tacitus Opera Hain 15218	Venice V. de Spira				
	München BSB 2° Inc.s.a.1110				
Bound not before 1473:					
5.iv.1473 Bonifacius VIII Liber sextus Decretalium GW 4853	Mainz P. Schoeffer				
	Frankfurt StUB, *Sack 16B*	Schoeffer 1471		★	★
23.xi.1473 Gregorius Decretales GW 11451	Mainz P. Schoeffer				
	München BSB 2° L impr. membr. 3ª		★	★	★
Bound not before 1474:					
10.ix.1474 Henricus de Herpf Speculum aureum Hain-Cop. 8523	Mainz P. Schoeffer				
	Darmstadt LB, *Sack 57*	Schoeffer 1473		★	★

		printer's waste	Mainz painting	flourishing	rubrication
Bound not before 1475:					
14.iv.1475 Bernardus Claravallensis Sermones GW 3940	Mainz P. Schoeffer München BSB B-320 3rd copy				★
1475 Johannes de Imola In Clementinas Hain 9143	Venice J. Rubeus Würzburg UB, Hubay 1275 Sack 62				
Bound not before 1476:					
1474-76 Breviarium Moguntinum (a part only) GW 5392	Marienthal Fratres Vitae Communis Mainz StB, Sack 23	binder's waste ms. Mainz			
P.aestivalis (dated 12.iii.1473)	New York, H. P. Kraus Cat. 193 no. 6				★
9.iv.1476 Lactantius Opera Hain-Cop. 9812	Rostock Fratres Domus Viridis Horti Frankfurt StUB, Sack 66				
10.vi.1476 Gratianus Decretum GW 11356	Basel B. Richel Würzburg UB, Hubay 943/2 Sack 44				
18.xii.1476 Michael de Dalen Casus summarii Decretalium Hain 4657	Cologne P. in Altis de Olpe Frankfurt StUB, Sack 71				

		printer's waste	Mainz painting	flourishing	rubrication
1476 Bonifacius VIII Liber sextus Decretalium GW 4856	Venice N. Jenson Würzburg UB, Hubay 490 *Sack 17*	Jenson			
1476 Clemens V Constitutiones GW 7098	Venice N. Jenson Würzburg UB, Hubay 657 *Sack 26*	Jenson + Mentelin			
c. 1476 Articella seu Opus artis medicinae GW 2678	Padua N. Petri Bamberg SB *Sack 8*				

Bound not before 1477:

31.v.1477 Corpus iuris civilis Infortiatum GW 7679	Venice J. Rubeus Bamberg SB *Sack 31*				
21.viii.1477 Corpus iuris civilis Novellae GW 7751	Mainz P. Schoeffer Köln UB *Sack 32*				
21.xi.1477 Corpus iuris civilis Digestum vetus GW 7657	Venice J. Rubeus Bamberg SB *Sack 30*				
10.xii.1477 Bonifacius VIII Liber sextus Decretalium GW 4859	Basel M. Wenssler Darmstadt LB *Sack 18*		★	★	★

		printer's waste	Mainz painting	flourishing	rubrication
1477 Antoninus Florentinus Summa theologica P. III GW 2185	Venice N. Jenson Darmstadt LB Inc. IV/421				
c. 1477 Decisiones rotae Romanae GW 8202	Basel B. Ruppel, M. Wenssler, B. Richel Würzburg UB, Hubay 750 Sack 37				

Bound not before 1478:

2.v?.1478 Clemens V Constitutiones GW 7092	Basel M. Wenssler Sack 27				
bound with: c. 1470/72 Bonifacius VIII Liber sextus Decretalium GW 4849	Strasbourg H. Eggestein Frankfurt StUB Sack 16				
27.vi.1478 Nicolaus de Ausmo Supplementum Summae Pisanellae	Nuremberg A. Koberger Würzburg UB, Hubay 1521 Sack 72				
19.viii.1478 Gregorius IX Decretales GW 11456	Basel M. Wenssler Bamberg SB Sack 48 Frankfurt StUB Sack 49 Würzburg UB, Hubay 972 Sack 50				

		printer's waste	Mainz painting	flourishing	rubrication
29.xi.1478 Corpus iuris civilis Novellae GW 7752	Basel M. Wenssler Erlangen UB Sack 33				
(pt. I)	Frankfurt StUB Sack 34				
Bound not before 1479:					
26.ii.1479 Bartolus de Saxoferrato Super II p. Digesti Veteris GW 3596	Venice J. de Colonia & J. Manthen Erlangen UB Sack 11				
10.iii.1479 Gregorius IX Decretales GW 11457	Mainz P. Schoeffer Erlangen UB Sack 51				
	Annmary Brown Memorial Library, RI		★	★	★
6.v.1479 G. Duranti Speculum judiciale GW 9154 (3 vols)	Padua J. Herbort Würzburg UB Sack 40				
	Nürnberg GMN Sack 41			★	★
11.vi.1479 Barth. Platina Vitae Pontificum Hain-Cop. 13045	Venice J. de Colonia & J. Manthen Neuburg (Donau) SB Sack 76				
3.ix.1479 Joh. Turrecremata Meditationes Hain-Cop. 15726	Mainz (?) J. Numeister Stuttgart LB Sack 91				

		printer's waste	Mainz painting	flourishing	rubrication
23.ix.1479 Joh. Marchesinus Mammotrectus Hain-Cop. 10559	Venice N. Jenson Frankfurt StUB Sack 69				
1479 Corpus iuris civilis Digestum novum GW 7704	Padua P. Maufer Bamberg SB Sack 29				
n. a. 1479 Dominicus de S. Geminiano Super sexto Decretalium GW 8648 (P.1, 2)	Speyer P. Drach Würzburg UB, Hubay 779 Sack 38				
n. a. 1479 G. Duranti Rationale GW 9118	Strasbourg G. Husner Bamberg, Dombibl. Sack 39				
c. 1479 Henr. de Gorichem Conclusiones Hain-Cop. 7810	Reutlingen M. Greyff Darmstadt LB Sack 56				
c. 1479 (?) Joh. Melber Vocabularius predicantium Hain 11026	Basel J. Amerbach Darmstadt LB Sack 70				
c. 1475-80 Lud. Pontanus Singularia Hain-Cop. 13267	Strasbourg H. Eggestein Hubay 1765/3 Sack 77				

	printer's waste	Mainz painting	flourishing	rubrication
bound with: not before 1475 Nicolaus de Tudeschis Consilia Hain 12343 Strasbourg H. Eggestein Würzburg UB, Hubay 2096/3 Sack 88				

Bound not before 1480:
 	
3.i.1480   Venice
Gratianus   J. de Colonia
Decretum   & J. Manthen
GW 11360   Dillingen KrBibl.
      Sack 45
 	
26.iv.1480   Venice
Joh. de Imola   J. de Colonia
In Clementinas   & J. Manthen
Hain 9144   Sack 63
 	
bound with:
c. 1478   Lyon
Nic. de Tudeschis   M. Huss
Super rubrica
de translatione
Hain 12370   Erlangen UB
      Sack 90
 	
1480   Speyer
Petrus de Aquila   P. Drach
Quaestiones
Hain 1325   München BSB
      2° Inc.c.a.916a				

Bound not before 1481:
 	
24.vii.1481   Vienne
Joh. de Turrecremata   E. Frommolt
Quaestiones
evangeliorum
Hain-Cop. 15716   formerly
      Donaueschingen HB
      Sack 92 (Sotheby's
      London, 1 July 1994,
      lot 316)				

		printer's waste	Mainz painting	flourishing	rubrication
17.viii.1481 Bonifacius VIII Liber sextus Decretalium GW 4867	Speyer P. Drach Frankfurt StUB Sack 19				
19.viii.1481 Gratianus Decretum GW 11362	Basel M. Wenssler Frankfurt StUB Sack 46		*	*	*
19.xi.1481 Olradus de Ponte Consilia et quaestiones Hain-Cop. 9935	Vienne E. Frommolt Sack 73				
bound with: c. 1476/77 Nic. de Tudeschis Glossae Clementinae	Basel M. Wenssler Nuremberg StB Sack 89				
24.xii.1480 Ant. Andreae Scriptum in artem veterem Aristotelis GW 1669	Venice O. Scotus Sack 5				
bound with: 24.xii.1481 Ant. Andreae Quaestiones super Metaphys. GW 1660	Venice A. de Strata Sack 4				
bound with: 12.xii.1481 Joh. de Magistris Quaestiones Hain-Cop. 10447	Parma D. de Moyllis Frankfurt StUB Sack 68				
1481 W. Rolewinck Fasciculus Temporum Hain-Cop. 6929	Cologne H. Quentel München BSB				

		printer's waste	Mainz painting	flourishing	rubrication
c. 1480-1481 Ant. Florentinus Summa theologica GW 2187	Venice L. Wild & R. de Novimagio Frankfurt StUB Sack 6				
Bound not before 1482:					
12.iii.1482 Bonifacius VIII Liber sextus Decretalium GW 4868	Nuremberg A. Koberger Stuttgart LB Sack 20				
15.iii.1482 Gregorius IX Decretales GW 11463	Basel M. Wenssler Frankfurt StUB Sack 52 München BSB Sack 53				
23.xi.1482 Codex iuris civilis Codex Justinianus GW 7728	Lyon J. Siber München BSB 2° Inc.c.a. 1188				
Bound not before 1483:					
25.i.1483 Gratianus Decretum GW 11365	Venice P. de Piasiis Frankfurt StUB Sack 47				
17.v.1483 Horatius Opera Hain-Cop. 8883	Venice J. de Gregoriis Sack 61				
bound with: 6.xii.1482 Persius Flaccus Satyrae Hain-Cop. 12721	Venice B. de Tortis Sack 74				

		printer's waste	Mainz painting	flourishing	rubrication
bound with: 22.vii.1483 Juvenalis Satyrae Hain-Cop. 9695	Venice B. de Tortis Erlangen UB *Sack 65*				
Bound not before 1484: 12.x.1484 Cicero De officiis GW 6954	Venice B. Rizus & B. Celerius Erlangen UB *Sack 25*				
1484 Bernardus Parmensis Casus longi GW 4095	Strasbourg Pr. Jordanus de Quedlinburg Frankfurt StUB *Sack 13*				
Bound not before 1485: 1485 Livius Historiae Romanae Decades Hain-Cop. 10136	Treviso J. Rubeus Augsburg SB *Sack 67*				
No bindings on record for books printed in the years 1486, 1487 and for 1489 only for a book completed at the end of the year					
Bound not before 1489: 22.xii.1489 Baldus de Ubaldis Super I. et II Decretalium Hain 3214, p. 1 and 2	Milan U. Scinzenzeler Frankfurt StUB *Sack 95*				
Bound not before 1490: 13.i.1490 Bonifacius VIII Liber sextus Decretalium GW 4885	Venice J. & G. de Gregoriis *Sack 21*				

		printer's waste	Mainz painting	flourishing	rubrication
bound with: 16.ii.1490 Clemens V Constitutiones GW 7116	Venice J. & G. de Gregoriis Frankfurt StUB *Sack 28*				
19.vi.1490 Marianus Soncinus de Senis Tractatus de citationibus Hain-Cop. 14857	Pescia Pr. of Canaro Bamberg SB *Sack 78*				
Bound with 15 other incunabula, not specified.					
17.ix.1490 Thomas Aquinas Opuscula Hain-Cop. 1541	Venice H. Liechtenstein Frankfurt StUB *Sack 83*				
23.ix.1490 Bartolus de Saxoferrato Super I. parte Digesti novi GW 3555	Venice A. Torresanus de Asula Mainz Gutenb. Mus. Ink 2535				
Bound not before 1491:					
1491 Cassiodorus Expositio psalterii GW 6163	Basel J. Amerbach Frankfurt StUB *Sack 24*				
Bound not before 1492:					
8.viii.1492 Hieronymus Epistolae (2 vols.) Hain 8561	Basel N. Kessler Frankfurt StUB *Sack 60*				

		printer's waste	Mainz painting	flourishing	rubrication
Bound not before 1493:					
11.ii.1493 Avicenna Canon lat. Lib. 3 GW 3124	Venice B. de Tortis Erlangen UB *Sack 9*				
22.iv.1493 Terentius Comoediae Cop. 5747	Lyon A. Lambillion Frankfurt StUB *Sack 80*				
Bound not before 1494:					
26.vi.1494 Gregorius IX Decretales GW 11489	Venice B. de Tortis Frankfurt StUB *Sack 54*				
20.viii.1494 Christoph. Barzizius Introductorium GW 3672	Pavia A. de Carcano for O. Scotus ErlangenUB *Sack 12*				
9.iii.1486 Petrus de Crescentiis Ruralia commoda GW 7824	Strasbourg Pr. Jordanus de Quedlinburg *Sack 35*				
bound with: after 28.viii.1494 Joh. Trithemius De scriptoribus ecclesiasticis Hain-Cop. 15613	Basel J. Amerbach Frankfurt StUB *Sack 87*				
1.ix.1494 Bonifacius VIII Liber sextus Decretalium GW 4890	Basel J. Froben Darmstadt LB Inc. II/851				

		printer's waste	Mainz painting	flourishing	rubrication
c. 1494 Vivianus Tuscus Casus longi super Digesto vet. Cop. 6276(I) = 1486	Freiburg i. Br. K. Piscator (Fischer) *Sack 94*				
bound with: c. 1494 Vivianus Tuscus Casus longi super Codice Cop. 1485	Freiburg i. Br. K. Piscator (Fischer) *Sack 93*				
bound with: c. 1494 Franc. Accursius Super Digesto novo GW 186	Freiburg i. Br. K. Piscator (Fischer) *Sack 1*				
bound with: c. 1494 Guido Casus longi super Institut. Hain 4663	Freiburg i. Br. K. Piscator (Fischer) Fulda LB *Sack 55*				
No bindings on record for books printed in the year 1495.					
Bound not before 1496:					
9.v.1496 Bonifacius VIII Liber sextus Decretalium GW 4895	Venice B. de Tortis Frankfurt StUB *Sack 22*				
1.xi.1496 Terentius Comoediae Hain-Cop. 15431	Strasbourg J. Grüninger Frankfurt StUB *Sack 82*				

		printer's waste	Mainz painting	flourishing	rubrication
Bound not before 1497:					
1497 Hieronymus Commentaria in Bibliam Hain 8581 (I)	Venice J. & G. de Gregoriis Stuttgart LB *Sack 58*	Schoeffer			
Bound not before 1498:					
11.ii.1498 Magister Adam Summula GW 215 *bound with:* c. 1489-93 Terentius Comoediae Hain-Cop.- Reichling 15389	Cologne H. Quentell *Sack 2* Strasbourg J. Prüss Frankfurt StUB *Sack 81*				
Bound not before 1499:					
19.viii.1499 Bartholomaeus Sibylla Speculum peregrinarum quaestionum GW 3460	Strasbourg J. Grüninger Würzburg UB, Hubay 312 *Sack 10*				
Bound not before 1500:					
7.vii.1500 Johannes de Sacro Bosco Opus sphaericum Hain-Cop. 14124 *bound with manuscripts*	Cologne H. Quentell Frankfurt StUB *Sack 64*				

		printer's waste	Mainz painting	flourishing	rubrication
Bound not before 1502:					

1502
Biblia latina
Cum postillis
GW 4285
	Basel
	J. Amerbach for
	A. Koberger
	   Frankfurt StUB
	   (six volumes)
	   Sack 14				

Bound not before 1504:					
20.vii.1498 Albertus Magnus Paradisus animae GW 707	Cologne H. Quentell *Sack 3*				
bound with 9 other incunabula and one work printed in 1504, in chronological order:					
1493 Jac. de Jüterborg De valore missarum Hain-Cop. 9341	Heidelberg H. Knoblochtzer *Ohly-Sack 1554*				
21.vii.1494 Joh. Trithemius De laudibus S. Annae Hain 15633	Mainz P. Friedberg *Ohly-Sack 2816*				
c. 1494/95 Franc. Diedus Vita S. Rochi Hain-Cop. 10546	Mainz P. Friedberg for J. Nell *Ohly-Sack 1013*				
c. 1495 Ars moriendi GW 2610	Cologne H. Quentell *Ohly-Sack 274*				
6.i.1497 Hier. Baldung Aphorismi compunctionis GW 3211	Strasbourg J. Grüninger *Ohly-Sack 358*				

LOTTE HELLINGA

		printer's waste	Mainz painting	flourishing	rubrication
c. 1497 Hilduinus Vita Dionysii Areopagitae Hain-Cop. 6237	Nuremberg C. Hochfeder *Ohly-Sack 1468*				
2.iii.1499 Cato Disticha (German) GW 6348	Strasbourg J. Prüss *Ohly-Sack 838*				
14.ii.1500 ps. Methodius Revelationes divinae Goff M-525	Basel M. Furter *Ohly-Sack 1985*				
c. 1500 Nicodemus Evangelium de passione Hain-Cop. 11750	Cologne C. de Zierikzee *Ohly-Sack 2075*				
and an unspecified book printed in 1504 Frankfurt StUB					

Bound in 1511 (binder's date):

*11 works, including 5 incunabula
(in chronological order):*

c. 1492 Petrus Popon Libellus facetus Unrecorded	Leipzig M. Landsberg *Ohly-Sack 2407*				
1494 Theod. Gresemundus Lucubratiunculae Hain-Cop. 8047	Mainz P. Friedberg *Ohly-Sack 1315*				
1499 Augustinus Datus Elegantiolae GW 8133	Speyer K. Hist *Ohly-Sack 995*				

		printer's waste	Mainz painting	flourishing	rubrication
after 1.ix.1499 Jacob Wimpfeling De hymnorum auctoribus Hain-Cop. 16176	Mainz P. Friedberg *Ohly-Sack 3028*				
c.1497-1500 Fr. Petrarcha Ars punctandi Reichling 1317	Leipzig W. Stöckel *Ohly-Sack 2253*				

and 6 other works printed after 1500,
of which only one specified:

| 1510
Suetonius
De viris illustribus | Strasbourg
J. Knoblouch
Frankfurt StUB
Sack 79 | | | | |

Bent Juel-Jensen

THREE ETHIOPIAN BINDINGS

How very difficult for an amateur who knows little about bindings to write anything of the slightest interest to a celebrated binding expert! Forgive me for trying, Anthony; it is well-meant and I can at least claim that the subject is obscure.

In the late fifteen twenties disaster struck Ethiopia. The country which had been Christian since 330 was overrun by Muslim fanatics, led by Ahmed Grañ "the left-handed". They pillaged and burnt churches, church furniture and manuscripts. Therefore relatively few pre-Grañ manuscripts have come down to us, and few of these are in their original bindings, for many have been rebound. In the West, manuscripts became obsolete with the advent of printing with movable type. Although a few books were printed in Ethiopic type in Rome relatively early (*Potken's Psalter* 1513, and the *New Testament* 1548-49), printing only reached Ethiopia in the second half of the nineteenth century. Until very recently, manuscripts were still being written and bound as they had been for centuries. No manuscript earlier than the eleventh century has survived. Sydney Cockerell pointed out that the way manuscripts were bound did not appear to have changed from the twelfth century to the present.

Nearly all Ethiopian manuscripts are bound in wooden boards; a cover of tough leather is the exception. The boards are commonly made from *wanza* (*Cordia africana*) which is light, or from cedar or *wayra* (*Olea africana*) which is very hard. All have the advantage of not being damaged by insects. The vellum sheets are not sewn on cords. The sewing thread, of cotton, linen or goat's or sheep's gut, is anchored in holes drilled with an awl near the inner edge of the board, to emerge on the inner edge. The sewing starts at the front cover and continues from sheet to sheet, finishing in corresponding holes drilled near the inner edge of the back cover. This gives a very flexible binding. Ancient codices in the West were bound similarly; St. Cuthbert's Gospels is an example.[1]

Most manuscripts are merely protected by the wooden boards; the back is bare. More elaborate bindings have a back made of goat skin, and expensive books such as those commissioned by kings and nobles are

---

1. Sydney M. Cockerell, Ethiopian Bindings, *Designer Bookbinders Review*, 10 Autumn 1977, pp. 5-9. The illustration in this paper makes the Ethiopian method of sewing quite clear.

bound in full leather. Normally, the bindings of all manuscripts are protected by a cloth cover. This accounts for the relatively good condition of many bindings of even some age. Goat skin is the usual material used for binding. In the past, goat skins for better bindings were sent to Arabia for tanning and dying. The colour is usually red or brown. Sergew Hable-Selassie remarks that he has "not come across a manuscript covered with black leather".[1] Most skins have been home tanned during this century.

I have chosen three bindings separated in time by about a quarter of a millennium as examples of the remarkable tradition of an ancient African Christian community.

The First Binding (Fig. 1) is on a *Psalter*[2] illustrated with many miniatures, a small folio measuring 280 x 205 mm. from the middle of the fifteenth century. Miraculously the original binding has survived. The stout wooden boards are made of *wayra*. Marks of the adze which was used to fashion the covers are obvious. The volume is "quarter bound". Brown goatskin covers the spine and the inner third of the boards. The leather on the sides is decorated with a symmetrical pattern of blind-tooled parallel and diagonal lines. The back is flat, as one would expect from the nature of the sewing, and faint diagonal blind-tooled lines can be seen. The inside of the boards is covered in the inner third with plain goat-skin. Mediaeval Ethiopian manuscripts in their original bindings are very uncommon. The Oxford University Expedition to Tigray in 1974 found an example on the Mariam Magdalawit Gospelbook[3] which is dated 1363. The volume which measures 364 x 270 mm has been re-backed, but enough of the front and back covers remains to enable one to distinguish the blind-tooled patterns. On the front cover is a design of parallel lines and stylized leaves, on the back parallel and diagonal lines similar to the patterns seen on the present binding. The rebacking which must be early, has also been decorated with a blind-tooled pattern of parallel and diagonal lines.

The Second Binding (Fig. 2) is on a *Ta'amre Maryam, Miracles of The Virgin Mary*, a small folio measuring 280 x 225 mm. This manuscript, illustrated with miniatures in the "Second Gondarene style", dates from the second quarter of the eighteenth century. It is bound in high quality brown goatskin, and is a good example of a type of fine binding which

---

1. SERGEW HABLE-SELASSIE: *Bookmaking in Ethiopia*, Leiden 1981, p. 24.
2. This manuscript is described more fully in *Three Illuminated Ethiopian Manuscripts. The Book Collector*, Summer 1987, pp. 210-18.
3. *Rock-Hewn Churches of Eastern Tigray*. An Account of the Oxford University Expedition to Ethiopia 1974. Ed. Bent Juel-Jensen & Geoffrey Rowell. Oxford, 1975, pp. 73-82; frontispiece and figs. 97-112 and 117-118, the latter two of the binding.

Fig. 1. Front Cover, *Psalter*, Ethiopia, c. 1450.

Fig. 2. Back Cover, *Miracles of the Virgin Mary*, Ethiopia, c. 1725.

became fashionable in the seventeenth century and has remained popular ever since for volumes of any consequence. The brown leather is carefully decorated with an all-over design in blind, arranged round a central cross. At first sight it is tempting to think that the four concentrically arranged borders are made with rolls. Whilst this may be true of the outer two borders, the inner two are in fact produced with a small stamp, repeated over and over again. Sergew Hable-Selassie in his account of Ethiopian bookbindings illustrates several tools. The inside of the boards has a wide doublure, with a central panel of red velvet. Elegant bindings usually have such a panel of material, almost certainly imported from the Indian subcontinent. Richard Pankhurst has discussed these textiles in two essays in *Azania*.[1] The wide doublures are decorated with seven parallel triple blindstamped fillets.

The Third Binding (Fig. 3) is from our own time. During a stay in Tigray in the autumn of 1974 I commissioned a copy of *Henok, the Book of Enoch*, which in its entirety is only known in Ge'ez (Ancient Ethiopic). The manuscript cost 100 birr (Ethiopian dollars), and the binding was 5 birr extra. The scribe, the deacon Amaha Selassie Gebre Kristos, went to Makalle Market and selected and bought ten goat skins, took them to his monastery (Menewie in Tembien) and cured the skins, made vellum out of the nine and a half, and tanned and dyed the remaining half and used it for the binding. Fairly thick boards of *wanza* are covered with red goat skin. The manuscript is a quarto and measures 265 x 205 mm. There are doublures, rather more rough and ready than those on the previous binding, and a central panel of tartan material. The sides are decorated with blind-stamped tooling. Two frames, one inside the other, enclose a central cross. There are four additional rectangles with diagonal lines, the lower two with "roofs", in the central panel. It might be tempting to think that the frames and the cross are made with rolls. Not so: small tools have been repeated over and over again.

Gold is hardly ever used on Ethiopian bindings. The use of gilt tooling is mostly recent, and then always on *The Gospels*. Sometimes bindings have studs of brass or silver, probably to protect the binding when they lie on lecterns. Many smaller books have leather cases with a strap, so that they can be hung from a peg or carried slung over the shoulder. The plate of the Abyssinian Library in the Monastery of Souriani in Robert Curzon's *Visits to Monasteries of the Levant*, 1849, shows many manuscripts, some quite large, hanging in their cases from pegs on the wall. I have

---

1. RICHARD PANKHURST, *Imported textiles in Ethiopian sixteenth and seventeenth century manuscripts in Britain*, Azania 5, 1980, pp. 43-55; idem, *Imported textiles in eighteenth-century Ethiopian manuscripts in Britain*, Azania 16, 1981, pp. 131-150.

Fig. 3. Front Cover, *The Book of Enoch*, Ethiopia, December 1450.

several times stayed with an Ethiopian monk in his little house (and a great luxury it was, for there were none of God's smaller creatures that otherwise so often give you little peace in humbler rural Ethiopian homes). Above the bed, on pegs on the wall were his manuscripts and printed books, in their leather cases.

Piccarda Quilici

LEGATURE DEL PICCOLPASSO E LEGATURE VISCONTEE NELLA BIBLIOTECA AMBROSIANA DI MILANO

La Biblioteca Ambrosiana di Milano conserva un gruppo di manoscritti quattrocenteschi ancora felicemente provvisti della loro legatura originale, che provengono dalla biblioteca privata di Francesco Piccolpasso, e che meritano di essere studiati dettagliatamente; le legature del Piccolpasso, tutte eseguite nella prima metà del secolo, negli anni in cui questo prelato fu arcivescovo di Milano, vengono ad integrare il quadro tracciato dalle legature viscontee a loro contemporanee, già studiate dalla Pellegrin e dal De Marinis, con le quali dividono età, caratteristiche ed anche la provenienza dalle stesse botteghe artigiane, e costituiscono con questo uno dei primi gruppi omogenei di legature decorate che il nostro Rinascimento abbia prodotto.[1]

La raccolta del Piccolpasso rappresenta uno dei più importanti e consistenti fondi storici dell'Ambrosiana; il cardinale Federico Borromeo, tornato stabilmente a Milano nel giugno del 1601, aveva incominciato subito a mandare ovunque persone di sua fiducia, con l'incarico di reperire ed acquistare codici e libri per la biblioteca da lungo tempo desiderata, su esempio della nuova splendida sede della Vaticana fatta allestire da Sisto V, e nel 1603 aveva iniziato la costruzione dell'edificio.[2]

Negli anni della sua permanenza a Milano l'attività del card. Borromeo nel raccogliere libri e soprattutto manoscritti era continuata inten-

---

1. Per notizie relative alle legature lombarde, in particolare viscontee e sforzesche, cfr. Th. GOTTLIEB, *Grolier Studien*, «Jahrbuch der Einbandkunst», Bd. 2, 1928, pp. 63-99 (in particolare p. 73, T. 20, per una legatura del Piccolpasso); BIBLIOTECA NAZIONALE BRAIDENSE. *Mostra bibliografica. Manoscritti e libri miniati. Libri a stampa rari e figurati dei sec. XV e XVI. Legature artistiche. Autografi.* Catalogo a cura di Tommaso GNOLI, Domenico BASSI e Paolo NALLI. Milano, 1929; H. WIESER, *Zwei Bände aus dem Besitz Blanca Maria Sforzas*, «Biblos», 5, 1956, pp. 98-104; BIBLIOTECA DELL'ARCHIVIO STORICO E CIVICO E TRIVULZIANA. *Mostra storica della legatura*. Milano, 1953. Catalogo a cura di Caterina SANTORO. Milano, 1953; E. PELLEGRIN, *La bibliothèque des Visconti et des Sforza ducs de Milan, au XVe siècle*. Paris, 1955, e *Supplément*, Firenze, 1969; T. DE MARINIS, *La legatura artistica in Italia nei secoli XV e XVI. Notizie ed elenchi*. Firenze, 1960 (per Milano, v. 3, pp. 9-16, n. 2541-2663 bis, tav. A$_1$-A$_6$, CCCCXXV-LXXXIII); F. JUNTKE, *Ein Mailänder Einband des 15. Jahrhunderts*, «Gutenberg Jahrbuch», 1960, pp. 380-2; A.R.A. HOBSON, *Humanists and bookbinders. The origins and diffusion of the humanistic bookbinding. 1459-1550*. Cambridge - New York - Port Chester - Melbourne - Sydney, 1989 (in particolare per il card. Piccolpasso cfr. p. 16, nota 11).

2. Cfr. A. PAREDI, *Storia dell'Ambrosiana*. Vicenza, 1981, pp. 7-14.

sa; entrarono così a far parte dell'Ambrosiana i manoscritti bobbiesi, la collezione del bibliofilo Gian Vincenzo Pinelli ed altri; nella zona di Milano il cardinale Federico fece acquistare gruppi di codici sia dalla biblioteca del Capitolo del Duomo, sia dal convento agostiniano di S. Maria Incoronata: si tratta proprio, almeno in parte, dei manoscritti appartenuti al Piccolpasso. Altri acquisti, più modesti come entità, ma non meno importanti da un punto di vista storico e scientifico, furono fatti presso privati, perloppiù familiari ed eredi di celebri studiosi ed uomini di cultura: Maffeo Vegio, Gerolamo Mercuriale, Francesco Ciceri, Pier Candido Decembrio, Gaudenzio e Filippo Merula, Ottavio Ferrari, il senatore Cesare Rovida ed altri, attraverso le cui biblioteche nei primi anni del '600 furono assicurati all'Ambrosiana non pochi manoscritti di epoca e di provenienza viscontea.[1]

Francesco di Nicolò Filippo de' Piccolpassi, nato a Bologna da nobile famiglia intorno al 1370, dopo anni di intensa attività politica e diplomatica tutta svolta al servizio della Chiesa, in quel periodo lacerata dal grande Scisma, fu per la prima volta nominato vescovo da papa Martino V nel 1423, per la diocesi di Dax, in Guascogna.[2] Resasi poi vacante la sede di Pavia nel 1426 per la morte del vescovo Pietro Grassi, lo stesso Martino V con bolla del 26.11.1427 lo nominò alla diocesi della città lombarda. L'opera religiosa e politica del Piccolpasso a Pavia e poi Milano si è svolta quindi tutta, fino al 1443, anno della sua morte, in una situazione di delicato equilibrio, in tempi in cui in Lombardia il potere era esercitato dai Visconti con lotte e contrasti senza fine; Filippo Maria (1392-1447), ereditato il ducato dal fratello Giovanni Maria, e cacciati da Milano Estorre e Gianpiccino, rispettivamente figlio e nipote di Bernabò Visconti, grazie ad un'abile preparazione diplomatica ed all'aiuto di Niccolò Piccinino, di Francesco Sforza e del Carmagnola, era riuscito a recuperare buona parte dei territori persi dal fratello: il che gli aveva suscitato contro i timori e le invidie di Venezia e Firenze che, anche con l'appoggio del papa, lo vinsero nella battaglia di Maclodio nel 1426 (come ricorda la tragedia di Manzoni «Il conte di Carmagnola»): per questo Filippo Maria oppose la più netta resistenza all'insediamento del Piccolpasso, considerato uomo di fiducia del pontefice, nella diocesi di Pavia, tanto che il prelato poté prendere possesso della sua sede solo nel 1430, e a difficili condizioni. Pavia era allora già uno splendido centro di studi umanistici, la biblioteca del castello possedeva nel 1426 un migliaio di codici, ma il Piccolpasso rimase nella città solo un anno, perché dovette presto partire per partecipare al Concilio di Basilea; nominato da Eugenio IV arcivescovo di Milano nel 1435 conti-

1. Cfr. A. PAREDI, *op. cit.*, p. 12.
2. Per notizie dettagliate sulla vita del Piccolpasso ed i suoi tempi, cfr. A. PAREDI, *La biblioteca del Piccolpasso*, Milano, 1961, pp. 3-65.

nuò invece, ancora per lungo tempo, a seguire i lavori del Concilio. Solo nei suoi ultimi tre anni di vita, dal 1440 al 1443, il Piccolpasso poté risiedere stabilmente a Milano, e dedicarsi al riordinamento della sua diocesi, occupandosi anche sia della sua libreria privata che delle altre biblioteche milanesi, in particolare di quella annessa a S. Ambrogio. Non sappiamo quanto profonda fosse la sua cultura umanistica, è certo però che fu amico ed ebbe stretti rapporti con umanisti famosi, in particolare con il Cusano; prima di morire, fece dono della sua raccolta privata alla biblioteca del Capitolo dei canonici ordinari del Duomo di Milano. Nei primi anni del Seicento il Borromeo acquistò in gran parte (ma non tutta) la biblioteca del Piccolpasso, per farne dono all'Ambrosiana: degli 83 codici elencati nell'inventario redatto nel 1443 in occasione della consegna alla Biblioteca Capitolare, e pubblicato dal Magistretti, 56 sono oggi ancora conservati in Ambrosiana. Intanto, dopo la nuova sconfitta ad Anghiari nel 1440 (la ricorda il celebre cartone di Leonardo), e la pace di Cavriana nel 1441, in compenso dei buoni uffici prestati Francesco Sforza aveva ottenuto da Filippo Maria il possesso della città di Cremona e la mano della figlia naturale Bianca Maria divenendo, per i suoi meriti mercenari, l'erede di un ducato che si spegneva senza figli legittimi; finiva così, nel 1447, pochi anni dopo la scomparsa dello stesso Piccolpasso, la signoria dei Visconti su Milano, e cedeva il posto alla nuova signoria di Francesco Sforza e dei suoi discendenti; la storia milanese del Piccolpasso s'intreccia quindi compiutamente con quella dei Visconti: sia nei suoi manoscritti che nelle legature che li rivestono non c'è da meravigliarsi se compaiono contemporaneamente lo stemma dell'arcivescovo in un ferro che ripetuto compone delle cornici, o delle strisce, il più noto stemma visconteo, con la biscia che divora un bambino, ed altre imprese della famiglia ducale. Né bisogna dimenticare che il Piccolpasso aveva in precedenza, dal 1427 al 1433, retto il vescovato di Pavia, di quella città lombarda cioè nel cui castello i Visconti avevano stabilito la sede della loro famosa biblioteca, e che era un po' il cuore del loro potere.

Della biblioteca Visconti-Sforza, poi in gran parte acquisita da Luigi XII e trasportata a Blois nel 1499, si è occupata a più riprese Elisabeth Pellegrin.[1] È merito della Pellegrin aver pubblicato gli inventari della biblioteca di Pavia, ed aver reperito ed identificato molti dei manoscritti che vi sono elencati.[2] Del Piccolpasso invece l'autrice si occupa in modo

---

1. Cfr. il già citato E. PELLEGRIN, *La bibliothèque des Visconti et des Sforza ducs de Milan, au XVe siècle*. Paris, 1955 e *Supplément*. Firenze, 1969.
2. Il primo inventario della biblioteca del castello è del 1426, ed esso contiene, oltre all'elenco dei codici, una descrizione delle legature; è il ms. AD. xv. 1. 8. 4. della Biblioteca Braidense. Nessuna o quasi notizia sulle legature si trova invece sui successivi inventari del 1459 e del 1469, cfr. il ms. Lat. 11400 della Nazionale di Parigi.

del tutto marginale, per l'evidente motivo che la biblioteca dell'alto prelato non ha preso, come per la maggior parte quella viscontea, la via della Francia. La Pellegrin cita un solo manoscritto del Piccolpasso, elencato nell'inventario di Pavia del 1459, ma questo pezzo dovrebbe essere pervenuto nella biblioteca viscontea soltanto dopo la morte dell'arcivescovo (†1443) molto probabilmente, quindi, senza seguire le diverse vicende della sua intera raccolta; il codice è stato identificato con il ms. Lat. 5068 della Nazionale di Parigi.[1] Dell'intera biblioteca del Piccolpasso si è invece occupato, dopo il Sabbadini[2] ed il Magistretti[3] Angelo Paredi, attento studioso della storia ambrosiana, ma con un taglio essenzialmente bibliografico, e con scarse notizie sulle legature.[4] Le legature invece, che recano come contrassegno di proprietà, sui piatti, il ferro con lo stemma del Piccolpasso (spesso in corrispondenza con lo stemma miniato all'interno, uno scudo inquartato a 1 e 4 d'argento a tre caprioli azzurri, e 2 e 3 d'oro, a tre pali rossi) sono state notate anche se di sfuggita dal De Marinis, nella parte relativa a Milano e a Pavia: il De Marinis elenca una legatura del Piccolpasso non conservata all'Ambrosiana ma nella British Library, e citata nell'inventario visconteo del 1459; anche questo manoscritto quindi, come l'altro studiato dalla Pellegrin, non ha seguito la nota via della raccolta dell'arcivescovo, dalla Biblioteca Capitolare di Milano all'Ambrosiana.[5] Del resto, parte di questa raccolta è andata dispersa, ed altri manoscritti del Piccolpasso sono senza dubbio conservati in altre biblioteche, sia lombarde che di altri paesi. Recentemente infine l'argomento è stato ripreso da A. R. A. Hobson nel suo magistrale *Humanists and bookbinders*.[6] Già il De Marinis, nell'introduzione al capitolo relativo a Milano ed alla Lombardia, e poi descrivendo la legatura della British Library, nota che oltre che con la biscia viscontea, usuale elemento decorativo nelle legature milanesi del tempo, questa è adorna con il ferro alle armi del Piccolpasso, e rileva la stretta connessione che intercorre con altre legature, quelle descritte ai n. 2544-47 e 2559; quasi gemelle alla legatura del Piccolpasso sono le due corrispondenti ai n. 2544 e 2545 (la prima ricopre uno Svetonio del 1444, appartenuto a Giovanni Visconti, figlio di Vercellino, morto nel 1453, ed è ornata con la biscia viscontea), che, con i n. 2546-47 e 2559 (quest'ultima ricopre un codice del 1460), ven-

1. Cfr. PELLEGRIN, p. 316, n. 580 e nota 4.
2. Cfr. R. SABBADINI, *Spogli ambrosiani latini*, «Studi italiani di filologia classica», 11, 1903, pp. 377-83.
3. Cfr. M. MAGISTRETTI, *Due inventari del Duomo di Milano nel sec. XV. 1. Inventario della biblioteca dell'arcivescovo Piccolpasso († 1443)*, «Archivio storico lombardo», 36, 2, 1909, pp. 302-13.
4. Cfr. A. PAREDI, *La biblioteca del Piccolpasso*, Milano, 1961.
5. Cfr. T. DE MARINIS, 3, pp. 9-16 e n. 2541, tav. CCCCXXV.
6. Cfr. p. 16.

gono a costituire un gruppo omogeneo, proveniente dalla medesima bottega, attiva dai tempi dell'apostolato religioso del Piccolpasso (1433-43) fino ad almeno il 1460. Poiché anche le legature del Piccolpasso che ho esaminato all'Ambrosiana presentano caratteristiche costanti, questa più antica bottega milanese, evidenziata dal De Marinis, deve aver lavorato regolarmente per la biblioteca dell'arcivescovo. Scopo di questo studio è di fissarne le caratteristiche tecniche e decorative. Fra i codici del Piccolpasso conservati all'Ambrosiana ho avuto modo di esaminare 19 legature, che ho elencato e descritto nella lista A; purtroppo, i lavori di restauro e ristrutturazione della Biblioteca recentemente iniziati e la relativa chiusura dei fondi manoscritti alla consultazione, mi hanno costretto ad una drastica scelta, ed impedito di effettuare ulteriori controlli su tutte le legature con lo stemma del Piccolpasso segnalate dal Paredi; il materiale reperito tuttavia mi è sembrato così interessante, che ho deciso di mantenere inalterata la lista, limitandomi a segnalare molto brevemente le legature, la cui descrizione è rimasta per cause di forza maggiore incompleta (e di queste involontarie lacune spero che mi perdonino i lettori).

Nella lista B invece ho elencato una serie di legature del Quattrocento, sempre conservate in Ambrosiana, delle quali alcune portano i contrassegni viscontei, e che comunque appartengono alla stessa area geografica, cronologica e stilistica. Salvo qualche raro caso di pezzi interessanti su cui c'era ancora qualcosa da dire, e dei quali do una descrizione il più possibile completa, di quelle già pubblicate dal De Marinis fornisco solo l'indicazione, dilungandomi invece sulle inedite; anche qui ho mantenuto l'ordine topografico, per dare a chi vorrà ampliare questa ricerca una comoda possibilità di movimento nelle raccolte dei manoscritti ambrosiani, oltre quelli citati dal De Marinis, ed oltre quelli descritti in questo contributo. Vorrei inoltre chiarire che non mi sono spinta fino ad elencare il gruppo delle sforzesche, quelle tipiche decorate al centro dei piatti con rosoni di cordami intrecciati, perché queste ultime, già pienamente rinascimentali, ormai esulano dallo svolgimento del nostro discorso, e potrebbero piuttosto divenire argomento per altri studi; ho cercato invece di fornire nelle due liste tutti gli elementi attualmente in nostro possesso per riuscire ad avere una più precisa conoscenza della legatura milanese del pieno Quattrocento. Non sfuggirà, nell'insieme, la stretta analogia tecnica e stilistica riscontrabile fra le legature del Piccolpasso, e fra queste e le legature milanesi a loro contemporanee: segno non solo di una certa uniformità culturale vigente nella città dei Visconti e degli Sforza, ma anche di un'appartenenza spesso accertata alla stessa legatoria e segno, infine, che le botteghe da legatoria, come del resto le prime tipografie, non dovevano essere numerose, e che in realtà si contavano sulla punta delle dita.

Torniamo al Piccolpasso: le sue legature (lista A) ricoprono volumi di dimensioni abbastanza grandi (dall'altezza minima di 17,5 cm del n. 9, a quella massima di 40,5 cm per il n. 19); sono montate quasi esclusivamente su assi di legno, e quasi sempre le assi hanno la stessa dimensione del blocco delle carte: nelle legature milanesi del secondo quarto del secolo l'unghiatura non sembra ancora molto diffusa. Le coperte sono prevalentemente in robusto cuoio marrone, spesso in bazzana di montone, in vacchetta, una è in vitello (n. 12); ancora abbastanza raro il marocchino (ne sono stati riscontrati tre esempi, i n. 1, 3, 14). I dorsi purtroppo risultano quasi tutti rifatti, o in condizioni molto precarie: hanno comunque quasi sempre cuciture a doppi cordoni, da tre a sei, che per il fissaggio s'infilano nel bordo dell'asse (n. 2, 4, 10-11). I capitelli meritano una nota a parte: in alcuni casi sono, come ci si potrebbe aspettare da delle legature ancora monastiche, in canapa grezza, ma alcuni di essi risultano rifatti in occasione di successivi restauri; i capitelli che si possono considerare originali si distinguono perché, su un'anima di canapa rustica, sono in seta spesso elaborata, con uno spiccato gusto per il colore e una certa sontuosità: in seta bianca e rossa (n. 2), rossa e verde (n. 5), rosa, verdazzurra e oro (n. 10), bianca e azzurra (n. 11), rossa e verde a doppia anima (n. 18). Questo gusto per la seta applicata alle legature, non solo per i capitelli ma, come vedremo, anche per fermagli e le coperte stesse dei volumi, è una caratteristica peculiare dell'artigianato milanese, in zone in cui l'industria della seta, fino ai nostri giorni, ha avuto una grande fioritura ed è stata una delle basi dell'economia.[1] I fermagli, alla maniera monastica, sono metallici; si tratta quasi sempre di fermagli in pelle a punta d'ottone, di solito quattro, due sul lato anteriore, uno alla testa e al piede del volume secondo una proprietà, forse derivata dal mondo tardoantico, rimasta nelle legature italiane e spagnole; scomparsi per la maggior parte, fermagli e finiture hanno lasciato le loro tracce sui piatti. In un caso i fermagli sono tre, uno sul lato anteriore, uno alla testa e al piede (n. 5): si tratta per la verità di un elemento non troppo raro per le legature milanesi, come avremo modo di constatare anche nella lista B; in un altro, al posto dei fermagli abbiamo dei legacci in pelle (n. 18): in conclusione, si nota nelle legature del Piccolpasso la costante dei quattro fermagli in pelle a punta d'ottone, pur con qualche rara eccezione. Le strisce in pelle sono fermate sul piatto anteriore con dei chiodini pure d'ottone a forma di fiorellino, e sul piatto posteriore corrisponde l'attacco o tenone in pieno metallo. Le punte dei fermagli ed i tenoni, che sono rettangolari o a forma di foglia, quando si sono conservati risultano

---

1. Dall'argomento si è occupato in particolare F. MALAGUZZI VALERI, nella sua monumentale *La corte di Ludovico il Moro*. Milano, 1913,-23, cfr. v. 1 e 4.

decorati; il n. 14 ha fermagli a punta d'ottone con la scritta AUG, riferentisi all'autore del testo, S. Agostino, mentre i tenoni sul piatto posteriore, lavorati a sbalzo, recano alternamente le figure della Madonna col Bambino (la protettrice della città di Milano), e l'*Agnus Dei*, motivo ricorrente anche nella decorazione dei piatti. L'attaccatura è di solito dal piatto anteriore al posteriore, alla maniera latina ma talvolta i piatti si allacciavano dal piatto posteriore all'anteriore, alla maniera nordica (n. 5-6, 13). Riguardo al verso dell'aggancio, di questa caratteristica tecnica si sono occupati J. B. Oldham e più recentemente H. Nixon. Secondo il Nixon è fondamentale, per stabilire l'area geografica di una legatura, dalle legature medioevali fino al sec. XVI, il *test* relativo alla posizione dei fermagli e delle borchie metalliche introdotto per la prima volta da Oldham:[1] in Italia, come in Francia ed in Inghilterra, era d'uso comune lasciare chiuso un libro d'officio sull'altare, o un libro secolare sul banco, con quello che noi chiamiamo piatto posteriore: i fermagli erano agganciati dal piatto anteriore al posteriore in modo che, quando il libro era chiuso, era il piatto anteriore ad essere visibile; in Germania e in Olanda questa posizione era al contrario, ed i fermagli erano fissati a degli attacchi sul piatto anteriore; questa caratteristica, riscontrata in alcune legature del Piccolpasso, vi farebbe presupporre un certo influsso nordico, germanico, comune del resto in tutta l'Italia settentrionale. Vi sono poi da notare i cartellini pergamenacei con l'indicazione del testo, inchiodati con minuscole bollette d'ottone (o incollati) in alto sul piatto posteriore: essi stanno ad indicare che, una volta che il volume era posato a piatto, era il piatto posteriore quello visibile, e del resto si nota bene che il piatto posteriore di queste legature, non soggetto ad abrasioni, è quello che si è sempre meglio conservato.

Per quanto riguarda i tagli, ci troviamo di solito di fronte a dei tagli rustici, uno solo reca tracce di doratura (n. 1); frequenti i titoli a penna, di solito trascritti sul taglio anteriore. Un solo taglio si può dire decorato: è rustico, e reca dipinto un bel serto di fogliami e rose, in rosso e verde (n. 12).

La decorazione, che è sempre a secco, è costituita dalla ripetizione e composizione di ferri singoli (l'uso della rotella è molto più tardo). Nell'impostazione decorativa c'è subito un particolare da evidenziare: lo schema più frequente, uguale per i due piatti, è quello tipico delle contemporanee legature italiane, a cornici rettangolari concentriche formate da fasce di filetti che racchiudono ferri singoli impressi in successione; al centro resta uno spazio rettangolare, più o meno ampio, che non viene

---

1. Cfr. la presentazione di H. Nixon alla ristampa del volume di BERNARD A. MIDDLETON, *A history of English craft bookbinding technique*, London, The Holland Press, 1988, pp. VI-VII.

mai lasciato vuoto ma viene riempito con dei fregi longitudinali, con seminati di piastrelle o doppie catene di cordami intrecciati; spesso però le legature del Piccolpasso rivelano un forte influsso francese nella decorazione dello spazio centrale a strisce verticali e parallele con motivi ripetuti (n. 2-3, 10, 12). Gli stretti rapporti culturali intercorsi tra la Francia e la signoria milanese risalgono almeno ai tempi di Valentina Visconti (1366-1408), figlia di Giangaleazzo e sposa nel 1387 di Luigi di Valois duca d'Orléans, al quale aveva portato in dote i diritti di successione al ducato di Milano, diritti di cui si varrà Luigi XII nel 1498, una volta estinta la linea legittima dei Visconti. Che le legature milanesi del tempo risentissero dell'influsso francese lo ha rilevato da tempo la Pellegrin, nel riferire che nell'inventario del 1426 i manoscritti della biblioteca di Pavia vengono indicati come realizzati *ad modum parisinum*, il che potrebbe significare rilegati e decorati nello stile francese, ma per la verità anche trascritti e rilegati in Francia.[1] A volte allo spazio rettangolare al centro viene conferita una forma più quadrata mediante due strisce alla testa e al piede, con ferri impressi in successione.

I ferri usati benché abbastanza variati si ripetono costantemente, e ricalcano la gamma già descritta dal De Marinis come usuale per il territorio milanese. In quasi tutte le legature si ripete costantemente il grosso ferro quadrato con le armi del Piccolpasso, che viene di solito usato per formare una cornice rettangolare, o anche una banda centrale. Lo stemma del Piccolpasso non è il solo elemento araldico che si trovi su queste legature: spesso è accompagnato da imprese ed emblemi viscontei come l'aquila, la biscia sia piccola, racchiusa in un ferro romboidale, sia più grande in un grosso ferro rettangolare; fra gli altri simboli viscontei la colomba sormontata da una corona e la cerva in corsa, emblemi di Bianca Maria Visconti (1425-68, anche se la colomba è per la verità una delle più antiche imprese viscontee), il cane, la scritta IHS sormontata da una corona, emblema di Filippo Maria Visconti (1392-1447).[2] Sembrerebbero figure emblematiche, o imprese, il ferro rettangolare con una volpe, e quello con un gallo (?) e una volpe affrontati, anche se le ricerche effettuate in questo senso non mi hanno dato risultati; bisogna specificare anche che il grande numero di appartenenti alla famiglia Visconti (che si divise in una moltitudine di rami collaterali) rende ardua l'identificazione dei singoli personaggi: come sottolinea la stessa Pellegrin, la vipera che inghiotte il bambino ed altri emblemi viscontei furono adottati dai figli naturali (per es. la colomba, usata da Filippo Maria e poi, con la corona, dalla figlia Bianca Maria che resse il granducato dalla morte del marito

1. Cfr. PELLEGRIN, p. 20.
2. Cfr. PELLEGRIN, pp. 490-1.

nel 1466, alla sua morte, nel 1468), e dai figli cadetti dei duchi di Milano, e furono anche concessi alle loro favorite, o anche a dei privati cittadini che s'intendeva così ricompensare dei servizi prestati.[1]

Fra i simboli religiosi costante è l'uso dell'*Agnus Dei*, peraltro comune in tutta l'Italia settentrionale; si distingue dagli altri il grosso punzone con la figura, a contorno libero, della Madonna con il Bambino (n. 4); costanti alcuni motivi floreali, come il tipico ferro rettangolare con il rametto fiorito regolarmente usato per le cornici,[2] la rosetta quadrilobata racchiusa in un cerchio, una viola, un fiore a quattro lunghi petali,[3] la palmetta, un ferro con un nastro avvolto intorno ad un ramo fiorito; fra le figure geometriche ed astratte le crocette, i piccoli rombi con i lati concavi, che il De Marinis chiama «dadi stellati», utilizzati sia per le decorazioni a seminato che per formare, insieme a dei cerchietti, dei fregi compositi, infine l'ampia serie dei cordami a uncino o barretta, che formano motivi intrecciati, o incrociati a serpentina. Per i ferri rimando alle tavole qui accluse, ed anche alla già citata legatura pubblicata dal De Marinis, decorata alla francese, con cui sono visibili lo stemma del Piccolpasso, il piccolo ferro romboidale con la biscia, ed all'interno le strisce con l'*Agnus Dei* ed il grosso ferro rettangolare con la biscia.[4] Gli stessi ferri ritroveremo in parte più avanti, in non poche legature viscontee della lista B.

Prende così una connotazione più chiara la bottega (o l'artigiano) che ha prodotto queste legature, perché è evidente, dalle caratteristiche costanti, che si tratta di un'unica bottega, che ha lavorato per diversi anni, almeno fino al 1460, sia per l'arcivescovo di Milano che per alcuni personaggi della famiglia Visconti. Aggiungendo alle legature già citate dal De Marinis, in tutto sei, di cui una sola eseguita per il Piccolpasso (n. 2541, 2544-47 e 2559), le diciotto sicuramente del Piccolpasso della lista A ed i n. 25 e 30 della lista B qui riportate, possiamo già attribuire a quello che propongo di chiamare «Maestro del Piccolpasso» dal nome del suo più noto committente, il non piccolo numero di 27 legature identificate (più le ulteriori sei citate dal Paredi per l'Ambrosiana), cui se ne potranno sicuramente aggiungere molte altre, ancora conservate nelle biblioteche milanesi e lombarde).

Nella lista B ho elencato alcune legature viscontee o di età visconteo-sforzesca, che dovrebbero comunque contribuire a completare il quadro della produzione milanese dell'epoca, anche per il fatto che presentano

---

1. Cfr. PELLEGRIN, p. 56.
2. Questo ferro è stato usato per molto tempo a Milano.
3. Questo ferro, che a me sembra un fiore a quattro petali, potrebbe anche rappresentare un motivo a quattro foglie, cfr. F. A. SCHMIDT KÜNSEMÜLLER, *Die abendländischen romanischen Blindstempeleinbände*. Stuttgart, 1985, pp. 251-2, n. 259.
4. Cfr. DE MARINIS, 3, n. 2541, tav. CCCCXXV.

grosse affinità con le contemporanee (o di poco anteriori) legature eseguite per il Piccolpasso; due, come ho già accennato, hanno la stessa provenienza. Si tratta quasi sempre di legature su assi di legno (molto raramente cartone), coperte in cuoio, bazzana di montone, o capra, capretto, vitello, spesso (sei casi) in marocchino; il colore è costantemente marrone, tranne che per il n. 36 che è in pelle giallastra, color senape, e per delle notevoli pelli scamosciate bianche, tipiche della produzione lombarda, che troviamo in due casi: al n. 32 una legatura in vitellino rovesciato bianco su assi, che ricopre una *Chronica* di Benvenuto da Imola della 2ª metà del sec. XV, e la cui decorazione consiste esclusivamente in applicazioni metalliche, al centro dei piatti un rosone in ottone sbalzato con la scritta IHS, e tutt'intorno l'*Agnus Dei*, agli angoli la IHS e lunghi petali lanceolati, con un trifoglio a traforo nel mezzo; al n. 33 altra legatura in pelle scamosciata bianca, forse cervo, che è decorata esclusivamente con una punta metallica, tracciando dei filetti che dividono il piatto in croci, rettangoli e successivamente triangoli. Curiosa la legatura descritta al n. 27, che ricopre un Cornelio Nepote di scuola lombarda del 1456, e che è «damaschinata»: su un fondo in cuoio argenteo sono disegnati dei fiori rossicci in oro ramato, tracciati a *criblé* con una punteggiatura ottenuta con un punzone: il disegno imita perfettamente certi damaschi o velluti operati che possiamo vedere riprodotti in quantità sul Malaguzzi Valeri, a foglie e fiori raggruppati e raccordati da grandi linee ondulate; in questa legatura anche i fermagli, di cui sono rimaste le tracce, sono in stoffa. L'industria delle stoffe, sete, velluti, damaschi, broccati, fiorente in Lombardia nel Quattrocento, risente dell'ispirazione orientale che influenza all'epoca l'artigianato veneto perché, pur essendo già praticata nella regione, sembra aver ricevuto nuovo impulso a Milano, per iniziativa di Filippo Maria Visconti, da artigiani veneti, toscani e ferraresi che, almeno nei primi tempi, avrebbero continuato a lavorare secondo le tecniche e le decorazioni apprese nei luoghi d'origine. La prima corporazione degli artigiani della seta e dei tessitori, filatori e tintori fu organizzata nel 1460. Come ho già notato per le legature del Piccolpasso, quest'arte viene spesso applicata alle coperte, ma anche per le bellissime strisce che fungono da legacci, e per i capitelli: abbiamo capitelli in seta verde-azzurra (n. 1), gialla e celeste (n. 22), bianca e azzurra (n. 23), verde (n. 24) gialla e marrone (n. 25); fermagli in seta rossa, fissati con chiodini in ottone lavorato, e capitelli a doppia anima, rustici ed in seta marrone (n. 26), fermagli in velluto rosso con chiodini d'ottone (n. 27), un fermaglio in seta rossa e capitelli in seta rosa e azzurra (n. 28), capitelli in seta azzurra e rossa (n. 30), o solo rossa (n. 34), fermagli in seta rossa e capitelli a tripla anima in seta verde e rossa (n. 36), capitelli in seta rossa (n. 39), fermagli in stoffa rossa (n. 40). Nel complesso si può notare, con il trascorrere dei decenni, un graduale aumento della tendenza a usare la seta o comunque la stoffa per impreziosire le legature, secondo un gusto già ben stabilizzato in tempi più antichi, e rilevato anche nelle legature del Piccolpasso. Come qualche volta per il Piccolpasso i fermagli a punta metallica, quando non sono in stoffa, sono in pelle allumata tinta in rosso, e pure in pelle allumata sono qualche volta i rinforzi dei cordoni sul dorso. Un altro elemento importante nelle legature milanesi del Quattrocento è la decorazione metallica: borchie, cantonali, fermagli sono di solito in ottone e spesso, come abbiamo già visto, con decorazioni a sbalzo; della lista B vorrei ricordare i n. 21, 26, 29 e 33 che hanno tre fermagli, mentre il n. 28 ne ha uno solo, in seta rossa: ma di solito vi sono quattro fermagli, due sul lato anteriore, uno alla testa e al piede, in pelle o in stoffa, ma con punta metallica, che si agganciavano dal piatto anteriore al posteriore; nelle legature descritte ai n. 27 e 29 l'aggancio è dal piatto posteriore all'anteriore. Il n. 25 reca al centro le tracce di una placca metallica a lobi, il già citato n. 32 è caratterizzato da applicazioni metalliche agli angoli ed al centro dei piatti, lavorate a sbalzo; il n. 37 ha tenoni in ottone, di forma triangolare, con la scritta IHS inclusa in un sole radiante, il n. 38 tenoni rettangolari lavorati a rilievo con il motivo dell'*Agnus Dei*, ed una scritta sulle punte dei fermagli; i tenoni possono essere rettangolari, a triangolo, a forma lanceolata; sui piatti, in qualche caso, si notano i fiori e gli agganci per la catena di fissaggio. Sussistono sul piatto posteriore i cartellini pergamenacei con l'indicazione del testo (n. 39-40); i tagli sono rustici, con l'eccezione del n. 34, che ha un taglio dorato e inciso, e dei n. 1 e 26, che hanno il taglio dorato e liscio.

La decorazione delle coperte è a secco; come per le legature del Piccolpasso si tratta di cornici rettangolari concentriche (da 2 a 4), delimitate da fasce di filetti che vanno digradando dall'esterno verso il centro, mentre per ottenere un effetto di profondità diminuisce progressivamente anche la dimensione dei ferri; lo spazio centrale rimane di solito rettangolare, ma può anche assumere una forma quadrata, o quasi, per l'aggiunta di due strisce, oppure perché la cornice aumenta di spessore sui due lati alla testa e al piede, mentre rimane sottile sui due lati lunghi; il centro viene riempito o alla maniera francese, a strisce verticali, o con una composizione di cordami a forma di stella, o con i soliti fregi romboidali disposti in senso longitudinale, o con rosoncini o con un seminato di piccoli ferri, rombi con i lati concavi o crocette. Per i ferri: la legatura descritta al n. 30, assai simile a quelle del Piccolpasso, tanto che si può ipotizzare una provenienza dalla stessa bottega, è decorata alla francese con gli stessi ferri già visti, il rettangolo con il rametto fiorito, la rosetta quadrilobata inclusa nel cerchio, l'*Agnus Dei*, la IHS con la corona; ugualmente i n. 31 e 40 sono caratterizzati dallo stemma visconteo che forma una cornice, con l'alternarsi di due ferri, il rombo con la biscia ed il ferro quadrato con l'aquila; il già più volte ricordato ferro con la biscia viscontea si arricchisce ai lati con le iniziali B/M (Bianca Maria, non mi sembrerebbe G/M come riporta il De Marinis, da riferire al figlio Giovanni Maria).[1] Il ferro quadrato con il cervo, ed un ferro con un dragone supino che si morde la coda, non sembrerebbero invece pienamente delle imprese viscontee (n. 22). Fra i motivi religiosi, si ripete costantemente il ferro quadrato con l'*Agnus Dei*; un ferro insolito, con la figura di un vescovo, o un santo, forse S. Ambrogio, vescovo e patrono di Milano, forma una striscia all'interno del n. 31. Fra i motivi floreali, rosette di tutti i tipi, ma in particolare la rosetta quadrilobata inclusa nel cerchio, tipica della produzione milanese, poi rosette a contorno libero, a otto petali e di forma romboidale; un altro ferro molto comune, che si ripete costantemente sia nelle legature del Piccolpasso che in molte di questa lista, è il rettangolo che include un rametto fiorito.[2] Citerò ancora un ferro quadrato con uno strano fiore, forse un garofano sulla legatura n. 30, al n. 31 e al n. 40 un rombo quadrato con un fiore stilizzato, a quattro petali, o quattro foglie, già notato, al n. 35 un ferro quadrato con un fiore di melograno, al n. 38 un rosoncino incluso in un cerchio, al n. 39 una palmetta a contorno libero. Per i motivi astratti e geometrici, sempre frequentissimi i piccoli rombi concentrici con i lati concavi, e le crocette, arricchiti da cerchietti anche dorati; infine cordami di tutti i tipi, formati dalla composizione di barrette dritte e uncinate, o a mezzaluna, che s'intrecciano a catena o a serpentina. Tipica una piastrella romboidale con dei motivi a croce; molto particolare, ma già abbastanza tardo, mi sembra il ferro elicoidale che forma la cornice del n. 37, ad effetto simulato, quasi tridimensionale.

È possibile risalire, per qualche legatura, alla bottega che l'ha prodotta. A quella stessa da cui sono venute le legature del Piccolpasso e le poche altre citate dal De Marinis, appartiene la viscontea descritta al n. 25, che ricopre un manoscritto della metà del sec. XV, contenente i *Carmina* di Claudio Claudiano; l'appartenenza a questa bottega potrebbe essere suffragata con i punti in comune che la legatura presenta con i n. 2544-45 (in particolare), 2546-47 e 2559 del De Marinis, sia per il ferro romboidale con la biscia, piuttosto calligrafico nei particolari, sia per i giochi di cordami. Lo stesso si può ipotizzare per la legatura descritta al n. 30, pubblicata dal De Marinis al 2557 bis, per le cornici rettangolari che mostrano ferri già molto noti (il rametto fiorito, la rosetta quadrilo-

---

1. Cfr. DE MARINIS, 3, n. 2581 bis.
2. Cfr. DE MARINIS, 3, n. 2577 bis: questo ferro venne ripreso più tardi per le legature commissionate dal Grolier (cfr. anche nota 18).

bata, l'*Agnus Dei*), per l'uso francesizzante di riempire lo spazio centrale con strisce simmetriche di ferri: partendo dal centro la striscia con la scritta IHS sormontata da una corona, due strisce con il garofano, e alle estremità due con l'*Agnus Dei*. Ugualmente fra le più antiche, ma non della stessa bottega, è la legatura descritta al n. 22 che, oltre al seminato centrale composto da rombetti ed una cornice di cordami a catena (formata da due ferri a mezzaluna incrociati fra loro), ha una seconda cornice con uno strano ferro, il dragone che si morde la coda, ed una terza con un cervo. La legatura, che è eccezionale anche per la decorazione del dorso, proviene da S. Maria Incoronata.

Due legature sono molto simili: alla prima, al n. 38, già pubblicata dal De Marinis al n. 2581 bis, è caratterizzata dal ferro romboidale con la biscia viscontea affiancata dalle iniziali B/M; all'interno un fregio longitudinale, formato da tre rombi di cordami intrecciati; quasi gemella la legatura al n. 21, che contiene la stessa cornice con la biscia viscontea e le iniziali B/M e, al centro, un fregio longitudinale di cordami.

Allo stesso gruppo della legatura descritta al n. 29 e famosa perché già appartenuta al Grolier (è stata pubblicata da Gottlieb, De Marinis e Fritz Juntke), sembrano potersi ascrivere diverse legature, in elenco ai n. 23, 31, 35, 39 e 40, tutte accomunate dal gusto per i bei rosoni impressi sui piatti, sia formati dall'unione di alcuni rombetti con i lati concavi, sia da rosette a otto petali, ed a contorno libero.[1] Nel n. 29 i rosoncini riempiono lo spazio vuoto in mezzo alle cornici rettangolari, nei n. 23 e 30 vanno a formare un fregio longitudinale nello specchio centrale, nel n. 31 arricchiscono le punte della croce centrale, che è pure costituita da rombi e cerchietti, e lo stesso si rileva nei n. 35 e 40. Il n. 31, oltre ad avere la già citata cornice con il ferro di S. Ambrogio, si avvicina al n. 40 per i due ferri alternati, il rombo con la biscia viscontea e l'aquila, che qui vanno a costituire due strisce alla testa ed al piede dello spazio centrale. Altri ferri usati in questo gruppo, il solito *Agnus Dei*, la rosetta quadrilobata, il rombo con il fiore stilizzato a quattro petali, il fiore di melograno, la palmetta, i cordami. A questa anonima bottega si richiama anche, con ogni probabilità, una legatura della lista A, il n. 4, che reca, oltre al ferro con la colombina coronata di Bianca Maria Visconti, dei rosoni formati da rombetti concavi nel fregio centrale; la legatura copre un manoscritto del Piccolpasso, ma è più tarda. Certo, un'identificazione meno vaga delle botteghe milanesi sarà attuabile quando il censimento delle legature anteriori al sec. XVI, attualmente in corso per iniziativa dell'Istituto Centrale per la Patologia del Libro, avrà consentito di quantificare e analizzare tutti i pezzi rimasti, che non sono pochi, anche se pochi si sono salvati da malaugurati

---

1. Cfr. Gottlieb, p. 73; Juntke, pp. 380-2; De Marinis, 3, n. 2574 bis.

restauri, che hanno alterato le cuciture ed appiattito le decorazioni a secco. Un secondo passo, altrettanto necessario, sarà quello del completamento delle ricerche d'archivio che, nonostante la benemerita opera della Pellegrin e di altri, non può certo dirsi esaurito. Il fervore di studi sulle legature antiche che si è recentemente risvegliato in Italia dopo vent'anni di silenzio (dalla morte del De Marinis), lascia bene sperare per il futuro delle legature che tuttora numerose sono conservate nelle nostre biblioteche; il contributo che ciascuno di noi saprà dare andrà a colmare, come in un gioco di tasselli, i vuoti rimasti nelle nostre conoscenze.

La ricerca sulle legature della Biblioteca Ambrosiana è stata svolta con la collaborazione scientifica di Francesco Cossu.

LISTA A: LEGATURE DEL PICCOLPASSO

1. ORIGENES. *Commentaria in Cantica Canticorum Salomonis* [in tres libros e Greco in Latinum traductos], ms. membr. inizi del sec. XV. 240 x 165 mm. (Fig. 1)

Legatura coeva in marocchino marrone su assi di legno. Decorazione a secco: sui piatti due cornici rettangolari concentriche, formate da filetti racchiudenti ferri singoli in successione, la cornice esterna un ferro rettangolare con due animali affrontati (forse un gallo, e una volpe), la cornice interna un grifone; lo specchio centrale è decorato con un seminato di piastrelle romboidali, con un'aquila rivolta verso destra. Cartellino pergamenaceo con il titolo incollato sul piatto posteriore. Dorso a 3 doppi cordoni, rifatto in antica data; capitelli rustici; taglio con tracce di doratura, e titolo trascritto sul lato anteriore. Restaurata in antica data e nel 1966.

Provenienza: Dono del Piccolpasso alla Chiesa Metropolitana di Milano (lo stemma dell'arcivescovo è miniato all'interno del volume); all'Ambrosiana dal 1605.

Bibliografia: CERUTI, 2, pp. 731-8; PAREDI, 1961, n. 1; CIPRIANI, p. 4.

(A 96 sup.)

2. LEO I papa, santo. *Epistulae* [seguono epistole di altro Autore], ms. membr. 1ª metà del sec. XV. 290 x 205 mm.

Legatura coeva in cuoio marrone chiaro (bazzana) su assi di legno della stessa dimensione delle carte. Decorazione a secco: sui piatti quattro cornici rettangolari concentriche, formate da filetti racchiudenti ferri singoli in successione, dall'esterno rispettivamente lo stemma del Piccolpasso, un ferro rettangolare con un rametto fiorito, l'*Agnus*

LEGATURE DEL PICCOLPASSO E VISCONTEE NELL'AMBROSIANA 207

Fig. 1. Origenes. *Commentaria in Cantica Canticorum*,
ms. 1ª metà sec. XV (n. 1)

Dei, e un ferro rettangolare con un dragone, probabilmente la biscia viscontea. Lo specchio centrale è decorato a strisce verticali, non perfettamente simmetriche: da sinistra un ferro con un frutto (forse una pigna), delle rosette, lo stemma dell'arcivescovo, delle rosette. Cartellino pergamenaceo con il titolo incollato sul piatto posteriore. Tracce di 4 fermagli in pelle (due sul lato anteriore, due alla testa e al piede), fermati con dei chiodini, e che si allacciavano dal piatto posteriore all'anteriore. Dorso a 4 doppi cordoni che s'infilano nel bordo dell'asse, rifatto; capitelli in seta bianca e rossa; taglio rustico, con titolo trascritto a penna sul lato anteriore. La legatura risente di un forte influsso francese nell'impostazione decorativa. Restaurata in antica data; meglio conservato il piatto posteriore.

Provenienza: Dono dell'arcivescovo Piccolpasso alla Chiesa Metropolitana (lo stemma del prelato si ripete miniato all'interno del volume alla c. 3 e 88); all'Ambrosiana dal 1605.

Bibliografia: CERUTI, 2, p. 768; PAREDI, 1961, n. 2; CIPRIANI, p. 6.

(A 142 sup.)

3. HIERONYMUS, santo. *Psalterium* [seguono altri scritti dello stesso Autore], ms. membr. 1ª metà del sec. XV. 300 x 210 mm. (Fig. 2)

Legatura coeva in marocchino marrone scuro su assi di legno. Decorazione a secco: riquadrature rettangolari (notevole la successione del ferro con la biscia viscontea) racchiudono lo specchio centrale decorato a strisce verticali parallele: dal centro verso i lati si ripetono simmetricamente un ferro con una rosetta quadrata a 8 petali, il ferro con la biscia viscontea, e lo stemma dell'arcivescovo Piccolpasso. Sui piatti fori per quattro fermagli, due sul lato anteriore, due alla testa e al piede. Titolo sul piatto anteriore. Dorso a 4 doppi cordoni, rifatti; capitelli rifatti; taglio rustico. La legatura risente di un forte influsso francese nell'impostazione decorativa. Restaurata dall'ICPL nel 1970; rilievo molto appiattito.

Provenienza: Dono del Piccolpasso alla Chiesa Metropolitana; all'Ambrosiana dal 1605.

Bibliografia: CERUTI, 3, pp. 74-5; PAREDI, 1961, n. 2; CIPRIANI, pp. 10-11.

(B 120 sup.)

4. IOANNES Chrysostomus, santo. *De dignitate sacerdotale*, ms. membr. 1ª metà del sec. XV. 310 x 208 mm. (Fig. 3)

Legatura coeva, o di poco posteriore, in cuoio marrone su assi di legno della stessa dimensione delle carte. Decorazione a secco, differente per i due piatti: sul piatto anteriore tre cornici rettangolari concentriche formate da filetti, racchiudenti ferri singoli impressi in successione:

Fig. 2. Hieronymus, santo. *Psalterium*, ms. 1ᵃ metà sec. XV (n. 3)

Fig. 3. Ioannes Chrysostomus, santo. *De dignitate sacerdotale*,
ms 1ª metà sec. XV (n. 4)

dall'esterno rispettivamente una piastrella romboidale racchiudente un fiore a quattro petali, il ferro della colombina volante e della corona (riferentisi a Bianca Maria Visconti, 1425-68, moglie di Francesco Sforza), ed infine dei grossi cordami intrecciati; al centro, nello specchio, un fregio longitudinale formato da un piccolo ferro forma di rombo con i lati concavi, che forma dei rosoni. Sul piatto posteriore le stesse cornici, ma in ordine diverso; al centro è impressa la figura intera della Vergine con Bambino. La decorazione sul piatto posteriore è più accurata ed importante perché il volume era poggiato sull'anteriore, come dimostra anche il cartellino con il titolo fissato con due chiodini al piatto posteriore. Tracce di 4 fermagli, due sul lato anteriore, uno alla testa ed uno al piede, che si allacciavano dal piatto anteriore al posteriore. Dorso a 6 doppi cordoni in canapa, che s'infilano nel bordo del piatto; capitelli rustici; taglio rustico. Male conservata sul piatto anteriore; pelle del dorso quasi del tutto staccata.

Provenienza: Dono del Piccolpasso alla Chiesa Metropolitana; acquistato dal Borromeo per l'Ambrosiana nel 1605 (nota ms. a c. 12); secondo la Cipriani all'Ambrosiana dal 1601.

Bibliografia: CERUTI, 3, pp. 198-99; PAREDI, 1961, n. 9; KRISTELLER, I, p. 329; CIPRIANI, pp. 20-1. (*C 99 sup.*)

5. PROSPER Aquitanus, santo. *Pro predicatoribus gratie Dei contra librum Cassiani presbiteri qui prenotatur de protectione Dei* [seguono testi di altri Autori], ms. membr. 1ª metà del sec. XV. 210 x 145 mm. (Fig. 4)

Legatura coeva in cuoio marrone su assi di legno della stessa dimensione delle carte. Decorazione a secco: sui piatti tre cornici rettangolari concentriche formate da filetti, racchiudenti ferri singoli impressi in successione, la cornice esterna un ferro rettangolare con un rametto fiorito, quella centrale lo stemma del Piccolpasso, quella interna l'*Agnus Dei*. Nello specchio centrale un seminato di piccoli rombi con i lati concavi. Targhetta pergamenacea attaccata con chiodini d'ottone al piatto posteriore. Tracce di tre fermagli, uno sul lato anteriore, uno alla testa e al piede, attaccati con quattro chiodini ciascuno e che si agganciavano dal piatto posteriore all'anteriore. Dorso a 3 doppi cordoni, rifatto; capitelli in seta rossa e verde, su un supporto di canapa; taglio rustico, con un titolo a penna. Stato di conservazione buono, vecchio restauro sul dorso.

Provenienza: Dono del Piccolpasso alla Metropolitana (lo stemma miniato dall'arcivescovo e sue note autografe al testo sono visibili all'interno del volume); all'Ambrosiana dal 1601.

Bibliografia: CERUTI, 3, pp. 224-5; PAREDI, 1961, n. 10; CIPRIANI, pp. 22-23. (*D 11 sup.*)

Fig. 4. Prosper Aquitanus, santo. *Pro predicatoribus gratie Dei*, ms 1ª metà sec. XV (n. 5)

6. LACTANTIUS, Lucius Caecilius Firmianus. *De ira Dei* [seguono altre opere dello stesso Autore], ms. membr. 1ª metà del sec. XV. 221 x 142 mm.

Legatura coeva in cuoio marrone (bazzana di montone), su assi di legno della stessa dimensione delle carte. Decorazione a secco: sui piatti quattro cornici rettangolari concentriche formate da filetti racchiudenti ferri singoli impressi in successione; dall'esterno rispettivamente un ferro rettangolare con un rametto fiorito, un ferro romboidale con la biscia viscontea, un ferro quadrato con i lati leggermente concavi, racchiudente un fiore a quattro petali, ed infine l'*Agnus Dei*; lo specchio centrale, particolarmente lungo e stretto, racchiude una decorazione formata da una doppia catena di cordami intrecciati a serpentina. Tracce di quattro fermagli, due sul lato anteriore, uno alla testa e al piede, fissati con quattro chiodini ciascuno, e che si allacciavano dal piatto posteriore all'anteriore dove è rimasta traccia di borchie rotonde. Dorso rifatto nel corso di un restauro seicentesco, a 3 cordoni; capitelli rustici, in canapa; taglio rustico, con titolo a penna. La legatura risente di un forte influsso francese nell'impostazione decorativa. Restaurata in antica data, meglio conservato il piatto anteriore.

Provenienza: Dono del Piccolpasso alla Chiesa Metropolitana (iniziale con lo stemma dell'arcivescovo alla c. 1); all'Ambrosiana dal 1605.

Bibliografia: CERUTI, 3, pp. 241-2; PAREDI, 1961, n. 12; CIPRIANI, p. 24

(*D 31 sup.*)

7. HIERONYMUS, santo. *Descriptio de formis Hebraicorum litterarum*, ms. membr. sec. XV [c. 1439]. 330 x 230 mm.

Legatura coeva in cuoio marrone rossiccio su assi di legno, della stessa dimensione delle carte. Decorazione a secco: sui piatti quattro cornici rettangolari concentriche formate da filetti racchiudenti ferri singoli in successione, dall'esterno rispettivamente un ferro rettangolare con un rametto fiorito, lo stemma del Piccolpasso, un ferro rettangolare racchiudente un fiore (una violetta?) ed infine l'*Agnus Dei*; lo specchio è decorato con una composizione longitudinale formata da un piccolo rombo dai lati concavi. Tracce di quattro fermagli fissati con fiorellini d'ottone. Sul piatto posteriore si sono conservati dei chiodini in ottone, che servivano a reggere la targhetta pergamenacea con il titolo. Dorso a 4 cordoni, rifatto; capitelli rustici; taglio rustico, con scritta. Il piatto anteriore è molto abraso, il posteriore in migliori condizioni.

Provenienza: Dono del Piccolpasso alla Chiesa Metropolitana milanese (lo stemma dell'arcivescovo si vede, oltre che sulla coperta, miniato a

c. 2v); acquistato dal cardinale Federico Borromeo per l'Ambrosiana nel 1605.
Bibliografia: Ceruti, 3, pp. 278-80; Paredi, 1961, n. 13; Cipriani, p. 30.

(*D 88 sup.*)

8. ISIDORUS arciv. di Siviglia, santo. *Libri soliloquiorum* [seguono altre opere dello stesso Autore] ms. membr. 1ª metà del sec. XV (c. 1430-35). 182 x 130 mm.
Legatura coeva in cuoio su assi di legno; decorazione impressa a secco: fra i ferri usati, lo stemma del card. Piccolpasso. Restaurata in antica data.
Provenienza: Dono del Piccolpasso alla Chiesa Metropolitana (a c. IV stemma miniato dell'Arcivescovo); all'Ambrosiana dal 1603.
Bibliografia: Ceruti, 3, pp. 320-22; Paredi, 1961, n. 16; Kristeller, I, p. 297; Cipriani, p. 35.

(*E 17 sup.*)

9. HIERONYMUS, santo. *Collectio ex dictis nonnullis*, ms. membr. 1ª metà del sec. XV [1439]. 175 x 125 mm.
Legatura coeva in cuoio marrone (vacchetta?), su assi di legno. Decorazione a secco: sui piatti tre cornici rettangolari concentriche formate da filetti racchiudenti ferri singoli impressi in successione; dall'esterno rispettivamente si alternano un ferro rettangolare con un rametto fiorito, un ferro con una cerva in corsa (impresa di Bianca Maria Visconti) ed ancora il rametto fiorito; nello stretto specchio centrale si ripete il ferro con la cerva. Cartellino pergamenaceo con il titolo fermato sul piatto posteriore con dei chiodini. Tracce di due fermagli sul lato anteriore del taglio, che si allacciavano dal piatto anteriore al posteriore, ma *sopra* il piatto, a circa 4 cm di distanza dal bordo. Dorso a 3 doppi cordoni; capitelli rustici in canapa; taglio rustico. Discretamente conservata, ma decorazione abrasa; tracce di restauro di antica data sul dorso.
Provenienza: Dono del Piccolpasso alla Chiesa Metropolitana (scritta autografa dall'arcivescovo, del 1439, a c. 1); alla Biblioteca Ambrosiana dal 1601.
Bibliografia: Ceruti, 3, pp. 587-88; Paredi, 1961, n. 21; Cipriani, p. 56.

(*H 5 sup.*)

H 37 sup. cfr. Paredi, *1961, n. 23*
H 59 sup. cfr. Paredi, *1961, n. 25*

10. ANSELMUS, archiepiscopus Cantuariensis, santo. *Monologium*, ms. membr. 1ª metà del sec. XV. 295 x 200 mm. (Fig. 5)
Legatura coeva in cuoio marrone (bazzana?) su assi di legno, della stessa di-

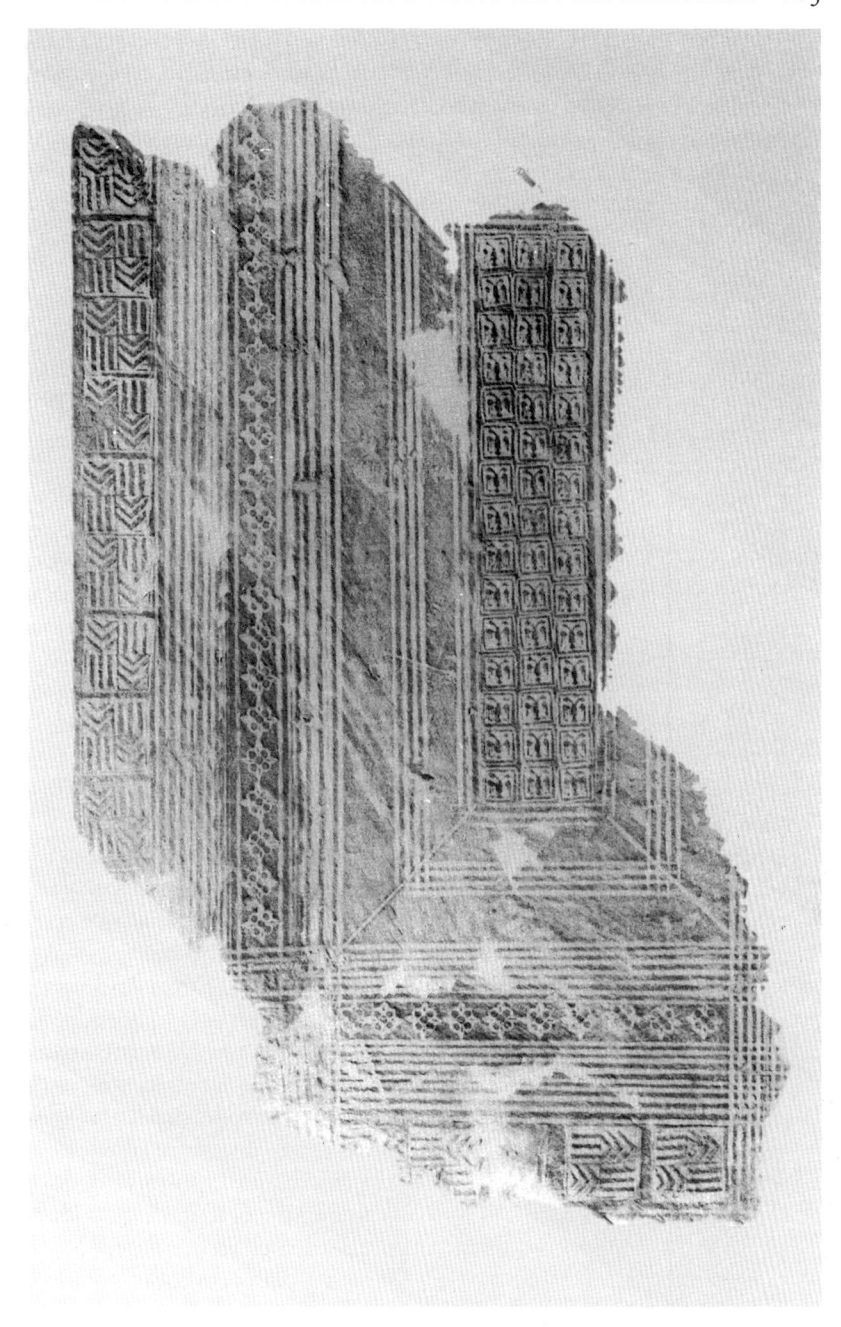

Fig. 5. Anselmus, archiepiscopus Cantuariensis. *Monologium*,
ms 1ª metàsec. XV (n. 10)

mensione delle carte. Decorazione a secco: sui piatti due cornici a ferri singoli alternate ad ampie fasce di filetti, digradanti dall'esterno verso l'interno; la cornice esterna reca il ferro con lo stemma del Piccolpasso, quella interna un fiorellino; lo specchio centrale, stretto e lungo, ospita, alla maniera francese, tre strisce verticali; anche se sono entrambe formate dalla ripetizione di un unico ferro, c'è una leggera differenza fra i due piatti: sull'anteriore si ripete un'aquila ad una sola testa, rivolta verso destra, sul posteriore un'aquila bicipite. Cartellino pergamenaceo con Autore e titolo fissato con sei chiodini d'ottone al piatto posteriore. Tracce di quattro fermagli, due sul taglio anteriore, uno alla testa e al piede, in pelle allumata bianca, che si agganciavano dal piatto anteriore (dove sono fissati con borchiette d'ottone a forma di fiore) al posteriore (con tenoni d'ottone). Dorso a 4 cordoni che s'infilano nel bordo dell'asse, rifatto; capitelli in seta rosa, verde-azzurra e oro, molto rovinati; taglio rustico, con titolo a penna. Decorazione molto abrasa; meglio conservato il piatto posteriore. Dorso restaurato.

Provenienza: Dono del Piccolpasso alla Chiesa Metropolitana milanese (lo stemma dell'arcivescovo ricorre miniato a c. IV); all'Ambrosiana dal 1605.

Bibliografia: CERUTI, 3, p. 640; PAREDI, 1961, n. 27; CIPRIANI, p. 66.

(*H 89 sup.*)

H 95 sup. cfr. Paredi, *1961, n. 28*

11. PLINIUS CAECILIUS SECUNDUS, Gaius. *Epistularum libri*, ms. membr. 1ª metà del sec. XV[circa 1440]. 270 x 184 mm. (Fig. 6)

Legatura coeva in cuoio molto abraso (bazzana di montone), su assi di legno della stessa dimensione delle carte. Decorazione a secco: quattro cornici rettangolari concentriche formate da filetti racchiudenti ferri singoli impressi in successione, dall'esterno rispettivamente il ferro rettangolare con il rametto fiorito, l'*Agnus Dei*, lo stemma del Piccolpasso, la rosetta quadrilobata; nello specchio un fregio longitudinale formato dalla composizione di un unico ferro, un piccolo rombo con i lati concavi. Cartellino pergamenaceo con il titolo incollato sul piatto posteriore; tracce di quattro fermagli in pelle marrone, due sul lato anteriore, uno alla testa e al piede, che dal piatto anteriore (dove sono fermati con due chiodini d'ottone) si allacciavano al posteriore, dove si sono conservati quattro minuscoli chiodini per ogni fermaglio. Dorso rifatto, a 3 doppi cordoni infilati nel bordo dell'asse; capitelli in seta bianca e azzurra; taglio rustico. Dorso a 3 doppi cordoni infilati nel bordo dell'asse, rifatto; capitelli in seta bianca e azzurra; taglio rustico. Rilievo molto appiattito, meglio conservato il piatto anteriore; restaurata.

LEGATURE DEL PICCOLPASSO E VISCONTEE NELL'AMBROSIANA 217

Fig. 6. Plinius Caecilius Secundus, Gaius. *Epistularum libri*,
ms. c. 1440 (n. 11)

Provenienza: Già del Piccolpasso (oltre che sulla legatura, lo stemma dell'arcivescovo è visibile, miniato, a c. IV).
Bibliografia: CERUTI, 3, p. 700; PAREDI, 1961, n. 29; CIPRIANI, p. 75.

(*I 75 sup.*)

L 8 sup. cfr. Paredi, *1961, n. 31*
R 68 sup. cfr. Paredi, *1961, n. 38*

12. CYRILLUS, Alexandrinus, santo. *Apologeticus* [seguono testi di altri autori], ms. membr. 1ª metà del sec. XV. 229 x 161 mm. (Fig. 7)
Legatura coeva, in vitello marrone su assi (di legno? il restauro ha alterato i dati). Decorazione a secco: sui piatti quattro cornici rettangolari concentriche formate da filetti, racchiudenti ferri singoli impressi in successione; dall'esterno, rispettivamente, un ferro rettangolare con un nastro che si avvolge intorno a un rametto fiorito, un grosso fiore a quattro petali, il ferro rettangolare con il rametto fiorito, la colombina (riferentisi a Bianca Maria Visconti, 1425-68, moglie di Francesco Sforza). Nello specchio diviso, alla maniera francese, in strisce verticali, la striscia centrale con lo stemma del Piccolpasso è accompagnata ai due lati, simmetricamente, dal motivo del nastro avvolto intorno al ramo fiorito. Sul piatto posteriore si notano le tracce del cartellino pergamenaceo con il titolo, inchiodato. Si notano le tracce di quattro fermagli (due sul lato anteriore del taglio, uno alla testa e al piede) che si allacciavano dal piatto anteriore al posteriore. Dorso a 4 cordoni, rifatto; capitelli rifatti; taglio rustico, dipinto con un serto di rose e fogliami, in rosso e verde. Restaurata nel 1977, con pesanti rifacimenti.
Provenienza: Già del Piccolpasso (oltre che sulla legatura lo stemma dell'arcivescovo è miniato a c. 2v); all'Ambrosiana dal 1603.
Bibliografia: CERUTI, 5, p. 3; PAREDI, 1961, n. 40; KRISTELLER, 1, p. 342; CIPRIANI, p. 118. (*S 7 sup.*)

13. LACTANTIUS, Lucius Caecilius Firmianus. *Institutiones* [seguono testi dello stesso autore], ms. membr. 1ª metà del sec. XV. 335 x 235 mm. (Fig. 8)
Legatura coeva in cuoio marrone (bazzana di montone), su assi di legno della stessa dimensione delle carte. Decorazione a secco; sui piatti quattro cornici rettangolari concentriche formate da filetti, racchiudenti ferri singoli impressi in successione; dall'esterno, rispettivamente, un ferro quadrato con un fiorellino a quattro petali, lo stemma del Piccolpasso, un cane, un'aquila volta verso sinistra; lo specchio, delimitato da una cornice che su tre lati è impressa con un ferro con un dragone e sul lato inferiore con un ferro rettangolare con una volpe, è

Fig. 7. Cyrillus Alexandrinus, santo. *Apologeticus*, ms. 1ª metà sec. XV (n. 12)

Fig. 8. Lactantius, Lucius Caecilius Firmianus. *Institutiones*,
ms. metà sec. XV (n. 13)

decorato all'interno con un seminato di crocette. Anche qui si nota il cartellino pergamenaceo con il titolo, inchiodato sul piatto posteriore; tracce di quattro fermagli in ottone, fermati con dei chiodini sul piatto posteriore; si agganciavano all'anteriore, dove sono rimasti dei tenoni metallici di forma arrotondata. Dorso a 4 doppi cordoni, rifatto; capitelli rustici, in canapa; taglio rustico. Restaurata; meglio conservato il piatto posteriore.

Provenienza: Dono del Piccolpasso alla Chiesa Metropolitana milanese (testo forse di mano dello stesso arcivescovo); acquistato per l'Ambrosiana nel 1605.

Bibliografia: CERUTI, I, p. 115; PAREDI, 1961, n. 43; KRISTELLER, I, p. 280; CIPRIANI, p. 156. *(A 212 inf.)*

14. AUGUSTINUS, Aurelius, santo. *De civitate Dei*, ms. membr. 1ª metà del sec. XV [1439]. 375 x 260 mm.

Legatura della seconda metà del sec. XV, in marocchino marrone su assi di legno, provvista di unghiatura. Decorazione a secco: sui piatti quattro cornici rettangolari concentriche formate da filetti, racchiudenti ferri singoli impressi in successione; dall'esterno, rispettivamente un cordame intrecciato, un ferro con una rosetta a quattro petali, una doppia foglia egizia, una catena formata da cordami incrociati a serpentina. Nello specchio un lungo fregio derivato dalla composizione di piccoli ferri a cordami. Dei quattro fermagli originali (due sono stati rifatti) si è conservato un aggancio in ottone con la scritta AUG, riferentisi all'Autore del testo; sul piatto posteriore quattro tenoni lavorati a rilievo con le figure, alternate, della Madonna con il Bambino e dell'*Agnus Dei*. Dorso a 5 doppi cordoni, rifatto; capitelli in canapa rustica, rifatti; taglio rustico, con il titolo. Pesantemente restaurata.

Provenienza: Manoscritto già del Piccolpasso (lo stemma dell'arcivescovo, miniato, è a c. 17v); la legatura è stata eseguita in data posteriore, nella 2ª metà del sec. XV.

Bibliografia: CERUTI, I, p. 162; PAREDI, 1961, n. 5; CIPRIANI, p. 165.
(B 16 inf.)

15. SULPICIUS SEVERUS. *De vita sancti Martini ad Desiderium*, ms. membr. 1ª metà del sec. XV. 295 x 210 mm.

Legatura coeva su assi, in cuoio impresso a secco; fra i ferri usati, delle imprese viscontee (la biscia), manca però una cornice con lo stemma del Piccolpasso; sul piatto posteriore cartellino con il titolo. Restaurata sul dorso.

Provenienza: Già del Piccolpasso (suo stemma miniato a c. 3); all'Ambrosiana dal 1603.

Bibliografia: CERUTI, 1, pp. 228-30; PAREDI, 1961, n. 46; CIPRIANI, pp. 180-1. *(C 67 inf.)*

16. CYPRIANUS, Thascius Caecilius, santo. *Epistulae*, ms. membr. 1ª metà del sec. XV. 320 x 230 mm.

Legatura coeva in pelle marrone su assi di legno, della stessa dimensione delle carte. Decorazione a secco: quattro cornici rettangolari concentriche formate da filetti, racchiudenti ferri singoli impressi in successione; dall'esterno, rispettivamente, un rametto fiorito, un ferro quadrato con una crocetta, lo stemma del Piccolpasso, l'*Agnus Dei*; al centro un fregio longitudinale formato dalle crocette racchiuse in un quadrato. Targhetta pergamenacea con il titolo sul piatto posteriore; tracce di quattro fermagli in pelle (due sul lato anteriore del taglio, uno alla testa e al piede), fissati con dei chiodini al piatto anteriore; si agganciavano al posteriore mediante dei tenoni metallici a forma di foglia, di cui restano le tracce. Dorso liscio, rifatto; capitelli rifatti; taglio rustico con titolo a penna. Stato di conservazione pessimo, il rilievo è molto appiattito, e ormai poco visibile.

Provenienza: Già del Piccolpasso; il suo stemma, oltre che sulla legatura, miniato a c. IV.

Bibliografia: CERUTI, 1, pp. 266-67; PAREDI, 1961, n. 47; CIPRIANI, p. 188. *(C 131 inf.)*

17. HIERONYMUS, santo. *Commentatio in XII prophetas.*, ms. membr. 1ª metà del sec. XV. 370 x 255 mm.

Legatura coeva in cuoio su assi di legno, impresso a secco; fra i ferri usati lo stemma del Piccolpasso. Cartellino con il titolo sul piatto posteriore. Restaurata.

Provenienza: Già dono del Piccolpasso alla Metropolitana; all'interno (c. 1r) suo stemma miniato; all'Ambrosiana dal 1605.

Bibliografia: CERUTI, 1, pp. 298-99; PAREDI, 1961, n. 48; CIPRIANI, p. 194. *(C 177 inf.)*

18. HIERONYMUS, santo. *Epistulae*, ms. membr. 1ª metà del sec. XV. 368 x 250 mm.

Legatura coeva in pelle marrone su assi di legno, della stessa dimensione delle carte. Decorazione a secco, molto simile al n. 17: sui piatti quattro cornici rettangolari concentriche formate da filetti, racchiudenti ferri singoli impressi in successione; dall'esterno, rispettivamente, il ferro rettangolare con il rametto fiorito, una crocetta racchiusa in un quadrato, lo stemma del Piccolpasso, un ferro quadrato con la scritta IHS sormontata da una corona, impresa di Filippo Maria Visconti;

nello specchio un fregio longitudinale formato dalla composizione di piccole losanghe con i lati concavi. Sul piatto posteriore cartellino con il titolo; legacci in pelle. Dorso a 5 doppi cordoni, rifatto; capitelli doppi, in canapa e in seta verde e rosa; taglio rustico. Conservazione discreta, restaurata.

Provenienza: Dono del Piccolpasso alla Chiesa Metropolitana milanese; all'Ambrosiana dal 1605.

Bibliografia: CERUTI, 1, p. 337; PAREDI, 1961, n. 52; CIPRIANI, pp. 204-5.

(*C 250 inf.*)

C 305 inf. cfr. Paredi, *1961, n. 53*

19. ORIGENES. *Omeliae super Pentatheucum, Leviticum, Numeros,* ecc., ms. cart. sec. XV [c. 1425]. 405 x 288 mm.

Legatura coeva in cuoio su assi di legno, impresso a secco con vari motivi; fra i ferri usati, lo stemma del Piccolpasso. Cartellino pergamenaceo con l'indicazione del testo sul piatto posteriore.

Provenienza: Dono del Piccolpasso alla Chiesa Metropolitana milanese (suo stemma in oro e argento, con le iniziali F/P all'interno del volume).

Bibliografia: CERUTI, 1, pp. 678-79; PAREDI, 1961, n. 54; CIPRIANI, p. 255.

(*C 523 inf.*)

LISTA B: LEGATURE VISCONTEE E MILANESI

20. LACTANTIUS, Lucius Caecilius Firmianus. *De falsa religione* [seguono altre opere dello stesso autore] ms. membr. metà del sec. XV [1459]. 312 x 183 mm.

Legatura coeva in cuoio (bazzana di montone), su assi di legno. Decorazione a secco: tre cornici rettangolari concentriche formate da filetti racchiudenti ferri singoli impressi in successione; dall'esterno rispettivamente un ferro che forma una treccia di cordami, nel mezzo l'usuale rosetta a quattro petali racchiusa in un cerchio, all'interno barrette diritte e curve formano un cordame intrecciato a serpentina, arricchito da cerchietti. Lo specchio è decorato in alto e in basso da una striscia con il ferro dell'*Agnus Dei* che si ripete per 10 volte; nel centro dei filetti formano i contorni di una stella a 8 punte, riempita di cordami a forma di barrette e uncini, e di cerchietti. Tracce di quattro bindelle in seta verde, attaccate ai piatti con bollette d'ottone, a forma di stelline a 8 petali. Dorso rifatto, con cucitura a 4 doppi cordoni; capitelli in canapa rustica ricoperta in seta verde-azzurra; taglio dorato, liscio. Restaurata; pelle molto abrasa, meglio conservato il piatto anteriore.

Provenienza: all'Ambrosiana dal 1603.
Bibliografia: CERUTI, 3, pp. 103-4; CIPRIANI, pp. 12-3.   (*B 154 sup.*)

21. ISIDORUS arciv. di Siviglia, santo. *De summo bono*, ms. membr. metà del sec. XV. 248 x 165 mm. (Fig. 9)

Legatura coeva in capretto castano scuro su assi di legno. Decorazione a secco: sui piatti due cornici rettangolari concentriche, formate da filetti racchiudenti ferri singoli impressi in successione, dall'esterno rispettivamente un rombo con la biscia viscontea affiancata dalle iniziali B/M (cfr. anche il n. 38) riferentisi a Bianca Maria Visconti, 1425-68, moglie di Francesco Sforza, e dei piccoli rombi con i lati concavi. Nello specchio un fregio romboidale formato dalla composizione di cordami ad uncino e a barretta; cerchietti concentrici sparsi qua e là, ed agli angoli. Ogni piatto presenta le tracce di cinque borchie metalliche rotonde, quattro gli angoli ed una centrale; tre fermagli (uno sul lato anteriore, uno alla testa ed uno al piede) che si agganciavano dal piatto anteriore al posteriore. Dorso a 3 doppi cordoni, rifatto; capitelli in canapa rustica; taglio rustico. Volume sconnesso, con attacchi di tarli; nervature recise.

Provenienza: Dagli eredi di Francesco Ciceri; all'Ambrosiana dal 1603.
Bibliografia: CERUTI, 3, p. 264; CIPRIANI, p. 28.   (*D 66 sup.*)

E 67 sup. cfr. De Marinis, *3, n. 2548 bis*
E 110 sup. cfr. De Marinis, *3, n. 2587*
F 150 sup. cfr. De Marinis, *3, n. 2572*
G 22 sup. cfr. De Marinis, *3, n. 2543*

22. STEFANO da Pavia. *Expositio Canonis Missae*, ms. membr. sec. XV [1455]. 270 x 200 mm. (Fig. 10)

Legatura coeva, quasi sicuramente milanese, in bazzana di montone su assi di legno della stessa dimensione delle carte. Decorazione a secco: quattro cornici rettangolari concentriche, formate da filetti racchiudenti ferri singoli impressi in successione, dall'esterno rispettivamente una cornice con un ferro rettangolare con un cordame intrecciato, impressa in doppio, un ferro quadrato con un dragone che si morde la coda, un cervo in un quadrato, un piccolo rombo con un fiore dentro; nello specchio centrale un seminato di piastrelle formate da una composizione di rombetti con i lati concavi uniti a cerchietti, alternati a un fiore a quattro petali. Cartellini pergamenacei inchiodati ed incollati sul piatto posteriore; due fermagli in pelle sul lato anteriore del taglio, che si allacciavano dal piatto anteriore al posteriore (sono rimaste le tracce dei tenoni di forma lanceolata sul piatto posteriore, fermati con tre chiodini); sul piatto anteriore si notano delle forature, forse per la

Fig. 9. Isidorus arciv. di Siviglia santo. *De sommo bono*,
ms. metà sec. XV (n. 21)

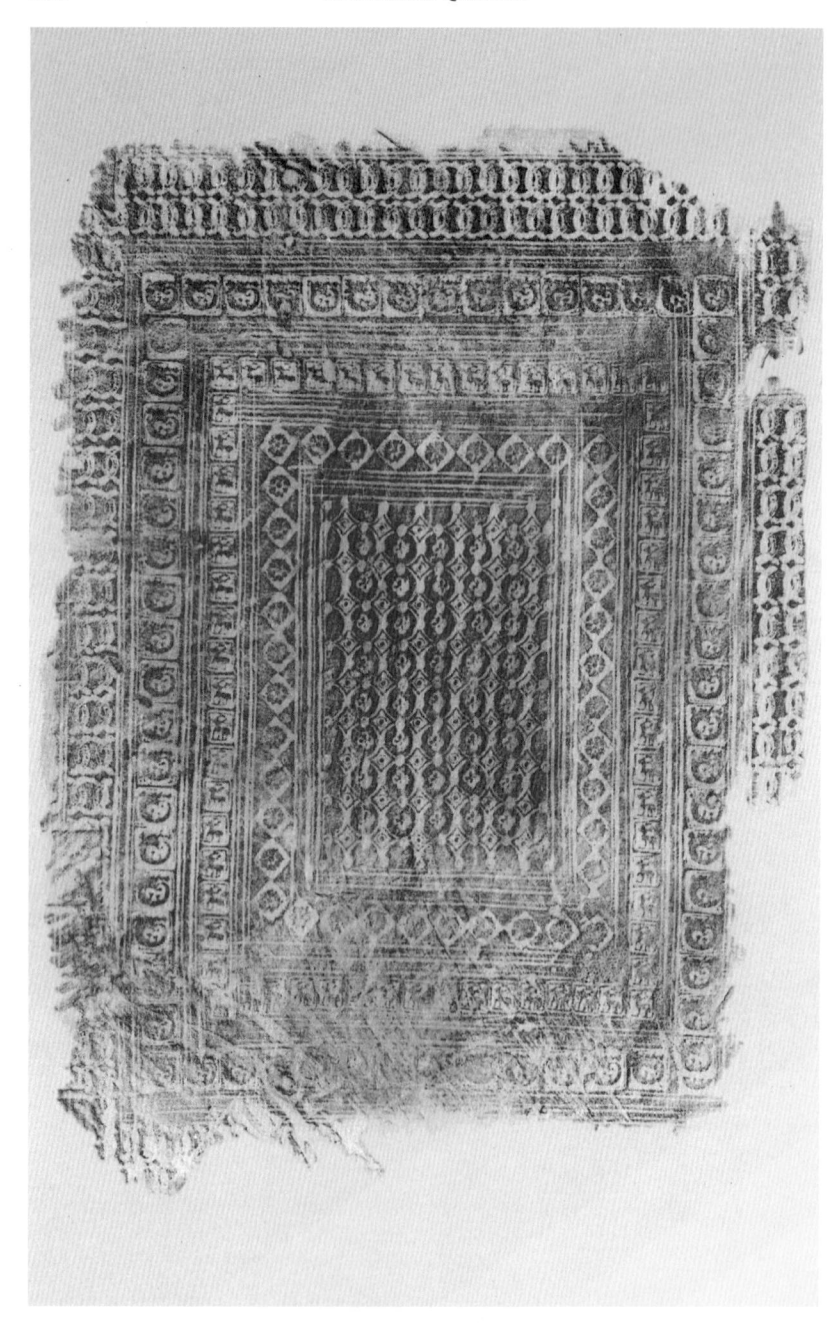

Fig. 10. Stefano da Pavia. *Expositio Canonis Missae*,
ms. sec. XV, c. 1455 (n. 22)

catena che fissava il volume al pluteo. Il dorso, a 4 doppi cordoni che s'infilano nel bordo dei piatti, è decorato con un motivo a reticolato, arricchito da cerchietti, capitelli in seta gialla e celeste; taglio rustico. Abrasioni e tagli sulla pelle; rilievo appiattito.

Provenienza: Convento agostiniano di S. Maria Incoronata; all'Ambrosiana dal 1607.

Bibliografia: CERUTI, 3, pp. 629-30; CIPRIANI, p. 62. *(H 72 sup.)*
L *104 sup. cfr.* De Marinis, *3, n. 2564*

23. CICERO, Marcus Tullius. *De senectute* [seguono altre opere dello stesso autore] ms. membr. metà del sec. XV. 235 x 165 mm. (Fig. 11)

Legatura coeva in bazzana di montone rossiccia, molto abrasa, su assi di legno della stessa dimensione delle carte. Decorazione a secco: tre cornici rettangolari concentriche formate da filetti racchiudenti ferri singoli impressi in successione; dall'esterno, rispettivamente, una cornice di cordami incrociati a serpentina, una di cordami a treccia e, ultima, una cornice con un ferro quadrato con una rosetta a quattro petali. Nello specchio un fregio longitudinale di tre rosoni sovrapposti, formati dalla composizione di piccoli rombi dai lati concavi. Tracce di quattro fermagli (due sul taglio anteriore, due alla testa e al piede): sul piatto anteriore erano fissati semplicemente con due chiodini, e si allacciavano al posteriore, dove sono rimaste le tracce di quattro rettangoli metallici fermati con cinque bollette. Dorso rifatto in antica data, cucitura a 3 doppi cordoni infilati nel bordo dell'asse; capitelli in seta bianca e azzurra; taglio rustico. Stato di conservazione critico; decorazione molto abrasa; meglio conservato il piatto anteriore. Dorso restaurato in antica data.

Provenienza: Dal 1464 di Onofrio Gallarati, poi di Cesare Rovida; all'Ambrosiana dal 1606.

Bibliografia: CERUTI, 4, p. 644; CIPRIANI, p. 111. *(R 39 sup.)*
R *46 sup. cfr.* De Marinis, *3, n. 2552*

24. ALCHABITIUS. *Introductorium ad magisterium iudiciorum astrorum; Ad invenienda loca planetarum; Modus perspiciendi radios et aspectus planetarum,* ms. cart. metà del sec. XV [1444-49]. 247 x 165 mm.

Legatura coeva in cuoio marrone su assi di legno della stessa dimensione delle carte. Decorazione a secco: due cornici rettangolari concentriche, formate da filetti racchiudenti ferri singoli impressi in successione, dall'esterno rispettivamente dei fiori e delle crocette; nello specchio, delimitato da una larga fascia di filetti, una cornice rettangolare a crocette più piccole racchiude nello stretto e lungo spazio centrale una fascia di fiorellini: il progressivo decrescere nella dimensione dei

Fig. 11. Cicero, Marcus Tullius. *De senectute*, ms. metà sec. XV (n. 23)

ferri crea quasi un effetto prospettico. Tre fermagli, uno sul lato anteriore, uno alla testa e al piede, si agganciavano dal piatto anteriore al posteriore. Dorso rifatto, con cucitura a 3 nervi doppi (ora semirecisi), che s'infilano nel bordo; capitelli (a doppia anima) in canapa rustica ed in seta verde; taglio rustico. Il piatto anteriore è staccato; vecchio intervento di restauro al dorso.

Provenienza: Forse appartenuto agli Sforza; all'Ambrosiana dal 1603.
Bibliografia: CERUTI, 5, p. 28; CIPRIANI, p. 121.   (*S 54 sup.*)

25. CLAUDIANUS, Claudius. *Carmina*, ms. membr. metà del sec. XV. 288 x 205 mm.

Legatura coeva in marocchino marrone sui piatti di legno provvisti di unghiatura (ma il volume risulta pesantemente restaurato). Decorazione a secco: una cornice rettangolare impressa con un unico ferro in successione, un rombo con la biscia dei Visconti, racchiude un ampio decoro pure rettangolare, a cordami diritti e curvi e cerchietti, più stretto ai due lati e più alto alla testa e al piede; nello spazio centrale, di dimensioni molto modeste, ed ornato solo ai quattro angoli, è rimasta la traccia rotonda di una placca metallica, a lobi. Dorso a 4 doppi cordoni, rifatto; capitelli in seta gialla e marrone; taglio rustico. Restaurata nel 1976; decorazione appiattita.

Provenienza: A c. 2, al piede, uno stemma miniato (scudo blu con camicia argentea in campo rosso) con le lettere IO/ST ai due lati; pervenuto in Ambrosiana nel 1605.
Bibliografia: CERUTI, 5, pp. 34-5; CIPRIANI, p. 122.   (*S 66 sup.*)

26. PIUS II papa. *Libri IV de institutione principis ad Ladislaum Pannoniarum et Bohemiae regem.*, ms. membr. 2ª metà del sec. XV. 210 x 150 mm.

Legatura in marocchino marrone su assi di legno. Decorazione a secco: due cornici rettangolari concentriche formate da filetti racchiudenti ferri singoli impressi in successione; dall'esterno rispettivamente dei cordami che s'incrociano a serpentina, ed all'interno dei cordami a treccia; al centro, nello specchio rettangolare, un fregio composto da tre rombi, formati da cordami diritti e curvi e da cerchietti. Tre fermagli in seta rossa, uno sul lato anteriore, uno alla testa e al piede, erano fissati al piatto anteriore con due chiodini in ottone lavorato; sul piatto posteriore si sono conservati due tenoni in ottone, con l'*Agnus Dei*. Dorso a 3 doppi cordoni, rifatto; capitelli a doppia anima, rustici e marrone; taglio dorato. Pelle abrasa; meglio conservato il piatto posteriore.

Provenienza: Visconti e Sforza (a c. 2r nella cornice a bianchi girari medaglioni con simboli viscontei e sforzeschi, e stemma dei Visconti al piede); poi di M. A. Brugnoli (nota a c. iv).

Bibliografia: Ceruti, 5, p. 139; Malaguzzi Valeri, 3, pp. 118-22 e fig., Pellegrin, 1955, p. 61, 373; De Marinis, 3, n. 2556; Kristeller, 1, p. 315; Cipriani, p. 125 e tav. xix. (*T 7 sup.*)

27. CORNELIUS NEPOS. *Vitae illustrium Imperatorum a Baldo Martorello perstrinctae*, ms. membr. metà del sec. XV [c. 1456]. 205 x 150 mm.

Legatura coeva in cuoio su assi di legno; decorazione ad effetto damaschinato: su un fondo argenteo sono punteggiati con la tecnica del *criblé*, e dipinti in rosso ramato, dei fiori e delle volute ad imitazione di una stoffa operata. Tracce di tre fermagli, uno sul lato anteriore del taglio, uno alla testa e al piede, che si allacciavano dal piatto posteriore all'anteriore: in velluto rosso, erano fissati al piatto anteriore con due chiodini a forma di fiore; tenoni rettangolari, in ottone, sul posteriore. Dorso rifatto. Restaurata in data non recente; meglio conservato il piatto anteriore.

Provenienza: A c. 1 iniziale miniata con l'impresa della bilancia, con le iniziali BAL/MAR (Baldo Martorello, precettore dei duchi Galeazzo Maria e della sorella Ippolita).

Bibliografia: Ceruti, 5, p. 146; Kristeller, 1, p. 315; Cipriani, p. 126.
(*T 16 sup.*)

28. LUCIANUS Samosatensis. *De amicitia* [traduzione latina anonima] ms. membr. metà del sec. XV. 200 x 140 mm.

Legatura in cuoio marrone su assi di legno, della stessa dimensione delle carte. Decorazione a secco: due cornici rettangolari concentriche formate da filetti racchiudenti ferri singoli impressi in successione, dall'esterno rispettivamente dei cordami a torciglione ed all'interno dei cordami a treccia. Nello specchio rettangolare alla testa ed al piede due strisce, con il ferro dell'*Agnus Dei* ripetuto più volte. Al centro un fregio romboidale, formato dalla composizione di filetti diritti e curvi, e di cerchietti. Tracce di un fermaglio in seta rossa, fissato con un chiodino, che si allacciava dal piatto anteriore al posteriore. Dorso a 3 doppi cordoni, rifatto; capitelli in seta rosa e azzurra; taglio rustico. Restaurata; meglio conservata la decorazione sul piatto anteriore.

Provenienza: Visconti (a c. 2r, al piede, putti e insegne viscontee fra le lettere I/V; due stemmi gentilizi, uno con torre a due merli su scudo d'oro e verde, l'altro scudo argenteo con tralci di vite). Acquistato nel 1824.

Bibliografia: Ceruti, 5, pp. 159-60; Kristeller, 1, p. 343; Cipriani, p. 127. (*T 39 sup.*)

29. BIGLIA, Andrea. *Historia Mediolanensis.*, ms. membr. 2ª metà del sec. XV. 210 x 150 mm.

Legatura coeva in marocchino marrone su assi di legno provviste di unghiatura (ma il volume è stato restaurato). Decorazione a secco: sui piatti una cornice rettangolare a ovuli incrociati a catena, sottolineata da filetti; uno spazio vuoto, decorato con bei rosoni formati dalla composizione di piccoli ferri (si alternano rombi con i lati concavi, e rosette a otto petali); infine, all'interno, una seconda cornice di cordami incrociati a serpentina. Nello specchio centrale, decorato alla testa e al piede con il ferro dell'*Agnus Dei* ripetuto tre volte, un fregio longitudinale formato dalla composizione dei soliti rombetti con i lati concavi. Grosso fermaglio in ottone, allacciato dal piatto posteriore all'anteriore (in origine i fermagli erano tre, sono rimaste le placche di metallo sul piatto posteriore). Dorso a 4 cordoni, rifatto; capitelli rifatti; taglio rustico, con la scritta a penna sulla parte inferiore: MLI. *de Vicecomitum.*

Forse la più nota delle legature viscontee dell'Ambrosiana, pubblicata per la prima volta dal Gottlieb nel 1928; presenta, per la singolare decorazione a rosoni, forti attinenze con una legatura conservata in Ambrosiana, quella del Cicerone segnato ms. R 39 sup. (n. 22 di quella lista) e con altre. Dei ferri che si notano su questa legatura, si può dire che ci troviamo di fronte a motivi molto comuni nelle legature lombarde di età viscontea: forse il meno frequente è quello a intreccio che forma la cornice esterna; gli altri, l'*Agnus Dei*, il fiore a 8 petali e il piccolo rombo dai lati concavi, li abbiamo incontrati spesso, contrariamente a quel che sembrava a Fritz Juntke. Pesantemente restaurata nel 1968.

Provenienza: A c. 2r iniziale a fogliame su oro, con il ritratto di Gian Galeazzo Visconti; alla c. 2v altra iniziale dorata su fondo a colori, con il ritratto di Filippo Maria Visconti; appartenuto a Girolamo Varadei, poi a Jean Grolier (nota di possesso all'interno del piatto posteriore), ed infine al conte Pertusati; acquistato dall'Ambrosiana nel 1824.

Bibliografia: CERUTI, 5, pp. 160-1; GOTTLIEB, p. 73; JUNTKE, pp. 380-2; DE MARINIS, 3, n. 2574 bis; KRISTELLER, 1, p. 315; CIPRIANI, p. 127.

(*T 42 sup.*)

30. PHILELPHUS, Franciscus. *Orationes in Cosmum Medicem ad exules optimates Florentinos* [e altri testi], ms. membr. sec. XV. [1437-1438]. 210 x 150 mm. (Fig. 12)

Legatura coeva in vitellino marrone su piatti di cartone. Decorazione a secco, di evidente influsso francese: sui piatti due cornici rettangolari concentriche formate da filetti racchiudenti ferri singoli impressi in successione, dall'esterno rispettivamente un ferro rettangolare con un

Fig. 12. Philelphus, Franciscus. *Orationes in Cosmum Medicem*, ms. 1ᵃ metà sec. XV, 1437-38 (n. 30)

rametto fiorito, e all'interno un ferro con la rosetta quadrilobata; nello specchio cinque cornici verticali, disposte simmetricamente, dal centro un ferro con l'invocazione IHS sormontata da una corona, emblema di Filippo Maria Visconti (1392-1447), poi ai due lati un fiore a calice (per De Marinis forse un garofano), ed infine all'esterno l'*Agnus Dei*. Tracce di quattro bindelle in pelle allumata bianca. Dorso liscio, cucito su canapa; capitelli in seta azzurra e rossa; taglio rustico.

Provenienza: *Ex libris* di un fra Bartolomeo da Saronno dell'Ordine dei Minori.

Bibliografia: CERUTI, 5, pp. 242-3; DE MARINIS, 3, n. 2577 bis; KRISTELLER, 1, p. 315. *(V 10 sup.)*

31. ANTONIO, santo. *De peccatis in generali (Summa de virtutibus et vitiis)*, ms. cart. sec. XV [c. 1460]. 370 x 245 mm. (Fig. 13)

Legatura coeva, in marocchino marrone rossiccio su assi di legno. Decorazione a secco: due cornici rettangolari concentriche formate da filetti racchiudenti ferri singoli impressi in successione, quella esterna un ferro con dei rombi racchiudenti un fiore a quattro petali, l'altra con un piccolo rombo racchiudente un cerchio entro cui è un rosetta; lo specchio rettangolare è decorato in alto e in basso da due file di ferri, particolare quella con la figura di un vescovo (S. Ambrogio?); nell'altra striscia si alternano aquile volte verso sinistra, e la biscia viscontea. Al centro un fregio a forma di croce, formato dalla composizione di piccoli rombi con i lati concavi e cerchietti; piccoli fregi con rombi e cerchietti si alternano anche nello spazio vuoto che corre intorno ai piatti. Due fermagli, rifatti, si allacciano dal piatto posteriore all'anteriore. Dorso a 5 doppi cordoni, rifatti; capitelli rifatti; taglio rustico. Pesantemente restaurata.

Provenienza: Eredi di Francesco Ciceri, all'Ambrosiana dal 1603.

Bibliografia: CERUTI, 1, pp. 102-3; CIPRIANI, p. 155. *(A 191 inf.)*

32. BENVENUTO da Imola. *Cronica a principio mundi usque ad adventum Christi*, ms. membr. fine del sec. XV. 440 x 270 mm.

Legatura coeva in vitello rovesciato bianco, su assi; la decorazione è costituita da applicazioni metalliche agli angoli ed al centro dei piatti: al centro un rosone in ottone sbalzato, con la IHS di S. Bernardino, e tutt'intorno l'*Agnus Dei* (si è conservato solo quello del piatto posteriore); gli angoli hanno la stessa IHS e lunghi petali laceolati con un trifoglio a traforo. Dorso in pelle, rifatto.

Provenienza: Forse da S. Eustorgio; poi di Annibale da Corte fino al 1597, e di J. Donato Coppa (nota a c. 283).

Bibliografia: CERUTI, 1, pp. 168-9; CIPRIANI, p. 167. *(B 24 inf.)*

Fig. 13. Antonio, santo. *De peccatis in generali* (*Summa de virtutibus et vitiis*), ms. sec. XV, c. 1460 (n. 31)

33. CASSIODORUS, Flavius Magnus Aurelius senator. *Opus variarum libri XII* [Segue il *De anima* dello stesso autore], ms. membr. sec. XIII. 245 x 175 mm.

Legatura del sec. XV, in pelle scamosciata bianca su assi di legno, decorata a secco con l'aiuto di una punta metallica: sui due piatti sono stati incisi dei filetti formanti croci, rettangoli, triangoli. Tracce di tre fermagli in pelle allumata tinta in rosso, che si allacciavano dal piatto anteriore al posteriore; sul piatto posteriore sono rimaste le tracce dei tenoni, di forma lanceolata. Dorso a 3 doppi cordoni con rinforzi in pelle allumata tinta in rosso, rifatto.

Provenienza: Biblioteca di Gian Vincenzo Pinelli.

Bibliografia: Ceruti, 1, p. 200; Rivolta, n. 199; Cipriani, p. 177.

(*C 19 inf.*)

C 21 inf. cfr. De Marinis, *3, n. 2548*
C 121 inf. cfr. De Marinis, *3, n. 2571*

34. CASSIODORUS, Flavius Magnus Aurelius, senator. *Historia ecclesiastica tripartita*, ms. membr. metà del sec. XV. 315 x 224 mm.

Legatura coeva in marocchino marrone su assi di legno, della stessa dimensione delle carte; decorazione a secco: cornice rettangolare esterna formata da filetti racchiudenti un ferro rettangolare impresso in successione che, ripetuto, forma un motivo ad archetti gotici; all'interno lo spazio è decorato con due grandi rettangoli alla testa e al piede, uniti fra loro da due strisce di cordami incrociati (formati da ferri diritti e curvi), e riempiti di cordami diritti e curvi e da cerchietti. Al centro un esiguo spazio rettangolare, delimitato da filetti, racchiude un rombo pure formato da bordami a barretta ed a uncino e da cerchietti. Quattro fermagli in pelle rossa fermati sul piatto anteriore con due chiodini a forma di stella, tracce di tenoni metallici rettangolari sul piatto posteriore. Dorso liscio, rifatto; capitelli in seta rossa; taglio dorato e inciso. Restaurata; taglio sconnesso.

Provenienza: a c. 11 stemma con l'aquila imperiale, dei Visconti?

Bibliografia: Ceruti, 1, p. 277; Cipriani, p. 190. (*C 142 inf.*)

35. CAESAR, Gaius Julius. *De bello gallico* ms. membr. metà del sec. XV. 335 x 235 mm. (Fig. 14)

Legatura coeva in cuoio marrone (bazzana), su assi di legno della stessa dimensione delle carte. Decorazione a secco: tre cornici rettangolari concentriche formate da filetti racchiudenti ferri singoli impressi in successione; dall'esterno rispettivamente una cornice a cordami ricurvi che formano una treccia, una con un fiore (un melograno, secondo la Cipriani), e quella interna con l'*Agnus Dei*; nello spazio centrale una

Fig. 14. Caesar, Gaius Julius. *De bello Gallico*, ms. metà sec. XV (n. 35)

grande croce, formata dalla composizione di tanti rombetti con i lati concavi, che sulle quattro estremità formano dei rosoni; al centro, nel punto dell'incrocio delle braccia della croce, il ferro dell'*Agnus Dei*. Tracce di quattro fermagli fissati con dei chiodini sul piatto anteriore, e sul posteriore tracce di tenoni rettangolari. Sul piatto anteriore, in alto, vicino al dorso, è rimasto l'aggancio metallico per la catena che fissava il volume al pluteo. Dorso a 5 cordoni, rifatto; capitelli rustici; taglio rustico. Restaurata in vecchia data; pelle molto abrasa, meglio conservato il piatto posteriore.

Provenienza: Dalla biblioteca di Francesco Ciceri; acquistato per l'Ambrosiana nel 1603.

Bibliografia: CERUTI, 1, p. 368; CIPRIANI, pp. 208-9. (*C 304 inf.*)

36. BOETHIUS, Anicius Manlius Torquatus Severinus. *De consolatione philosophiae*, ms. membr. sec. XV *in.* [1400, cfr. c. 72]. 300 x 200 mm.

Legatura della metà del sec. XV, in marocchino marrone su assi di legno della stessa dimensione delle carte. Decorazione a secco: due cornici rettangolari concentriche, formate da filetti racchiudenti ferri singoli impressi in successione; dall'esterno, rispettivamente, un cordame ricurvo che forma un motivo a torciglione, ed all'interno dei cordami a treccia; nello spazio centrale, in alto e in basso, una striscia in cui il ferro dell'*Agnus Dei* si ripete per otto volte; poi una terza cornice, con due ampi rettangoli riempiti con cordami diritti e curvi e cerchietti, ed uniti ai lati da due strisce di cordami a treccia; al centro altre due strisce in cui si ripete, per otto volte, una piccolissima rosetta a otto petali, e che racchiudono un rombo formato da cordami a barretta e ricurvi. Tracce di quattro fermagli in seta rossa lavorata in oro, fissati con due chiodini sul piatto anteriore, tenoni triangolari sul posteriore; agli angoli dei due piatti tracce di borchie rotonde. Dorso rifatto; capitelli in seta bianca e azzurra; taglio rustico. Stato di conservazione discreto; meglio conservato il piatto posteriore.

Bibliografia: CERUTI, 1, p. 401; CIPRIANI, p. 216. (*D 40 inf.*)

37. IUSTINUS, Marcus Iunianus. *In Trogi Pompei historiam libri XLIIII*, ms. membr. sec. XV. 285 x 200 mm.

Legatura della 2ª metà del secolo, in pelle giallo senape, su assi di legno fornite di una stretta unghiatura. Decorazione a secco e dorata; molto particolare, perché crea un effetto tridimensionale, l'ampia cornice rettangolare che circonda i piatti, e che è formata dalla ripetizione di un ferro elicoidale in cui minute strisce di cordami si sovrappongono a girandola. Nello stretto spazio centrale una composizione di cordami a barrette diritte e curve, e cerchietti dorati. Quattro fermagli in seta rossa, fermati sul piatto anteriore con tre chiodini, mentre sul piatto posteriore si sono conservati i tenoni in ottone, di forma triangolare, con la scritta IHS dentro un sole radiante. Dorso a 4 cordoni, doppi; capitelli a tripla anima, in seta verde e rosa; taglio rustico. La pelle è così abrasa da sembrare scamosciata.

Bibliografia: Ceruti, 1, pp. 406-7; Cipriani, p. 217.   (*D 50 inf.*)

38. TERENTIUS AFER, Publius. *Comoediae cum proemiis...Francisci Petrarcae et Jacopini de Mantua*, ms. membr. 2ª metà del sec. XV [1477]. 320 x 230 mm.

Legatura coeva in cuoio marrone su assi di legno, fornite di una stretta unghiatura. Decorazione a secco: tre cornici rettangolari concentriche formate da filetti racchiudenti ferri singoli impressi in successione, dall'esterno rispettivamente dei cordami a torciglione, una cornice con un ferro a rombo racchiudente la biscia viscontea affiancata dalle iniziali B/M (non mi sembra G/M, come riporta il De Marinis), riferentisi a Bianca Maria Visconti moglie di Francesco Sforza, 1425-68; all'interno la terza cornice è formata da un piccolo ferro rotondo racchiudente una rosetta. Nell'ampio spazio centrale un fregio longitudinale, formato da tre rombi composti da cordami a barretta diritti e curvi, e da cerchietti. Quattro fermagli in pelle allumata tinta in rosso, fissati con due chiodini a stella sul piatto anteriore (si è conservata anche la punta in ottone con la scritta *ave*); sul piatto posteriore tenoni rettangolari, pure in ottone, lavorati a bassorilievo con il motivo dell'*Agnus Dei*. Dorso a 3 doppi cordoni in pelle allumata, che s'infilano nel bordo dei piatti; capitelli in seta bianca e azzurra; taglio rustico. Meglio conservato il piatto posteriore.

Provenienza: Già dei Visconti-Sforza (a c. 9 un angelo miniato sostiene lo stemma visconteo con le iniziali G/V, Giovanni Visconti).

Bibliografia: Ceruti, 1, pp. 700-01; Pellegrin, 1955, p. 371; De Marinis, 3, n. 1581 bis; Kristeller, 1, p. 289; Cipriani, p. 232.   (*E 7 inf.*)

39. CICERO, Marcus Tullius. *Rhetorica* [seguono altre opere dello stesso autore], ms. membr. 2ª metà del sec. XV. 395 x 270 mm. (Fig. 15)

Legatura coeva, in pelle di capra marrone su assi di legno provviste di unghiatura. Decorazione a secco: tre cornici rettangolari concentriche formate da filetti racchiudenti ferri singoli impressi in successione, dall'esterno rispettivamente una cornice con un ferro con una particolare palmetta, poi due cornici a losanghe differenti tra loro in qualche particolare, ma ugualmente con i lati concavi; nel centro un fregio longitudinale, formato da tre bei rosoni di losanghe con i lati concavi, racchiudenti un fiore a quattro petali (si tratta delle stesse

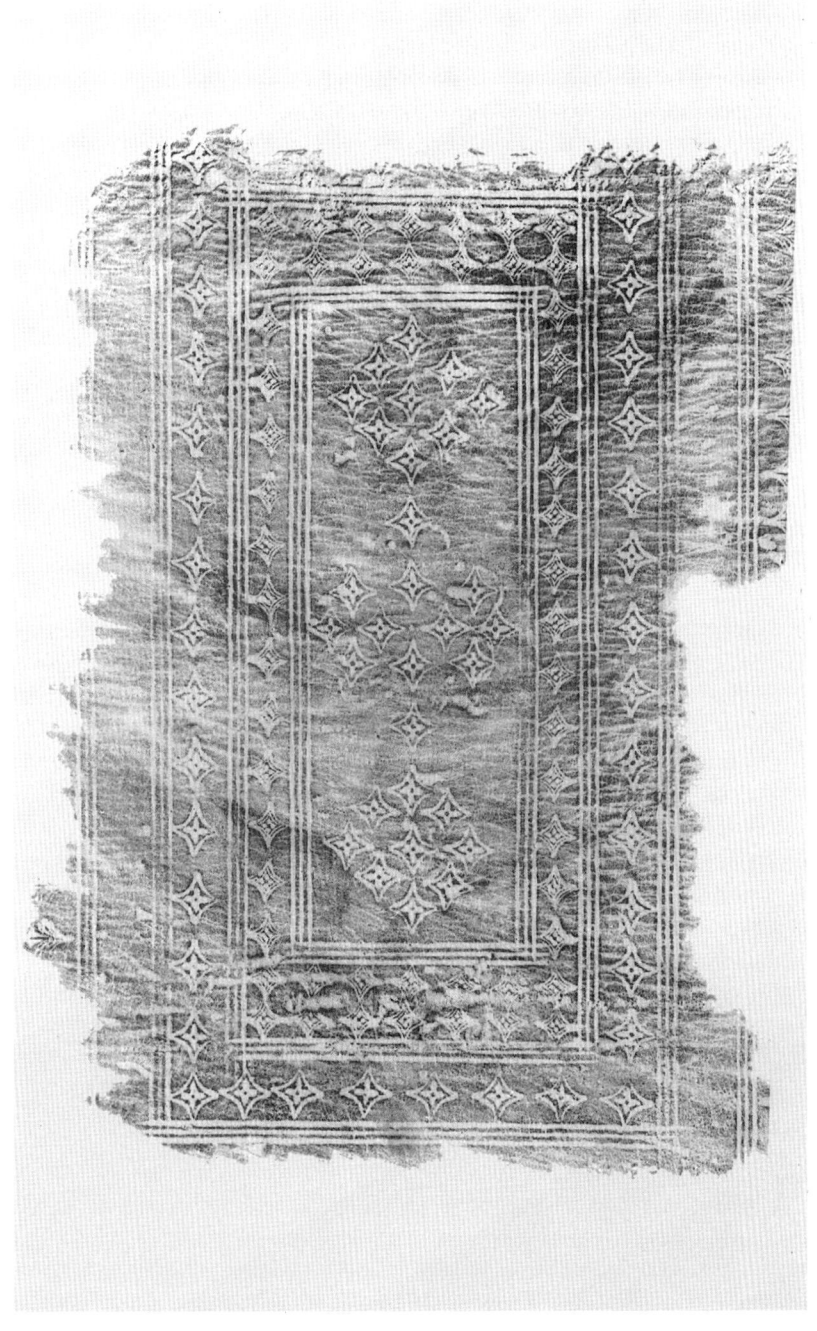

Fig. 15. Cicero, Marcus Tullius. *Rhetorica*, ms. 2ª metà sec. XV(n. 39)

losanghe della corniche mediana). Cartellino pergamenaceo inchiodato sul piatto posteriore, in alto; quattro fermagli in pelle allumata tinta in rosso, fermati con dei chiodini a stella sul piatto anteriore, si agganciano al piatto posteriore. Dorso a 4 doppi cordoni, ben conservato, con un motivo a filetti incrociati negli scomparti; capitelli in canapa rustica, ricoperti in seta rossa; taglio rustico. Pelle abrasa, in migliori condizioni il piatto posteriore.

Provenienza: Acquisito dagli eredi di Francesco Ciceri; all'Ambrosiana dal 1604.

Bibliografia: CERUTI, 1, pp. 704-5; MALAGUZZI VALERI, 4, pp. 141-2; CIPRIANI, pp. 232-33.   (*E 14 inf.*)

H 147 inf. cfr. De Marinis, *3, n. 2584*

40. PIUS II papa. *Epistulae*, ms. membr. sec. XV [1464, fine del testo]. 350 x 240 mm. (Fig. 16)

Legatura coeva in bazzana di montone su assi di legno della stessa dimensione delle carte. Decorazione a secco: sui piatti due cornici rettangolari concentriche, formate da filetti racchiudenti ferri singoli impressi in successione; dall'esterno rispettivamente una cornice di rombi con un fiore a 4 petali, ed una cornice di rombi racchiudenti la rosetta a 4 petali inclusa in un cerchio. Nell'ampio spazio rettangolare due strisce, in alto e in basso, in cui si alternano un'aquila rivolta verso sinistra, e la biscia viscontea racchiusa in un rombo. Al centro un ampio fregio longitudinale a forma di croce, formato dalla composizione di piccole losanghe con i lati concavi, e da cerchietti. Cartellino pergamenaceo inchiodato sul piatto posteriore; quattro fermagli in stoffa rossa, fermati con tre chiodini sul piatto anteriore, sul piatto posteriore tenoni in ottone, lavorati a traforo con un motivo a trifoglio. Dorso in cuoio, rifatto; taglio dorato. Carte di guardia pergamenacee incollate sui piatti. Lacerazioni sulla pelle.

Provenienza: Proprietà Giasone del Majno; acquistata nel 1709 da Giovanni Battista del Majno.

Bibliografia: CERUTI, 2, pp. 404-5; KRISTELLER, 1, p. 294; CIPRIANI, p. 257.   (*H 249 inf.*)

Fig. 16. Pius II, papa. *Epistulae*, ms. sec. XV, c. 1464 (n. 40)

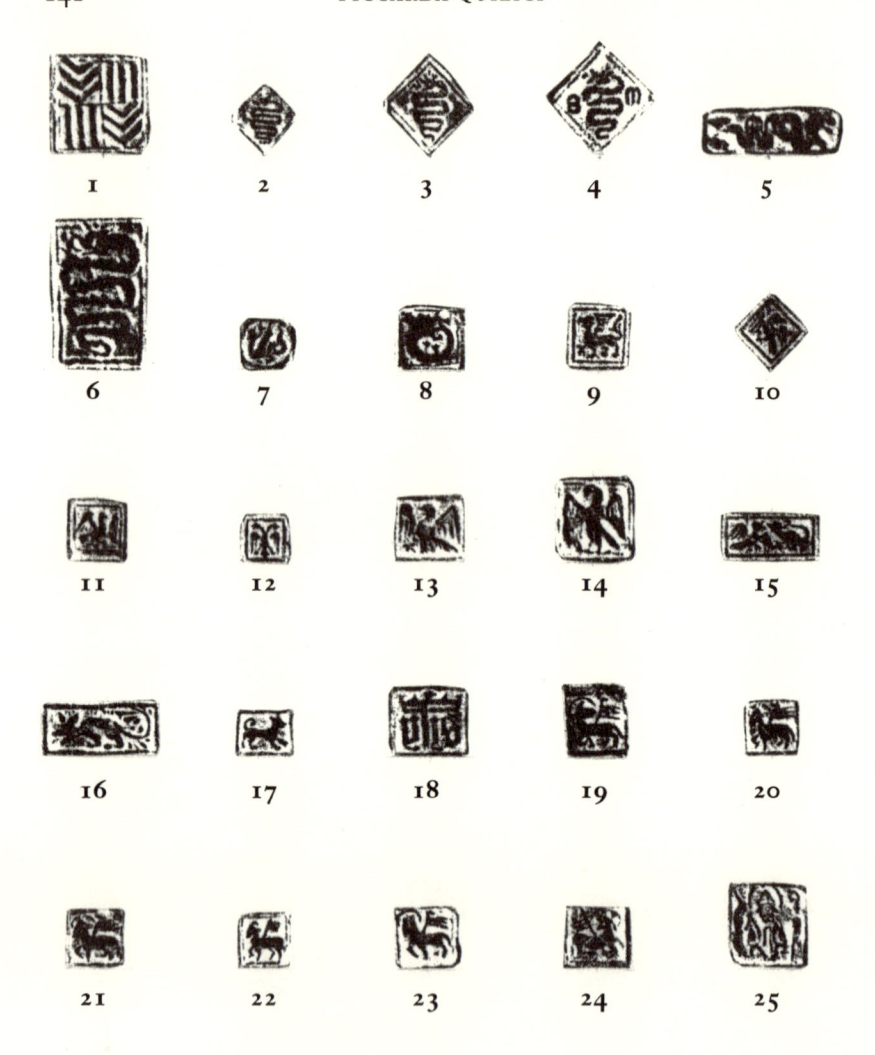

Ferri   1. Stemma del Piccolpasso, n. 2-3, 5-8, 10-13, 15-19.   2. Biscia viscontea, n. 6.   3. Biscia, n. 25, 31, 40.   4. Biscia, n. 21, 38.   5. Biscione visconteo, n. 2.   6. Biscione, n. 3.   7. Drago, n. 13.   8. Drago, n. 22.   9. Grifone, n. 1.   10. Aquila, n. 1.   11. Aquila, n. 10.   12. Aquila bicipite, n. 10.   13. Aquila, n. 13.   14. Altra aquila, n. 31, 40.   15. Gallo e volpe affrontati, n. 1.   16. Volpe, n. 13.   17. Cane, n. 13.   18. «IHS» coronato, n. 18, 30.   19. *Agnus Dei*, n. 2, 6, 29, 36.   20. *Agnus Dei*, n. 5, 7.   21. *Agnus Dei*, n. 11, 30.   22. *Agnus Dei*, n. 28.   23. *Agnus Dei*, n. 20.   24. *Agnus Dei*, n. 35.   25. S. Ambrogio, n. 31.

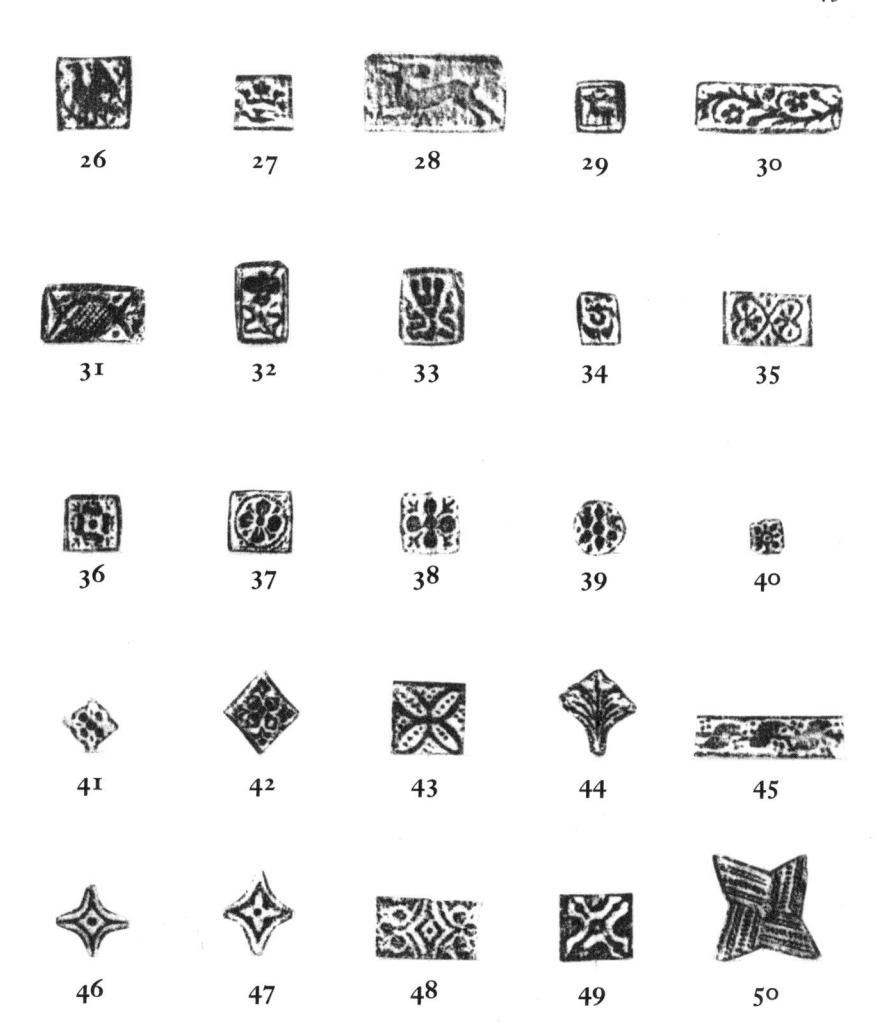

Ferri **26.** Colomba, n. 12. **27.** Colombina coronata, n. 4. **28.** Cerva, n. 8. **29.** Cervo, n. 22. **30.** Ramo fiorito, n. 2, 5, 7, 9, 11-12, 16, 18, 30. **31.** Pigna, n. 2. **32.** Viola, n. 7. **33.** Garofano, n. 30. **34.** Melograno, n. 35. **35.** Foglie cuoriformi, n. 14. **36.** Rosetta quadrilobata, n. 14. **37.** Rosetta quadrilobata nel cerchio, n. 20, 31, 40. **38.** Rosetta a contorno libero, n. 14. **39.** Altra rosetta, n. 38. **40.** Fiore a otto petali, n. 3, 29, 36. **41.** Fiore a otto petali, n. 10. **42.** Altro fiore, n. 4. **43.** Altro fiore, n. 12. **44.** Palmetta, n. 39. **45.** Nastro avvolto intorno a un ramo, n. 12. **46.** Rombo con i lati concavi, n. 5, 7, 31, 40. **47.** Altro rombo, n. 39. **48.** Rombo in cornice, n. 34. **49.** Crocetta, n. 24. **50.** Cordame elicoidale, n. 37.

BIBLIOGRAFIA

Biblioteca dell'Archivio Storico Civico e Trivulziana. *Mostra storica della legatura. Milano, 1953*. Catalogo a cura di Caterina Santoro. Milano, 1953.

Biblioteca Nazionale Braidense. *Manoscritti e libri miniati. Libri a stampa rari e figurati dei sec. XV-XVI. Legature artistiche. Autografi.* Catalogo a cura di Tommaso Gnoli, Domenico Bassi, e Paolo Nalli. Milano, Sperling & Kupfer, 1929.

Ceruti, Antonio. *Inventario Ceruti dei manoscritti della Biblioteca Ambrosiana*. Trezzano sul Naviglio (Milano), Editrice Etimar, 1979.

Cipriani, Renata. *Codici miniati dell'Ambrosiana. Contributo a un catalogo*, con 26 tavole fuori testo. Milano, Neri Pozza Editore, 1968.

De Marinis, Tammaro. *La legatura artistica in Italia nei secoli XV e XVI. Notizie ed elenchi*. Firenze, Alinari, 1960.

Gottlieb, Theodor. *Grolierstudien*, «Jahrbuch der Einbandkunst», Bd. 2, 1928, pp. 63-99, tav. 20.

Hobson, Anthony R. A. *Humanists and bookbinders. The origins and diffusion of humanistic bookbinding. 1459-1559*. Cambridge - New York - Port Chester - Melbourne - Sydney, Cambridge University Press, 1989.

Juntke, Fritz. *Ein Mailänder Einband des 15. Jahrhunderts*, «Gutenberg Jahrbuch», 1960, pp. 380-2.

Kristeller, Paul Oskar. *Iter Italicum. A finding list of uncatalogued or incompletely catalogued humanistic manuscripts of the Renaissance in Italian and other libraries*. London-Leiden, Warburg Inst. - E. J. Brill, 1963 -.

Magistretti, Marco. *Due inventari del duomo di Milano nel sec. XV*, «Archivio Storico Lombardo», 36, 1909, pp. 302-13.

Malaguzzi Valeri, Francesco. *La corte di Ludovico il Moro*. Milano, Hoepli, 1913-23.

Paredi, Angelo. *La biblioteca del Pizolpasso*. Milano, Editore Ulrico Hoepli, 1961.

Paredi, Angelo. *Storia dell'Ambrosiana*. Vicenza, Neri Pozza Editore, 1981.

Pellegrin, Elisabeth. *La bibliothèque des Visconti et des Sforza, ducs de Milan au XV siècle*. Paris, Service des publications du C.N.R.S., 1955 e *Supplément*, Firenze, Olschki, 1969.

RIVOLTA, Adolfo. *Catalogo dei codici pinelliani dell'Ambrosiana*. Con una presentazione di Giulio Bertoni. Milano, Tip. S. Giuseppe, 1933.

SABBADINI, Remigio. *Spogli ambrosiani latini*, «Studi Italiani di Filologia Classica», 11, 1903, pp. 377-83.

SCHMIDT-KÜNSEMÜLLER, Friedrich Adolph. *Die abendländischen romanischen Blindstempeleinbände*. Stuttgart, A. Hiersemann, 1985.

WIESER, Hans. *Zwei Bände aus dem Besitz Blanca Maria Sforzas*, «Biblos», 5, 1956, pp. 98-104.

Dennis E. Rhodes

SOME ENGLISH, WELSH, SCOTTISH AND IRISH BOOK-COLLECTORS IN ITALY, 1467-1850

From the late Middle Ages onwards, Englishmen have flocked to Italy in large numbers: firstly on pilgrimages to Rome and subsequently to the Holy Land; then as students to the universities of Padua, Bologna and Ferrara; often on various diplomatic missions, as the Venetian series of State Papers makes clear; and finally (as is most relevant to the present essay) gentlemen on the Grand Tour, which began in the seventeenth century and reached its heyday in the eighteenth.[1] But whereas a large dictionary could be compiled of such British travellers, it is not nearly so easy to compile lists of the books which they bought. It is my purpose here to bring together the notes which I have made over many years on books now in British and American collections which their owners acquired in Italy; and I stress that this is only a fraction of the whole, since it obviously represents only those books which have come to my notice. I include as 'bookcollectors' some people who are known to have acquired only one book, for it may be assumed that the same person also acquired others which have not come to light.

But first let us consider a number of celebrated literary names in British history, of men (are there to be no women on my list?) who certainly travelled to Italy and who must have picked up some books at least, but of whose libraries there is the scantiest information. Sir Thomas Hoby, who lived a very short life from 1530 to 1566 and was the first translator into English of Castiglione's *Courtier*, first published in 1561, was in Verona in July 1555. Nicolas Barker (*In Fair Verona*, 1972, pp. 7-8) has written: "He bought a copy of the first printed book about Verona, Sarayana's [sic for Sarayna's] *Le Historie e Fatti de Veronesi* (Verona 1542),

---

1. For the Grand Tour, and English travellers abroad in general, see John W. Stoye, *English Travellers Abroad, 1604-1667* (London, 1952, reprinted New York, 1968); Edward Chaney, *The Grand Tour and the Great Rebellion. Richard Lassels and 'The Voyage of Italy' in the seventeenth century*, Geneva, 1985. These books do not, of course, deal especially with the book-collecting activities of the travellers. See also Edward Chaney's excellent article, The Grand Tour and Beyond: British and American Travellers in Southern Italy 1545-1960, in: *Oxford, China and Italy. Writings in honour of Sir Harold Acton*. London, 1984, pp. 133-160, and the bibliography there cited. It is always possible that some books bought by some of the many travellers discussed by Dr Chaney and others may turn up in the future. John Lievsay, *The Englishman's Italian Books 1550-1700* (Philadelphia, 1969) does not mention a single book which is known to have been acquired in Italy.

while he was there and inscribed it with his name and motto, and the date". But where is this book now? Fynes Moryson (1566-1617?) the traveller, was in Italy from October 1593 to 1595, visiting Naples, Rome and Northern Italy, but where are any surviving books of his? Sir Henry Wotton (1568-1639), diplomatist and poet, was in 1592 in Rome, Naples, Genoa, Venice, Florence and Siena. On his second visit to Italy he settled in Venice, and later in Florence. He was Ambassador at Venice 1604-1612, 1616-1619 and 1621-1624. He became Provost of Eton on 26 July 1624. A friend of John Donne and later of Isaak Walton, Wotton left his manuscripts to Eton; but what of his printed books? John Donne (1573-1631), Dean of St Paul's, travelled abroad when a young man, but nothing is recorded in detail about his travels.[1] He is presumed to have been in Italy and Spain. Over two hundred of Donne's books have survived; they have been studied in detail by Sir Geoffrey Keynes, John Sparrow, and Donne's biographer R.C. Bald; but there is no indication in any of them that he bought them abroad.

John Milton (1608-1674) is also a difficult case. He was in Italy for a lengthy stay in 1638 and 1639: Genoa, Livorno, Pisa, Florence for two months, then Rome for two months, then Naples, back to Rome and Florence, and finally to Venice. It was from Venice that Milton sent home a consignment of books and music. This is all the D.N.B. says about his foreign acquisitions. Do we learn more from his most up-to-date biography by Parker?[2] The answer is that nowhere in all the 1,489 detailed pages of Parker can we point to a book which Milton is known to have acquired in Italy. One book shipped home from Venice may have been Joannes Bartholomaeus Marlianus, *Urbis Romae topographia* (Venice, 1588). A copy with the inscription 'Jo. Milton' is described in the Catalogue (1921, item 172) of the library of Wynne E. Baxter.[3] Then there is the case of a copy of Boiardo's *Orlando innamorato* (Venice, 1608) now in the University of Illinois Library which may or may not have been Milton's; it bears no marks of ownership apart from this faded inscription on a flyleaf: 'Bought at Venyce by Mr Francis Gherard for Daniel Oxenbridge and by hym sent to his good Freynd Mr. John Milton, in London,

---

1. It is a curious fact that R.C. Bald in his definitive life of Donne (Oxford, 1970) accepts without comment the old tradition that Donne travelled abroad between 1589 and 1591, hereby ignoring completely John Sparrow's article on 'The Dating of Donne's Travels' published in *A Garland for John Donne: 1631-1931*, ed. Theodore Spencer (Harvard U.P., Oxford U.P., 1931, pp. 121-151). Sparrow concluded that Donne could only have been on the Continent for any length of time between November 1594 and June 1596. Strangely, Bald does refer to this article, but in another context.

2. WILLIAM RILEY PARKER, *Milton. A biography*, Oxford, Clarendon Press, 1968, 2 vols.

3. Parker, p. 830.

p. ye Golden Lyon, Thomas Whiteing, Mr., ye 19th June, 1643, in Lyvorne.' Harris Fletcher rightly queried the allegation of Milton's ownership; the inscription has a spurious ring, and Daniel Oxenbridge, father of John, the Puritan divine, died on 24 August 1642.[1]

As Parker later remarks, any old book with the initials J. M. or I. M. written on its titlepage will almost inevitably, sooner or later, be considered by its owner or seller as once having been Milton's.[2] Nothing more can be said about Milton's Italian purchases at this stage.

Another uncertain case is that of Archbishop William Sancroft (1617-1693). Like his homonymous uncle before him, he was for a short time Master of Emmanuel College, Cambridge (1662-1664), and he gave many books to Emmanuel when he left Lambeth in 1691 for St. Paul's as Archbishop of Canterbury. He had travelled to Venice, Padua and Rome in 1657, and was in Rome when he heard of the Restoration in 1660.

Amongst Sancroft's books now at Emmanuel are a number which it is most likely he bought in Italy, including a very rare, if not unique, collection of tracts on the Battle of Lepanto and the war against the Turks (1572): these could hardly have been picked up elsewhere than at Venice. But Sancroft scarcely ever wrote his name in a book, let alone the date or place of acquisition.[3]

Two of the major bequests of antiquarian books now at Eton College have certain connections with book-collecting in Italy, but it seems that neither of the collectors in question ever went himself to that country. These are Richard Topham (1671-1730) and Anthony Morris Storer (1746-1799).

Richard Topham was Keeper of the Records in the Tower, who lived all his life at Windsor. He had been a pupil at Eton from about 1685 to 1689. He left just under 1,500 books to Eton, but although he died in 1730, the books did not arrive there until 1736. They include many classical texts, 'and a most remarkable collection of guide books to towns in Italy and France during the seventeenth and eighteenth centuries.' But although Robert Birley wrote that 'Topham bought books and drawings in Rome', it seems that his buying must have been done through agents, and

1. Parker, p. 861.
2. Parker, pp. 1121-3.
3. I am grateful to F. H. Stubbings, Fellow and former Librarian of Emmanuel College, Cambridge, for the suggestion that Sancroft most probably acquired in Italy a book on Trajan's column and another on the Raphael murals in the Vatican. He certainly owned these, as well as a few more volumes which contain ms. notes of earlier Italian ownership such as his copy of LEONE HEBREO, *Dialogi di amore*, Venice 1558, which had previously belonged to one Antonio del Cozzo; but there is no direct evidence of Sancroft's acquisition of any book in Italy. It is less likely that he bought such books as these in London.

that he never left England. Most of his books are in English bindings.

In the Storer collection is a copy of L. Annaeus Florus, *Rerum Romanarum Epitome*, printed 'in usum Delphini' at Paris 'apud Fredericum Leonard' in 1674. This book has a neatly written note on a flyleaf: "I bought this book at Rome in the year 1746 it formerly belong'd to the Queen of Sweden's Collection, as appears by the arms & was perhaps a present to her from the Editor." The book certainly has the arms of Queen Christina; but who wrote the note in 1746, the year of Storer's birth, is a mystery still unsolved. Above the note is an unexplained and indeed unreadable monogram.[1]

Other well-known figures in English literature about whose possible book-buying activities in Italy there is complete obscurity include the following: Izaak Walton (1593-1683) may have travelled to Italy, but it is not certain. Jonquil Bevan's article on books from Walton's library has no indication that any of them were acquired there.[2] In 1626 Walton married Ann Ken, a forebear of Thomas Ken (1637-1711), Bishop of Bath and Wells, who died at Longleat, leaving his library partly to Longleat and partly to Bath Abbey. He bequeathed 'to the Library at Bath all my French, Italian and Spanish books': they are now in Wells Cathedral Library. But where did he obtain them?[3] The Hon. Robert Boyle (1627-1691) was at Florence during the winter of 1641-2 to learn Italian. His library was dispersed, and nothing is recorded about Italian purchases.[4] Gilbert Burnet (1643-1715), Bishop of Salisbury, was in Italy in 1685. I have yet to locate a book which he bought there; but I have not extended my researches to Salisbury Cathedral Library. Nor do I have details about the books of Dr. Conyers Middleton (1683-1750), head librarian of the University Library at Cambridge from 1721 to 1750, who travelled in Italy in the 1720s and acquired manuscripts there.[5]

---

1. ROBERT BIRLEY, The Storer Collection in Eton College Library, *The Book Collector*, 5, 1956, pp. 115-126; ROBERT BIRLEY, *The History of Eton College Library* (1970), p. 38; K. JAMES MCCONNELL, ed., *Treasures of Eton* (1976), p. 36; see also *Treasures of Eton College Library. 550 years of collecting*. By Paul Quarrie. Ed. Michael F. Robinson. The Pierpont Morgan Library, New York; The Provost and Fellows of Eton College. Exhibited in New York, 26 September-25 November 1990.

2. JONQUIL BEVAN, Some Books from Izaak Walton's Library, *The Library*, September 1980, pp. 259-263. None of the books on this list is in Italian, and only one is by an Italian author (Paolo Sarpi), but in English translation.

3. E.H. PLUMPTRE, *Life of Thomas Ken*, second edition, London, 1980, II, pp. 294-301.

4. JOHN F. FULTON, *A Bibliography of the Honourable Robert Boyle*, second edition, Oxford, Clarendon Press, 1961, p. VI.

5. C.E. WRIGHT, Manuscripts of Italian provenance in the Harleian Collection in the British Museum, *Cultural Aspects of the Italian Renaissance. Essays in honour of Paul Oskar Kristeller*, ed. C. H. Clough, Manchester & New York, 1976, pp. 470-1.

Horace Walpole (1717-1797) travelled in Italy in 1739-41 with Thomas Gray (1716-1771), who had been his friend at Eton and Cambridge. Do we know of any books which either of them acquired there?

Henry Hare, third Baron Coleraine (1693-1749) and his father bequeathed a collection of books on Italian history and topography to Corpus Christi College, Oxford.[1] The influence of the Grand Tour is apparent in the bequest to Oriel College of Edward, fifth Baron Leigh (1742-1786), who became Chancellor of Oxford University.[2] I have not had an opportunity to investigate further these two collections, and there may well be scope for a future researcher to find amongst them some indication of purchases in Italy.[3]

William Beckford (1760-1844) the rich and eccentric author of *Vathek*, of Fonthill and later of Bath, left at his death one of the largest private libraries in the country, which sold for over £ 70,000 in 1883. He made two Grand Tours in Italy, one in 1780 and the other in 1782. What, if anything, is known about book purchases which he could have made there? The various biographies are silent on this point. Anthony Hobson has written two excellent articles, one on Beckford's library and the other on his binders. It is clear that no information has survived on possible book-purchases in Italy, for, as Mr Hobson writes: "Beckford's first purchases of rare books and manuscripts on a large scale were made in April 1783, when he was twenty-two, at the Reverend Thomas Croft's sale." In 1784 Beckford attended personally the La Vallière sale. Thus we conclude that in Italy he bought nothing.

What of the Romantics? We seem to know surprisingly little about their libraries. Perhaps Shelley and Keats had no libraries. Percy Bysshe

---

1. PAUL MORGAN, *Oxford Libraries outside the Bodleian. A guide.* Oxford, 1973, p. 38.
2. Morgan, op. cit., pp. 98-99.
3. For our complete ignorance of the identity of Italian bookdealers who supplied English customers (booksellers or private collectors), see my article 'Some notes on the import of books from Italy into England, 1628-1650', *Studi secenteschi*, VII (1966), 131-138, reprinted in the volume *Studies in Early Italian Printing*, London, The Pindar Press, 1982, pp. 319-326. If only the English had had the bibliographical instinct of the Sienese gentleman-scholar-book-collector Belisario Bulgarini (1539-1620), who in his tireless activity of book-buying in Italy almost always wrote the name of the bookseller, the day of purchase, and the price, into his purchases. Thereby he reveals to us a number of booksellers whose names have never been recorded in print. Some of these may not have had a regular shop, but merely a daily stall, rather like David's in Cambridge, or the 'bancherelle' of a present-day Italian piazza. (Of course, David's have two shops as well; but one wonders whether the stall in the market-place sells more books on a fine day than the indoor shop.) See my article 'Per la biblioteca di Belisario Bulgarini', reprinted in the volume *Studies in Early European Printing and Book Collecting*, Pindar Press, 1983, pp. 211-220. A major desideratum in the history of book-collecting in Italy is a complete recostruction of the library of Belisario Bulgarini. He only just missed knowing personally Sir Kenelm Digby. (See below, p. 258.)

Shelley (1792-1822) was not quite thirty when he was drowned off Livorno , and John Keats (1795-1821) was not yet twenty-six when he died of consumption in Rome on 23 February 1821, having been in Italy for only a few months. Walter Savage Landor (1775-1864) lived in Florence from 1821 to 1835 and again from 1858 until his death. I have not come across any books acquired by him in Italy before 1850. Lord Byron (1788-1824) was probably not actively interested in collecting books. Arthur Hugh Clough (1819-1861) who died in Florence, is really too late for my period, as are Alfred Lord Tennyson (1809-1892), Robert Browning (1812-1889) and Elizabeth Barrett Browning (1806-1861). Professor Brand has written: "Thomas Moore, shortly after arriving in Italy, bought a small edition of Ariosto and an Italian dictionary, and Anna Jameson made a point of reading only Italian while in Italy. Macaulay occupied himself with Boiardo, Scott with Neapolitan ballads, Keats with Alfieri. Coleridge bought books in Italy, and Southey had more than a hundred sent from Milan. Byron and Landor read widely in the literature of their adopted country."[1]

S. T. Coleridge (1772-1834) travelled in Europe from 1804 to 1806. The British Library has a great many books which belonged to him, disfigured with his marginalia, largely written in pencil; but having looked at those by Italian authors, Petrarch, Dante, Girolamo Ruscelli and one or two more, I find no indication of where Coleridge acquired them. As for Southey (1774-1843), he never visited Italy, so he must have ordered his books through an agent. Although I have found about twenty of Southey's books in the British Library, they were nearly all bought while he was living at Keswick.[2] Thus the Romantics do not play a large part, if indeed any part at all, in the story of British book-collectors in Italy.

I now intend to look at the lives and travels of about forty British visitors to Italy, some famous and others unknown, about whose book

---

1. C.P. BRAND, *Italy and the English Romantics*, Cambridge University Press, 1957, p. 18.
2. Coleridge and his family had occupied one of the houses at Keswick since 1800, and then Southey lived at Greta Hall from 1803 until his death. Books were presumably ordered from London dealers. In a letter to Daniel Stuart, dated 25 September, 1813, Coleridge wrote: "I am compelled to sell my library." The editor of his letters in 1895, Ernest Hartley Coleridge, commented in a footnote: "This could only have been carried out in part. A large portion of the books which Coleridge possessed at his death consisted of those which he had purchased during his travels in Germany in 1799, and in Italy in 1805-06." If some of these books are now in the British Library, I have not found one in which Coleridge noted the place or date of purchase. He was much more interested in writing his copious and untidy comments on the text, and his bibliographical references are usually vague and unidentifiable.

purchases there we have much more positive evidence; and I will take them as far as possible in chronological order, beginning with the one man who is known to have bought books in Italy on any scale during the fifteenth century.

I. *John Shirwood* (c. 1425-1493)

John Shirwood took his M.A. at Oxford in 1450, became an Apostolic Protonotary at Rome in 1476, and was Bishop of Durham from 1484 until his death in 1493. He is the first recorded Englishman to have acquired printed books in Italy on a systematic scale. Twenty-three incunabula bought by him in Rome between 1474 and 1487 have survived: all but one of them are now in Corpus Christi College, Oxford, the one exception being in Magdalen College. They are almost all inscribed with the exact date of purchase in Rome, but unfortunately no bookseller is named. There is no need to list all the books here, because they have been published twice: 1. P.S. ALLEN, Bishop Shirwood of Durham and his library, *English Historical Review*, XXV (1910), pp. 445-456. 2. D. E. RHODES, *A catalogue of incunabula in all the libraries of Oxford University outside the Bodleian* (Oxford, 1982), pp. XXVI-II, 422-3.

The books which Shirwood bought in Rome were printed as follows: Milan one, Florence two, Venice seven, Rome thirteen. Of the Roman books, nine were printed by Sweynheim and Pannartz.

II. *James Goldwell, Bishop of Norwich* (c. 1420-1499)

Fellow of All Souls, 1441. Of the 29 incunabula given or bequeathed by Goldwell to All Souls College, Oxford, none states specifically that he acquired it in Italy. But it is generally assumed that after his appointment as King's proctor at the papal court and his arrival in Rome in 1467, he bought printed books as well as manuscripts there. The only book which he annotated in detail is the Durandus of Mainz, 1459, which he bought in Hamburg in 1465.

See Sir EDMUND CRASTER, *The History of All Souls College Library*, ed. E.F. Jacob, London, Faber & Faber, 1971, p. 32; D.E. RHODES, *A Catalogue of Incunabula in all the Libraries of Oxford University outside the Bodleian*, Oxford, Clarendon Press, 1982, p. XXI and p. 406. I do not believe, as Craster claims, that as many as 35 incunabula owned by Goldwell are still in All Souls. It is a great pity that he did not tell us precisely where he acquired all his books.

III. *John Taylor* (c. 1470-1534)

An incunable in Cambridge University Library was bought by John Taylor in Ferrara in 1500. This is Antonio Roselli, *Monarchia*, Venice, Herman Liechtenstein, 23 June 1487 (Oates 1886). John Taylor had been a fellow-student at Ferrara with Edward Yonge, who became Master of the Rolls in 1508. Taylor followed Yonge in this office, and was executor to the wills of both Edward and John Yonge, to the latter in 1516. Like so many people of his age, John Taylor was also a cleric. On his return from Italy he held the livings of All Hallows the Great and S. Gabriel, Fenchurch St. in London, and those of Shottesbroke, Berkshire, Bishop's Hatfield in Hertfordshire, and Halifax in Yorkshire. He died in 1534.

See R. J. MITCHELL, English Students at Ferrara in the fifteenth century, *Italian Studies*, 1 (1937), pp. 75-82.

IV. *Henry (or Harry) Lambert*. fl. 1542

The identity of this Englishman is unknown to me, but on 10 January 1542 he was in Venice when he acquired: I diletteuoli dialogi, le facete epistole di Luciano...in volgare tradotte per M. Nicolo da Lonigo. Vinegia per Francesco Bindoni, & Mapheo Pasini compagni, January 1536. On the verso of the last leaf is written: Libro de me harigo lambert ingleze scripto alj 10 de jenaro 1542 in venegia.

British Library, 720. c. 15.

V. *Humphrey Lloyd* (c. 1527-21 August 1568)

A native of Denbigh, he took his M. A. at Brasenose College, Oxford, in 1551. He worked for Henry Fitzalan, Twelfth Earl of Arundel, and married Barbara, sister of John Lord Lumley, Arundel's son-in-law. Lloyd was in Italy with Arundel between the early spring of 1566 and the late spring of 1567. He spent much time collecting books for his brother-in-law, John Lord Lumley. Sixty-four volumes in the British Library (about twenty of these are manuscripts) and one in the Bodleian still bear his signature, but only two of them are known to have been bought in Italy:

1. COSIMO BARTOLI, *Del modo di misurare le distantie*. Venetia, Francesco Franceschi, 1564. 4°. British Library, 531. g. 5. Bought by Lloyd in Venice on 23 May 1566.

2. ALFONSO ADRIANO, pseud. [i.e. Aurelio Cicuta.] *Della disciplina*

militare libri III. Venetia, Lodouico Auanzo, 1566. 4°. British Library, 534. e. 1 (1). Bought by Lloyd in Venice on 24 May 1566.

See R. GERAINT GRUFFYDD, *Humphrey Llwyd of Denbigh: some documents and a catalogue*. Denbighshire Historical Society. Transactions, vol. 17 (1968), pp. 54-107. (See especially p. 83.)

VI. *John Dee* (1527-1608 or 1609)

One of the British Library's four copies of Jacopo Silvestri, Opus nouum vtilissimum pro cipharis describentibus interpretandisq., Romae, 1526, is inscribed: Joannes Dee 1563. Junij 10 Venetijs. (556. b. 20 (2).) This is Roberts and Watson no. 700.

Cf. Roberts and Watson, p. 9: Dee visited Padua, Venice and Urbino briefly in the summer of 1563. By September of that year he was in Bratislava, and he does not appear to have visited Italy again. This is the only book in Dee's catalogue which (as far as I can see) he acquired in Italy. Incidentally, the British Museum's Italian S.T.C. of 1958 is wrong in describing this copy as 'a variant dated 1626'. It is merely a copy of the 1526 edition in which the date has been tampered with by hand: this does not constitute a variant, because the new date '1626' is not entirely type-set. The 'C' of 'M.D.CXVI' is in ink.

Bibl.: John Dee's Library Catalogue. Edited by Julian Roberts & Andrew G. Watson. London, The Bibliographical Society, 1990.

VII. *Thomas Savile* (died of a fever in London, 12 January 1592/93)

Of York. Brother of Sir Henry Savile, founder of the Savilian Chairs at Oxford. Thomas was a Fellow of Merton College, Oxford, from 1580 until his untimely death at an early age. He was buried in the College Chapel. In 1589 he sent home a consignment of books from Italy. On 14 September 1589 Fellows of Merton were summoned after evening prayers to the vestry by the Vice-Warden to check these books. The short list of titles as published in the College Register gives only the briefest of titles, but most of these titles can be identified with books which are still on the shelves of Merton Library. However, most of these books have no manuscript notes explaining their provenance. They are in a uniform English binding on wooden boards. The only set of printed books which I have come across in Merton bearing Thomas Savile's name as owner is the big edition of the works of Aristotle in eleven volumes (bound in four), shelf-mark 121. A. 4-7, with the commentaries of Averroes, printed at Venice by the Giunta press between 1550 and 1552. With slight variation in the wording from one volume to another, they are inscribed: Thomas Sauile Procurator ac socius huius domus iuuenis moriens dono dedit Collegio. On the titlepage of vol. 1 is painted a bishop's coat of arms (not identified). It is most probable that Savile bought these books in Venice and had them sent home to Oxford in unbound sheets. Those which he bought specifically for the College were not inscribed, but the Aristotle was inscribed soon after his death because in his final illness he gave instructions for it to be given to the College Library.

Bibl.: *Registrum Annalium Collegii Mertonensis 1567-1603*, p. 248. (Oxford Historical Society. New Series. vol. xxiv. Edited by John M. Fletcher.)

Thanks are due to my friend John Burgass, Assistant Librarian of Merton College, for all his help during many visits there, on this and on other subjects of bibliographical investigation.

VIII. *Cardinal William Allen* (1532-16 October 1594)

William Allen and Robert Parsons arrived in Rome on November 4, 1585. Allen was created Cardinal on 7 August 1587. He left the following book to the English College, having presumably bought it in Rome when it was new:

NICHOLAS SANDERS, *De claue Dauid seu Regno Christi libri sex contra calumnias Acleri pro visibili Ecclesiae Monarchia.* Romae, in Aedibus Populi Romani, apud Georgium Ferrarium, 1588. 4°. The vellum binding bears William Allen's arms in gold. There is a manuscript shelfmark inside the front cover: F 11 41.

I do not know when the English College in Rome disposed of this or other books, but the British Museum bought it on 22 September 1849.
British Library, 3901. g. 27.

IX. *Sir William Dethick* (1542-1612)

Matriculated at St. John's College, Cambridge, in 1559. B.A. 1562-3. Rouge Croix pursuivant in 1567, York Herald in 1570, Garter King of Arms in 1586. He was knighted on 13 May 1603. 'Often travelled professionally', says Venn: we now know that he was in Naples on 10 April 1568, when he bought the following book:

LAURA TERRACINA, *Discorso sopra il principio di tutti i canti d'Orlando Furioso.* Vinegia, appresso Domenico Farri, 1561. 8°. The manuscript note on the titlepage is somewhat cropped, but reads: Emptū Napoli 10 Aprilis 1568. Guil. Dethick a/Rougecros/ British Library, 1073. f. 13.

X. *Sir Arthur Throckmorton* (1556/7-1626)

He arrived in Italy in May, 1581, and bought books in Padua in June, then others in Venice and later in Florence in September of the same year. His books were left to his old college, Magdalen College, Oxford, in 1626, and are still there. Among the annotated ones are:

1. ALESSANDRO PICCOLOMINI, *Della filosofia naturale*. Vinetia presso Giorgio de' Caualli, 1565. For this he paid 40s at Padua on 7 June 1581.

2. G. B. PIGNA, *Historia dei Principi di Este*. Ferrara, Francesco Rossi, 1570. Bought at Florence on 23 September 1581.

3. BERNARDINO SCARDEONI, *De antiquitate urbis Patauii*. Basle, apud Nicolaum Episcopium iuniorem, 1560. Bought at Florence on 24 September 1581.

Two other books were probably bought by Sir Arthur in Italy, but are not so inscribed:

LIVY, *Deche*. (Italian translation of Iacopo Nardi.) Venetia appresso i Giunti, 1575.

JOSEPHUS in Italian. Two volumes: Venetia per Baldassar Salviani, 1570. With the printer's device of Domenico Farri. Venetia appresso Francesco Lorenzini da Turino, 1560.

Bibl. A. L. ROWSE, *Ralegh and the Throckmortons* (London, 1962), pp. 89-91.

XI. *Inigo Jones* (1573-1652)

Inigo Jones made his principal visit to Italy in 1613 and the whole of 1614. He was at Vicenza on 23 September, 1613, at Naples on 1 May 1614, and at Venice on 30 July 1614. There is a list of forty-one Italian books published by Gotch, and it seems possible that Jones acquired all of these in Italy, although he does not say so. He probably acquired his copy of Palladio (Venice, 1601) in Venice or Vicenza.

The following two books were certainly acquired by him in Italy:

1. TORELLI SARAYNAE VERONENSIS *De origine et amplitudine ciuitatis Veronae*. Verona, 1540. fol. On the titlepage is written: Inigo Jones. Venetia 30 Juli 1614. 2^{li} 1/2

2. GIO. ANTONIO SUMMONTE, *Historia della città e Regno di Napoli*. 2 vols. Naples, 1602, 1603. 4°. 'Napoli 1 mayio 1614: 14 Carlini 2 voll.'

Bibl.: J. ALFRED GOTCH, *Inigo Jones* (London, Methuen, 1928): Appendix A. Inigo Jones's books at Worcester College, Oxford, pp. 248-252.

See J. H. WHITFIELD's review of J.W. Stoye, *English Travellers Abroad, 1604-1667* (London, 1952) in *Italian Studies*, VIII (1953), p. 91.

XII. *John Morris* (c. 1580-1658)

Inscriptions in some of John Morris's books now in the British Library show that he visited Paris, Madrid, Genoa, Padua, Venice and Rome. He was in Italy in 1610 and 1611. In Rome he met the English Catholic Nicholas Fitzherbert (1550-1612) evidently only a short time before the latter's death, and was given a copy of one of Fitzherbert's own books. Five books in the British Library were acquired by Morris in Italy, one a gift and the others presumably bought:

1. JACOPO SANNAZARO, *Opera*. Lyons, 1592. 'Johannes Mauritius Venetijs 1610.' 1213. a. 13 (1)

2. NICHOLAS FITZHERBERT, *Descriptio Academiae Oxoniensis*. Rome, 1602. 731. b. 7. 'Johannes Mauritius Donū [not 'Domi' as transcribed by Birrell] Authoris Romae 1611.'

3. GIO. PIETRO CAPRIANO BRESCIANO, *Della vera poetica libro vno*. Vinegia, 1555. 'Giouanni Morris In Vinegia. 1611.' 1087. c. 1 (1).

4. LODOVICO DOLCE, *Libri tre ne i quali si tratta delle diuerse sorti delle Gemme, che produce la Natura*. Venetia, 1565. 972. e. 3. 'Giouanni Morris, 1611. A Padoua.'

5. FABRITIO CAROSO, *Il Ballarino*. Venetia, 1581. 558*. c. 17. 'Giouanni Mauritio pretio 3s in Genoua.'

Bibl. T. A. BIRRELL, *The Library of John Morris*. London, The British Library, 1976.

XIII. *Sir Kenelm Digby* (1603-1665)

Sir Kenelm Digby was in Italy in 1620 and again after 1640. As Petersson writes: 'In Florence and other cities, he spent much of his time enlarging his collections of books and cooking recipes, and his knowledge of art and sciences as well. In Siena he was made a member of a learned society, the Accademia dei Filomati, before which he delivered two very ornate, very learned, very obscure orations on secret modes of writing among the ancients.' He only missed by a year or two meeting the Sienese bibliophile and scholar Belisario Bulgarini (1539-1620) in Siena, and seems to have made a special effort to collect works by this author. The British Library volume 630.h.19 contains three works by Bulgarini, dated respectively 1602, 1608 and 1616, and all printed in Siena. It has Digby's name on the first titlepage, and a price, 'pret. 6 reals. 4 crowns'. Then there is Bulgarini's *Alcune considerationi* on Dante, Siena 1583, of which the copy now in the Bodleian belonged to Digby. But he was not a careful or precise annotator of his purchases, and did not normally write in them the place where he had acquired them. He gave most of his manuscripts to Bodley in 1634, and a number of books to Harvard, all but one of which were burned in a fire in 1764. Anyone attempting to reconstruct Digby's library, especially in the British Library, seems doomed to failure, or at least to considerable disappointment. At least one book which belonged to him is now missing from the shelves in the British Library; and even more aggravating, a typescript list of books from his library now in the British Museum, compiled in 1955, has been missing for the past five or six years. Who compiled it, and how this was achieved, and how many titles it contained, is now unknown.

See JOHN F. FULTON, M. D., *Sir Kenelm Digby. Writer, bibliophile and protagonist of William Harvey*, Peter & Katharine Oliver, New York, 1937. The section 'Bibliophile', pp. 39-55, does not mention any books acquired by Digby in Italy. D. E. RHODES, 'Sir Kenelm Digby and Siena', *British Museum Quarterly*, XXI, no. 3 (1958), pp. 61-63; reprinted in the volume *Studies in Early European Printing and Book Collecting*, London, The Pindar Press, 1983, pp. 161-2. R.T. PETERSSON, *Sir Kenelm Digby, the ornament of England, 1603-1665*, London, Jonathan Cape, 1956, p. 54.

XIV. *John Bargrave* (c. 1610-1680)

Born in Kent about 1610, he became a Fellow of Peterhouse, Cambridge, from which he was ejected in 1643. In 1646 and 1647 he was in Italy, and was again in Rome in 1650, 1655 and 1659-60. In 1662 he was made a canon of Canterbury, where he died on 11 May 1680. His will in Canterbury Cathedral, dated 29 April 1676 and proved 28 May 1600, shows that he left his cabinet of medals to Canterbury Cathedral and a few books to the library of Peterhouse. These included "two volumes of Matthiolus on Dioscorides in Italian – a rare peece, presented formerly by the States of Venice to the King of England's eminent imbassador Sir Henry Wootton". This is the edition printed at Venice in 1604. The Peterhouse copy, shown to Canon James Craigie Robertson for his book of 1867, contains copious notes by various members of the Bargrave family. John Bargrave also left to Peterhouse "an hundred thirty-three sheets of the cutts in print of Trajan's Pillar, together with the small treatise that explaineth them. They cost me four pistolls at Roome, and are now more hard to be gott."

Bibl.: Pope Alexander the Seventh and the College of Cardinals. By John Bargrave, D.D. Canon of Canterbury [1662-1680]. *With a catalogue of Dr. Bargrave's Museum*. Edited by James Craigie Robertson, Canon of Canterbury. Printed for the Camden Society, 1867. Cf. pp. XVIII-XIX.
Article on John Bargrave in D N.B. by Richard Garnett.

XV. *Henry Bennet, Earl of Arlington* (1618-1685)

The British Library has a tract-volume, bought by the British Museum on 7 January, 1869. Lord Arlington's coat of arms is impressed on the binding. It contains seven tracts (one manuscript and six printed), all on the subject of the notorious quarrel between Pope Paul V and the Republic of Venice in 1605-06, which ended in the excommunication of the Serenissima. There are various ms. notes written inside the volume, such as:

'The Earl of Arlington was employed on many foreign missions K. G. &c. &c. He was one of the Cabinet Council known by the name of the *Cabal*, which word was formed of the Initials of the several names or Titles composing the Council – L^{ds} Clifford, Ashley, D. of Buckingham, Lds Arlington and Lauderdale. Collected by Ld Arlington at Venice.'

Later: 'This collection was evidently made by Lord Arlington at Venice & many of the pieces at this period could not be obtained at any price.'

Lord Arlington was in Rome throughout 1645, but must at some unspecified date, probably during the same year, have also visited Venice. He may have been a Catholic all his life, but this is uncertain.

Bibl.: VIOLET BARBOUR, *Henry Bennet, Earl of Arlington, Secretary of State to Charles II*, Washington, 1914. D. E. RHODES, Roberto Meietti e alcuni documenti della controversia fra Papa Paolo V e Venezia, *Studi secenteschi*, I (1960), 165-174, reprinted in *Studies in Early Italian Printing*, London, Pindar Press, 1982, 302-311.

XVI. *John Evelyn the Diarist* (1620-1706)

John Evelyn was born at Wotton House, near Dorking, Surrey, on 31 October 1620, and educated at Balliol College, Oxford. A man of wealth, he spent some years abroad. He was in Italy from October

1644 to May 1646. In 1652 he made his home at Sayes Court, Deptford. He died at Wotton on 27 February 1706.

Although Evelyn amassed a large library, he was not a methodical, neat or very informative annotator of his books. He usually wrote his motto in them: *Omnia Explorate, Meliora Retinete*; but rarely the place or exact date of purchase. His books were predominantly English, but many were French. He acquired a fair number of books in Paris, and a few at Geneva; many more were donations to him. In 1970 the British Library purchased over a hundred of Evelyn's books, and a quick check through these has revealed only four which he bought in Italy:

1. ANTONIO ZANTANI (editor), *Primorum XII Caesarum verissimae imagines*. Romae, apud Iacobum Mascardum impensis Antonij Caranzani et Matthaei Greuterj, 1614. 'Ex collectione Euelyni R[omae?] 1644. Inscription partly mutilated. Eve. a. 108.

2. IO. BAPT. FERRARII SENENSIS, *De florum cultura libri IV*. Romae excudebat Stephanus Paulinus, 1633. A beautiful botanical book. 'E libris Euelyni emptus Romae 17 Mart. 1644.' Eve. a. 142.

3. GUIDO BENTIVOGLIO, Cardinal, *Historia di Fiandra*. Venetia, per Giunti, e Baba, 1645. 'E libris Euelynis emptus Venetijs 1645.'
Eve. b. 6.

4. GIOVANNI BATTISTA CASALIO, *De veteribus AEgyptiorum ritibus*. (*De veteribus Christianorum ritibus*.) Romae, ex Typographia Andree Phaei, 1644, 45. 'Catalogo Euelyni Inscriptus. Romae. 4°. Aprilis 1645'. pret.: 19 Julios. Eve. a. 108.

It is interesting to note that the three books acquired by Evelyn in Rome were all printed there; and likewise the one book acquired by him in Venice in 1645 had only just come off the press in that city. Evelyn did not collect Italian literature as such. These four books show his interest in botany and history. Before acquiring the above-named books, the British Museum already owned Evelyn's copy of Ioannes Henricus a Pflaumern, *Mercurius Italicus*, printed at Lyons by Pierre Anard in 1628, which he bought in Rome on 14 November 1644. This is inscribed: Ex libris J Euelyni emptus Romae 14. ixbris. 1644. *Omnia Explorate Meliora Retinete*. Pret: 4: Jul. British Library, C. 97. a. 22.

This is so far the only book known to me to have been bought by Evelyn in Italy which was printed outside Italy. On 11 November 1644 Evelyn bought in Rome a copy of Alessandro Donati, *Roma vetus ac recens*, Roma, ex Typographia Manelphi Manelphij, 1639. He wrote in it his usual half-motto '*Meliora Retinete*'. This copy was offered by Bernard

Quaritch, Catalogue 1130, 1990, no. 135. On 28 March 1645 Evelyn bought in Rome a copy of the poems of Pope Urban VIII, printed at the Jesuit Press, 'Typis Vaticanis', in Rome in 1631. This copy was recently acquired by the Library of Eton College.

Bibl.: J. EVELYN, *The Diary*, ed. E.S. de Beer, II (1955), p. 214, n.1.

XVII. *Sir Thomas Isham* (1657-1681)

Third Baronet. Of Lamport Hall, near Northampton. He travelled with his cousin and tutor, Rev. Zacheus Isham. They were in Italy from December 1676 to May 1678, staying in Venice in February and March, 1677, and spending the last ten months in Rome and Frascati. Sir Thomas was primarily a collector of pictures, but also bought some books, including the anti-papal works of Gregorio Leti. At Rome he bought G. P. BELLORI, *Vite dei pittori*, pt. 1 (no more published), Rome, 1672; and books at Lamport include: MARCO BOSCHINI, *Le ricche minere della pittura veneziana*, Venice, 1674; CARLO RIDOLFI, *Le maraviglie dell'arte*, Venice, 1648; GIORGIO VASARI, *Vite de' pittori*, etc., Bologna, 1647; G. B. MARINI, *La galeria del Cavalier Marino, distinta in pitture e sculture*, Venice, 1675. These books were all presumably bought either in Venice or Rome.

Bibl.: GERALD BURDON, Sir Thomas Isham. An English collector in Rome in 1677-8, *Italian Studies*, XV (1960), pp. 1-25 (especially at p. 18). H.A.N. HALLAM, Lamport Hall revisited. (Unfamiliar libraries. XII.) *The Book Collector*, Winter 1967, pp. 439-449.

XVIII. *John Barker* (1670)

A volume which the British Museum acquired in 1850 contains four plays:

1. G. F. SAVARO DI MILETO, *L'Anna Bolena*. Roma, Iacomo Fei d'And. F. Ad istanza di Bartolomeo Lupardi. 1667. 12°.

2. *Il Novello Giasone*. Dramma per musica. Roma, per il success. al Mascardi. Si vendono in Piazza Nauona da Bartolomeo Lupardi. 1671. 12°.

3. BATTISTA GUARINI, *Il Pastor Fido*. Venetia, appresso Gio. Battista Brigna, 1665. 12°.

4. GIACINTO ANDREA CICOGNINI, *La Forza del Fato*. Venetia [for Bartolomeo Lupardi in Rome?] c. 1670. 12°.

British Library, 11715. b. 57 (1-4)

Manuscript notes in the various plays read: 1. Roma, 29. Nov. 1670. J. Barker. 2. 2 Febraro 1671. di Sig.re Worley. J. B. 4. (cropped) Barker. Johis Barker 1 Julio.

The books were thus quite new when Barker bought them. I have not identified him. Who was Mr. Worley? An Italian would not have written 'di Sig.re Worley', but 'del Sig. Worley'. It is not clear whether Barker acquired this book from Worley, or vice versa; or whether it means that Barker gave it to Worley. Perhaps they were travelling companions together in Rome.

XIX. *Richard Mead* (1673-1754)

Richard Mead was born in Stepney on 11 August 1673, and at the age of sixteen went to the Universities of Utrecht and Leyden. In 1693 he made a tour of Italy and took a degree at Padua. On his return to England he set up in practice in Stepney, becoming Physician to St. Thomas's Hospital and Fellow of the Royal Society in 1703. He then took his M. D. at Oxford in 1707, and was a Fellow of the College of Physicians in 1716. He built up a most lucrative practice and spent his money freely. He acquired many of his books, all of which were beautifully bound, in Rome. The books were all sold in a sale which began on 18 November 1754 and lasted 20 days. The catalogue lists 6827 items.

I have not yet come across any of these books, since none of them appears to be either in the British Library or the Royal College of Physicians of London. Only one book in the latter library bears a pencil note reading: J. Letherland Coll. Med. London, Socii 1754. E Bibliotheca Dris Mead. This is a copy of Guido de Cauliaco, Cyrurgia parua [and other works], Venice, Bonetus Locatellus for the Heirs of Octavianus Scotus, 27 January 1500/01; but this is not in a special binding, and the pencil note is not contemporary.

Bibl.: ALAIN BESSON, Private medical libraries, in: *Thornton's Medical Books, Libraries and Collectors*. Third edition, revised. Gower Publishing Co., Aldershot, Hants., 1990, pp. 278-9.

XX. *Joseph Smith* (1682-1770)

He first took up residence at Venice as a merchant in 1700, and was British Consul there from 1740 to 1760. He died and was buried in Venice. As a collector he was too omnivorous to be of great interest. The British Library, for instance, has many dozens of books containing his armorial bookplate, but no indication of when or from whom he acquired the books. His great friend and colleague, Giambattista Pasquali, the Venetian publisher and bookseller, was responsible for drawing up the massive catalogue *Bibliotheca Smithiana, seu Catalogus librorum D. Josephi Smithii Angli*, which he published in 1755. Pasquali probably supplied Smith with most of his Italian books; but Smith was also a close friend of the Marquis Giovanni Poleni of Padua, who knew a great deal about the collecting of rare books.

Frances Vivian has done much research on both Pasquali and Smith, but she has not yet given us details about booksellers who supplied Smith with books unless they all came through Pasquali.

Bibl.: FRANCES VIVIAN, *Il Console Smith mercante e collezionista*. (Traduzione di Marisa Padoan.) Vicenza, Neri Pozza Editore, 1971. Cf. ch. 5: 'Gli amici veneziani e la stamperia Pasquali'. This book has not been published in English.

We now await with interest the publication of a lecture given by Dr. Lotte Hellinga to the Bibliographical Society of London on 16 February 1993 under the title 'The Incunabula of Consul Joseph Smith: the beginning of the King's Library'. These lectures are normally published in *The Library*.

But no sooner had I written the above two sentences than I received a most pleasant surprise: on 15 March 1993 was published by the British Library a new book entitled *The Italian Book 1465-1800*. Studies presented to Dennis E. Rhodes on his 70th birthday, ed. Denis V. Reidy. In it (pp. 335-348) is the essay by LOTTE HELLINGA-QUERIDO, 'Notes on the Incunabula of Consul Joseph Smith. An exploration'.

XXI. *W. Wentworth* (1710)

ANGELO GABRIELLI, *Lettere di complimenti semplici*. Lucca, per i Marescandoli, 1700. 12°. British Library, 10910. aa. 5. Written inside front cover: W. Wentworth, Florence, 12 September 1710.

Could this be Sir William Wentworth, who allowed £ 40 a year for seven years to the painter and architect William Kent (1685-1748), who is known to have gone to Rome in 1710, the same year as the inscription in this book? The two may well have met in Florence or Rome in 1710. (See M. S. BRIGGS, *Men of Taste*, 1947, p. 146.)

XXII. *W. Wood* (1751)

Inscribed his name and the note of purchase 'Venice, July 24, 1751' in G. ALBRIZZI, *Forestiere illuminato intorno le cose più rare, e curiose, antiche, e moderne della città di Venezia*, Venezia, presso Giovambatista Albrizzi, 1740.

This copy later belonged to Dante Gabriel Rossetti, and was offered by Bernard Quaritch in Catalogue 1145 (1991), Italian Books XV-XVIII centuries, no. 110.

XXIII. *William Gordon* (1770)

Bought a copy of VENERONI, *Il Maestro Italiano*, Venezia, presso Lorenzo Baseggio, 1760, in Rome in 1770. Probably a student learning Italian, because he has quite a childish hand.   British Library, 1507/478.

XXIV. *Sir Horace Mann* (1701-1786)

Horace Mann, British Minister to Florence, first arrived there in 1738 and remained in the Tuscan capital until his death in 1786. He collected pictures and antiques, and although he may not have been an avid book-collector, he certainly owned a respectable library, and it was inevitable that in his position he would receive some valuable gifts, including books. Thus on 8 December 1746 his physician, Dr. Antonio Cocchi, inscribed for him a copy of the first Florence edition of Machiavelli's *Prince* (Firenze, Bernardo Giunta, 1532), bound with the *Discorsi* of 1531. This copy, bound in eighteenth-century vellum with marbled endpapers and containing Sir Horace Mann's book-label and mark (a left hand inside a horseshoe with Mann's name) was offered for sale for £32,000 in the Spring Short List of Bernard Quaritch Ltd., London, 1993, p. 21, no. 29.

In 1757 Mann reciprocated this gift by presenting Cocchi, on behalf of Walpole, with a copy of the poems of Thomas Gray. Mann was a friend and correspondent of Horace Walpole, Thomas Gray and Mrs. Piozzi. 'In 1745 Gray despatched his "good dear Mr. Mann" a heavy box of books.' (D.N.B.)

Bibl.: BRIAN MOLONEY, Horace Mann in Florence: 1738-86. *Italian Studies presented to E.R. Vincent on his retirement from the Chair of Italian at Cambridge*, ed. C.P. Brand, K. Foster, U. Limentani (Cambridge, W. Heffer & Sons, 1962), pp. 154-165.

XXV. *Thomas Brand* (1719-1804)

Educated at Felsted School and University of Glasgow. He was a wealthy man who owned a beautiful house with a large estate called The Hide, near Ingatestone, Essex. On 19 July 1748 he set out with his great friend Thomas Hollis (1720-1774) on a Continental tour. His second tour abroad was made alone between the autumn of 1750 and the summer of 1753. F.R.S. 3 June 1756, F.S.A. 31 March 1757. His portrait was drawn by Pozzi in Rome in 1752, and an engraving from it, made in 1807 by E. Bocquet, is used as a frontispiece in *Memoirs of Thomas Brand-Hollis Esq.*, London, 1808. He cannot be the same person as Sir Thomas Brand who had a bookplate dated 1735 (for whom see BERNARD QUARITCH, *Contributions towards a dictionary of English book-collectors*, London 1892-1921, reprinted 1969, p. 325). This Thomas Brand was never a knight, and in 1735 he was only sixteen years of age.

In 1751 Brand and Hollis were in Rome and Naples together, and later they visited Verona. When Hollis died on 1 January 1774, he left his property to Brand, who was also appointed executor to Hollis's will on 7 November 1767. Brand then took the name of Brand-Hollis, together with Hollis's arms.

Brand bought the following book from the Casa Serlupi in Rome on 22 May 1756, through Pagliarini the bookseller:

ALDUS MANUTIUS, *Vita di Cosimo de' Medici*, Bologna, Aldo Mannucci, 1586. This book was sold at auction in October 1938, and is now in Harvard University Library. It contains many manuscript notes, including a letter of Torquato Tasso. Then Brand owned a copy of OTTAVIO LIONI, *Ritratti di alcuni celebri pittori del secolo XVII*, Roma, Antonio de' Rossi, 1731, which later belonged to Kenneth Clark (Lord Clark of Saltwood): see BERNARD QUARITCH, *Italian books, XV-XVIII centuries*, Catalogue 1145 (1991), no. 133.

Bibl. *Memoirs of Thomas Brand-Hollis Esq.* London, 1808. *Memoirs of Thomas Hollis Esq.* London, 1780.

E. R. Vincent, An unpublished letter of Torquato Tasso and other mss. in an annotated copy of the 'Vita di Cosimo de' Medici' by Aldus Manutius, *Italian Studies*, III (1946), pp. 21-27.

XXVI. *Inglesina Davies* [not before 1771]

A copy of the first edition of CARLO BARBIERI, *Direzione pe' viaggiatori in Italia*, Bologna, Battista Sassi, 1771, with text in Italian and French, is inscribed:

Sig.ra Inglesina Davies. This appears in E.P. Goldschmidt, London, Catalogue 171, 1992, no. 224, with the comment: "This prettily bound handbook was the companion of an unknown 'Signorina Inglesina Davies' who must have accompanied her father on the Grand Tour."

At last we have found a woman to add to our list! But she is a very mysterious woman, and it would be fascinating to learn who she was. If the inscription really reads 'Sig.ra', this stands for 'Signora', not 'Signorina', and hence it was most probably an English lady travelling with her husband, not a young lady with her father. Again, 'Inglesina' is a Christian name which the present writer has never before encountered, and as it means 'little English woman', it could well be a name which the lady in question invented to disguise her real identity. We need to find out who these Davieses were.

XXVII. *Joseph Jekyll* (?) (1752?-1837) - identification uncertain

The British Library owns a curious printed poem with the following title: *A Rhapsody on Antique Rings written in Rome*. (Then a quotation from Juvenal, Satire VI, lines 156-7, about a famous diamond).

The book is a large quarto of eight leaves (the last blank) signed A B⁴, with pp. 14. It has no imprint or date, but the typography shows clearly that it was not printed in England. The most likely place for its printing is Rome. The paper has a watermark with a fleur de lis in a double circle, and the initials AMC. I know nothing about late eighteenth-century Italian watermarks.

Written on the titlepage are three helpful ms. notes, evidently all in different hands and in different ink. First there is the date '1780' written in heavy black ink below the words 'in Rome' of the title. Lower down, in less heavy ink, is written: Supposed to be by Thresham & Hippisly.

Although the British Library hazards no guess as to authorship, these two persons appear quite plausible as authors. Sir John Coxe Hippisley (1748-1825) was in Italy in 1779 and 1780, and in the latter year married his first wife in Rome. He was in Italy again between 1792 and 1796. Henry Tresham (1749?-1814), the Irish painter, was in Rome for quite a long residence between about 1775 and 1789. They may well have written the poem between them, and had it privately printed in Rome. But who was the Englishman who acquired the book in Rome probably in the same year 1780? His signature, written as the third ms. note on the titlepage in a very flowery eighteenth-century hand, is very difficult to read. It might be 'J. Tekell' or 'J. Jekell', or the initial of the Christian name might not be a J, but a T. But there are no known surnames nearer than Tickell and Jekyll. On the whole, I am inclined to read it as 'J. Jekell', and I suggest a possible identification with the politician Joseph Jekyll (1752?-1837), who took his M.A. at Christ Church in 1777 and is known to have been in

France in 1775, although he is not recorded as having ever been in Italy. Therefore such an identification is far from being a certainty.

XVIII. *Stearne (or Sterne) Tighe* (1787)

Probably a member of the old family of Tighe from Co., Wicklow, Ireland. The British Library has a sale catalogue of his 'prints, capital drawings, and elegant illustrated books', sold on Tuesday, March 24, 1800, and the eleven following days, by William Richardson, at no. 31, the Corner of Villiers-Street, in the Strand. But this catalogue consists almost exclusively of prints and drawings, with very few books, not including that named below. Tighe is not named except in manuscript: he is styled simply 'a Gentleman gone abroad'.

At Florence on 27 February 1787 he bought a copy of the two volume edition of the Laws of Sardinia and Piedmont, published at Turin in 1770. This is now British Library, 660. i. 5, 6.

XXIX. *Henry Swinburne* (1743-1803)

Traveller, born at Bristol on 8 July 1743. Studied in France, and then went to study art and antiquities in Turin, Genoa and Florence. In 1777 and 1778 he travelled with his family to Naples and Sicily. Author of *Travels in the two Sicilies, 1777-1778*, published in two volumes, 1783 and 1785. He died in Trinidad on 1 April 1803. His library was sold by Leigh & Sotheby in 1802. He bought a copy of DIODORUS SICULUS, *Della libraria historica, tradotta dal greco in latino... & nella nostra lingua da M. Francesco Baldelli*, Vinegia, 1574.[1]

The sale catalogue comprises 1586 items, very miscellaneous and not by any means specializing in Italian books. It is not possible to estimate how many of his books Swinburne acquired in Italy.

1. This book is entered as no. 412, 'Didoro (*sic*) Siculo... Vineg. ap. Giolito, 1547 (*sic* for 1574) on p. 15 of 'A Catalogue of the... valuable library... of Henry Swinburne... which will be sold by auction, by Leigh, Sotheby, & Son... on Monday, January 10, 1803, and seven following days'. This same book was sold again in London in 1991.

XXX. *Sylvester Douglas, Baron Glenbervie* (1743-1823)

Of Aberdeenshire. He gave up medicine for a political career. He married Lord North's daughter. He amassed a large library, for which he had an elaborate and beautiful bookplate. He was in Florence in August and September, 1815, and again in 1819. He was buying books in Rome in 1816. Examples are:

1. PAULUS OROSIUS, *Historiae adversus paganos*. Venice, Octavianus Scotus, 30 July 1483. Corpus Christi College, Oxford. Bookplate, but no note of purchase. (Rhodes 1276 a.)

2. G. PICO DELLA MIRANDOLA, *Opera*. Bologna, Benedictus Hectoris, 20 March 1496; 16 July 1495 [1496]. Queen's College, Oxford. Bought in Rome, January 1816. (Rhodes 1400 c.)

3. ANTONIO PERABO, *Valsei ossia l'Eroe Scozzese, Tragedia*. Parma, [1774?] Bought in Florence, August 1815.
British Library, 839. g. 42.

4. G. SACCO, *I passatempi d'una musa faceta*. Parma, 1693. Bought in Rome, 27 Jan. 1816. British Library, 11429. c. 55.

5. P. A. ROLLI, *Marziale*. Firenze, 1776. Bought in Rome, January 1816.
British Library, 1463. c. 10.

6. *Rime e prose*. Genova, 1797. Bought in Florence in 1819.
British Library, 12226. a. 25.

7. FLAVIUS JOSEPHUS, *De bello Judaico*. In Italian. Florence, Bartolomeo de' Libri, 6 July 1493. B.M.C. vi, 649-650. Bought at Florence in September 1815. British Library, IB. 27297.

8. In August, 1815, at Florence, a local archaeologist, Filippo Nesti, presented to Lord Glenbervie copies of two of his recent publications on fossilized bones. These are now in a tract-volume (T. *15) at the British Library.

Baron Glenbervie's purchases are sufficiently numerous as to suggest that he was permanently resident in Italy in those years.

XXXI. *Sir Richard Colt Hoare* (1758-1838)

Historian of Wiltshire who lived at Stourhead. 'In September 1785 he left England, passed through France and Italy to Naples, and, after exploring the classic ground in the vicinity of that city and Rome, returned by Genoa to the south of France. In 1788 he left England a second time, and devoted a considerable time to the exploration of Rome and Naples and their vicinity, visited Sicily, Malta and Gozo, Capri, Ischia and Elba, and returned to England in August 1791. In 1825 he presented to the British Museum a collection of books on the history and topography of Italy, of which he printed a catalogue in 1812.' (D.N.B.)

This catalogue is entitled: *A Catalogue of Books relating to the History and Topography of Italy, collected during the years 1786, 1787, 1789, 1790,* London, printed in only twelve copies by W. Bulmer and Co., Cleveland-Row, St. James's. Of these twelve copies the British Library now has two; and the second of these has the following note in Hoare's own handwriting: "Anxious to follow the liberal example of our gracious Monarch George the Fourth, of Sir George Beaumont Bart., of Rich.ᵈ Payne Knight Esqr, (tho' in a very humble degree) I do give unto the British Museum *this* my collection of Topography, made during a residence of five years abroad – and hoping that the more modern publications may be added to it hereafter." (Signed:)

Rich.ᵈ Colt Hoare. A.D. 1825.

Then there is a pencil note at the beginning reading: 'The books ticked off with pencil – received. The books marked with a x received Mar. 1828'. At the end, after the colophon, is written: 'The catalogue contains 1733 articles.' After this are 8 1/2 pages of manuscript addenda, listing some 112 further items. Thus by the munificence of Sir Richard Colt Hoare the British Library has a splendid collection of some 1850 books on Italian topography (one of the best in existence in any single library), all in a standard vellum binding. None of them, however, was annotated at the time of acquisition by Hoare, so that we cannot tell from which booksellers he bought any of his volumes.

XXXII. *John Woodlocke* (1790)

The British Library owns: *Breve istoria del primo principio del progresso della Religione Protestante raccolta dai migliori scrittori Protestanti per via d'interrogazione e di risposta.* (A short history of the first beginning and progress of the Protestant religion, etc.) Arezzo, Michele Bellotti, 1767.

This is a book of parallel texts in English and Italian. This copy is covered all over both titlepages with the most unsightly manuscript notes, including: Rᵗ Revᵈ John Woodlocke Conf.ʳ and Prof.ʳ of Divinity & c; Ancona April yᵉ 16th A. Dñi 1790. The same note is on p. 273, but dated April 14, 1790.

John Woodlocke is not recorded as an alumnus of either Oxford or Cambridge; nor does he appear to have published any books. Who was he, and why did he buy a book in an unacademic town such as Ancona? John Nicholas Woodlock was an Irish Catholic, who became a novice at

Callan (co. Kilkenny) in 1782. He was sent to Perugia as a cleric to begin studies there on 31 May 1783. After two years' logic, he moved to Ancona in 1785 and stayed there until 1794. At Ancona he had two years' philosophy and one of theology before promotion to *cursor* in 1788. *Defendens* as *cursor secundi anni*, 1789-90. On 9 April 1790 he was made lector after dispensation '*super anno*', presumably his third year as *cursor*. He remained at Ancona as lector of metaphysics (1790-1791), as *lector moralium* (1791-92) and lector of philosophy (1792-93). Declared bachelor by customary patent on 4 August 1792. Again *lector moralium* at Ancona from summer 1793 until permitted to return to Ireland on 22 January 1794.

The book which he acquired in 1790 is now British Library, 3938. aaa. 59.

Bibl.: HUGH FENNING, O. P., *Irish Friars in the Augustinian schools of Italy: 1698-1808*, Analecta Augustiniana, XLIV (1981), pp. 329-362: see p. 353.

I am very grateful to my colleague Mr. R.K. Browne for this reference.

XXXIII. *Th. P. Walter* (1792)

A copy of the comedies of Terence in Italian verse translation by Niccolò Fortiguerri, published at Venice by Simone Occhi in 1774, is inscribed: Th. P. Walter - Bought at Venice July 1792.

Nothing further seems to be recorded about him.

British Library, 1001. d. 15.

XXXIV. *John Carr* (1793)

In 1950 the British Museum Library bought a copy of GIROLAMO DONZELLINI, *Epistolae principum, Rerumpublicarum, ac sapientum virorum*, printed at Venice by Giordano Ziletti in 1574. Written on the titlepage in a small hand is the note: John Carr Florence Jan 5 1793, and below this what appears to be the price paid (possibly 'p'd 1ᵖ 4ⁱ').

It is not possible to identify this John Carr further.

XXXV. *George Frederick Nott* (1767-1841)

See article in D.N.B. Fellow of All Souls College, Oxford, 1788. He spent much time in Italy after 1817, where he purchased many pictures and books. His library, consisting of 12.500 volumes and many prints and pictures, was sold at Winchester between 11 and 25 January 1842. The British Library now owns a few dozens of his book, and it is clear that he obtained many of them in Italy, some as donations from their authors.

For example the following three books are all inscribed in the same hand: Al Chiarissimo Sig.ʳ D.ʳ Nott Salvadore Leonardi da Catania:

1. FRANCESCO AVOLIO, *Saggio sovra lo stato presente della poesia in Sicilia*. Siracusa, 1794.

2. SALVADORE SCUDERI, *Tragedie*. Catania, 1816.

3. GIUSEPPE LEONARDI, *Poema supra di lu vinu*. Catania, 1789. Perhaps he acquired these while on a visit to Sicily. One of them contains a mutilated example of his bookplate, which displays a dove of peace.

It is probable that in Milan he met the poet Vincenzo Monti (1754-1828), since one of the British Library's two copies of Monti's book *Saggio diviso in quattro parti dei molti e gravi errori trascorsi in tutte le edizioni del Convito di Dante* (Milano, 1823) is inscribed: Al Sigʳᵉ Dʳ Nott in attestato di stima V. Monti.

For further details about Nott and his library, including references to a few more books which he may well have acquired in Italy, see ROBERTO L. BRUNI, ROSARIA CAMPIONI and DIEGO ZANCANI, *Giulio Cesare Croce dall'Emilia all'Inghilterra* (Firenze, Leo S. Olschki, 1991) p. 29. Five works by Croce which Nott owned are listed here.

XXXVI. *Sir Mark Masterman Sykes*, M.P. (1771-1823)

Of Sledmere, Yorks. Matriculated from Brasenose College, Oxford, in 1788. In 1820 he retired owing to ill-health as M.P. for the City of York. We now know that in that same year he bought a book in Italy, but whether he went there in person or bought through agents is not clear. He possessed one of the finest private libraries in England. At least thirteen of his incunabula are now in the British Library, and three more are in Oxford college libraries. These contain his bookplate, but do not indicate where he acquired them.

At Eton College is a large-paper copy of the *Rime* of Petrarch, vol. 1 (Padova, Tipografia del Seminario, 1819) which has a piece of paper stuck into it, reading: 'I bought this Copy of Sʳ Brizzolara at Milan in 1820 and it was then esteemed one of the rarest modern Books in Italy.' Signed: Mark Masterman Sykes.

This Milanese bookseller was Carlo Brizzolara, who published a catalogue of books for sale in 1829.

XXXVII. *Hon. George Matthew Fortescue* (1791-1877)

M.P. Travelled in Europe and bought books widely. He purchased the following volume frome the Roman bookseller Mariano de Romanis in 1820: ULPIANUS, *Commentarioli in Olynthiacas, Philippicasque Demosthenis orationes*. Venetiis, in aedibus Aldi et Andreae Soceri, June 1527.

Bibl.: JEREMY M. POTTER, *Catalogue of the Travers Collection in the University of Sussex Library*, Brighton, 1990, p. 106, no. 174.

XXXVIII. *Alexander Glynn Campbell* (1814)

His armorial bookplate and inscription are in a copy of Juvenal, Venice, Aldus Manutius, 1501, offered by Patrick King (Catalogue 15: Printing in Venice 1501-1564, Stony Stratford, Bucks., 1991, no. 33). This inscription is dated: Rome, 1814.

Alexander Campbell, of Gatcombe House, Isle of Wight, married Jane Worsley in 1795. Cf. Franks Collection of bookplates, no. 4970.

XXXIX. *Alexander Thomson* (1798-1868)

A volume containing two works bound together, and containing the bookplate of Alexander Thomson, Florence, 1828, was offered for sale as no. 194 in E.P. Goldschmidt, Catalogue 171, London, 1992. The two works are:

GIROLAMO SAVONAROLA, *Prediche utilissime per la quadragesima*, Venice, Bernardino Benalio, 12 December 1517; and ROBERTO CARACCIOLO, *Prediche*, Venice, Giovanni Rosso da Vercelli, 11 August 1509.

Alexander Thomson was born on 21 June 1798 at Banchory House, near Aberdeen, and died there on 20 May 1868. He resided in Florence from 18 October 1827 to 19 March 1828. 'His valuable museum and noble library were bequeathed to the Free Church College, Aberdeen.'

Bibl.: Rev. GEORGE SMEATON, *Memoir of Alexander Thomson of Banchory*, Edinburgh, 1869.

XL. *George Cornwall Legh* (1834)

He bought in Rome in 1834 three works by Giovanni Paolo Lomazzi bound together, and printed in Milan respectively in 1585, 1590 and 1591. Cf. BERNARD QUARITCH, Catalogue 1145, *Italian Books XV-XVIII centuries* (1991), no. 48.

George Cornwall Legh was possibly a son of George John Legh (1787-1832) of High Legh, Cheshire, whose father's name was Henry Cornwall, and whose brother was Henry Cornwall Legh (1775-1795, died of wounds in Jamaica). The Franks Collection includes a bookplate for

Henry Cornwall Legh, but none for George, although the volume bought in Rome contains a bookplate.

XLI. *William Hodge Mill* (1792-1853)

Scholar of Trinity College, Cambridge, 1811. Fellow 1814, M.A. 1816. Ordained Deacon 1817. Priest 1818. First Principal of Bishop's College, Calcutta, 1820-38. Canon of Ely, 1848-53. Regius Professor of Hebrew, Cambridge, 1848-53. Well known as a Sanskrit and Arabic scholar. Died Christmas Day, 1853, and was buried in Ely Cathedral. Probably visited Florence on his way back from India in 1838, since he bought the following book at Florence on 30 October 1838:

Acta apocrypha S. Romuli cum notis variorum ex XII. volumine deliciarum eruditorum v. cl. Ioannis Lamii Florentini. Florentiae, 1742.

British Library, 4831. a. 38.

XLII. *Thomas Stewart* (1803-1846)

Of Little Dunkeld, Scotland. Educated at Christ Church, Oxford. Knight of St. John of Jerusalem. He may well have lived in Rome for several years, because he bought in that city:

1. ROLANDINUS DE PASSAGERIIS, *Summa artis notariae.* Venice, Bernardinus Benalius, 30 Nov. 1485. 4°. Bought 1837.

Cambridge U.L. (Oates, 1914)

2. ST. BERNARD OF CLAIRVAUX, *Modus bene vivendi.* Venice, Bernardinus Benalius, 30 May 1494. 8°. Bought 1839.

Cambridge U.L. (Oates, 1921)

3. ST. ANTONINUS, *Confessionale volgare.* Venice, Petrus de Plasiis, Cremonensis, 18 July 1486. 4°. B.M.C. v, 269. Bought 1836.

British Library, IA. 20852.

4. ANTONIUS MANCINELLUS, *Epitoma seu regulae constructionis.* Milan, Antonius Zarotus, [not before 1496.] 4°. B.M.C. vi, 724. Bought 1837.　　　　　　　　　　　　　　British Library, IA. 26096.

It would be interesting to learn more about his life. He published several poems, no doubt at his own expense, in London; and he was at Monreale in Sicily on 12 January 1830, when he finished a poem entitled *Elegy on the Convent of the Grotto at Amalfi.* This he had privately printed at Palermo in 1830. He clearly had a love of incunabula.

XLIII. *Sir Woodbine Parish* (1796-1882)

He visited Naples in 1815. He then became first British Consul-General at Buenos Aires, 1825-1832. Published a book on Buenos Aires in 1839. He was in Naples again in 1840 when he acquired:
Duca della Torre, *Gabinetto Vesuviano*. Edizione seconda. Napoli, 1796. 8°.
British Library, 1509/1450.

Bibl.: Hon. NINA L. KAY SHUTTLEWORTH, *A life of Sir Woodbine Parish, K.C.H., F.R.S.*, London, 1910. This shows (chapter XII: Naples and Florence) that Parish arrived at Naples on 19 December 1840.

It is regrettable that not more than one or two of these forty and more book-collectors were sufficiently bibliographically minded to tell us anything about the booksellers from whom they bought their books in Italy. My notes have brought to light not one single name of a bookseller before the year 1700.[15]

In the eighteenth century, the brothers Niccolò and Marco Pagliarini at Rome were active booksellers and publishers from at least 1724 to 1762. Their printing-press, the Stamperia di Pallade, was in the district known as 'a Pasquino' (after the famous statue), a favourite location for many in the book – trade. They were clearly very successful, and they no doubt received many British customers.

In Venice Giambattista Pasquali is well documented, and his name is closely linked with that of his friend Consul Joseph Smith.

In the early nineteenth century we find Carlo Brizzolara, bookseller at Milan, c. 1820-30, and at Rome Mariano de Romanis in 1820.

Florence was, of course, a favourite haunt of the British traveller, who bought quite a sizeable number of books there, but never mentioned the booksellers. Smaller cities in which British collectors purchased a number of books include Naples, Padua, Genoa and Ancona; but strangely enough, I have so far found nothing bought by them in Bologna or other cities of Emilia, Tuscany and the Veneto, with the exception of one book bought at Ferrara in 1500.

Addendum (June 1994)

The British Library has a four-volume set of the *Opere drammatiche* of Pietro Metastasio (Rome, 1741), in which each volume is inscribed: J. Trapp, Rome, March 30, 1742. This is presumably Joseph Trapp the younger (died 1769), who in 1741 wrote a poem on 'Virgil's Tomb, Naples'.

INDEX OF BOOK-COLLECTORS IN ITALY

Allen, William, Cardinal
Arlington, Earl of
Bargrave, John
Barker, John
Bennet, Henry, *see* Arlington
Brand, Thomas
Campbell Alexander Glynn
Carr, John
Davies, Inglesina
Dee, John
Dethick, Sir William
Digby, Sir Kenelm
Douglas, Sylvester, Baron Glenbervie
Evelyn, John
Fortescue, Hon. George Matthew
Goldwell, James, Bishop of Norwich
Gordon, William
Hoare, Sir Richard Colt
Isham, Sir Thomas
Jekyll, Joseph (?)
Jones, Inigo
Lambert, Henry
Legh, George Cornwall
Lloyd, Humphrey
Mann, Sir Horace
Mead, Richard
Mill, William Hodge
Morris, John
Nott, George Frederick
Parish, Sir Woodbine
Savile, Thomas
Shirwood, John, Bishop of Durham
Smith, Joseph, Consul
Stewart, Thomas
Swinburne, Henry
Sykes, Sir Mark Masterman
Taylor, John
Thomson, Alexander
Throckmorton, Sir Arthur
Tighe, Stearne
Trapp, Joseph
Walter, Th. P.
Wentworth, W.
Wood, W.
Woodlocke, John

David J. Shaw

BOOKS BELONGING TO WILLIAM WARHAM, ARCHDEACON OF CANTERBURY, c. 1504-1532

The Warham family in the early Tudor period seems to have had a special affection for the first name William. The most famous of them, William Warham senior, was the last pre-Reformation archbishop of Canterbury, holding the office from 1503 until his death in 1532, following a typical late-medieval climb through the *cursus honorum* of university, church and state. He was fellow of New College, Oxford, and later Chancellor of the University; he held many ecclesiastical appointments, including the bishopric of London, before his elevation to the see of Canterbury. In civil affairs, he had been Master of the Rolls, was a frequent envoy to foreign parts for both Henry VII and Henry VIII and was Chancellor of England until supplanted by Wolsey.

In his will, Archbishop Warham made bequests to two nephews named William.[1] To William, son of his brother Hugh, he left the tapestries from his bedroom at the archiepiscopal palace at Knole. To the other William, archdeacon of Canterbury (who was the son of his other brother Nicholas),[2] he left his two best gowns and all of his books currently in William's possession.[3] He also left books to his old colleges and specified in one clause that books left to All Souls and to St Mary's [i.e. New College] at Oxford should be chained. A substantial list of Archbishop Warham's surviving books (especially those given to All Souls and to New College) can be found in Emden and in Ker's *Records of All Souls College Library*.[4] He had previously made a gift of books to

---

1. *Wills from Doctors' Commons*, ed. John Gough Nichols and John Bruce, Camden Society, 1863, pp. 21-27. The will was made in November 1530.

2. A pedigree of the Warham family of Malsanger (near Southampton) can be found in G. Steinman Steinman, 'An account of the manor of Haling in the parish of Croydon, Surrey', *Collectanea topographica & genealogica*, vol. III, 1836, p. 6.

3. 'Item, lego magistro Willielmo Warham nepoti meo Cantuariensi Archidiacono duas optimas togas meas cum penulis, et omnes libros meos quos modo habet in possessione sua' (p. 23).

4. A. B. EMDEN, *A biographical register of the University of Oxford to A.D. 1500*, vol. 3, Oxford, 1957, pp. 1990-91. N.R. KER, *Records of All Souls College Library, 1437-1600* Oxford, 1971. Ker (pp.24-26) transcribes the entries from the Vellum Inventory and the Benefactors' Register for the 91 books given to All Souls. Some are manuscripts; there are many incunables, and a number of sixteenth-century printed books, one (Pagnini's Bible) printed as late as 1528.

New College in 1508[1] and a gift of plate, jewels and vestments in 1516.[2]

Many of the Archbishop's books must have been located in his various palaces, particularly at Knole where other items mentioned in his will were kept. Those books which he left to his nephew, the Archdeacon, were presumably in the latter's house in St Stephen's, Canterbury, where the old man is recorded as having died in 1532 (a few hundred yards from the present writer's house).

The biography of archdeacon William is not well known. Emden's *Biographical register, 1501-1540* makes an entry for him in an appendix which lists figures who are presumed to have had an English university education but do not appear in the Cambridge lists and are assumed to have been at Oxford at a time for which the records are rather patchy.[3] Since his uncle went to Winchester and then to New College, there is some likelihood that the nephew followed the same or a similar route. William is likely to have been appointed Archdeacon of Canterbury in 1504 or 1505,[4] no doubt as an act of nepotism by his uncle who had become archbishop at the end of 1503 but was not enthroned until 1505. It has been suggested that the elder Warham had a strong partiality for fellow alumni of Winchester, especially if they were family.[5] There seems to be no record of the precise date of the archdeacon's appointment;[6] Le Neve has no record of him before 1511 but he must have been appointed within a year or two of the death of his predecessor Hugh Peynthwyn on 25 July 1504.[7] It seems likely that he was not appointed by his uncle un-

---

1. SEARS JAYNE, *Library catalogues of the English Renaissance*, re-issue with new preface and notes, 1983, p.94, referring to the New College Benefactors Register.

2. New College *Liber albus*, f. 16ᵛ; Emden, *Biographical register to 1500*, p. 1990.

3. A. B. EMDEN, *Biographical Register of the University of Oxford, A.D. 1501-1540*, Oxford, 1974, pp. 707-8.

4. Seventeenth, eighteenth and nineteenth-century accounts all give the date of his appointment as 1504 but cite no sources for this; see, for example, G. Steinman Steinman, 'An account of the manor of Haling', p. 5.

5. M. J. KITCH, 'The Chichester Cathedral chapter at the time of the Reformation', *Sussex Archaeological Collections*, 116, 1977-78, p. 288. Of Richard Warham, canon of Chichester 1524-45, he states that 'consanguinity with the archbishop was enough to account for his Chichester prebend'. The MS *Registrum custodum, sociorum, et scholarium Collegii Novi* at New College shows three sixteenth-century fellows called Warham, all from Compton in Dorset, who may have been members of another branch of the family: Thomas, 1516-26; Elizeus, 1520-25; and Robert, 1551-58. I am grateful to the College Archivist, Mrs C. M. Dalton, for making available her index to the Register.

6. Miss Ann Oakley of the Cathedral Archives, Canterbury, has checked T. S. Frampton's Extracts from the registers of the Archbishops of Canterbury prior to 1888 relating to institutions, admissions, collations and directions relating to the clergy. There is no record for the appointment to the archdeaconry.

7. JOHN LE NEVE, *Fasti Ecclesiae Anglicanae, 1300-1541*, vol. IV, Monastic cathedrals (Southern Province), compiled by B. Jones, London, 1963, p. 9.

til after the enthronement in 1505, as the installation of the archbishop, which was normally one of the archdeacon's tasks, was performed by the prior of Christ Church, presumably because there was no archdeacon in office at the time.[1] Appointment to the archdeaconry in about 1505 suggests that William junior was born no later than the early 1480s. He would have received an Oxford education at the time that his uncle was making his way in ecclesiastical administration after serving as fellow of New College (1475-1488).[2]

Steinman records that William was not a priest when appointed to the archdeaconry. He obtained a papal dispensation for not proceeding beyond the order of deacon for seven years, which was renewed in 1510 for a further six years and no doubt renewed again after that.[3] The earliest date discovered for him acting in an official capacity is 20 March 1508/9 when he made a presentation of Nicholas Hillington to the perpetual vicarage of the parish church of St Clement, Sandwich, of which living he was patron as archdeacon.[4] Some trace of his official activities in the archdeaconry can be found in the records of the Kentish visitations by the archbishop in 1511 and 1512 for which he acted as deputy.[5]

In addition to his archdeaconry, William started to acquire a series of other benefices. Le Neve lists him as a prebendary of St Paul's: he is recorded (possibly in error) as prebendary of Brownswood from 1515 to 1516; from 1516 to his death he is recorded as prebendary of Newingham, possibly in exchange for Brownswood.[6] By September 1516 he was also a canon of Exeter, again until his death.[7] In May 1520 he was collated to the Provostship of the College of Wingham, a few miles from Canterbury. This office was held by several other archdeacons of Canterbury, including Thomas Chichele and Edmund Cranmer. It seems to have been essentially a sinecure: Warham held a dispensation for non-residence.[8]

William also had the livings of a series of parishes in the south-east.

---

1. Canterbury Cathedral Archives U39/3/7, drawn to my attention by Miss Ann Oakley.
2. EMDEN, *Biographical Register to 1500*, p. 1988.
3. STEINMAN, 'Account of the manor of Haling', p. 5.
4. *Letters and Papers foreign and domestic of the reign of Henry VIII*, vol. 1, part 1, 1509-1515, London, 1862. This reference was brought to my notice by Miss Ann Oakley.
5. *Kentish Visitations of Archbishop William Warham and his deputies 1511-12*, ed. K.L. WOOD-LEGH, Kent Archaeological Society Records, vol. 24, 1984.
6. JOHN LE NEVE, *Fasti Ecclesiae Anglicanae, 1300-1541*, vol. v, 'St Paul's, London', compiled by Joyce M. Horn, 1963, pp. 22 and 52.
7. LE NEVE, *Fasti*, vol. IX, 'Exeter Diocese', comp. by Joyce M. Horn, 1964, p.62.
8. BL Stowe Charter 590; Frampton's Extracts, p. 111.

He was collated as rector of Orpington in December 1511.[1] From 1516 he was also rector of Hayes near Croydon; Battley records that his uncle founded a perpetual vicarage there for him, 'and thereby converted the Rectory into a rich *sine curâ*, as we term it'.[2] He was vicar of Shoreham in Kent from 1526 to 1527; rector of Wrotham, also in Kent, from 1527 to 1532; and rector of Harrow-on-the-Hill, in Middlesex, from 1532 to 1537.[3] He is also on record as being the patron of the Poor Priests Hospital, Canterbury, with the church of St Mary (1528), and as patron of Westhithe (1531), and of St Clement's, Sandwich, (1531).[4]

Warham's position as archdeacon gave him access to the world of national domestic politics. His uncle recommended him to Wolsey on a number of occasions, for example in 1523. In the same year, the Archbishop wrote to Wolsey saying that his nephew was with him at Knole, having failed to see Wolsey at Eltham on the Archbishop's business; he was about to return to Canterbury 'where his promotions and livelode lieth'. This letter also states that the Archdeacon is still 'not yet in priest's orders and therefore can do small service as chaplain'.[5] He travelled abroad on official business. Battley states that 'he attended upon Cardinal Wolsey in his Embassy to the French King, *Anno* 1527'.[6] In 1529 he was a member of Wolsey's suite in Calais and had been present in the Parliament Chamber earlier that year when the bishop of Lincoln presented the Pope's commission on the royal divorce to Cardinals Wolsey and Campeggio.[7]

Following his uncle's death, William resigned his archdeaconry and the provostship at Wingham, in return for annual pensions totalling £80. These payments were maintained for most of the rest of his life by the succeeding archdeacons.[8] The College at Wingham was still making payments in 1546.[9]

---

1. Frampton's Extracts, p. 59.
2. N. BATTLEY, *Cantuaria Sacra* (part II of the 1703 edition of William Somner's *Antiquities of Canterbury*), p. 158. See also Steinman, 'Account of the manor of Haling', cited above. Frampton's Extracts from the Archbishops' Registers give his collation as 4 October 1516 (p.93).
3. EMDEN, *Biographical register, 1501-1540*, p. 707. Frampton's Extracts, pp.149, 153, 155, 177.
4. Frampton's Extracts, pp. 157, 173, 175.
5. *Letters and Papers foreign and domestic*, Henry VIII, vol. 3. London, 1867, documents 2767 and 2795.
6. BATTLEY, *Cantuaria Sacra*, p. 158.
7. *Letters and Papers foreign and domestic*, Henry VIII, vol. IV, London, 1876, documents 5613 and 3216.
8. BATTLEY, *Cantuaria Sacra*, p.154.
9. E.L. HOLLAND, 'The Canterbury Chantries and Hospitals in 1546', *Kent Archaeological Society, Kent Records*, XII, Supplement, 1934, p. 45.

Warham had vacated the archdeaconry by 9 March 1534 when his successor Edmund Cranmer's collation is recorded.[1] A document of this year recorded that Laurence of Canterbury, scribe of the archdeacon of Canterbury, did penance at Paul's Cross for making a copy of Dr Bocking's book attacking the royal marriage; it is not clear whether this man was an officer of the outgoing archdeacon or of his successor.[2] As mentioned above, Warham seems to have moved to Middlesex following these resignations. After vacating the living of Harrow-on-the-Hill in 1537 (but retaining that of Hayes and his two canonries), he went abroad.

Emden refers to a grant of 18 July 1537 which states that 'Will. Warham, parson of Heyes, now in parts beyond sea by the King's licence. License to remain in foreign countries for the attainment of learning, and, after his return to England to be non-resident'.[3] In a further document of the same year, W. Frankeleyn, priest' (i.e. William Franklin, Dean of Windsor) petitions Cromwell that 'his house at Windsor is too close and small; [he] asks Cromwell to help him to get the house of the parson of Hayes who is absent'.[4] This suggests that Warham had a residence at Windsor Castle which was grander than that of the Dean.

At the end of 1538 one of Cromwell's agents, Thomas Theabold, writes from Venice that he was about to depart for England in some secrecy, using the pretext of a visit to Warham in Cologne concerning the permutation of a prebend.[5] Warham was still in Cologne in 1545, again in contact with the King's diplomatic agents: in a letter of 15 October 1545 to William Paget, Secretary of State and joint master of the posts, Stephen Vaughan, the King's financial agent in Antwerp, writes that 'on the 13th inst [he] received Paget's letters, by Francis, the King's post, together with one to Mr Warham, which (knowing that Warham was departed from Loveyn [Louvain] to Cullen [Cologne]), he forthwith sent to Cullen, but as it is 28 great leagues hence, [he] does not expect answer these five days'. Four days later, Vaughan wrote again to Paget, enclosing Warham's answer.[6] Paget was at this time involved in negotiations with the German protestants; it is possible that Warham was sending

---

1. Le Neve, *Fasti 1300-1541*, vol. IV, p. 9.
2. *Letters and Papers foreign and domestic*, Henry VIII, vol. VII, 1534, London, 1883, document 72.
3. Emden, *Biographical register, 1501-1540*, p. 708, citing *Letters and Papers foreign and domestic*, Henry VIII, 1537, vol. XII, pt. II, London, 1891, grant 411(32), p. 168.
4. *Letters and Papers foreign and domestic*, Henry VIII, 1537, vol. XII, pt ii, London, 1891, document 783.
5. *Letters and Papers foreign and domestic*, Henry VIII, vol. XIII, pt ii, London, 1893, document 1034, 12 December 1538.
6. *Letters and Papers foreign and domestic*, Henry VIII, 1545, vol. XX, pt 2, London, 1907, documents 597 and 618.

intelligence on this matter. The licence of 1537 and this involvement in diplomacy (or even espionage) suggest something of Warham's skills and his connections with the royal administration, though tantalisingly nothing more detailed is known about these incidents.

Warham was still recorded as patron of Hayes and Orpington in 1554.[1] In the same year Nicholas Harpsfield, Cranmer's successor as archdeacon and provost, refused to pay him his £40 pension.[2] William Warham died in October 1557, according to the dates of appointment of his successors to the canonries of St Paul's and Exeter.[3]

It seems that the archdeacon, though not in priestly orders, was a scholarly man. Some of the books which constituted his working library can be identified. Dennis Rhodes listed two among the incunables in his Oxford catalogue.[4]

1. ANDREAS BARBATIA, *Commentaria conscripta in titulum de foro competenti usque ad titulum de litis contestatione.*
Bologna, Justinianus de Ruberia, 17 January 1497, 2°.
Rhodes 261b; H 2445; GW 3362.
New College Ω. 30.6(1): in a contemporary blind-stamped binding by the Dragon binder on wooden boards.
At head of leaf a1ʳ: 'Liber d[omi]ni guilielmi cant. Archidiaconi relictus in custodia R[euerendissi]mi d[omi]ni guilielmi cant. Archie[pisco]pi'
Bound with:
Andreas Barbatia, *Tractatus de praestantia cardinalium.*
Bologna, Ugo de Rugeriis, 12 October 1487, 2°.
Rhodes 258; GW 3351; Pell. 1827.

2. BARTOLUS DE SAXOFERRATO, *Consilia, disputationes necnon tractatus.*
[Lyons, Johann Siber, not after 1492], 2°.
Rhodes 288b; BMC VIII, 254; GW 3542.
New College, Founders Library B.9.1(1): in a contemporary blind-stamped binding.
On blank a1ᵛ, following a MS list of contents in a different contemporary hand: 'Liber d[omi]ni guilielmi Warh[a]m Cant. Archidiaconi re-

---

1. *Sede Vacante Institutions*, ed. C. E. Woodruff, 1923, pp. 57, 67, 95. I am grateful to Ann Oakley for this and the following reference.
2. *Sede Vacante Institutions*, ed. C. E. Woodruff, 1923, p. 24.
3. LE NEVE, cited above.
4. DENNIS E. RHODES, *A catalogue of incunabula in all the libraries of Oxford University outside the Bodleian*, Oxford, 1982. I am grateful to Sandra Cromey, the Librarian of New College, for making these books available to me.

lictus in manib[us] R[euerendissi]mi d[omi]ni guilielmi Cant. Archie[pisco]pi'
Bound with:
Bartolus de Saxoferrato, *Lectura super autenticis*.
[Lyons, Johann Siber, c. 1495], 2°.
Rhodes 278; H2621; GW 3486.

There are in fact several more incunables at New College with the same inscription (or close variants):

3. UBALDIS, Baldus de, *Super Digesto nouo*.
Venice, Andreas de Torresanis de Asula, 18 August 1495, 2°.
Rhodes 1764.
New College, Founders Library B.8.12(1): in a contemporary blind-stamped binding on wooden boards.
On A1^r:
(1) 'Liber Collegij S[anc]tae marie winton. in Oxon.'
(2) 'Liber he[n]rici Cole'
(3) 'Liber d[omi]ni guilielmi Warha[m] cant. Archidiaconi relictus in manibus R[euerendissi]mi d[omi]ni Guilielmi Cant. Archie[pisco]pi.'
Bound with:
Ubaldis, Baldus de, *Super I et II Infortiati*.
Venice, Bernardinus Stagninus de Tridino, pt 1: [1494], pt 2: 5 February 1494, 2°.
Rhodes 1767; H*2308; Goff U26; IGI 9988.

4. UBALDIS, Baldus de. *In primum, secundum et tertium librum Codicis*.
Venice, Georgius Arrivabenus and Paganinus de Paganinis, 31 October 1485, 2°.
Rhodes 1758(1); H*2283; Goff U14; IGI 9945.
New College, Founders Library B.9.3(1): in a contemporary blind-stamped binding on wooden boards.
On blank a1^r:
(1) 'Liber Collegij S[an]ctae Marie Winto[n] in Oxo[n].'
(2) 'Liber d[omi]ni guilielmi Warh[a]m cant Archidiaconi relictus in manibus R[euerendissi]mi d[omi]ni Guilielmi Cant.'
On final leaf: 'Liber noui collegij Winton in Oxon.'
Bound with:
Ubaldis, Baldus de, *In quartum et quintum librum Codicis*.
Venice, Georgius Arrivabenus and Paganinus de Paganinis, 1485, 2°.
Rhodes 1758(2); H*2283; Goff U14; IGI 9949.

5. UBALDIS, Baldus de. *De materia statutorum*.
Venice, Andreas de Torresanis de Asula, 5 September 1486, 2°.

Rhodes 1773; H 2332; Goff U34; BMC v, 308; IGI 9938.
New College, Founders Library B.9.8(1): in a contemporary blind-stamped binding.
On blank a1^r 'Liber d[omi]ni guilielmi cant Archidiaconi relictus in manibus R[euerendissi]mi d[omi]ni guilielmi Cant. Archie[pisco]pi.'
Bound with:
(2) Ubaldis, Angelus de, *Opus ac lectura auctenticorum.*
Pavia, Christophorus de Canibus and Stephanus de Georgiis, 16 July 1484, 2°.
Rhodes 1753; H 15876; IGI 9917.
(3) Pontanus, Ludovicus, *Singularia.*
Venice, Johannes de Colonia and Johannes Manthen, 1475, 2°.
Rhodes 1461; HC *13270; Goff P928; BMC v, 231; IGI 8011.
Imperfect: lacks the final three leaves.

6. JOANNES DE IMOLA, *Super Clementinis.*
Venice, Johannes de Colonia and Johannes Manthen, 26 April 1480, 2°.
Rhodes 1019; HC *9144; Goff J344; BMC v, 236; IGI 5280.
New College, Founders Library A.14.4: in a contemporary blind-stamped binding.
At head of a2^r: 'Liber d[omi]ni gulielmi cant. Archidiaconi relictus in custodia R[euerendissi]mi d[omi]ni guilielmi Cant. Archie[pisco]pi.'

These inscriptions state that these are books belonging to Archdeacon Warham which he had left in the care of his uncle the archbishop ('in manibus' or 'in custodia'). They must have been written during the Archbishop's lifetime and while William was still Archdeacon (i.e. not later than 1532), before the books found their way to New College. It is possible that they record the ownership of books left in the Archbishop's care on the occasion of one of the Archdeacon's foreign trips. It is not clear whether the books passed to New College with the Archbishop's bequest. This is unlikely, as none of the books has the form of inscription which is found in New College books recording the Archbishop's bequest, for example:

> 'Hunc librum donauit R[euerendissi]mi p[ate]r Will[el]mus Warh[a]m Cant. Archiep[iscopu]s nouo collegio Beate marie Winton. in Oxon ad vsu[m] socioru[m] & scolariu[m] in libraria ibidem q[uam?] primum cathenandum'.[1]

---

1. Founders Library C.2.3(1), L. Pontanus, *Lectura super prima parte Infortiati*, [Milan], J. A. Scinzenzeler, for J. J. Legnano and his brothers, 1523, 2°. A similar inscription is recorded for Archbishop Warham's New College manuscripts: see H. O. Coxe, *Catalogus codicum MSS Collegii Novi*, 1845.

It would seem more probable that archdeacon William himself gave books to New College, books which he had previously entrusted to his uncle's keeping and which he allowed to enter the college either at the same time as his uncle's bequest or, more likely, on his departure for Cologne. In either event, the younger William might have made such a gift because he too was a former student at New College.

Fourteen of the surviving books given to All Souls by the Archbishop seem to have a standard inscription which does not refer to the nephew:

> Liber collegii animarum omnium fidelium defunctorum in Oxon' ex dono Reuerendissimi in cristo patris domini Willelmi Warham Cant' Archiepiscopi.[1]

No books belonging to either of the Warhams can currently be traced at Winchester College: the liturgical books which the Archbishop left in his will presumably disappeared at the time of the Reformation.[2]

Another book which definitely belonged at one time to William Warham the younger is an edition of a French politico-historical text:

7. JEAN LEMAIRE DE BELGES, *Illustrations de Gaule et singularitez de Troye*, Paris, Geoffroy de Marnef, 1512, 4°
British Library 492.i.1.
On the final verso are the following inscriptions:
(1) 'Ce liure est a moy s^r Thomas Boleyn.'
(2) 'Ce liure ma donne mons^r guyllaume Warham archediacre de cantorberie nepueu a mons larcheuecque de cantorberie.'

On the title-page, a monogram 'HR'.

It seems likely that this book first belonged to Archdeacon Warham (if it did not belong to his uncle before that) and that he gave it (in the lifetime of the Archbishop) to Sir Thomas Boleyn who recorded the gift. The book subsequently found its way into the Old Royal Library before the death of Boleyn's son-in-law Henry VIII whose initials 'HR' (Henricus Rex) are found on the title-page. Henry had married Boleyn's daughter Ann in 1533; Sir Thomas himself died at Hever Castle in Kent in 1539. It is interesting to note that Boleyn wrote the inscriptions in this book in French. This would seem to be because of a desire to match the language of the book itself, a very common practice at this time. Boleyn's knowledge of French is not surprising. He had been abroad on

---

1. KER, *Records of All Souls Library*, pp. 134-5.
2. Letter from the Fellows' Librarian, Mr Roger Custance.

diplomatic missions for Henry on several occasions; he was in Mechelen (Malines) in 1513 negotiating with Marguerite de Savoy and was in France in 1519-20.[1]

A further book belonging to Boleyn which found its way into the Old Royal Library is the *Revelationes sancte Brigitte*, Lübeck, 1492, 2° which has (also on the final verso) the inscription 'Liber Thome Boleyn'.[2] In this case the book did not arrive in the Old Royal Library until the reign of James I, as it has on the first blank leaf the signature of Lord Lumley whose books came into the possession of the crown in the early seventeenth century.[3]

The connection between Sir Thomas Boleyn and Archdeacon Warham is not clear. It may be simply that they were both involved in political and diplomatic affairs in the same sphere at the same time, or else that they came into contact as members of the same south-eastern group of gentry, since Warham's ecclesiastical affairs no doubt took him to the parts of Kent and Surrey where Boleyn resided as well as to the court. It is interesting to note that the future Secretary of State William Paget had been supported by the Boleyn family while at Cambridge (DNB), reminding us of the complexity of these circles of patronage and affiliation at the time.

The books which are known to have been either owned by Archdeacon Warham or loaned to him by his uncle suggest that he might have had a significant working library as an ecclesiastical administrator. The surviving books at New College are very substantial folio volumes bound in heavy wooden boards and must have required special shelving wherever they were kept. His revenues and houses show him to have been a wealthy man. The donations to New College are of course of books suitable for an academic library of the time, though as they are mainly commentaries on canon and civil law and the decretals, they would have become out of date almost at the time they were given. The gift to Boleyn shows another side of Warham's interests: contemporary literature in French. It is more than likely that he would have had recreational reading in English and probably in Latin too. So far nothing of this sort has come to light, but what has survived throws an interesting light on the career of a little-known Tudor cleric.

1. DNB.
2. British Library IB. 9861; BMC II, pp. 554-5.
3. *The Lumley Library. The catalogue of 1609*, ed. by Sears Jayne and Francis R. Johnson, London, 1956, no. 779.

Jan Storm Van Leeuwen

SOME OBSERVATIONS ON DUTCH PUBLISHERS' BINDINGS UP TO 1800

De luxe bindings from various times and countries have been the subject of many studies by bookbinding historians. These studies enable us to date many extensively tooled bindings within some ten to twenty years and ascertain their country or even place of origin. From time to time the ideas on the decoration and binding in some period can be drastically changed, as Anthony Hobson's recent study on Renaissance bindings in Italy and France has shown.[1] Drastically in this context, however, means the ascription of a group of bindings to someone known by name, the shifting of a group of bindings from one binder or bindery to another, the dating of about ten years earlier or later of a limited number of bindings or, at the most, the presentation of a theory why some pieces cannot have been made in one country but must come from another. Revolutionary findings to the specialist, but not to the non-specialist reader of *Humanists and Bookbinders* who will rather be struck by the enormous amount of information Hobson presents on beautiful bindings made 450 to 550 years ago. Similar data on fine bindings from other places and times have been published by him and various other authors. The history of fine binding, although far from complete, is not a closed book. Still, we are talking about the relatively small percentage of special pieces, made by order of book collectors, who wanted their bindings to reflect their refined taste, or of authors and publishers who wished to draw the attention of the persons to whom they donated copies of their books to these gifts, by the luxurious appearance of the covers.

The same cannot be said for the history of bookbinding as such, for the less elaborately decorated bindings did not receive comparable attention; even less did the undecorated ones. The majority of bindings from former times remain almost unstudied, not only because of lack of decoration, but also because of their vast quantity and our lack of knowledge of common binding practices in former times. Little is known about how the book left the publisher, in sheets, as Goldschmidt states not without reason,[2] in quires already folded, in quires simply stitched

---

[1]. Anthony Hobson, *Humanists and Bookbinders; the Origins and Diffusion of the Humanistic Bookbinding 1459-1559* (Cambridge, 1989).

[2]. Ernst Philipp Goldschmidt, 'Prinzipien zur Lokalisierung und Datierung alter Einbände,' *Jahrbuch der Einbandkunst*, 2 (1928), pp. 3-13; E. Ph. Goldschmidt, Gothic & Renaissance Bookbindings (London, 1928; reprint Nieuwkoop, 1967), pp. 116-118.

together, sewn and put in plain covers, given some sort of wrapper, not considered to be the definitive binding and therefore taken off when the 'real' binding was to be applied, or put into some more permanent binding. Did several traditions exist at the same time, the one each publisher adhered to depending on his means and output at a certain time? I think this rather probable, but even the question has seldom been put and answers have only sometimes been given, for some publications of some publishers, not all.[1]

Did a publisher's binding exist before about 1825 when the combination of binder's cloth (calico), case-binding and new machinery made it attractive?[2] If so, in what shape, where and when did the binding put on several copies of the same book by order of the publisher, to be thus sold, come into being? We do know something about the fifteenth century. For, although Goldschmidt rightly claimed that books were not bound before sale in the fifteenth and sixteenth centuries, this 'rule' did not always apply. Conclusive proof has been presented that the German publisher Schöffer at the end of the fifteenth century had sturdy publisher's bindings in blind-tooled calf over wooden boards made by the Mainz binder Hanns Oisterreicher.[3] Another kind of publisher's binding originated in Germany too (Augsburg) and at the same time, consisting of woodblock-printed paper wrappers – the slightly later Italian paper bindings apparently were not made by order of the publisher. Through a lack of technical descriptions and the fact that most of them survived only in part, pasted in a more permanent binding, we do not know the precise character of these most interesting pieces. Yet it is clear they consisted of covers and spine.[4] The oldest binding of this kind may date from 1482.[5]

---

1. Much of the information for this article was collected during my sabbatical stay at the Netherlands Institute for Advanced Studies in Wassenaar.

2. On the nineteenth century publisher's binding, see DOUGLAS BALL, *Victorian publisher's bindings* (London, 1985); ELEANORE JAMIESON, *English embossed bindings, 1825-1850* (Cambridge, 1972); FONS VAN DER LINDEN, *In linnen gebonden, Nederlandse uitgeversbanden van 1840 tot 1940*, met medewerking van Albert Struik (Veenendaal 1987); RUARI MCLEAN, *Victorian publishers' book-bindings in cloth and leather* (London, 1974); SOPHIE MALAVIEILLE, *Reliures et cartonnages d'éditeur en France au XIXe siècle (1815-1865)*, (Paris, 1985); MICHAEL SADLEIR, *The evolution of publishers' binding styles, 1770-1900* (London, New York, 1930).

3. HERMANN KNAUS, 'Über Verlegereinbände bei Schöffer', *Gutenberg Jahrbuch 1938*, pp. 97-108; VERA SACK, 'Über Verlegereinbände und Buchhandel Peter Schöffers', *Archiv für Geschichte des Buchwesens*, 13 (1973), coll. 249-287.

4. *The History of Bookbinding, 525-1950 A.D.* [catalogue of the] exhibition at the Baltimore Museum of Art [by Dorothy Miner] (Baltimore, 1957), no. 193a and 193b; PAUL NEEDHAM, *Twelve centuries of bookbinding: 400-1600* (The Pierpont Morgan Library, New York, London, 1979), no. 33 and 45.

5. MAX MÜLLER, 'Der älteste bisher bekannte Buchumschlag', *Festschrift für Georg Leidinger, zum 60. Geburtstag* (München, 1930), pp. 195-197.

But the earliest preserved on several copies of the same book dates from around 1488 and is to be related directly to the publisher, woodcutter and binder Jörg Schapff, who may have been its inventor.[1] These very early publisher's bindings in paper stand totally isolated. Only in the eighteenth century did this kind of binding occur again.

And what about the more luxurious publisher's bindings, like those of Oisterricher in leather, but with the device or name of a publisher on the covers, that are known? Already in 1967 Anthony Hobson warned the readers of *The Book Collector* not too easily to draw the conclusion that a binding with a publisher's device on the covers, in his case the pelican of (probably) Richard Jugge (working in London, 1552-77), Alexander Arbuthnot or Thomas Finlayson (both working in Edinburgh, 1579-84 and 1604-09), was necessarily a trade binding, made by order of publisher or bookseller.[2] Recently Georges Colin made it clear that there is no reason why the bindings with Plantin's *Compas d'or* in gold in the centre of the covers, held by several authors to be good examples of a publisher's bindings, should be such; none of them regularly covers the same title.[3] Nor do the extant data on other so-called publisher's bindings, where the device or name of a publisher forms part of the decoration, prove that they could only have been made to order of the publisher with the intention of being sold en masse. As regards Johannes Veldener and Ludovicus Ravescot at Louvain (end of the fifteenth century),[4] Claude Chevallon[5]

1. OTTO LEUZE, 'Mit Holzschnitten verzierte Buchumschläge des 15. Jahrhunderts in der Württ. Landesbibliothek in Stuttgart', *Festschrift für Georg Leidinger, zum 60. Geburtstag* (München, 1930), pp. 165-169. See also FERDINAND GELDNER, *Bucheinbände aus elf Jahrhunderten* (Zweite Auflage, München, 1959), p. 26; LEO BAER, *Mit Holzschnitten verzierte Buchumschläge des XV. und XVI. Jahrhunderts* (Frankfurt am Main, 1923), and HOWARD M. NIXON, *Broxbourne Library, styles and designs of bookbindings* (London, 1956), no. 6.

2. A.R.A. HOBSON, 'Bindings with the device of a pelican in its piety', Note 291 in *The Book Collector*, 16 (1967), pp. 509-10.

3. GEORGES COLIN, 'Le compas d'or sur des reliures', *De Gulden Passer*, 66-67 (1988-89), pp. 325-336; see also GEORGES COLIN, 'La fourniture de reliures par l'Officine plantinienne', *Gutenberg Jahrbuch 1990*, pp. 346-359, especially p. 351.

4. For Veldener, see *De vijfhonderdste verjaardag van de boekdrukkunst in de Nederlanden*, catalogus tentoonstelling, (Koninklijke Bibliotheek Albert I, Brussels, 1973) no. 74 d; for Ravescot, see LEONIDE J. MEES in *De vijfhonderdste op. cit.*, no. 194 and LUC INDESTEGE, 'New light on Ludovicus Ravescot', *Quaerendo* 1 (1971), pp. 16-18.

5. GOLDSCHMIDT, *Gothic & Renaissance Bookbindings cit.*, no. 73; another binding in *Livres anciens et modernes, Littérature - Histoire...*, Librairie Giraud Badin, Paris, [ca. 1990], no. 135. See also Jos. M.M. HERMANS, 'Oude banden, aantekeningen over vroege uitgeversbanden uit Parijs en Keulen', in: *Codex in context, studies over codicologie kartuizergeschiedenis en laat middeleeuws geestesleven, aangeboden aan Prof. Dr. A. Gruijs* (Nijmegen, 1985), pp. 175-197. Hermans's other example, a binding he related to the Cologne publisher Franz Birckmann (1526-1530), is not mentioned here because I am not sure the device can really be interpreted as that of Birckmann.

and Charles l'Angelier[1] (Paris, first half of the sixteenth century), no two copies of the same work in the same binding have been found. These bindings could equally well have been made for the publisher's own library, for donation by him to some person by whom he wanted his name to be remembered, or for sale in the bookshop he would normally have owned.

Two bindings with Jean Bogard's device (Southern Netherlands, second half of the sixteenth century) with the same contents have been found. They were not made for his own library; presentation or sale in the publisher's own shop may have been their purpose. The same can be said of the identical vellum bindings on two copies of *Historiarum Sacrarum Encolpodion*, printed for Peder Andersen in Copenhagen in 1634.[2] Only with the three identical calf bindings on James Howell's *Dodona's Grove, or The Vocall Forest* (London, for Humphrey Moseley, 1650) do we come close to certainty that they were publisher's bindings. The centre of the covers is decorated with an oval silver plaque especially made for this purpose, depicting three trees with the text DODONAS GROVE in a laurel wreath.[3] But even then it cannot be excluded that they were made for presentation purposes.

As to the (Northern) Netherlands, the earliest binding said to be a publisher's binding is decorated with the device of the Amsterdam publisher Pieter Hendricksz and the Amsterdam coat of arms (c. 1540). The book covered, however, is an edition by Simon de Colines (Paris, 1540?), which shows that the binding must have served another purpose.[4] From the end of the sixteenth century date two uniform vellum bindings decorated with a stamp of an Amsterdam panorama, on Linschoten's *Itinerario*, published by Cornelis Claesz in 1594-95. De la Fontaine Verwey considered them to be publisher's bindings, but also published other bindings with the same

---

1. BARON J. PICHON, *Documents pour servir à l'histoire des libraires de Paris* (Paris, 1894); YVES DEVAUX, *Dix siècles de reliure* (Paris, 1977), p. 364; LÉON GRUEL, *Manuel historique et bibliographique de l'amateur de reliures* (2 vols., Paris, 1887-1905), vol. 1, p. 42; GOLDSCHMIDT, *Gothic...cit.*, no. 186; GEORGES COLIN, 'Reliures à la marque de Jean Bogard', *Gutenberg Jahrbuch 1966*, pp. 372-373 (an 'Angelier' binding on a book from another publisher). An interesting Angelier-binding is to be found in The Royal Library, The Hague, on GILLES D'AURIGNY, *Le livre de police humaine...* Paris, 1546, 8vo., 145 G 26: see *Boekbanden in de Nationale Bibliotheek* [exhibition catalogue] ('s-Gravenhage, 1941), p. 49, no. 4.

2. HEINZ PUMMER, 'A 17th-century Danish publisher's binding', *The Book Collector* 36, (1987), pp. 72-76.

3. *Catalogue of valuable printed books...the property of Major J. R. Abbey*, Sotheby & Co., London, 21-23 June 1965, no. 399, mentions the identical copies in the British Library and the Bodleian Library, Oxford.

4. GRUEL, *Manuel...op. cit.*, vol. 2, pp. 92-93; Herman de la Fontaine Verwey, 'Amsterdam publishers' bindings from about 1600', *Quaerendo* 5 (1975), p. 284.

Amsterdam stamp.[1] This indicates that they could equally well have been made by Claesz as bookbinder, or for Claesz's own bookshop. The same can be said for Verwey's other examples, the identical bindings on Claesz's Latin and French editions of Waghenaer's *Spieghel der zeevaerdt* (1586 and 1600), the two bindings on copies of both his editions of Willem Barendts's *Nieuwe beschrijvinghe* with a Charitas stamp on the covers, and a binding in calf on Claesz's edition of *Veelderhande liedekens* (1593 and 1598), with an emblematic block on the front cover, depicting a passage from the Gospel according to Saint Matthew 13. Verwey may have been right in describing especially the last of these as a publisher's binding, but they may as well have been made for the purpose of presentation or sale in Claesz's shop.[2] The same holds good for Verwey's last example: two bindings on Cyprianus de Valera's Spanish Bible (1602), published by Claesz's former apprentice Laurens Jacobsz, with the same Justitia stamp in the centre of the covers.[3]

Four bindings with the small device of Daniel and Lodewijk Elzevier (Leiden, third quarter of the seventeenth century) are known.[4]

One of them contains an edition of 1560.[5] These bindings will more probably have been made for the publisher's own collection.

Lastly we come to the famous *Atlas maior, sive Cosmographia Blaviana* (Amsterdam, 1662-1664) in 11 volumes, the *Tonneel der steden van de Vereenighde Nederlanden* in two volumes, and other similar publications by Blaeu. Many of them are covered by bindings that can be called publisher's bindings without any reservation. Anyone who saw several copies of the *Atlas* will have observed that they are usually bound and decorated identically. The large volumes are covered by gold-tooled sturdy limp vellum bindings. The text-blocks are sewn onto vellum bands, normally seven, laced through open joints and corresponding to the spine decoration. At first sight the tooling on the covers is the same too: two frames of stylized tendril rolls between rules, the corners being joined to each other by the same combination of roll and rules. Large triangular blocks

1. VERWEY, *op. cit.* in n. 16, pp. 283-302.
2. I found no proof of the existence of bookseller's binding in our country. If it did exist, it was certainly on a far smaller scale than in England, the book-trade being so widely diffused in the Netherlands.
3. VERWEY, *op. cit.* in n. 16, p. 297.
4. GRUEL, *Manuel...cit.*, vol. 1, pp. 94-95 (Willems no. 1187 and 1511), to which can be added a binding in Cambridge, St. John's College, Aa.2.54. (HENRICUS REGIUS, *Philosophia naturalis...* Amstelaedami, apud Ludovicum & Danielem Elzevieros, 1661, 4to., Willems no. 1274 and *Exhibition of bookbindings*, Burlington Fine Arts Club (London, 1891), no. 30, p. 93).
5. Binding in gold-tooled marbled calf, Fondation Custodia, Paris (TERENTIUS. *In quem triplex edita est P. Antesignani...* Lugduni, apud Mathiam Bonhomme, 1560, small 4to.).

of stylized tendrils decorate the corners of the inner frame and matching, even larger, lozenge-shaped blocks the centre. The same combination of roll and rules divides the spines into compartments, with a rosette in the centre and a small tool in each corner. Not without reason this type of binding is known as 'Dutch' or 'Atlas' binding. But, as Kyriss has shown, a closer inspection will reveal many small differences in the tools used. Further study still has to be done in order to ascertain which tools were those of Blaeu's regular binder and which belonged to other binders not employed by him.[1]

How then do we know that several of them should be considered as publisher's bindings? Blaeu's 1670-71 publisher's catalogue clearly shows this: the 12-vol. 'Atlas en François', the 11-vol. 'Atlas en Latin', the 'Atlas en Espagnol...sous la presse...dont les dix sont achevés', 'Le Theatre des Cités des XVII Provinces des Pays-bas...en Latin ou en Flamend' and other works are offered either 'illuminé & relié, doré sur la couverture & sur la tranche' or 'Le mesme...mais point illuminé', that is, always bound.[2] Actually as early as 1655 atlases were sold ready-bound by him.[3] Although the catalogue makes no mention of the fact, the atlases could also be obtained unbound, as was demonstrated by Herman de la Fontaine Verwey: 'to obtain the atlases unbound... was for the benefit of those who, not content with the standard mode of publication, preferred to call upon the services of a...master colourist.'[4] 'As soon as binding was completed a number of bound copies will have been dispatched to the 'regular customers' and the remainder, designed for new purchasers, will have been added to the series of ten bound volumes already lying awaiting buyers in the shop...The rest were stored in sheets...in the printing-office...'[5] For those of Blaeu's clients who wished it, Magnus decorated the vellum bindings with personal coats of arms, monograms...'[6] Albert Magnus, who

---

1. ERNST KYRISS, 'Amsterdamer Verlagseinbände des 17. Jahrhunderts', *Amor librorum...a tribute to Abraham Horodisch* (Amsterdam, 1958), pp. 133-136.

2. *Catalogue des Atlas, theatre des citez...* mis en lumiere par Jean Blaeu, à Amsterdam... The only known copy, in the Plantin Museum at Antwerp, is reproduced by C. KOEMAN, *A catalogue by Joan Blaeu, a facsimile with an accompanying text* (Amsterdam, 1967).

3. C. KOEMAN, *Joan Blaeu and his Grand Atlas* (Amsterdam, 1970), p. 32, on a sale to Sir John Scott: 'Atlas, 6 vols bound 196 gulden, the same printed and bound 216 gulden. Vol. V of the atlas, bound 25 gulden, the same printed and bound 36 gulden'; see also p. 46.

4. HERMAN DE LA FONTAINE VERWEY, 'The glory of the Blaeu Atlas and the 'Master Colourist', *Quaerendo* 11 (1981), pp. 197-229; especially p. 197.

5. HERMAN DE LA FONTAINE VERWEY, 'The Spanish Blaeu', *Quaerendo* 11 (1981), pp. 83-94, especially p. 88.

6. HERMAN DE LA FONTAINE VERWEY, 'The binder Albert Magnus and the collectors of his age', *Quaerendo* 1 (1971), pp. 158-78, especially p. 164.

after the death of Joan Blaeu in 1673 sold Blaeu's atlases, town books and other publications at his shop, was probably Dr. Blaeu's regular binder and made his publisher's bindings. Blaeu did not have a bindery himself.[1]

Let us try to understand why Blaeu, possibly the first Dutch publisher to do so on a regular basis, should want to go to the expense and trouble of having his monumental publications sold ready bound, because this makes us understand why some other complicated and large publications of the late seventeenth and early eighteenth centuries were probably sold ready bound also. Blaeu's reasons will have been due to the special problems related to the binding of this type of book: the difficult sewing of mostly loose sheets, many of which had to be mounted on guards or folded. Binding an atlas was considered to be one of the most complicated jobs a binder could face, especially if the vellum and the edges of the book had to be gilded. Blaeu certainly did several of his customers a favour by supplying his publications ready bound. Contrary to other publications, they were completely unusable unbound. Moreover in this manner he freed purchasers from the search for a binder equipped for this hard task, who could only be found in the larger cities of Europe.

At the same time Blaeu would be as good as certain that the sheets which make up the book would not get mixed up, pages be lost or spoilt by the binder, for his own binder was fully equipped for the job. He would have a reasonable certainty that his client could have no complaints about the completeness of the work. Bookbinders' treatises of the eighteenth century usually pay much attention to the collation of the book and the insertion of the plates in the correct places.[2] That the risk of loss, misplacement or even having an incomplete or damaged copy delivered by the client in order to be bound was very real, is made clear by the advice given to the binder in German treatises on bookbinding of that time: there are no such treatises for Holland. The anonymous author of *Anweisung zur Buchbinderkunst* (1762) may be quoted: 'Damit nun aber die Käufer und Buchbinder keinen Schaden und Verdruss dadurch leiden, so ist nöthig, dass so bald ein Buch zu binden gebracht wird, der Buchbinder solches collationire und zusehe ob es complet oder Vollständig sey, in dessen Ermanglung er solches dem Käufer wieder zustelle, welcher der Ergänzung von dem Buchhändler verlangen kann. Doch wäre es weit besser, dass der Käufer des Buches solches in dem Buchladen selbst verrichten thäte...'[3]

1. VERWEY, 'The glory... *op. cit.*', p. 220.
2. See, for example, HENDRIK DE HAAS, *De Boekbinder* (Dordrecht, 1806: new edition Amsterdam, Utrecht, 1984), pp. 1-6 on folding, 7-8 on collating, 9-18 on cutting out and inserting all kinds of plates.
3. *Anweisung zur Buchbinderkunst* (2 vol., Leipzig, 1762), p.5. See also JOHANN GOTTFRIED ZEIDLER, *Buchbinder-Philosophie, oder Einleitung in die Buchbinderkunst*

Yet the fire in one of his warehouses, which destroyed large quantities of printed and unprinted sheets, but no bound books, shows Blaeu to have had the larger part of the copies of his publications in stock unbound.[1] Thus he could always sell them in this form, or bound to the special request of the customer without risking too high an investment in the binding (and, for that matter, the colouring). Nor would his binder be confronted with too large a task at a time, even for his shop, which was certainly large. Each time his supply of bound atlases was running out, Blaeu would, we may safely assume, have more copies bound.

Did Blaeu possess tools characterising the contents, comparable to the block with the figure of Atlas which the collector Laurens van der Hem had put in the centre of the covers of his famous 50-volume Atlas?[2] Probably not. Kyriss's only tell-tale tool, also the only one I have been able to find, is a celestial globe, printed in the centre of a large tendril block. He found it on the eleven volumes of Jodocus Hondius's *Novus atlas absolutissimus*.[3] I found it not only on Blaeu's *Atlas maior*, but also on two copies of the *Theatrum Statuum Regiae...Sabaudice ducis* and the *Toneel der Vermaerste Koop-Steden*, both publications by Blaeu's heirs (1682), on *Voorne, Caart-Boeck*, by Romeyn de Hooghe (1695) and the *Toneel der Heerschappyen van...den Hartog van Savoyen*, published by Adriaan Moetjens in The Hague in 1697, all of them in the Royal Library.[4] All these bindings have most other tools in common and will probably have to be dated after Magnus's death in 1689. Blaeu's standard tools may rather have been those on the Latin *Atlas maior* Kyriss mentions (1662-1665) – the central block shows a crowned angel. They can also be found on a copy of Blaeu's *Toonneel des aerdriicx* in five volumes (Amsterdam, 1649-1654) and on a copy of his two-volume *Novum et magnum theatrum urbium Belgicae-regiae*...[5] Another set of blocks, rolls and tools, not mentioned by Kyriss, may equally have belonged to Magnus, on Blaeu's *Groote Atlas* 1664 (fig. 1) and on the second volume only of his *Tonneel der Steden* in The Hague, and on his *Theatrum urbis terrarum* (1650-1655) and *Toonneel des aerdrycx*...(1658) in Ghent.[6]

(Hall im Magdeburgischen, 1708), p. 15, and J.J.H. BÜCKING, *Die Kunst des Buchbindens* (Stendal, 1785; reprint Leipzig, 1983), pp. 1 and 4.

1. KOEMAN, *Joan Blaeu op. cit.*, p. 96.
2. *Een wereldreiziger op papier*, De atlas van Laurens van der Hem (1621-1678). [Exhibition catalogue.] (Amsterdam , 1992), pp. 12-14.
3. KYRISS, 'Amsterdamer Verlagseinbände *op. cit.*', p. 134 and pl. 1 A.
4. Royal Library, The Hague, 1046 B 1-11, 1051 B 2-3 and 1045 B 3-4, 395 B 23, 395 B 16, 1045 B 5-6.
5. In Maaseik, the monastery of the *Domini Crucis* and in the Royal Library, The Hague (395 B 14-15).
6. Royal Library, The Hague, 1050 B 5-13 and 1049 B 15. Ghent, Seminarium, A 187 and A 188.

Fig. 1. Front cover and spine of gold-tooled vellum binding, on *Groote Atlas*, vol. 1, Amsterdam, Ioannes Blaeu, 1664. Royal Library, The Hague, 1050 B 3. (Photograph: Royal Library, The Hague.)

Blaeu had no tell-tale tools, but almost certainly some Amsterdam publishers, or rather their binders, at the turn of the century did, and had them put on some of their works, complicated but far less so than Blaeu's *Atlas*, in-folio or in-plano and containing large amounts of prints or maps. In one case documentary evidence exists that copies were supplied ready bound. We may safely assume that one of the others was sold bound too, but for the other three too little proof has been found. Surprisingly enough, on the basis of the tools all these bindings must be ascribed to only one Amsterdam workshop, possibly the only one capable after Magnus's death of executing this type of work in large quantities in a relatively short time, an anonymous binder, working from about 1692 to about 1738, and called Roset-dubbelwiegevoetgroep, 'Rosette-double-drawer-handle-group' by me. The many products found show this bindery to have been very important indeed: in 1984 I was able to publish 65 groups of bindings. Since then I have found some 35 more.[1]

In my 1984 publication I stated that eight bindings on copies of Jacobus Basnage's *Histoire du Vieux et du Nouveau Testament* (1704?), the translation into Dutch *'t Groot waerelds tafereel* (1705) and later re-editions (in French as *Le grand tableau de l'univers*) had to be publisher's bindings. It is known from an advertisement that the publisher, Jacobus Lindenberg, sold the edition of 1707 both sewn and bound in a so-called tortoise binding, which means polished marbled calf, with an allegorical design. For the eighth edition of 1714 (?) he announced the choice of having the book also bound and printed on large paper, and with the addition of the text of the Bible.[2] The allegorical calf bindings mentioned are the eight found, one from the 1704 edition in French, one from the 1705 edition in Dutch, one from the third Dutch edition (1707), four from the eighth French edition (1714) and one from the tenth edition in Dutch, 1721.[3] To these six more can now be added, one of the 1705 edition, one of 1707, one of 1714, one of 1715 and two of 1721.[4]

---

1. JAN STORM VAN LEEUWEN, 'Un groupe remarquable de reliures amstellodamoises ou contribution à l'étude des reliures du XVIIIe siècle', *De libris compactis miscellanea* (Bruxelles, 1984; *Studia Bibliothecae Wittockianae*, 1) pp. 321-374; my observations on Dutch bindings of the eighteenth century are based on my forthcoming publication on the subject, *De Nederlandse boekband in de achttiende eeuw, met catalogus van relevante banden (uitgezonderd Den Haag) in de Koninklijke Bibliotheek te Den Haag* (provisional title).

2. I will not go into the numbering of the editions (which seems dependent on Lindenberg's desire to show how popular his work was) and give them as recorded on the titlepages.

3. STORM VAN LEEUWEN, 'Un groupe...*op. cit.*', pp. 347-350.

4. Respectively in the Municipal Archives of Den Bosch (Mag H, M 30); in Ghent Seminarium (A 821) and in Ghent Seminarium (A 821); Van Gendt Book Auctions,

All covers are decorated by means of a very large block obviously made specifically for this project (Fig. 2). Jesus and Moses are depicted under the sign of the Holy Trinity and sitting on a celestial globe, with the text 'libera nos a malo' and borne by angels. Underneath a man chained to a large globe lies between a devil and an angel. The further decoration of the covers is very similar, consisting of two frames of rolls, connected to each other at the corners by means of a roll and with a small tool in the corners of the inner one. On each spine, with six or seven raised cords, the second field contains the book title, whereas the other fields are decorated in the corners and the centre with the typical straight edged triangular and lozenge-shaped tools that were meant for these spaces. On closer inspection, however, details differ in the tools used. These differences do not only occur between bindings on different editions, which would be logical since they need not be bound at the same time, but also between copies of one and the same edition. The covers of two of the three copies of the 1721 edition are the same, but the spines show small differences, whereas the third has totally different tools. The two copies of the 1705 edition and the two of the 1707 edition differ even more in this respect. Only copies of the French 1714 edition show consistency, i.e. four bindings are almost the same, while the fifth has totally different tools.

Just as with Blaeu's Atlas, the bindings on Basnage's work, lavishly illustrated by Romeyn de Hooghe, were certainly made in order to spare the customer the trip to the binder and to allow the publisher the certainty that the volumes he sold had the plates in due order. Lindenberg was evidently proud of his product and showed this in his huge emblematical block. Directly after publication he will have had several copies of each edition bound and tooled to the same design, with the same tools in the same place. But many copies will have remained in stock to be bound as the need arose. At that time the binder will have remembered the layout of the decoration, but forgotten about the details or temporarily not have had some tools available, so that he used others, causing the difference in details mentioned. Clearly Lindenberg's publisher's binding is something quite other than the standard product made nowadays, which, after all, is only to be expected of pieces made by hand.[1]

A similar case is presented by bindings on the history of the Bible, in two volumes, written by David Martin and richly illustrated by several Dutch engravers. Both editions, in Dutch *Historie des Ouden en Nieuwen*

Amsterdam, May 3rd-4th 1988 (cat. 280), no. 841; in 1990 at the antiquarian bookshop Librije in IJmuiden and in Ghent Seminarium (A 822).

1. KNAUS, 'Über Verlegereinbände, *op. cit.*', p. 98, observed the same with publisher's bindings in the incunable period.

Fig; 2. Front cover and spine of gold-tooled binding in marbled calf, on J. Basnage, *Le grand tableau de l'univers*..., Amsterdam, J. Lindenberg, 1714. Royal Library, The Hague, 199 A 2. (Photograph: Royal Library.)

Testaments, and in French *Histoire du Vieux et du Nouveau Testament*, were published by Pieter Mortier (Amsterdam, 1700). I know of five copies of the Dutch edition and one of the French in very similar bindings.[1] They have the same large allegorical panel in the centre of the covers, including the Ark of the Covenant and a praying angel (Fig. 3). Two borders surround the panel, the inner one with an angel's head tool in the corners. The second and third fields on the spines contain the title; the others have the angel stamp in the centre and a pair of matching angel's heads in the corners. Obviously all these tools were made especially for the bindings, but the other rolls and tools were not. They belonged to the 'Rosette-double-drawer-handle group', in which workshop the bindings were made. Although the composition of the tooling and many tools are the same, some rolls and some tools vary from copy to copy. Two advertisements for the 'Great Bible' are known, in which the publisher gives prices for two kinds of paper, both unbound.[2] Yet I see only one reason why he should have had the costly plate of the Ark and the angel tool made, i.e. for sale of copies bound by order of himself. The copies I studied at least show no sign of having been intended for presentation. Perhaps Mortier only sold a limited number of bound copies. The differences in tools suggest that the binder did not get them all at the same time, as with Lindenberg's books.

Only the sale of unbound copies is likewise recorded of Bonaventura van Overbeke's lavishly illustrated book in large folio format, *Reliquiae antiquae urbis Romae* (in Latin, 1708) and *Les restes de l'ancienne Rome* (in French, 1709), printed at the expense of Michel van Overbeke by Johannes Crellius in Amsterdam, both with a printed dedication to the English Queen Anne.[3] Yet every binding on the ten copies which I have seen or heard of, each in three volumes, is decorated in the centre of the covers with a huge block of the English Royal arms and two frames of two different rolls alternating British emblems and leaves (Fig. 4). The corners of the inner frame show Queen Anne's monogram and a crown, those of the outer frame either St. George or St. Andrew. Two fields on the spine contain the title; the tools with St. George and St. Andrew alternate in the centre of the other fields, whereas a flower decorates the

1. A copy of the Dutch edition in the Royal Library, The Hague, in vellum (579 A 9-10), the others in speckled calf, two in the Rijksmuseum Meermanno-Westreenianum, The Hague (17 B 2 and 33 C 1-2), one in Amsterdam University Library (237 A 15-16) and one at antiquarian bookdealers Forum (Utrecht, 1992). A copy of the French edition, in speckled calf, was sold by Maggs, London, 1991 (see catalogue 1125, *Fine continental books and bindings*...no. 135).
2. I.H. VAN EEGHEN, *De Amsterdamse boekhandel, 1680-1725* (Amsterdam, 1960-1978), vol. III, p. 263.
3. VAN EEGHEN, *op. cit.*, vol. III, p. 85.

Fig. 3. Front cover and spine of gold-tooled vellum binding, on *Historie des Ouden en Nieuwen Testaments*, vol. 1, Amsterdam, Pieter Mortier, 1700. Royal Library, The Hague, 579 A 9. (Photograph: Royal Library.)

Fig. 4. Front cover and spine of gold-tooled binding in marbled calf, on B. van Overbeke, *Reliquiae antiquae urbis Romae*, Amsterdam, M. van Overbeke, 1708. Royal Library, The Hague, 42 B 10. (Photograph: Royal Library.)

corners. The large block, the rolls on the covers, Queen Anne's calligraphic monogram and the tools with the saints must have been specially cut for this enterprise. Possibly the crown and the tool with thistle and rose were too; the three other rolls (printed on the spine and the edges of the boards) were certainly not. At any rate, the two tools and three rolls belonged to the standard stock of the 'Rosette-double-drawer-handle group'; the bindings must originate from this shop.

The red morocco copy of the Latin edition in the British Library will have been the dedication copy for the Queen.[1] The other copies, five of the Latin and three of the French edition and one each of both editions are covered in polished marbled calf. Anthony Hobson asked me for information on one of these nine years ago, and I answered him that they were probably publisher's bindings.[2] Contrary to what I said then and notwithstanding the comparatively numerous copies in the 'standard binding' that have come to light (one would not expect this with presentation bindings), I now think it less likely that they were made for purposes of ready bound sale: would the Queen allow her coat of arms to be thus (mis)used? Are they then copies presented by the publisher, or, as is more likely, was it the Queen who decided to whom the bindings covered with British Royal emblems were to be given? At any rate, the publisher must have had the books bound in Amsterdam and by the 'Rosette-double-drawer-handle group'. The history of only the two copies in Leiden can be traced to their origin. Old book-numbers and an entry in the 1716 catalogue prove them to have entered the university library before 1716: they will have been donated to the library.[3]

My 1984 study referred to two other works, copies of which are known in identical bindings of the 'Rosette-double-drawer-handle group', Hen-

---

1. Mentioned in the catalogue of the Franklin H. Kissner Collection, Christie, Manson & Woods, London, 3-4 October 1990, no. 319. Shelfmark 136.g.6; the copy has silk end-leaves; the cypher of George III has been added, which means that the binding belonged to his library. I thank Dr. M. M. Foot for supplying me with the relevant data on both Van Overbeke bindings in the British Library.

2. The Latin edition in the Royal Library, The Hague, 42 B 10-12; Leiden University Library, Plano 49 B 1-3; Sale Sotheby, Parke Bernet & Co., London, 27-28 Oct. 1975, no. 273; the British Library, 687.1.14 (belonged to the early nineteenth century British Museum benefactor Rev. C. M. Cracherode); the Chester Beatty Library, Dublin, 13.E (this copy was mentioned in Anthony Hobson's letter of 11 Nov. 1983). The French edition in Leiden University Library, Plano 44 C 1-3; the 1990 Christie sale, *op. cit.*, no. 319; and sale of Sotheby's, London, 28th Nov. - 1st Dec. 1983, 347. The other copies I saw in the Van Wassenaer collection (Castle Twickel near Delden) some fifteen years ago, but could not make notes at that time.

3. *Catalogus librorum...bibliothecae...Universitatis Lugduno-Batavae* (Lugduni apud Batavos, 1716), p. 497, no. 487 A and B. I thank R. Breugelmans, Leiden U.L., for this information and the theory about the Queen as donor of these books.

ri Chatelain's *Le grand théâtre généalogique* (circa 1720) and Nicolas Sanson's *Atlas nouveau*.[1] I am less inclined now to consider them as publisher's bindings, especially those on the *Théâtre*, which show no more than the normal tools of the bindery. At least those of the *Atlas* have in the centre of the covers a block depicting Atlas carrying the celestial globe, which may have been specially cut for these bindings.

An extensive study of gold-tooled Dutch bindings of the eighteenth century has revealed no other possible publisher's binding of the 'luxury type' on expensively illustrated books and most probably made in order to please the purchaser, to facilitate the sale, and give certainty to the seller that everything was in the right order. Neither could less luxurious publisher's bindings be found before 1776 – the bindings mentioned in a 1772 advertisement (see below) have not come to light. In 1776 the first of a totally different kind appears on the market: a cheap and simple product, meant for usually short-lived books.

Some authors have stated that from the beginning of the eighteenth century books were sold either sewn or bound.[2] Reasons must be given here why this is not true. The ever repeated description of collating and folding in eighteenth century binding manuals (see above) and the instructions to the binder, at the end of many an illustrated book, telling him where to put the plates and other pages delivered on separate sheets, prove that many books at that time were still published in loose sheets. The instructions can be quite detailed. To quote the end of a fairly extensive one: 'This volume consists of 57 sheets and a title in red, of 1 penny each, costing 2 guilders and 18 pence, one vignette... 18 geographical maps and plates... the price of this whole second volume, on small paper 5 guilders and 14 pence, or on large paper 8 guilders and 11 pence. But subscribers will not pay more than 4 guilders and 15 pence, small paper, and for the edition on large paper... 7 guilders and 2 pence.'[3] But often they are far simpler. The latest one I found dates from 1792.[4]

Many books in the eighteenth century were published, by subscrip-

---

1. STORM VAN LEEUWEN, 'Un groupe... *op. cit.*', pp. 337-8 and cat. 23a,b and 14,15.
2. E.G. VAN EEGHEN, *De Amsterdamse boekhandel, op. cit.* (especially vol. V-1, pp. 49, 131-177) came to this conclusion from the book-keeping of the Leiden firm of Luchtmans, but even a study of inventories and other booklists presented in her standard work proves that a large part of the books was sold unbound, the other part just sewn and only a smaller part bound.
3. In the second volume (1747) of *Historische beschryving der reizen, of nieuw en volkoome verzameling van... zee- en landtogten...* 21 vol. ('s Gravenhage. Pieter de Hondt, 1747 - Amsterdam, J. Hayman and others, 1767) – all the other volumes have similar instructions, if not always as extensive.
4. In the last volume of G. BONNET's *Verzameling van leerredenen* (Utrecht, Willem van Yzerworst, 1792).

tion, in instalments, as the above instructions show, which gave the buyer a financial advantage. But he could only have the volumes bound when all quires or groups of quires were published. Of course the publisher could and would sell part of the edition bound. An advertisement on a bifolium, afterwards pasted into the book, M. Magerus' 1772 quarto edition of Ovid, *Gedaantwisselingen*, offers his customers the choice of buying the book either in instalments or after completion of each volume.[1] Ready bound he could get the edition on 'Superroyal' or 'Imperial' paper, in a 'half English binding', a 'Burgomasters binding' or a 'French binding' – unfortunately I have not been able to trace copies thus bound. Matthijs van Loopik's bookbinding manual (1790; see below) was published in quires too, but never got beyond three.

The invoices for the library of stadholder William V provide another argument against the general existence of publisher's bindings in eighteenth century Holland. They show all his new books to have been bound after purchase, in sturdy vellum or simple marbled or speckled calf with gold tooling only on the spine. The stadholder had no interest in luxury and I do not think he would have had them bound had they been delivered in some sort of more permanent binding.[2] When the binder Hendrik de Haas (1806) deals with the folding of small books, 18° and smaller, and remarks that these, mainly *children's books and almanachs* (my italics), 'nowadays' usually present no more problems in this respect since they are delivered sewn or ready bound, he apparently refers to an exception![3]

From 1661 onwards the Utrecht university printer had, among other duties, to see to the sewing of at least 100 copies of dissertations, for students, professors and others. In a regulation of 1764 this simple method of binding is mentioned again and so is even the kind of paper to cover the thin quarto publications.[4] Many Dutch dissertations of the eighteenth century may be found stitched in wrappers of decorated paper, which shows that other universities had the same custom of having them distributed in this form. Here, however, we cannot speak of normal publisher's bindings, for they were not made in order to be sold, but to be given away by the student.

1. Royal Library, The Hague (760 A 2).
2. JAN STORM VAN LEEUWEN, *De achttiende-eeuwse Haagse boekband*...('s Gravenhage, 1976), pp. 137-197; JAN STORM VAN LEEUWEN, 'Over de bibliotheek van de stadhouders Willem IV en V', *Vereniging "Oranje-Nassau Museum", met het jaarverslag over 1977*, pp. 25-52.
3. DE HAAS, *De Boekbinder, op. cit.*, p. 6. His book, published in 1806, was written mainly in 1794, at the end of a long and fruitful life.
4. G.A. EVERS, 'Gegevens betreffende Utrechtsche staten-, stads-, en akademiedrukkers', *Het grafisch museum*, 1-5 (1930-1935). Offprint of the whole article separately published with its own pagination.

But more books were probably sold in our country thus provisionally bound than in France. True, in collections with older holdings one does find Dutch publications of the eighteenth century in wrappers or bindings in grey-blue or speckled paper. But they do not show who had them made: the publisher, the bookseller or the first owner. Later in the century some publishers added one or more printed title labels to the publication, to be glued on the spine of such a binding. The oldest example found dates from 1787, but they go on well into the nineteenth century.[1] The title labels, however, indicate that these bindings were not made by order of the publisher.

Actually the only certain publisher's binding in paper is the one with printing on the covers and/or spine, which brings us back to Germany in the late fifteenth century. It was apparently a totally isolated phenomenon. But in the eighteenth century it started anew and gradually grew in popularity. It originated, it seems, in France and Italy and soon spread to England and Holland.[2] The Paris 'revised bookbinders' code' of 1750, specifically gave publishers and printers the right to cover pamphlets and small books in paper or vellum without stiffening.[3] But the first paper binding found with preprinted decoration on covers and spine dates from 1764. At the same time in England schoolbooks were issued in simple bindings, covered with a coarsely woven cloth.[4] This may have given the London publisher William Pickering the idea to have at least part of publication bound in specifically prepared cloth in the early 1820s. Soon afterwards a combination with case-binding and the stamping of whole binding decorations by means of the press was made.[5] The new publisher's binding was born. But almost everything leading up to it originated in the eighteenth century. The role of the publisher in the process and the choice of cloth as covering material came from that period and, as will be shown, so does casebinding.

1. *Tael- en dichtlievende oefeningen, van het Genootschap...Kunst wordt door arbeid verkreegen...* [vol. 5], (Leiden, C. van Hoogenveen and others, 1787). The Royal Library, The Hague, (655 J 5).
2. GILES BARBER, 'L'évolution de la couverture imprimée', in: *La bibliographie matérielle*, présentée par Roger Laufer (Paris, 1983), pp. 63-74; idem, 'Continental paper wrappers and publisher's bindings in the eighteenth century', *The Book Collector* 24 (1975), pp. 37-49; WILLIAM A. JACKSON, 'Printed Wrappers of the Fifteenth to the Eighteenth Centuries', *Harvard Library Bulletin* 6 (1952), pp. 313-321. See also M. Sadleir, *The evolution...cit.*, and, for Italy, A.R.A. HOBSON, *French and Italian Collectors and their bindings*...(Oxford, 1953), no. 84.
3. See also D.T. POTTINGER, *The French Book Trade in the Ancien Régime* (Cambridge, Mass., 1958), p. 333.
4. ERIC QUAYLE, 'The Evolution of Trade Bindings', *Antiquarian Book Monthly Review* 4 (1977), pp. 320-325, 358-364.
5. D. BALL, *Victorian publishers' bindings...op. cit.* in n. 4, pp. 2-3.

Up till now Dutch publisher's binding in paper of that period has received little attention. Three examples covering type specimen books (of 1784, 1793, 1796, in the Broxbourne Library and now in the Bodleian Library, Oxford) were mentioned by Barber.[1] I have not been able to study them: no copies are available in the larger Dutch libraries. Here I shall give a list of 32 further examples, dating from 1776 to 1800. The list gives the titles of the books and some details on the bindings in chronological order. It can in no way be considered complete, based as it is on not much more than examples which I chanced upon in the stacks of Amsterdam University Library, the Royal Library at The Hague and Zeeuwse Bibliotheek, Middelburg. A more extensive search will undoubtedly reveal more. But even then it will be difficult to guess how many of them were ever made. Their provisional character will have caused many a collector to have more permanent bindings put in their place immediately, while others had them replaced after some time, after damage through wear and tear. Incomplete as the list is, I think the examples found give an idea of most of the varieties that existed, so that a first analysis can be provided.

There can be no doubt that these bindings are true publisher's bindings. The printing in ink of the paper cover is typically the work of a printer/publisher. Some bindings exist in several copies on the same book. A beautiful example is the series of Middelburg almanachs (in our list no. 1; fig. 5), known in three styles of execution: in paper with a decoration made up of loose pieces of decorative type, or in paper printed with a single block, or, the de luxe variant, in leather or silk printed with a single block. The first variety exists in ten copies, ranging from almost perfect to very imperfect. Every binding on the combined years 1791/92 belongs to the second style as does an incomplete series starting with the year 1778. The third style is known in five copies, one perfect and most of the others very imperfect. I will not go into questions about the use of a block for gold tooling for printing in ink, or what the de luxe bindings were made for, sale or presentation. It is more important that the Middelburg 1777 almanach, bound in 1776, is the earliest Dutch example of the publisher's binding under discussion: the number of copies found and the placing of the publisher's name on the back cover make it clear that they were made by order of the publisher. Although the practice started in 1776, it may have taken almost ten years to get fully under way.

More bindings were found in several copies. In chronological order they are: Pope Clement's published reflexions (no. 2), in paper as well as

---

1. PLOOS's *Epreuves de plusieurs sortes de caractères* (1784), the 1793 edition of Von Herdingh and Mortier's *Proeve van letteren* and Van Teeckelenburgh's *Proeve van letteren* of 1796, Broxbourne Library; see Barber, 'Continental...op. cit.', p. 43.

Fig. 5. Both covers and spine of printed paper binding, on *Zeelands chronyk-almanach* ... 1777, Middelburg, J. Dane, 1776. Royal Library, The Hague, 346 L 1. (Photograph: Royal Library.)

in silk (the latter possibly meant for presentation; fig. 6), the writings of Tollé in three identical bindings (no. 14), a political treatise on the stadholder in two copies (no. 17; one only partly preserved), a series of burlesque small political treatises (called almanach; no. 21) in two copies, one partly preserved and the other known only from a catalogue entry, and a children's book in two copies (no. 32; fig. 9). Several of the bindings listed here have the addresses where the book could be bought on the back cover (no. 1, 10, 14, 17; fig. 7). Others have a justification by the publisher in the same place (no. 6 and 32; fig. 9) or an advertisement on other publications by him (no. 11, 16, 22, 24, 26 and 28). This is further proof that they were made by order of the publisher. Printing material used on three bindings was also used in the books themselves (no. 1, 12, 27), which is definite proof that they are publisher's bindings.

The publisher's binding in paper, as has already been said, was intended to allow the buyer immediate use of a book whose value lasted for

Fig. 6. Back cover and spine of printed and coloured silk binding, on Pope Clement XIV, *Uitgeleezene gedagten*, Amsterdam, Yntema and Tieboel, 1779. Royal Library, The Hague, 1756 G 114.
(Photograph: Royal Library.)

only a short period of time (like almanachs) and to keep a cheap book cheap for new clients with a small purse. The printed covers gave them some decoration, showed the title of the book or advertised other publications of the same printer. The decoration varies between lavish and very simple. Four bindings are decorated only on the spines, with not much more than the title of the book (no. 3, 4, 19; fig. 8 and no. 23). The bindings on the Middelburg almanach mentioned (no. 1; fig. 5) and the treatise on stadholder Willem V (no. 17; fig. 7) are examples of extensive decoration. Three cover decorations were printed with a large block. With the first, Clement's reflexions (no. 2; fig. 6), the block shows the portrait of the Pope and was obviously made for these bindings; with the second (no. 17) the decorative block may have been meant for other octavo editions as well. And with the third the blocks are illustrations directly related to the contents of the book (no. 20). The decorated covers of the other bindings are either printed with only type (the title of the book), or, more often, with type within a border of separate decorative pieces. One style of border, a staff with rococo decoration in the corners and half way down the sides, decorates the oldest binding (no. 1; fig. 5) and the last three (no. 30, 31, 32; fig. 9) and was apparently popular.

From the point of view of technique this paper binding also presents a wide variety. Four wrappers were found where the pastedown is pasted directly on to the inside of the paper cover. The quires of the book are stitched with unsupported chain-stitches (no. 22, 25, 27); once a technique of stabbing and oversewing has been used (no. 23). Obviously these wrappers are strongly related to those covering separate quires of books published in instalments, like Van Loopik's *Volkomen handleiding* already mentioned. The only copy known is rebound in a modern library binding, while retaining at the front and back of each quire the original blue-grey paper cover.[1] Some bindings are almost as simple, sewn on two series of kettle-stitches too, but have cardboard covers. The paper is mostly just glued onto the covers and flat spine, without turn-ins (e.g. no. 6, 11 and 28). Many paper bindings, however, have one piece of cardboard, folded in order to make a hinge, for the covers and the slightly rounded spine. The covering paper has turn-ins all round, also at the top and bottom of the spine. The bookblock in most cases is sewn onto two vellum strips, pasted to the inside of the covers under the flange and the pastedown (e.g. no. 3, 4, 5, 12, 13, 14, 16, 19, 23, 32). Obviously the whole binding could be

1. M[ATTHIJS] VAN LOOPIK, *Volkomen handleiding tot de boekbindkonst...* (Gouda, M. van Loopik, 1790). Three quires published. The only copy known is in the library of the Vereeniging ter Bevordering van de Belangen des Boekhandels in Amsterdam University Library. HENDRIK DE HAAS, *De boekbinder, op. cit.*, pp. ix-x, says that van Loopik started the subscription in 1786, but did not publish more than three quires in 1790.

Fig. 7. Both covers and spine of printed paper binding, on *Het praaltoneel...voorgevallen 1787*, Amsterdam, J. Peppelenbos, 1791. Nijmegen University Library, 807 c 69. (Photograph: Royal Library.)

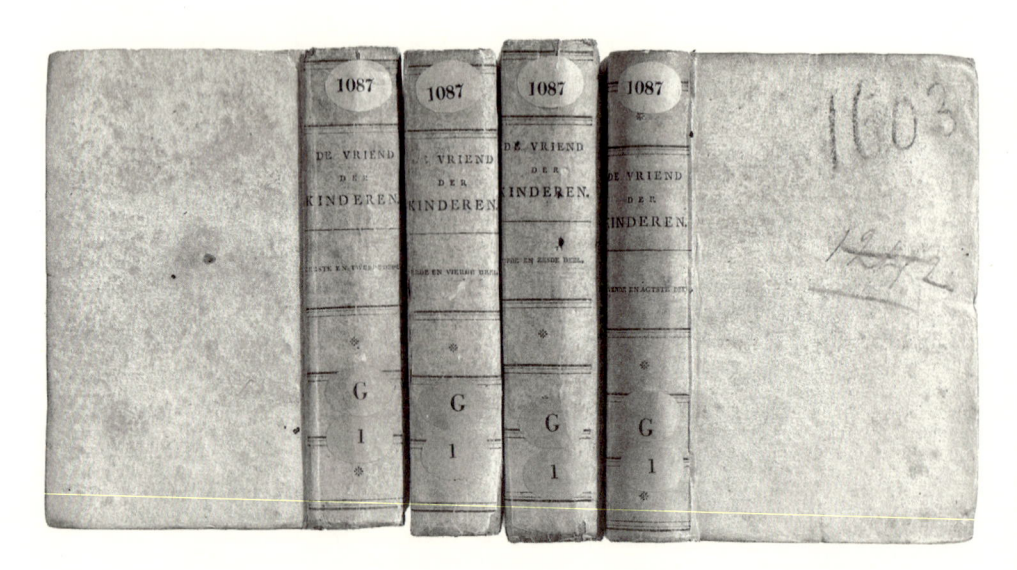

Fig. 8. Back cover, four spines and front cover of printed paper binding, on *De vriend der kinderen*, Haarlem, F. Bohn, 1791-92. Royal Library, The Hague, 1087 G 1. (Photograph: Royal Library.)

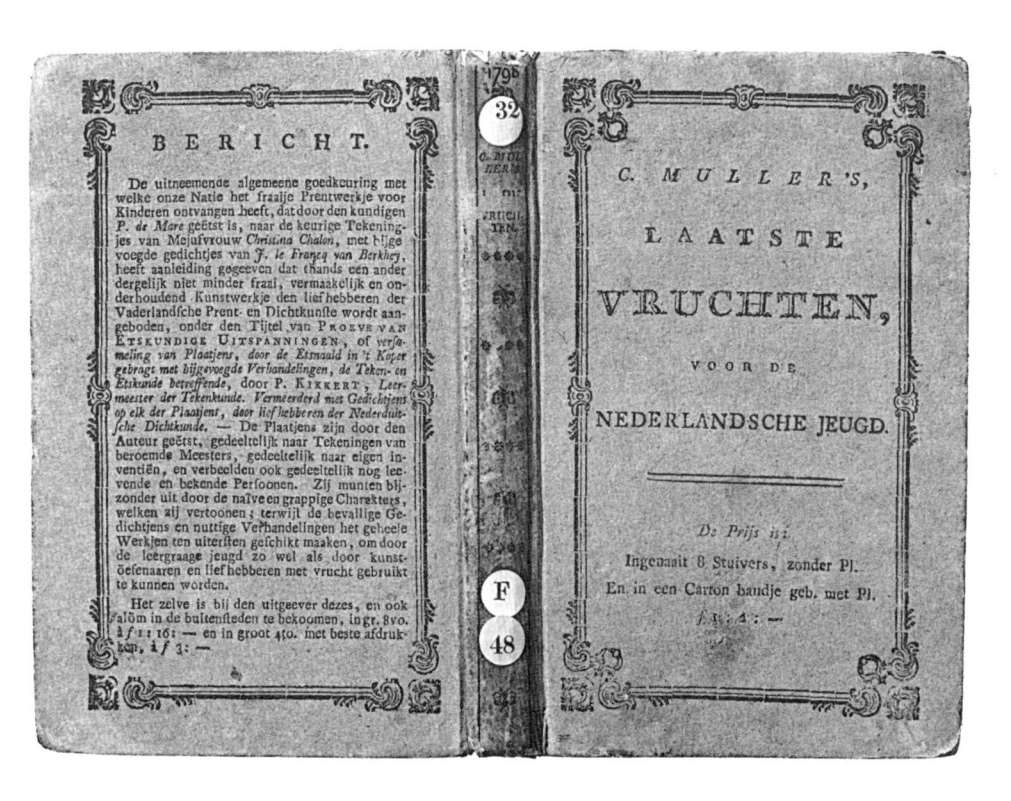

Fig. 9. Both covers and spine of printed paper binding, on C. Muller, *Laatste vruchten*..., Amsterdam, W. van Vliet, 1798. Royal Library, The Hague, 32 F 48. (Photograph: Royal Library.)

finished before putting the bookblock in it. Case-binding seems to be an invention of the eighteenth rather than the nineteenth century.

In many Dutch paper bindings of that century, both printed and not printed, we find a construction of the endpapers which seems to have been typical for precisely this type of binding. I did not find it in more permanent bindings. Often it consists of just one endpaper, the pastedown, sewn with a stub around the final quire of the book (no. 6, 7, 9, 11, 25, 27), but as often it consists of a double leaf, folded in such a manner that one leaf is ca. 2 cm. narrower than the other. This double leaf was folded for a second time ca. 1 cm. from the first fold, resulting in a double stub, with which the quire was sewn around the final quire of the book, the larger leaf forming the pastedown and the smaller a flyleaf. But the bindings with cardboard covers and spine usually have a more conventional construction of the end-leaves, consisting of two double leaves, sewn in the fold, whereby one leaf is the pastedown. Several variants, however, were also in use.

The edges of the bookblocks were seldom trimmed, which proves that most of these bindings were considered to be temporary: the buyer preserved every possibility of having the book definitely bound. But the edges of the three almanachs, still in their complete covering, are cut off and sprinkled, which is not surprising with this type of publication that would not be rebound because normally it had to last only one year (no. 1, 7, 26). Only three other pieces have also cut and sprinkled edges (no. 12, 30, 32).

It is not surprising that just over half (seventeen) of the books in these publisher's bindings should be printed in Amsterdam, the most important publishing city in the Netherlands, but it is surprising that no examples from the second most important city, The Hague, were found. Four books come from Haarlem, three from Leiden and two from Dordrecht, whereas other towns are represented by only one item or group of items each. While talking about the difficulty of establishing a general trend for paper bindings, Barber observed that various classes of publication were probably marketed in different ways: schoolbooks, prayer books, almanachs, periodicals each following their own trend, quite apart from those in the general fields of literature and science.[1] The books covered by the Dutch paper publisher's bindings bear this out. At the same time Hendrik de Haas's remark on the new way of supplying children's books and almanachs (referred to above) is proved correct; nine cover children's books and four almanachs. Eight of the books enclosed are collections of poems, four political treatises, all apparently of a short-lived character. The other seven books have different subjects. Hendrik de Haas's remark about the small size of the publications is also true. No sizes larger than octavo were found: 5 in small octavo, 5 in duodecimo, 4 in sixteen-mo and the rest in normal octavo.

Finally special attention may again be drawn to the bindings of the Middelburg almanach, because of the differences in execution found, the colour of the paper, the printing material used. This may, once again, warn us that the publisher's binding in the eighteenth century was something quite different from that of our time. At that time when many books were still published on several kinds of paper, and mass-production could still be adapted to the needs of groups of customers, it will have been logical to supply the publisher's bindings in variants too.

LIST OF SOME DUTCH EIGHTEENTH-CENTURY PAPER PUBLISHER'S BINDINGS

1. Zeelands chronyk-almanach voor den jaare 1777 [from 1781 'voor 't jaar']. Te Middelburg, by Jan Dane (1777-1784), by P. Gillissen en Zoon

---

1. BARBER, 'L'évolution...*op. cit.*', p. 64.

(1785-1790), by W. A. Keel en Comp. (the year 1791/1792). 16-mo (bound 1776-1791).[1]

A series of 14 bindings in the Royal Library (1777-1786, 1788-1791/92; 346 L 1-14; ill. 5), in pale yellow paper, over cardboard covers. a) The vols. for 1777-1790 have a baroque frame (*rocailles* over the corners and half way down the sides) on the covers and the title and the coat of arms of Zeeland (front) or the coat of arms of Middelburg and the imprint (back). b) Vol. 1791/92 has on both covers the impression of one large plate: a baroque frame around the circular coat of arms of Zeeland. The spines are divided into five compartments. Edges cut and sprinkled red-brown.

A series of 11 similar bindings in the Zeeuwse Bibliotheek (1778, 1779, 1781-85, 1787-90; 1029 D 3, 4, 5, 7), in brownish paper, with cover decoration type a.

A series of 3 similar bindings in the Zeeuwse Bibliotheek (1778, 1781, 1788; 1029 D 4), in brownish paper, with cover decoration a.

One similar binding in the Zeeuwse Bibliotheek (1788; 1092 D 6), in brownish paper, with cover decoration a.

A series of 11 similar bindings in the Zeeuwse Bibliotheek (1777, 1779-81, 1783-89; 1029 D 2, 3, 4, 5, 6), in orange/pink painted paper, with cover decoration a.

Two similar bindings in the Zeeuwse Bibliotheek (two of 1786; 1029 D 1, 5), in orange/pink painted paper, with cover decoration a.

A series of 4 similar bindings in the Zeeuwse Bibliotheek (1777, 1783, 1784, 1791/92; 1029 D 1, 2, 3), in yellowish paper, with cover decoration a and b.

A series of 11 similar bindings in the Zeeuwse Bibliotheek (1777, 1778, 1780-87, 1790; 1029 D 3, 4, 5, 6) in yellow-greenish paper, with cover decoration a.

A series of 3 similar bindings in the Zeeuwse Bibliotheek (1782, 1785, 1790; 1029 D 2, 6, 7), in yellow-greenish paper, with cover decoration a.

One similar binding in the Zeeuwse Bibliotheek (1790; 1029 D 6), in yellow-greenish paper, with cover decoration a.

A series of 9 similar bindings in the Zeeuwse Bibliotheek (1778-1782, 1785, 1788, 1789, 1791/92; 1029 D 5), in white paper, with cover decoration b on the covers of every volume, no decoration on the spines and blue coloured edges.

One binding similar to the above-mentioned in the Zeeuwse Bibliotheek (1791/92; 1029 D 3).

1. It is known from many entries in the *Extract uit de Notulen van de Maandvergadering* (Middelburg, May 1783 - December 1802) that the Almanach was bound at the end of the year preceding that for which it was compiled.

A complete series of de luxe bindings in the Royal Library (346 J 1), in gold tooled rose-pink morocco, over cardboard covers. French bindings with three raised cords. On both covers the impression of one block as described above under b. The fields on the spine have only a small tool in the centre. Edges gilt.

A series of 7 similar de luxe bindings, in the Zeeuwse Bibliotheek (1777-81, 1788; 1029 D 1).

Two similar de luxe bindings in the Zeeuwse Bibliotheek (1785, 1791/92; 1029 D 1), in dark green morocco.

Three similar de luxe bindings in the Zeeuwse Bibliotheek (1787, 1790, 1791/92; 1029 D 1,6), in marbled calf.

One similar de luxe binding in the Zeeuwse Bibliotheek (1782; 1028 B 19), in whitish silk.

The frames in cover decoration type a) are of the same sort as those surrounding the text-columns of the booklets. The printing material on Dane's and on Gillissen's covers differs only in details. The plate used for cover decoration type b) and always found on the vols. for 1791/92, seems identical to the gold-tooled block on the de luxe copies. Did the binder of the last almanach and of the incomplete series in Middelburg (1029 D 5) use the same block that had been used for gold-tooling the de luxe copies since 1777? This would be something totally unknown for our country at that time.

2. Clement XIV (Ganganelli), Pope. Uitgeleezene gedagten van - verzameld uit deszelfs brieven en redenvoeringen. Te Amsterdam, by Yntema en Tieboel, 1779. 12mo.

Copy in Amsterdam University Library (1072 G 13), in grey-blue paper, over cardboard covers and spine. On each cover the impression of one woodblock, depicting a large frame in Louis XVI-style, garlands and a central lozenge with the portrait of Pope Ganganelli. The book-title in the second compartment on the spine.[1]

De luxe copy in the Royal Library (1756 G 114; ill. 6), in greyish silk, printed and hand coloured in blue, yellow, red, green and violet, over cardboard covers and spine. Binding with hollow back; sewing on five recessed cords. Covers and spine printed with the same blocks. Headbands embroidered; edge made black.

The blocks, obviously made for the publisher's bindings, were also used for some luxury copies, probably for presentation purposes.

3. Abraham Blussé. Iets dichtmaatigs. Te Dordrecht, bij Pieter Blussé, 1784. 8vo.

Copy in the Royal Library (297 J 44) in grey-blue paper, over card-

---

1. I thank Joke Kuijpers and Anne-Dirk Renting for tracing this copy.

board covers and spine. Only the spine is decorated, the book-title in the second compartment.

An advertisement of the publisher added on a separate leaf with a stub around the last quire.

4. De patriotten. Tooneelspel. Te Amsterdam, bij Johannes Allart, 1785. 8vo.

Copy in the Royal Library (312 L 72) in bluish-grey paper, over thin cardboard covers and spine. Only the spine is decorated; the book-title in the third compartment.

5. Korte beschryving benevens eene naauwkeurige afbeelding... van 't koninglyke lusthuis 'T Loo... [re-edition of prints by Romeyn de Hooghe]. Te Amsterdam, by G.W. van Egmond, 1786. 8vo.

Copy in the Royal Library (587 D 33) in yellow paper, over cardboard covers and spine. On both covers a simple frame and the book-title (front cover), or an ornament (back cover). Spine divided into five fields.

6. Proeve van kleine gedigten voor kinderen [door H. van Alphen]. Vijftiende druk. Te Utrecht, bij de wed. Jan van Terveen en zoon, 1786. 8vo.

Copy in the Royal Library (1090 E 113) in bluish-grey paper, over cardboard covers. The book-title and price on the front cover and a justification of the edition on the back cover. The title also in the eighth compartment on the spine.

7. De naauwkeurige Hollandsche Almanach 1787. Te Amsterdam, by Louwerens Nutbey, [1786 or 1787] . 16mo.

Copy in the Royal Library (28 E 6: 1787), in whitish paper, printed in red-brown ink, over cardboard covers. On both covers a composition of frame, central and corner ornaments. The book-title in the second compartment on the spine. Edges cut off and sprinkled brownish.

8. Pieter Nieuwland. Gedichten. Te Amsterdam, bij P. de Hengst, 1788. 8vo.

Copy in the Zeeuwse Bibliotheek (1019 A 8), in grey-blue paper, printed in brown ink, cardboard covers and spine. On each cover a different composition of a frame and flowers in the centre. The book-title in the second compartment on the spine.

9. J.A. Schasz. Reize door Aapeland. [s.l.] 1788. 8vo.

Copy in Amsterdam University Library (3 D 21), in yellow paper over thin cardboard covers and spine. On both covers the book-title, which is also in one compartment on the spine.

10. Het [Amstels] driedaags, treur-toneel... 1787. [Amsterdam, 1789.] 8vo.[1]

1. *Het driedaags, treurtoneel, geöpend binnen Amsteldam, op den 29ste Mei...* 1787... Uit egte stukken... by een verzameld: Door een Vriend der Waarheid ... [Am-

In Amsterdam University Library (291 C 19:1), remains of a binding or wrapper of grey-blue paper covers, preserved at the front and back of the book in a half-leather binding of the early nineteenth century, which also contains two other, similar publications. On the covers two connected frames of the same typographical material as can be found in the book. On the front cover is the book-title; on the back cover the addresses of where the book was sold.

From instructions to the binder, giving the final arrangement, we learn that the book was sold in three parts, each containing one canto. Possibly the remaining covers originally belonged to one of these separately published parts.

11. J. Ahorner. Brieven aan de Jonge Carolina, een opvoedings schrift. Te Amsterdam, bij N.T. Gravius, 1789. Small 8vo.

Copy in the Royal Library (1088 B 100), in grey-blue paper, over cardboard covers. On the covers a border of leaves and tendrils. The book-title on the front cover and an advertisement on the back cover. The title also in the first compartment of the spine.

12. Echtzangen ter eere van... Willem Leonard Voorduin en Maria Huiberta van Meerten... door den Echt vereënigd den 28sten van Grasmaend 1790. [Te Leyden gedrukt, bij Cornelis Heyligert, 1790]. 8vo.

Copy in the Royal Library (recent acquisition),[1] in light grey paper, over cardboard covers and spine. Edge cut off and sprinkled light brown. On both covers a decorative border and the book-title in playful disposition (front cover) or decoration in lozenge form (back cover). The book-title along the spine.

On the front cover a block with a pair of clasped hands that can also be found above two of the poems in the booklet.

13. Jan van Dyk. Kunst- en historie-kundige beschryving van alle de schilderyen op het stadhuis van Amsteldam... Te Amsteldam, by I. de Jongh, 1790. 8vo.

Copy in the Royal Library (1295 G 27), in bluish-grey paper, over thin cardboard covers and spine. Only the spine is decorated; the book-title in the third compartment.

14. Hendrik Antoni Tollé. Iets, van -. Te Vere, bij C. M. van de Graaf, 1790. 8vo.

Three identical copies in the Zeeuwse Bibliotheek (1028 D 25, 1086 C 38, 1045 A 1) in grey-blue paper, over cardboard spine and covers. On both covers an identical frame, with the title (front cover) and the im-

---

sterdam, 1789.] Half-title: *Amstels driedaags treur-toneel*; engraved title: *Monumenten voor Amsterdam in drie zangen*, te Amsterdam, in de geplunderde boekwinkels. 8vo.

1. From antiquarian bookdealer Frits Knuf, Buren, cat. 141 (1982), no. 668 and cat. 154 (*Some interesting and remarkable bookbindings*, 1988), no. 24.

print (back cover). The title in the second compartment of the spine also.

15. Kransje van letter-bloempjes voor Nederlandsch Jufferschap. IIe stukie. Te Dordrecht, by N. van Eysden & Comp., 1791. Small 8vo.

Copy in the Zeeuwse Bibliotheek (1085 E 13), in grey-blue paper, over cardboard spine and covers. On the front cover a border and the book-title. On the back cover another border and a rose. The title also in the second compartment on the spine.

16. De lydens-geschiedenis van den Zaligmaker... door LII. prentverbeeldingen opgehelderd. Te Haarlem, by François Bohn, 1791. Small 8vo.

Copy in the Zeeuwse Bibliotheek (1057 C 15), in white paper, over cardboard covers. On the front cover the title of the book, on the back cover an advertisement of the publisher. The title in the second compartment on the spine.

17. Het praal-toneel, der gezeegende omwenteling in de Zeven Vereenigde Nederlanden, Voorgevallen... 1787... Te Amsterdam, by J. Peppelenbos, 1791. 8vo.

Copy in Nijmegen University Library (807 C 69; ill. 7), in grey-blue paper over cardboard covers. On the front cover the book-title, above the portraits of stadholder William V and his wife, Princess Wilhelmina of Prussia, their coat of arms under a crown and the price of the book. On the back cover two horizontal emblematic blocks and the addresses where the book was to be sold. The title also on the spine between some ornaments. Elaborate binding in very good condition.[1]

Fragments of a copy in Amsterdam University Library (236 B 3), in a binding re-bound in the present century, but preserving the covering of front and back cover.

18. A. Loosjes. Pz. Frank van Borselen en Jacoba van Beijeren. Tweede Druk. Te Haarlem, by A. Loosjes, pz., 1791. 8vo. Large paper.

Copy in the Zeeuwse Bibliotheek (1057 H 7), in grey-blue paper, over cardboard covers. On both covers the impression of one (?) block; a broad border and central lozenge around a flower. Spine repaired.

19. De vriend der kinderen. Eerste - [agste] deel. Te Haarlem, bij François Bohn, 1791-1792. 8 vol. in 4 bindings. 12mo.

Copy in the Royal Library (1087 G 1 : 1-8; ill. 8), in white paper, over cardboard covers and spine. Only the spine is decorated; the book-title in the second compartment and the volume numeration in the third.

20. Nieuw geschenk voor de jeugd. [Deel I, IIde and IIIde Deel]. Te Amsterdam, bij Johannes Allart, 1791-1794. 12mo.

---

1. Thanks are due to Dr. Robert Arpots of this library for kindly supplying the photographs and relevant data.

Copy in the Royal Library (30 K 27-29), in white paper over cardboard covers and spine. On the covers a frame of stars and the book-title (front cover) or a larger star (back cover). Spine divided into eight compartments.

21. Amurath-Effendi Hekim-Bachi. De lantaarn, voor 1792, [1793, 1796, 1798, 1800, 1801]. Te Amsterdam, in 't Nieuwe Licht, [1791?-1800?]. 16mo. Published by the physician P. van Woensel, in order to vent his political ('Patriot') ideas.

Fragments in the Royal Library (519 L 22-27), preserved as loose sheets, at the front and back of the books, in modern library bindings, with one block-print each.

The prints are of the same sort as those inside the booklets. Only the prints in front of the volumes for 1792 and 1793 are the same; 1796 shows also part of the imprint 't Nieuwe- Licht'.

An incomplete series of copies (1796, 1798, 1800 and 1801), 're-backed', at Van Stockum's sale, The Hague, 1-3 June 1988, no. 1282.

22. De Spiegel der Jeugd...in een Zamenspraak tusschen vader en Zoon door S.V.D.T. Te Amsteldam, by Ph. van Leeuwen, 1793. 8vo.

Copy in Amsterdam University Library (3 D 20), in white paper wrapper. On the front cover a decorative frame and the book-title, on the back cover a frame and an advertisement of the publisher. The title also in the second compartment of the spine.

23. I.D. Pasteur. Beknopte natuurlijke historie der zoogende dieren. Eerste [-derde] deel. Te Leyden, bij Honkoop en du Mortier, 1793-1800. 3 vol. 8vo.

Copy in the Royal Library (1087 D 27-29), in white paper, over cardboard covers and spine. Only the spines are decorated; the book-title in the third compartment.

24. Catechismus der Egaliteit en de rechten van den Mensch. Gedrukt in Nederland, [s.l.], 1794. 8vo.

Copy in Amsterdam University Library (3 E 8), in white paper wrapper. Stab-sewing in Japanese manner, through three small holes. Front cover with a decorative frame and the book-title, back cover with an advertisement of the printers.

25. Hoveniers of Tuinmans zakboekje...Vermeerderd...Te Leyden, bij A. en J. Honkoop, 1794. Small 8vo.

Copy in the Zeeuwse Bibliotheek (1074 D 7), in wrapper of grey-blue paper. On both covers a border and the title (front cover) or the contents of the book (back cover). The title along the length of the spine also.

26. Almanak, van vernuft en smaak voor het jaar 1795. [Te Amsterdam, bij de Wed. J. Doll, 1794?] 16mo.

Copy in the Royal Library (26 E 7: 1795), in light blue paper, over cardboard covers and spine. Sewing onto two cords. On the front cover the book-title, on the back cover an advertisement of the publisher. The title in the second and third compartments of the spine also. Edges cut off and sprinkled red-brown.

27. Hieronimus van Alphen. Kleine gedichten voor kinderen. Te Amsterdam, bij J. Wortman, [ca. 1794?]. Small 8vo.

Copy in the Royal Library (1090 E 98), in whitish-yellow paper wrapper. On the front cover a decorative frame and the book-title. On the back cover the same frame and a decoration of putti and a basket of flowers. The spine is decorated along its length.

The wrapper consists of wastepaper of a print. The putti and flowers (back cover) are also found on the titlepage.

28. J. Hazeu, Corn. Zoon. Het Psalm-gezang gemaklijk gemaakt... Te Amsterdam, bij Gravus en Hazeu, Cz., 1796. 12mo.

Copy in the Zeeuwse Bibliotheek (1057 C 15), in grey-blue paper, over cardboard covers. On both covers a border and the title (front) or an advertisement of the publisher (back). Spine divided into seven fields.

29. P. Nieuwland. Nagelaten gedichten. Te Haarlem, bij A. Loosjes, 1797. 8vo. Large paper.

Copy in the Zeeuwse Bibliotheek (1057 H 3), in grey-blue paper, over cardboard covers. On both covers a border and the title (front) or a flower (back). The title in the second compartment of the spine.

30. De vier stonden van den dag, vervat in zestien Afbeeldingen... voor Nederlands Jeugd. Te Delft, bij de Groot pz., 1798. 8vo.

Copy in the Royal Library (32 F 64), in grey-blue paper, over cardboard covers and spine. Sewing on two double cords. Bookblock cut off; edges sprinkled red. On both covers a rococo frame (as on no. 1), with the book-title (front) or the table of contents of the book (back). The title also in the second compartment of the spine.

31. Hieronymus van Alphen. Kleine gedichten voor kinderen. Te Amsteldam, by J. Woertman, 1798. 12mo.

Copy in the Royal Library (1090 E 116), in yellow paper, over cardboard covers. On the covers a rococo frame (as no. 1) with the book-title (front) and a basket of flowers (back). The book-title along the length of the spine.

32. C. Muller. Laatste vruchten, voor de Nederlandsche jeugd. Te Amsteldam, bij Willem van Vliet, 1798. 8vo.

Two copies in the Royal Library (32 F 48; 1090 G 59: ill. 9), in blue-grey paper, over cardboard covers and spine. Bookblock cut off; edges sprinkled red. On the covers a rococo frame (as no. 1), with the book-title (front) or the preface and an advertisement by the publisher (back). The title also in the first compartment of the spine.

Jeanne Veyrin-Forrer

NOTES SUR THOMAS MAHIEU

L'examen de quelques documents inédits ou publiés invite à former de nouvelles conjectures sur les origines du bibliophile Thomas Mahieu et à préciser certains aspects de sa carrière. C'est à quoi tendent les notes qui suivent.

Par un acte établi le 26 novembre 1527 à l'étude du notaire parisien Pierre Leroy, «Noble homme maistre Iehan grolier, conseiller du Roy nostre sire, tresorier de ses guerres et tresorier Receveur general de ses finances, tant ordinaires que extraordinaires, en ses pays et duché de milan», donne procuration générale à Antoine Grolier, élu du Lyonnais, pour exiger la remise des quittances qu'ils détiennent, auprès de tous ceux qui, entre le 1er octobre 1515 et le 31 décembre 1521, ont eu en charge, au nom du roi, les redevances du duché de Milan ou les sommes alors payées, à titres divers, «pour les affaires du Roy». Ceux-ci – fermiers, daciers, gabelliers et autres – doivent lui montrer les quittances des paiements qu'ils ont faits «a feu maistre Iehan mahieu, en son vivant commis dudit constituant [Jean Grolier] a l'exercice dudit office de tresorier et Receveur general desdites finances de ladite duché». Mission est donnée à Antoine Grolier de recouvrer ces quittances, précédemment remises par Jean Mahieu et signées de sa main, et d'en délivrer de nouvelles, servant de décharges et signées par Antoine Grolier, au nom et comme procureur de Jean Grolier, qui promet de les recevoir comme si elles étaient signées de sa propre main et de tenir quittes les fermiers, daciers, gabelliers et autres dont ont été reçues les sommes ainsi déclarées.[1]

Il est tentant de voir en Thomas un fils de ce défunt Jean Mahieu, commis aux finances de Jean Grolier pendant les six années de la seconde occupation française en Milanais. Né durant cette période – peut-être d'une mère italienne –, Thomas aurait vécu sa première jeunesse en Lombardie, éventuellement sous le nom de Maioli, mais bénéficiant de la protection accordée par Jean Grolier à un orphelin, issu de son représentant dans la péninsule. Hypothèse plausible au regard des préférences italiennes manifestées plus tard par Thomas Mahieu et des affinités rapprochant les deux hommes.

Il faut remarquer que le nouveau procureur de Jean Grolier cité dans ce document est son cousin germain, Antoine Grolier le jeune, nommé élu du Lyonnais le 17 août 1524, pour exercer cet office à sa place, en l'ab-

---

1. Paris, Arch. Nat., Min. Centr., CXXII, 13, 26 novembre 1527. Voir Annexe.

sence ou après la mort de son père, Antoine Grolier l'aîné.[1] Pour donner pleine valeur juridique à cette nomination, Antoine Grolier le jeune, résidant à Milan, avait lui-même passé procuration à son parent, Claude Grolier, devant trois notaires milanais, le 17 décembre 1524.[2] C'est donc celui-ci qui avait pris, à la place d'Antoine, possession de l'office à Paris, le 11 janvier 1525, n. st.[3] Antoine le jeune devait mourir au siège de Naples pendant l'été 1528, plusieurs années avant son père. Son frère François lui succédera en la charge en décembre suivant.[4]

Les Mahieu auxquels Thomas est vraisemblablement apparenté en France ont des attaches avec Montfort-L'Amaury (aujourd'hui département des Yvelines), où François Mahieu, qui a reçu en 1524 la charge de «payeur des mortes payes de Normandie»,[5] est concurremment détenteur en 1537 de l'office de grenetier du grenier à sel de Montfort-l'Amaury, l'un des plus convoités de France.[6] Devenu «trésorier des mortes payes

1. Nomination à l'office d'élu du Lyonnais d'Antoine Grolier le jeune, à la requête de son cousin, Jean Grolier, résignataire, et avec le consentement de son père, Antoine Grolier l'aîné, pour exercer cet office en l'absence et à la survivance l'un de l'autre. Valence, 17 août 1524. Paris, Bibl. Nat., ms fr. 2702, fol. 105 *r-v* (copie XVIe siècle); *Catalogue des actes de François Ier*, Paris, I, 1887, p. 386, n. 2061. (La similitude des prénoms a été parfois source de confusions chez les historiens de Jean Grolier.).

2. Procuration d'Antoine Grolier le jeune à Claude Grolier. Milan, 17 décembre 1524. Cette procuration passée devant un notaire de Milan, Cayme, est suivie de l'attestation de deux autres notaires milanais. Bibl. Nat., *ibid.*, fol. 107*r*.

3. Mise en possession de l'office d'élu du Lyonnais, par Claude Grolier, comme représentant d'Antoine Grolier le jeune. Paris, 14 janvier 1525. Bibl. Nat., *ibid.*, fol. 107 *r*.

4. Lettres de provisions de l'office d'élu du Lyonnais en faveur de François Grolier. Fontainebleau, 8 août 1528. Bibl. Nat., ms fr., 5501, fol. 387 *r-v* (copie XVIe siècle). Voir aussi sa nomination. Saint-Germain-en-Laye, 22 décembre 1528. Bibl. Nat., ms fr. 2702, fol. 144*v* - 145*r* (copie XVIe siècle). *Catalogue des actes de François I*, I, 1887, p. 625, n. 3271; VII, 1896 (Suppl.) p. 151, n. 23959.

5. Lettres de provisions de François Mahieu. Saint-Just-sur-Lyon, 11 novembre 1524. Bibl. Nat., ms fr. 5779, fol. 12 *v* (mention). *Catalogue des actes de François Ier*, V (Suppl.), 1892, p. 629, n. 17892. Voir aussi dans ce catalogue aux vol. II, III et VIII, différents mandements de paiement à François Mahieu, «receveur et payeur» ou «commis au payement des 339 mortes payes de Normandie» en 1532, 1536 et 1537. Les mortes payes étaient d'anciens soldats, souvent invalides, affectés à la défense des places fortes sous le commandement de capitaines (nommés parfois gouverneurs) ou de lieutenants. Voir R. Doucet, *Les Institutions de la France au XVIe siècle*, Paris, 1948, II, p. 647.

6. Bibl. Nat., Pièces originales, 1793, Mahieu (2ème numérotation: Mahieu de Normandie, n. 13). Il s'agit de très brèves notations du XVIII^esiècle, s'appuyant apparemment sur des actes notariés. On lit aux *l. 1 et 2*: «honorable homme francois Mahieu grenetier de Montfort l'Amaury 2 Xbre 1537; *l. 2 et 3*: «lui et thomas Mahieu 3 janvier 1537»; *l. 3 et en marge:* «ledit francois 7 8bre 1538 grenetier et tresorier des mortes payes de Normandie et Madeleine Pocquet sa femme 19 juillet 1539. Lui 8 mai et 11 juin et dernier juillet 1540»; *l. 4 et 5*: «Pierre Mahieu marchand à Coulombs 11 fevrier 1538, 27 septembre 1540»; *l. 6 et 7*: «Jacques Mahieu Religieux de labbaye de Coulombs, 1er mars 1539». Sur l'office de grenetier et celui de Montfort en particulier, voir G. Dupont-Ferrier, *Etudes sur les institutions financières de la France*, Paris, 1930-1933; *Reprint*, Genève, 1976, I, pp. 137-146.

de Normandie» l'année suivante, il porte toujours ce titre en 1547 lorsqu'il vend une pièce de terre, située à Montfort, au procureur du roi en l'élection et gabelle de Montfort, Etienne Berruyer.[1] Il habite alors à Coulombs, près Nogent-le-Roi (Eure-et-Loir), à quelque six lieues au sud-ouest de Montfort. Car c'est maintenant un Pierre Mahieu, qui, au moins depuis 1540, a la charge de grenetier et receveur du magasin à sel de Montfort-l'Amaury.[2] En 1557, ce dernier a pour commis Pierre Mahieu le jeune – probablement son fils – qui est alors redevable de 5043 livres tournois à la recette de la gabelle de Montfort-l'Amaury. Pierre Mahieu le jeune et sa femme, Isabeau Le Moyne, obtiennent le 18 décembre de la même année des lettres patentes qui laissent entrevoir une intervention de Jean Grolier, trésorier de France. Ces lettres donnent en effet mandement à Jean Grolier d'inscrire à la recette des receveurs généraux des finances à Paris la somme de 2000 livres en déduction de celle que doivent les époux Mahieu à la recette de la gabelle de Montfort.[3] Il s'agirait donc d'une sorte de virement. Le mois suivant, un très long délai est accordé aux débiteurs, puisque l'amortissement de leur dette est fixé à 400 livres par an.[4]

Ou trouve aussi, en décembre 1567, un Robert Mahieu, Normand, «l'un des gentilhommes retenus a faire le service du ban et de l'arriere ban», et à Paris, un Claude Mahieu, capitaine de trois cents hommes de guerre à pied, levés pour la garde de la ville, probablement le même que le "proviseur de la dépense des pages et chevaux de la grand écurie du roi" [François II], dit *Premor*, en 1560.[5]

1. Arch. Nat., Min. Centr., VIII, 73, 27 mars 1547, fol. 202r - 203r.
2. Cf. réf. n. 7: l. 8-10: «honorable homme Pierre Mahieu a present Grenetier de Montfort l'Amaury donne quictance a Pierre Mahieu son oncle, marchand à Coulombs, 23 juillet 1540».
3. Lettres patentes obtenues par Pierre Mahieu le jeune et sa femme Isabeau Le Moyne, portant mandement au Trésorier de France, Jean Grolier, d'inscrire en la recette des receveurs généraux des finances, ancien et alternatif, à Paris, la somme de 2000 livres tournois qu'ils recevront des mains dudit Mahieu en déduction de celle de 5043 livres tournois dont il était resté redevable au roi comme commis de Pierre Mahieu l'aîné en la recette de la gabelle de Montfort-l'Amaury. 18 décembre 1557. (Mention dans une copie du XVIIIe siècle du registre-journal de la Chambre des Comptes de Paris). Arch. Nat., P 2849, p. 192. D'après la suite encore inédite du *Catalogue des actes royaux*, dont la publication est préparée aux Archives Nationales. Je remercie vivement Mme Baudouin-Matuszek, Ingénieur de recherche au Centre National de la Recherche Scientifique, d'avoir bien voulu me communiquer les analyses relatives aux années 1550-1558.
4. Délai à Pierre Mahieu et Isabeau Le Moyne sa femme, commis de Pierre Mahieu l'aîné, grenetier et receveur du magasin à sel de Montfort-L'Amaury, pour le paiement de 5043 livres 3 sols en payant 200 livres par an jusqu'a l'entier paiement. Janvier 1558. Arch. Nat., PP 119, 42r.
5. Bibl. Nat., Pièces originales 1793, Mahieu de Normandie, n. 12; Mahieu, 3, 4; *Catalogue des actes de François II*, Paris, 1991, vol. 1, p. 352.

Pour revenir à Thomas Mahieu, le premier document ayant trait à sa carrière en France n'est connu que par une mention du XVIIIe siècle, mais puisée à la meilleure source, celle des archives des secrétaires du roi, alors conservées au couvent des Célestins à Paris, où l'assemblée de ce collège disposait de locaux depuis le XVIe siècle. Le rapport non daté du compilateur anonyme relate en substance qu'on a trouvé dans ces archives, au registre des années 1545-1552, trois documents transcrits par Thomas Mahieu: ses lettres de provisions du 1er septembre 1547, données à Compiègne et signées Marchand; au dessous, copie de la quittance des 61 livres 5 sols, remises par Mahieu, le 8 septembre suivant, à Eustache le Picart, notaire à Charenton, pour le demi-marc d'or payé lors de sa réception (correspondant au droit d'admission dans la compagnie). A la suite, Thomas Mahieu certifiait avoir transcrit ces deux actes de sa main et que la signature apposée au bas de son certificat était celle dont il entendait se servir dans l'exercice de ses fonctions.[1] L'ouvrage de Tessereau consacré à la Grande Chancellerie, que le compilateur cite en même temps, précise que la réception de Thomas Mahieu comme Conseiller Secrétaire du Roy, maison et couronne de France et de ses finances, a eu lieu le 7 septembre 1547, par résignation de Jacques de Saint-Mesmin.[2]

Dans l'importante étude qu'elle a publiée en 1967 sur la Grande Chancellerie, Hélène Michaud a consacré plusieurs chapitres très documentés aux 119 ou 120 notaires et secrétaires du roi, les uns gagers, les autres boursiers. «Les membres de cette compagnie, écrit-elle notamment, appartenaient à la Maison du Roi et portaient le titre d'officiers domestiques ou commensaux dont ils partageaient les bénéfices ... juridiques et financiers», juridiction particulière, exonération d'impôts, exemptions militaires. Ils étaient déclarés nobles. Les secrétaires gagers qui touchaient un salaire fixe étaient payés sur la base annuelle d'environ 300 livres tournois et 10 livres de droits de manteaux, mais ils pouvaient bénéficier en outre de gratifications.[3]

---

1. Bibl. Nat., Mss, dossiers bleus, 414 (Mahieu). *A la suite*: description des armes: De gueules, à la levrette d'argent, courante, annelée et colletée, au chevron d'or chargé de trois roses de gueules. Femme: N. Puis six courtes notices sur des «de Mahieu», dont trois commissaires des guerres en Languedoc. Sans date. Sur papier à la contremarque N♥B dans un cartouche, papier utilisé par les Benoît Vimal, père et fils, à Ambert entre 1702 et 1776. P. DELAUNAY, «Le papier du manuscrit de Blaise Pascal», *Bulletin de la librairie ancienne et moderne*, n. spécial 150 (1972), pp. 201-208. Je remercie M. Raymond Gaudriault pour cette information.

2. A. TESSEREAU, *Histoire chronologique de la Grande Chancellerie de France...revue et augmentée*, Paris, 1710, I, p. 110.

3. H. MICHAUD, *La Grande chancellerie et les écritures royales au seizième siècle*, Paris, 1967. Voir notamment pp. 90-126.

Pendant les premiers mois qui suivent sa réception, les actes dont Mahieu doit s'occuper et dont la mention a été conservée sont, le plus souvent, des confirmations de privilèges, confirmations qui suivent ordinairement l'avènement d'un roi. L'ensemble des actes relevés, qui atteint la quarantaine pendant les deux derniers mois de 1547, dépasse le chiffre de 150 en 1548. La moyenne annuelle tombe aux alentours d'une vingtaine entre 1549 et 1551. On ne compte plus que 14 actes en 1552 et moins d'une dizaine en 1553 et 1554. Mais on sait que les actes recensés ne représentent qu'une très faible partie de ceux qui ont été effectivement passés.[1] Par ailleurs, dès 1549, Thomas Mahieu cumule avec sa charge à la Chancellerie royale celle de premier secrétaire des finances de Catherine de Médicis, aux gages annuels de 500 livres, ce qui contribue nécessairement à diversifier ses activités.[2]

La Grande Chancellerie se déplace en même temps que le roi. On peut donc, grâce au relevé de sa signature sur les actes d'Henri II, connaître l'itinéraire que suit pendant quelques années le nouveau secrétaire royal à travers les villes de France, Anet, Fontainebleau, Nogent-sur-Marne, Aix-en-Othe (Aube), Meyzieux, Dijon, Abbaye d'Aynay, Lyon, Moulins, en 1547 et 1548; Saint-Germain-en-Laye, Paris, Amiens en 1550; Blois Amboise, Chateaubriant, Angers, Ville-au-chef (Villocher), Nantes, Chambord, Paris, Fontainebleau et Blois en 1551. Durant l'année 1552, ce seront Blois en janvier, Fontainebleau, Paris, Villers-Cotterêts, Soissons, Coucy en février, et Reims en mars, où Mahieu signe, apparemment pour la première fois, un privilège de librairie. Accordé au libraire lyonnais, Guillaume Rouille, le 12 mars 1552, n. st., pour les *Histoires* de Paolo Giovio, traduites en français par Denis Sauvage, ce privilège est valable pour dix ans.[3] Neuf jours plus tard, Mahieu est à Joinville où il signe une lettre de rémission. Il n'est plus mentionné ensuite cette année-là dans la série des actes royaux recensés. Il faut remarquer toutefois qu'en dehors du premier quart du XVIe siècle, si

---

1. Pour la période concernée, l'analyse de ces actes est publiée jusqu'à la fin de l'année 1549: *Catalogue des actes de François Ier*, vol. I-VII, Paris, 1887-1896; *Catalogue des actes de Henri II*, vol. I-III, (31 mars 1547 - 31 décembre 1549), Paris, 1979-1990. Pour la suite voir n. 10. A paru séparément le *Catalogue des actes de François II (1559-1560)*, Paris, 1991. 2 vol.

2. Bibl. Nat., Nouv. acq. fr. 9175, fol. 479. *Officiers domestiques de la maison de la reyne Catherine de Medicis depuis le 1er Juillet 1547 jusques en 1585.* «Secretaires. Le 1er à V^c ll., les autres à divers gages... M. Thomas Mahieu au lieu de Berthault en 1549 à V^c ll... Hors en 1560». Publié dans: *Lettres de Catherine de Médicis. Ed. G. Baguenault de Puchesse, E. Lelong, L. Auvray, A. Lesort*, Paris, vol. X, 1943, p. 504. Les secrétaires de Catherine de Médicis sont au nombre de six en 1547-1549, de douze en 1552, et de vingt en 1554-1555. Voir aussi: Bibl. Nat., ms fr. 7854, p. 2010 et ms fr. 7856, p. 1251.

3. P. Giovio, *Histoires*, 1552. 2°. Baudrier, *Bibliographie lyonnaise, Reprint*, Paris, 1964, IX, p. 197.

bien étudié par Elizabeth Armstrong,[1] les privilèges de librairie n'ont pas fait, en France, l'objet de relevés systématiques. C'est à Saint-Germain-en-Laye, et accessoirement à Paris, que Thomas Mahieu semble passer la première partie de l'année 1553, au cours de laquelle il est encore, le 31 mars et le 18 juin, le signataire de deux privilèges délivrés pour dix ans à Guillaume Rouille. Le premier concerne un ensemble de livres juridiques, médicaux et littéraires.[2] Le second est réservé au *Promptuaire des medailles*, oeuvre de Guillaume Rouille lui-même, dédiée à la soeur du roi et publiée «tant en langue latine, Francoise, Italienne que Espaignole», avec deux médaillons à chaque page.[3]

Cependant, le privilège que Mahieu signe à Compiègne, le 11 juillet 1553, pour l'*Epitome thesauri antiquitatum* et pour l'*Epitome du thresor de antiquitez*, au bénéfice de l'auteur, le numismate mantouan Jacopo de Strada, et de son libraire lyonnais, Thomas Guerin, retient particulièrement l'attention: sa durée est de douze années et, sur le livre imprimé, le nom de Mahieu s'y détache en gros caractères. A travers le long préambule qui ouvre l'ouvrage, l'auteur retrace la suite des démarches qu'il a dû entreprendre en Italie, en Allemagne et en France pour mener ses recherches. A Lyon notamment, il a eu de fréquents entretiens avec l'archéologue Guillaume Du Choul dont il vante, l'expérience, la mémoire et le jugement, aussi bien que la magnifique maison. A Paris, Strada a été émerveillé par «l'industrie de Monsieur le thresorier Iean Grolier...homme riche et docte, lequel on appelle communement le thresorier de Milan». Le recommandent spécialement à l'admiration ses nombreuses antiquités, «mais aussi...une tres grande multitude de livres tant Grecs que Latins...».[4] Deux mois plus tard, le 31 octobre 1553, Mahieu se trouve à Villers-Cotterêts au moment où il signe, au bénéfice de Guillaume Rouille, un nouveau privilège protégeant précisément deux ouvrages de Guillaume Du Choul, *Discours sur la castrametation et discipline des Romains*[5] et *Discours de la religion des anciens*

---

1. E. Armstrong, *Before Copyright. The French Book Privilege System, 1488-1526*. Cambridge, 1990.

2. GALIEN, *Libellus cui titulum fecit quos, quando purgare oporteat*, 1553. 16°; A. TIRAQUEAU, *De legibus connubialibus*, 1554. 2°; A. TIRAQUEAU, *De utroque retractu*, 1554. 2°; VERGILIUS, *Bucolica cum commentariis Richardi Gorraei*, 1554. 8°. BAUDRIER, IX, pp. 203, 210-211, 212, 218.

3. *Promptuarium iconum*, 1553. 4°; *Prontuario de le medaglie*, 1553. 4°; *Promptuaire des medailles*, 1553. 4°. BAUDRIER, IX, pp. 204-205, 205, 205-207.

4. *Epitome thesauri...*, 1554. 4°; *Epitome du thresor...*, 1554. 4°. BAUDRIER, IX, pp. 365 et 366; R. MORTIMER, *French 16th Century Books*, Cambridge (Mass.), 1964, vol. II, n.[s] 502 et 503.

5. *Discours sur la castrametation...des Romains*, 1555 ou 1556. 2°. BAUDRIER, IX, pp. 228-229.

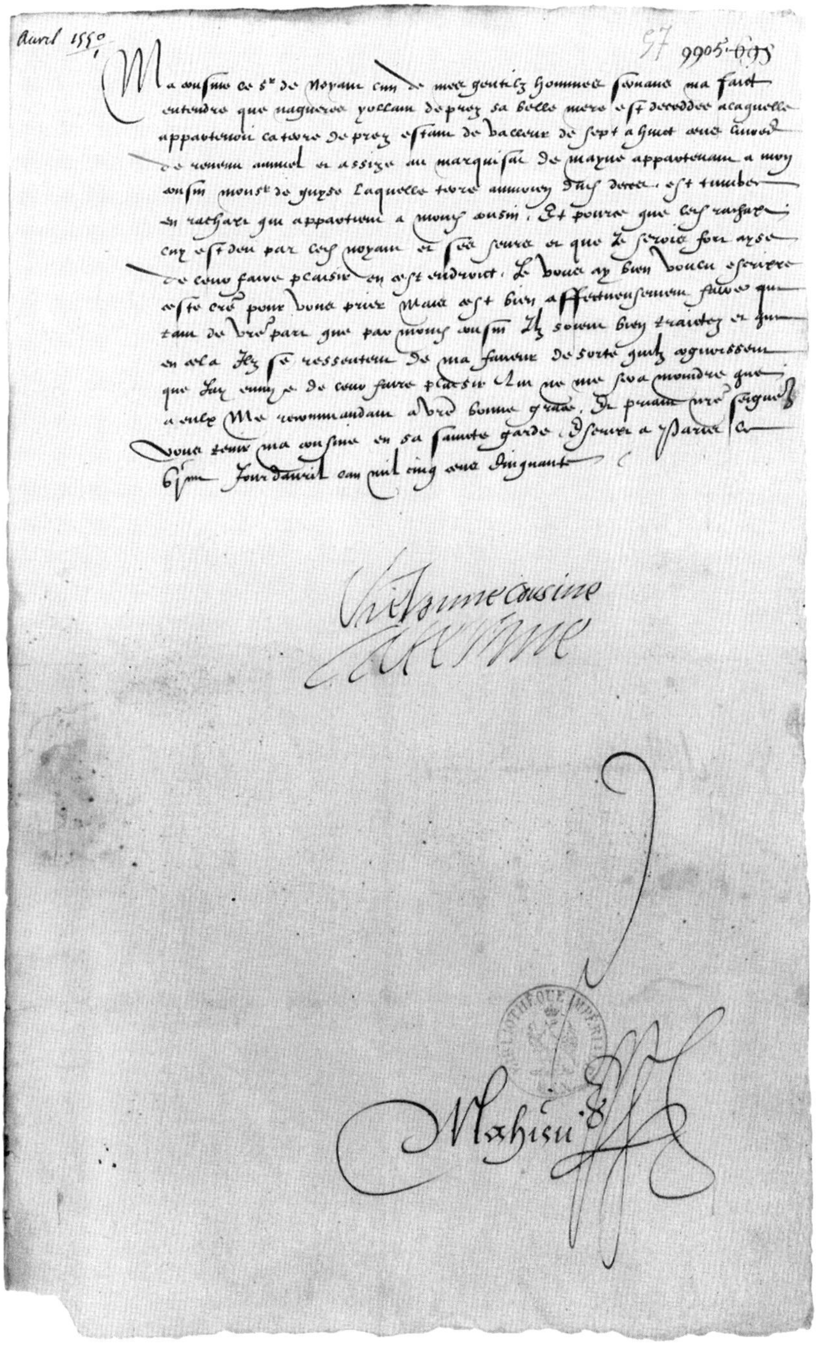

Fig. 1. Lettre de Catherine de Médicis à sa cousine Antoinette de Bourbon, épouse du duc Claude de Guise, 6 avril 1550. Celle-ci porte la signature de Catherine, et, au bas, celle de Thomas Mahieu qui a transcrit la lettre.
Bibl. Nat., ms Clairambault 344, fol. 57

Romains[1] de même qu'un commentaire galénique de l'Espagnol Andrès de Laguna.[2]

Les seuls actes portant la signature de Mahieu dont on a trace pour l'année 1554 émanent de Paris et sont des privilèges de librairie. Celui du 15 avril dont bénéfice encore pour dix années Guillaume Rouille intéresse quatre ouvrages.[3] Mais autrement important apparaît celui qui a été octroyé le 11 février précédent (1554, n. st.) à l'imprimeur parisien Michel de Vascosan «pour le temps et terme de dix ans pour tous les livres que ledit de Vascosan imprimera cy apres: lesquels n'auront esté auparavant imprimez en nostredit Royaume et six ans pour ceulx lesquels... auront esté remis, restituez et illustrez de notables corrections, emendations et annotations, à commencer du iour et date de la premiere impression de chacun desdits livres...». Sous diverses formes, ce privilège général est en effet invoqué pendant une décennie dans de multiples impressions de Vascosan, soit qu'on y trouve reproduits les termes mêmes des lettres patentes royales, selon l'original «seelé sur double queue du grand seau en cire iaune» et évoquant la personne du souverain, «Henry par la grace de Dieu Roy de France...»,[4] soit qu'y figure un extrait substantiel commençant par le rappel: «Par grace speciale... et auctorité royale...» et incluant l'année et le quantième des lettres patentes,[5] soit encore que l'extrait, fort abrégé, se borne à une déclaration: «Il est permis à...» et à une formule finale telle que celle-ci: «Comme plus amplement appert par le privilege general octroyé par le Roy audict de Vascosan. M D L III. Mahieu». (Il s'agit toujours de 1554, n. st.).[6] Enfin, dans

---

1. *Discours de la religion des anciens Romains*, 1556. 2°. BAUDRIER, IX, pp. 229-230. (Privilège cité par A. R. A. HOBSON, *French and Italian Collectors and their Bindings*, Oxford, 1953, p. 33, n. 2.)

2. *Epitome omnium rerum et sententiarum quae annotatu in Commentariis Galeni in Hippocratem extant*, 1554. 8°. BAUDRIER, IX, p. 213.

3. A. DE LAGUNA, *Annotationes in Dioscoridem*, 1554. 16°. BAUDRIER, IX, p. 212; DIAZ DE LUCO, *Regulae juris*, 1554. 8°. BAUDRIER, IX, p. 125; *L'histoire d'Herodian*. Trad. Jacques Des Contes, 1554. 2°. BAUDRIER, IX, pp. 217-218: HIPPOCRATE, *Les anciens et renommez aucteurs de la medecine et chirurgie*. Comment. Vidus Vidius, 1555. 8°. BAUDRIER, IX, pp. 223-224.

4. Exemples: Saint JUSTIN, *Les Euvres mises de grec en langage francois par Ian de Maumont*. 2ᵉ édition revue..., 1559. 2°; JUSTIN (L'historien), *Les Histoires universelles de Trogue Pompee abregees par Justin, translatees de latin en francois par Claude de Seyssel*, 1559, 2°; J. ZONARAS, *Les Histoires et Chroniques du monde mises en langage francois par Ian de Maumont*, 1561. 2°. Pour ces trois traductions, ce privilège est de dix ans.

5. Exemples: J. LE FRERON, *Catalogue des... ducs et connestables de France*, 1555. 2°. (Cité par A. R. A. HOBSON, *ibid.*); G. BUDÉ, *Annotationes Priores et Posteriores in Pandectas*, 1556. 2°.

6. Exemples: ARISTOTE, *Les Oeconomiques nouvellement traduictes en francois par J. Amelin*, 1554. 8°; Saint JUSTIN, *Les Oeuvres mises de grec en langage francois par Ian de Maumont* [1ᵉ édition], 1554. 2°. (Cité par A. R. A. HOBSON, *ibid.*); TITE LIVE, *Les Concions et Harengues nouvellement traduictes en francois par J. Amelin*, 1554. 8°. (Cité

la plupart des livres en latin se voit l'intitulé: «Privilegii Sententia», l'incipit «Cautum est...» et la date entière: «VII. Idus Februarii. M D L III).[1] Il arrive en outre que le privilège délivré à l'auteur ait été ensuite cédé par lui à Vascosan. C'est le cas des *Commentaires sur le faict des guerres* de François de Rabutin. Ici, la mention du privilège octroyé à Rabutin le 23 février 1555, n. st. et signée du secrétaire Fizes, est suivie de celle de la cession faite à Vascosan, et de celle du privilège général délivré à l'imprimeur et dont Mahieu avait été le signataire un an plus tôt.[2] De même, lorsqu'en 1559 l'historiographe d'Henri II, Pierre de Paschal, est chargé par Catherine de Médicis de composer un *Elogium* du roi, récemment décédé, il transporte sur Vascosan son privilège, signé le 11 décembre par De Vabres. Mais ici, probablement par révérence à l'égard du monarque célèbre, c'est le privilège général, octroyé de son vivant et portant la signature de Mahieu qui est cité le premier.[3]

Les deux exemplaires des *Commentarii* de Caesar, imprimés par Vascosan en 1543, et que Mahieu a fait relier à son nom, sont peut-être un don de l'imprimeur à l'occasion de la délivrance de ce privilège général. Toutefois, ainsi qu'en témoignent les devises différentes frappées sur le plat inférieur, plusieurs années séparent les commandes de ces deux reliures.[4] Mahieu possédait aussi un manuscrit des *Commentarii*, calligraphié par l'humaniste vénitien Giovanni Battista Egnazio,[5] vraisemblablement

---

par A. R. A. Hobson, *ibid.*); Arioste, *Le Premier volume de Roland furieux...mis en rime Francoise par Ian Fornier*, 1555. 4°; Thucydide, *L'Histoire...de la guerre qui fut entre les Peloponesiens et Atheniens translatee de grec en francois par feu Claude de Seyssel*, 1559. 4°. (Cité par M. Foot, *The Henry Davies Gift*, vol. I, Cambridge, 1978, pp. 184 et 190, n. 7).

1. Exemples: A. Le Ferron, *De rebus gestis Gallorum*, 1554. 2°. (Cité par A. R. A. Hobson, *ibid.*); *Aeschinis et Demosthenis contrariae orationes in Ctesiphontem...I. Perione interprete*, 1554. 4°. (Cité par A.R.A. Hobson, *ibid.*); R. Baynes, *In proverbia Salomonis tres libri Commentariorum*, 1555. 2°; H. Du Chastelet, *Oratio Lutetiae habita qua futuro medico necessaria explicantur*, 1555. 4°; Oppian, *De Venatione libri quatuor J. Bodino interprete*, 1555. 4°. N. de Grouchy (Gruchius), *De Comitiis Romanorum libri tres*, 1555. 4°;

2. F. de Rabutin, *Commentaires...*, 1555. 2°.

3. P. de Paschal, *Henrici II Gallorum regis Elogium. Eiusdem Henrici Tumulus*. 1560. 2°.

4. G.D. Hobson. *Maioli, Canevari and others*, London, 1926, n.os XXII et XXIII. La reliure du premier exemplaire, reproduite par M.J. Husung, portait la devise INGRATIS SERVIRE NEPHAS, datable de la décennie 1550, celle du second, conservé à la British Library, porte la devise INIMICI MEI MEA MICHI NON ME MICHI, plus tardive. M.J. Husung, *Bucheinbände aus der Preussischen Staatbibliothek zu Berlin in historischer Folge erläutert*, Leipzig, 1925, p. 18 et ill. 67, pl. XLII.

5. Manuscrit sur vélin, probablement écrit, selon H.M. Nixon, entre 1480 et 1510. La reliure porte au plat supérieur le titre: C. IVL. CAES. / .COMMENT. / .IO. BAP. AEGN. / MANV. / .SCR. / et l'ex-libris: THO. MAIOLI. ET AMICORVM. / le plat inférieur porte la devise: INIMICI. / .MEI. MEA. / .MICHI. / .NON. ME. / .MICHI. / G.D. Hobson, *Maioli*, n. XX;

celui que Jean Grolier avait prêté à Vascosan, et qui servit, avec plusieurs autres manuscrits anciens, au collationnement du texte en vue de l'impression.[1] La bibliothèque de Mahieu comptait au moins deux autres productions de Vascosan: le *De gestis Romanorum libri quatuor* de Florus, de 1534[2] et le *De Republica* d'Aristote de 1548.[3]

Tout incomplets qu'ils soient, les repères fournis par ses signatures officielles suggèrent que c'est peut-être dès 1550, mais surtout à partir de 1552, que la vie de Mahieu devient moins itinérante et que ses contacts avec deux grands libraires de Lyon et de Paris – et sans nul doute avec plusieurs autres – sont de nature à favoriser ses achats de livres et ses commandes de reliures. Cependant, en novembre 1554, des lettres patentes d'Henri II instituent quatre-vingts offices nouveaux de secrétaires du Roi, portant ainsi leur nombre à deux-cents,[4] augmentation qui mécontente fortement l'association professionnelle du collège. «La meilleure preuve de son opposition, écrit H. Michaud, c'est qu'en décembre 1556, la décision fut rapportée par un autre édit».[5] Faut-il voir dans les remous suscités par cette affaire un lien avec le ton amer de la devise que Thomas Mahieu adopte pour les premières reliures portant son nom: INGRATIS SERVIRE NEPHAS? Cette devise est aussi l'une de celles que le polygraphe florentin Gabriele Symeoni utilise et illustre en 1556, quand il projette un recueil de *Discours* et de nouvelles devises destiné à Catherine de Médicis.[6] Symeoni qui passe l'hiver 1556-1557 à Paris, a pu l'emprunter à

H.M. NIXON, *Twelve Books in fine Bindings from the library of J. W. Hely Hutchinson*, Oxford, 1953, p. 18; T. DE MARINIS, *Appunti e Ricerche bibliografiche*, Milano, 1940, p. 120, n. 21 et pl. n. CCXX.

1. Comme le souligne H.M. Nixon, l'avertissement «Lectori» de l'édition donnée par Vascosan en 1543 montre que l'éditeur a emprunté à Jean Grolier un ancien manuscrit des *Commentarii*, apporté de Venise et utilisé par Egnazio. Il est possible qu'il s'agisse du manuscrit cité ci-dessus. Le privilège accordé le 30 avril 1543 à Vascosan pour son édition indique en outre que celui-ci a collationné plusieurs manuscrits anciens corrigés par des savants: «...summa diligentia a Michaele Vascosano, multorum veterum codicum collatione facta, doctorumque hominum iudicio adhibitos emendatos ac typis excusos».

2. G.D. HOBSON, *Maioli*, n. XXXVII.

3. G.D. HOBSON, *Maioli*, n. VII.

4. Enregistré au Parlement de Paris, le 16 novembre 1554. Arch. Nat., XIA 1579, fol. 341; TESSEREAU, *op. cit.*, pp. 122-123.

5. Révocation de l'édit de novembre 1554 portant création de quatre-vingts offices de secrétaires du roi. Les offices déjà pourvus doivent disparaître par extinction. Saint-Germain, décembre 1556; TESSEREAU, *op. cit.*, pp. 125-126; MICHAUD, *op. cit.*, p. 101.

6. *Discours francois, toscan et latin du Seigneur Gabriel Simeon florentin sur la cognoissance des esprits et desseings des hommes suivant un dialogue italien imparfait de devises amoureuses et militaires de Monsieur Paul Jove,...avec l'adjunction de LXXX nouvelles devises...A la Royne de France. MDLVI.* Firenze, Bibl. Medicea Laurenziana, ms 1376.

Mahieu.[1] L'écrivain met ici l'ingratitude sous le signe de la vipère ovovivipare tuée par les vipereaux auxquels elle donne naissance. Seule subsiste de son projet initial une maquette à la plume aujourd'hui incomplète, mais on retrouve le thème de l'ingratitude et sa représentation graphique dans les différents livres d'emblèmes que Symeoni fera imprimer à Lyon par Guillaume Rouille à partir de 1559.[2]

Deux arrêts du Parlement de Paris, en date du 1er avril 1556, que me signale généreusement Mme Baudouin-Matuszek, Ingénieur de recherche au Centre National de la Recherche scientifique, permettent de voir que Thomas Mahieu gagne alors les actions en justice qu'il a introduites contre François Charles, puis contre Jean Huguet. Dans ce dernier procès, Mahieu agit comme représentant de Jérôme de Beaquis, «gentilhomme millanoys», qui, ainsi que le fait remarquer Mme Matuszek, travaille avec le célèbre banquier de Lyon, Albisse del Bene, devenu également depuis 1550, Surintendant des finances royales.[3] Cette récente découverte ouvre, semble-t-il, de nouvelles voies de recherche. Que Mahieu, en effet, ait entretenu des relations avec la banque lyonnaise, soit pour le compte du roi, soit pour lui-même, prend un relief particulier, dès qu'on évoque le faste des reliures alors exécutées à sa demande.

Le secrétaire du roi est bien placé pour suivre les changements que le souverain ne cesse d'introduire dans l'administration financière du royaume. Depuis la réforme de 1552, les Trésoriers et les Généraux des finances, chargés respectivement du domaine royal, et des aides, taille et gabelle, ont été remplacés par dix-sept «Trésoriers généraux», affectés aux dix-sept généralités du royaume. Ceux-ci ont l'obligation de résider dans leur généralité et de faire chaque année une tournée de trois mois pour surveiller l'activité de leurs subordonnés.[4] En 1557, l'ancienne distinction ayant été rétablie, les charges ont été dédoublées.[5] En avril 1558,

---

1. Date du séjour parisien de Symeoni, d'après T. RENUCCI, *Un aventurier des lettres au XVIe siècle, Gabriele Symeoni, Florentin, 1509-1570 (?)*, Paris, 1943, p. 89.

2. *Devises ou Emblemes heroiques et morales; Le Imprese heroiche et Morali; Le Sententiose imprese et Dialogo; Tetrastiches.* Voir BAUDRIER, *op. cit.*, IX, pp. 260, 270-271, 273, 277-278, 283, 289-291.

3. Arch. Nat., XIA 1582, fol. 253 *r-v*. Prononciations du mercredi 1 avril. Sur Albisse del Bene, voir en dernier lieu: M.-N. BAUDOUIN-MATUSZEK et P. OUVAROV, «Banque et Pouvoir au XVIe siècle: La Surintendance des finances d'Albisse del Bene», *Bibliothèque de l'Ecole des chartes*, t. 149 (1991), pp. 249-291.

4. S. FOURNIVAL, *Recueil général des titres concernant les fonctions, rangs, dignitez, seances et privileges des charges des presidens tresoriers de France, Generaux des Finances et Grands voyers des Généralités du Royame*, Paris, 1655, pp. 183, 193, 246; [J.-L. PATAS DE BOURGNEUF], *Mémoires sur les privilèges et fonctions des Trésoriers généraux de France*. Orléans, 1745, pp. 28-32. Voir aussi: R. DOUCET, *Les Institutions de la France au XVIe siècle*, Paris, 1948, I, pp. 290-303.

5. FOURNIVAL, *op. cit.*, p. 246.

Henri II a décidé d'ériger deux nouvelles généralités, à Orléans et à Limoges.[1] Pour celle d'Orléans, il a créé en septembre les deux offices de Trésorier de France et de Général des finances, aux gages annuels de 2500 livres et droits de bûche.[2] Ce n'est apparemment pas un hasard si, le 5 octobre suivant, Thomas Mahieu résigne sa charge de secrétaire du roi au profit de Raoul Moreau, père et fils par survivance.[3] A cette époque d'ailleurs, comme le montre un reçu, signé de sa main le 31 décembre 1557, ses émoluments chez la reine, réduits à 400 livres, ne correspondent plus à ceux de premier secrétaire:

> Je Thomas mahieu secretaire des finances de la Royne confesse avoir eu et receu comptant de Me Pierre de picquet tresorier de la maison dicelle dame La somme de Quatre cens Livres Tournois A moy ordonnee pour mes gaiges de Lannee finie le dernier Jour de decembre mil cinq cens cinquante sept De laquelle somme de IIII^c L tournois je me tiens pour contant et bien paié et en ay quicté et quicte ledit de Picquet tresorier susdit et tous autres Tesmoing mon seing manuel cy mict le dernier jour de decembre mil cinq cens Cinquante sept.
>
> *Signé*: Mahieu (fig. 2)

On lit au verso:

> Pour quictance de la somme de Quatre cens livres tournoy pour mes gaiges a cause de mon office de secretaire des finances de la royne pour lannee finie au dernier jour de decembre lan mil cinq cens cinquante sept.[4]

Le nom de Thomas Mahieu n'apparaît plus en 1560 parmi ceux des secrétaires de Catherine de Médicis,[5] mais il se retrouve alors, au premier rang, sur la liste des cinq secrétaires attachés à ses trois fils, les ducs d'Orléans, d'Angoulême et d'Anjou, puis en 1562, sur la liste personnelle du troisième d'entre eux, (Alexandre-Edouard, le futur Henri III), devenu duc d'Orléans après la mort de François II et l'accession au trône de Charles IX.[6] Les gages annuels de Mahieu se montent toujours à 400

---

1. Arch. Nat., AD+31 pièce 7; Bourgneuf, p. 33 (mention).
2. Enregistré au Parlement de Paris, le 17 septembre 1558. Arch. Nat., XIA 8622, fol. 73-75*v*. Fournival, p. 289; Bourgneuf, p. 33. Toutefois, en 1572, Mahieu signera un reçu sous le double titre de Trésorier de France et de Général des finances. Voir p. 341.
3. TESSEREAU, *op. cit.*, p. 130.
4. Bibl. Nat., Mss, Pièces originales 1793 (1ère numérotation, n. 2)
5. Voir n. 17.
6. Bibl. Nat., ms fr. 7854, p. 2129 et p. 2140; ms fr. 7856, pp. 1185 et 1196. En cette dernière occurence, les références à ces deux manuscrits sont empruntées aux notes manuscrites de Seymour de Ricci conservées à la Réserve des livres rares et précieux du département des Imprimés de la Bibliothèque nationale, Paris. Seymour de Ricci y fait allusion dans sa communication: «Les reliures dites de Maioli», *Compte-rendu de l'Académie des Sciences et Belles-Lettres*, 1926, n. 1. Je suis reconnaissante à M. Jean Toulet, Directeur de la Réserve, de me les avoir signalées.

Fig. 2. Quittance de Thomas Mahieu pour ses gages de secrétaire
de Catherine de Médicis pour l'année 1557, 31 décembre 1557.
Bibl. Nat., Pièces originales 1793, (n. 2)

Fig. 3. Quittance de Thomas Mahieu pour ses gages de Trésorier de France
et Général des finances en la charge et Généralité de Languedoil
pour le premier trimestre 1572, 4 avril 1572.
Bibl. Nat., Pièces originales 1793 (n. 5)

livres. Il semble, comme on le verra, que sa nomination au titre de « Conseiller du Roy, Tresorier de France et General de ses finances en la charge et Generalité Languedoil » soit intervenue dans le courant de l'année 1562.

Orléans vient d'être, de la mi-décembre 1560 à la fin de janvier 1561, la siège des Etats-Généraux auxquels a participé le très jeune duc d'Orléans, âgé de neuf ans. Mais, le 2 avril 1562, le prince Louis de Condé s'empare de la ville qui va devenir sous sa domination, pendant un an, la capitale de la Réforme en France.[1] Dès ses débuts, l'insurrection s'accompagne de violences et de pillages, bientôt connus dans la capitale et qui y provoquent une réaction extrêmement brutale. Le 18 août 1562, sur information du Procureur du roi, le Parlement de Paris ordonne la prise de corps d'une centaine d'Orléanais, habitants de la ville ou réfugiés, dont une soixantaine de seigneurs, quelque vingt-cinq officiers publics et dix femmes apparentées aux uns ou aux autres. Ceux-ci, à quelque endroit qu'on les trouve, doivent être amenés à la Conciergerie du Palais pour y être jugés. S'ils ne peuvent être pris, ils sont ajournés à comparaître dans les trois jours ».[2] Ce délai écoulé, le Procureur général du Parlement, Malon, *alias* Mallon, arrête ses conclusions « contre plusieurs habitans de la ville d'Orléans et contre plusieurs autres personnes qui ont pris les armes contre le Roy ». Il demande que, par défaut, les personnes déjà nommées – auxquelles s'ajoutent cinquante nouvelles désignations – soient condamnées comme contumax, criminels de lèse-majesté divine et humaine, rebelles et intestats, que leurs offices et dignités soient déclarés vacants, leur corps tiré à quatre chevaux et traîné à la voirie, leurs armes détruites en signe d'ignominie et leurs biens retournés à la couronne de France.[3]

Parmi les noms des officiers royaux figurant sur les deux listes se trouvent ceux d'Antoine Fumée, Président aux enquêtes de Bretagne, de Nicolas Compaing, Conseiller au Grand Conseil, de Pierre de Mondoré, garde de la librairie du roi, et de « Mahieu n'aguieres [*id. est* récemment] Général des finances ». Ainsi Thomas Mahieu se trouve-t-il inculpé

---

1. B. DE LACOMBE, *Les débuts des guerres de religion (Orléans 1559-1564). Catherine de Médicis entre Guise et Condé*, Paris, 1899.
2. Arrêt du Parlement de Paris contre les auteurs des troubles survenus à Orléans au mois d'avril 1562, 18 août 1562, signé Malon. Bibl. Nat., ms fr 3176, fol. 4 *r-v* (copie). Publié dans « Documents inédits sur les guerres de religion dans l'Orléanais recuellis par Baguenault de Puchesse, L. Auvray et B. de Lacombe », *Mémoires de la Société archéologique de l'Orléanais*, 28, (1902), pp. 47-48.
3. Conclusions du Parlement de Paris contre plusieurs habitans de la ville d'Orléans et contre plusieurs autres personnes qui ont pris les armes contre le Roy (s. d.) Bibl. Nat., ms fr. 3176, fol. 25 *r* -31 *r*. Publié dans les *Mémoires de Condé*. Ed. D. F. Secousse, vol. 4, 1743, pp. 94-101.

comme protestant rebelle. Cependant, lorsque le 16 et le 21 novembre, sont prononcés, par défaut, les arrêts de condamnation à mort contre les seigneurs «rebelles et contumaces»,[1] puis contre ceux qui sont «revêtus de charges de la ville d'Orleans», aussi «rebelles et contumaces», le nom de Mahieu n'apparaît plus.[2] Il ne figure pas davantage sur la longue liste que comporte, le 13 février 1563, un nouvel arrêt du Parlement portant même condamnation contre d'autres habitants d'Orléans «rebelles au Roy et contumaces», où l'on peut distinguer les noms de Théodore de Bèze, de François Petau, de Girard Bongars et de l'imprimeur Eloi Gibier.[3]

Plutôt que l'obtention d'une grâce spéciale, cette suppression semble indiquer la prise en compte d'une erreur de procédure, soit que Thomas Mahieu n'ait pu être convaincu de protestantisme, soit que les conclusions du Procureur du Parlement aient contrevenu aux privilèges juridiques des trésoriers de France. Selon un édit d'avril 1519, en effet, les procès des trésoriers ne pouvaient être intentés que par le «Chancelier de France, appelés avec lui les maîtres des Requêtes et aucuns Gens des comptes, ou par les cours de Parlement, appelés aucuns Gens des comptes».[4] On sait que l'édit de pacification, signé à Amboise le 19 mars 1563, devait rendre nuls et non avenus ces arrêts de condamnation et laisser un fragile répit à la guerre civile.

Mais la tension demeure grande dans la ville où la réaction catholique entend s'imposer progressivement dans les rouages d'une administration auparavant majoritairement protestante, notamment pour l'échevinage, les impôts, les indemnités et l'Hôtel-Dieu. Ainsi le nouveau gouverneur, Sipierre, décide-t-il, dès son arrivée, d'adjoindre douze échevins catholiques aux douze échevins réformés qui venaient d'être élus.[5]

Thomas Mahieu a laissé quelques traces livresques à Orléans. On pense à cet égard à trois in-folio reliés pour lui, qui n'ont pas quitté la ville

---

1. Arrêt du Parlement de Paris portant condamnation de mort contre le Seigneur de Chastillon, Amiral de France, et autres Seigneurs rebelles au Roy, contumaces, 16 novembre 1562, Bibl. Nat., ms Dupuy, vol. 137, pp. 65-66. Publié dans les *Mémoires de Condé, op. cit.*, pp. 114-115.

2. Arrêt du Parlement de Paris portant condamnation de mort contre les y denommez revêtus de charges dans la ville d'Orléans et autres rebelles au Roy, contumaces, 21 novembre 1562. Bibl. Nat., *Ibid.*, pp. 67-68. Publié dans les *Mémoires de Condé, Ibid.*, pp. 122-123.

3. Arrêt du Parlement de Paris portant condamnation de mort contre les y denommez, habitans de la ville d'Orléans, contumaces. Signé Mallon, 13 février 1563, n. st. Bibl. Nat., *Ibid.*, pp. 61-64. Publié dans les *Mémoires de Condé, Ibid.*, pp. 232-234.

4. BOURGNEUF, *op. cit.*, p. 80.

5. P. DE FÉLICE, «La réaction catholique à Orléans au lendemain de la première guerre de religion (1563-1565)», *Société de l'histoire du Protestantisme français, Bulletin*, 1903, pp. 483-554; B. DE LACOMBE et P. DE FÉLICE, *Correspondance*, (controverse autour de cet article et du livre cité n. 52), *Ibid.*, 1904, pp. 173-186.

depuis le XVIe siècle: les *Commentariorum urbanorum octo et triginta libri* de Raffaelo Maffei (Volaterranus), imprimés par Froben à Bâle en 1530 et qui portent l'ex-libris de l'abbaye Saint-Euverte,[1] l'*Ecclesiastica historia gentis Anglorum* de Beda, publiée à Anvers chez J. Gravius en 1550, où se lit le prix manuscrit «1 L. T.» (une livre tournoi)[2] et enfin, particulièrement intéressant, le *De Rebus gestis Alexandri* de Quintus Curtius, sorti également de l'officine de Froben en 1545, où se trouve inscrit de la même main, le prix «2 L. T.», et qui contient en outre l'ex-libris «I. Damain».[3] Sur la reliure de ces deux derniers livres a été frappée la devise INIMICI. MEI. / MEA. MIHI. / NON ME. / MIHI. (avec la variante MICHI pour le Quintus Curtius). Cette devise, la deuxième adoptée par Mahieu, paraît répondre aux haines, aux condamnations et aux meurtres que connurent les Orléanais à partir des années soixante.

Les Damain sont nombreux à Orléans au milieu du siècle. Nicolas, Euverte, le receveur, puis Antoine, y sont tour à tour échevins en 1547-1548, 1549-1550 et 1563-1564.[4] C'est assurément Euverte que les greffiers parisiens du Parlement entendaient désigner parmi les rebelles, en 1562, sous les appellations de «recepveur Daman» ou de «recepveur d'Avian».[5] Comme Mahieu, ce receveur, qui travaillait probablement en relation avec lui, ne figura pas sur les listes définitives de condamnation. L'ex-libris «I. Damain» est celui de Jacques Damain, né vers 1528, chanoine de la cathédrale Sainte-Croix, puis conseiller-clerc au présidial d'Orléans.[6] Lui reconnaissant la qualité d'«homme paisible et detestant les cruautés de sa religion», Jean Crespin lui empruntera ouvertement sa relation du massacre de la Saint-Barthélemy à Orléans.[7] «Flor. [Florent] Damain, de même que Jacques Damain, a possédé un livre portant au second plat le monogramme de Mahieu. Il s'agit des *Commentarii rerum gestarum Francisci Sfortiae* de Simoneta, imprimés à Milan par Zaroto vers 1482. Cet incunable, avant d'appartenir à Mahieu, avait été la propriété

---

1. G.D. HOBSON, *Maioli*, n. LXXXV; *Les richesses des bibliothèques de France*. Ed. P. Neveux et E. Dacier, Paris, 1932, vol. 2, p. 83.
2. G.D. HOBSON, *Maioli*, n. XI; *Les Richesses*, ibid.
3. G.D. HOBSON, *Maioli*, n. XXXIV; *Les Richesses*, ibid.
4. F. LEMAIRE, *Histoire et antiquitez de la ville...d'Orléans*, Orléans, 1645, vol. 1, pp. 482-484.
5. Voir n. 53 et 54.
6. D. LOTTIN, *Recherches historiques sur la ville d'Orléans*, Orléans, 1836, vol. 2, p. 18; A CHENAL, *Etude sur le Présidial d'Orléans*, Orléans, 1908.
7. J. CRESPIN, *Histoire des martyrs*. Ed. D. Benoist et M. Lelievre, Toulouse, 1889, vol. 3, pp. 692-704. «Ce que nous avons à réciter de l'estat de l'Eglise d'Orléans a esté recueilli de l'extrait qu'en dressa les jours du massacre un chanoine de S. Croix, homme paisible et detestant les cruautez de ceux de sa Religion, des conseils et actes desquels il fut auditeur et spectateur. Nous avons espargné son nom en cet endroit pour cause».

de Jean Grolier, qui y a inscrit son ex-libris au bas du colophon: «Io. Grolierij Lugdun et amicorum». Florent Damain devait en faire don au diplomate Jacques Bongars, fils de Girard, porté, on l'a vu, sur l'une des listes de condamnation en février 1563.[1]

Pendant la phase de demi-paix qui a suivi le traité d'Amboise, Thomas Mahieu a dû apprendre la mort, survenue le 22 octobre 1565, de celui qui fut pour lui un guide et un modèle, Jean Grolier. L'ancient trésorier de France, qui paraît en effet n'avoir pas été étranger à la carrière de Mahieu, a exercé sur lui une visible influence que manifestent notamment son amour des livres, son goût pour les reliures à décor et le choix des ateliers chargés de les exécuter, attribués à Claude de Picques, et aux relieurs dits «de Mansfeld», «du Cuspinianus de Grolier» et «de l'Esope de Mahieu».[2] Outre l'incunable milanais, déjà cité, on connaît deux impressions bâloises de Cicéron portant l'ex-libris de Grolier et dont la reliure fut faite pour Mahieu.[3] Sur le *De Officiis* de 1528, Mahieu a pris soin d'ajouter sur une garde son propre ex-libris, jumeau de celui de Grolier, «A Mahieu et a ses amys».

Particularité qui intrigue davantage, Mahieu a inscrit de sa main sur deux autres volumes reliés pour lui la devise même de Jean Grolier, «Portio mea domine sit in terra viventium», inspirée du Psaume 141,6. L'un, dont la reliure porte la devise INIMICI, contient précisément les *Psalmi di David*, traduits de l'hébreu en italien et commentés par Antonio Brucioli en 1534.[4] Mahieu y a inscrit aussi sur la page de titre une variante du Psaume 145,20, «Custodit dominus omnes diligentes et omnes impios

---

1. 2°. Berne, Stadtbibliothek. Dédicace manuscrite: «Bongarsii beneficio amicissimi Flor. Damani». H. STRAHM, «Bücher und Menschen», *Zeitschrift für Bücherfreunde* 37 (1933), pp. 248-251, ill.; G. AUSTIN, *The Library of Jean Grolier*, New York 1971, n. 493. 2; M. FOOT, *The Henry Davis Gift…A collection of bookbindings, op. cit.*, I, p. 184 et n. 20.

2. Sur ces rapprochements fondés sur l'étude des reliures et des ateliers qui ont travaillé pour les deux collectionneurs, voir les ouvrages déjà cités: G. D. HOBSON, *Maioli*, 1926; A. R. A. HOBSON, *French and Italian Collectors*, 1953; H. M. NIXON, *Twelve Books*, 1953; G. AUSTIN, *The Library of Jean Grolier*, 1971; M. FOOT, *The Henry Davis Gift*, 1978. Et en outre, G. D. HOBSON, *Bindings in Cambridge Libraries*, Cambridge, 1929; P. M. MICHON, *La reliure française*, Paris, 1951; *Bookbindings from the Library of Jean Grolier*. Ed. H. M. NIXON, London, 1965; H. M. NIXON, *Sixteenth Century gold-tooled Bookbindings in the Pierpont Morgan Library*, New York, 1971: A. HOBSON et P. CULOT, *La Reliure en France au seizième siècle*, Bibliotheca Wittockiana, 1990.

3. *De Officiis*, Bâle, J. Froben et N. Episcopius, 1528. 4°. Lyon, Bibl. Munic. G. D. HOBSON, *Maioli*, n. XXIX; AUSTIN, n. 111. *Tusculanae quaestiones*, Bâle, J. Froben et N. Episcopius, 1536. 4°. G. D. HOBSON, *Maioli*, n. XXX; AUSTIN, n. 121. 1.

4. Venise, A. Pincio pour A. Brucioli, mai 1534. 4°. Paris, Petit Palais, G.D. HOBSON, *Maioli*, n. LXVIII; AUSTIN, n. 451. Sur l'édition, voir: G. SPINI, *Bibliografia delle opere di Antonio Brucioli*, La Bibliofilia, 1940, n. 38.

disperset».[1] L'autre volume, dont la reliure est ornée du monogramme répété TDM, est largement postérieur à la mort de Grolier.[2] C'est un ouvrage du mathématicien Kaspar Peucer sur les divinations, traduit par l'actif pasteur genevois, Simon Goulart, qui l'a fait paraître en 1584 sous deux adresses différentes, celle du libraire lyonnais B. Honorati, ou celle de l'imaginaire Anversois, H. Connix, alors que Peucer, ami de Théodore de Bèze et accusé de «crypto-calvinisme», était prisonnier des luthériens.[3] Mahieu s'est procuré un exemplaire de l'édition clandestine. En même temps que la devise de Grolier, il y a laissé son ex-libris manuscrit sous la forme «Cest a Mahieu et a ses amys».

Les commentaires bibliques de Brucioli, parents de ceux de Martin Bucer, furent condamnés par l'index vénitien de 1549, par celui de Milan en 1554, par celui de Rome, dit de Paul V en 1559. Ils devaient l'être encore par l'index romain de 1564, dit du Concile de Trente, et par celui de 1590.[4] Mahieu possédait d'ailleurs aussi la Bible en italien de Brucioli, publiée en 1547.[5] Quant à l'oeuvre entière de Peucer, déjà condamnée en 1559 et en 1564, elle le sera à nouveau en 1590 et en 1594.[6] Même si, à cette époque, la France attachait peu d'importance aux index romains, il est curieux de voir que Mahieu a transcrit la devise de son aîné sur deux ouvrages considérés à Rome comme hérétiques.

Par ailleurs, la présence à Orléans de trois livres reliés pour Jean Grolier[7] n'aurait-elle pas un lien originel avec Thomas Mahieu? Deux d'entre

---

1. L'écriture de la devise, la même que celle du verset, n'est pas celle de Grolier, mais correspond à celle de Thomas Mahieu.

2. *Le devins, ou Commentaires des principales sortes de divinations... Tourné en vers François par S. G. S. [Simon Goulart, Senlisien]*, Anvers, H. Connix, 1584. 4°. A.R.A. HOBSON, *French and Italian Collectors*, p. 37, n. 17.

3. L.C. JONES, *Simon Goulart*, Genève, 1916. n. 24; BAUDRIER, *Bibliographie lyonnaise*, IV, p. 147. Les exemplaires au nom d'Honorati et les exemplaires au nom de Connix, celui-ci inconnu des répertoires d'imprimeurs belges ou hollandais, présentent un corps d'ouvrage identique. Seule diffère la composition typographique des préliminaires. La fausse adresse d'Anvers recouvre très probablement celle de Genève. Je remercie Ursula Baurmeister et Sylvie Postel-Lecocq de l'aide qu'elles m'ont apportée en cette recherche.

4. P.F. GRENDLER, *The Roman Inquisition and the Venetian Press, 1540-1605*. Princeton (N.J.), 1977, pp. 116-129; J. M. DE BUJANDA, *Index des livres interdits. III. Index de Venise, 1549, Venise et Milan, 1554*, Sherbrooke, Genève, 1987, *passim*; id., *Index des livres interdits. VIII. Index de Rome, 1557, 1559, 1564*, Ibidem, 1990, *passim*.

5. Venise. G. Scotto, 1547. 4°. Paris, Bibl. Nat., Rés. A 2442 bis. G.D. HOBSON; *Maioli*, n. 13 A; G. SPINI, *art. cité*, pp. 144-145, n. 14.

6. J. M. DE BUJANDA, *Index des livres interdits. VIII. Index de Rome*, op. cit., *passim*.

7. OVIDIUS, *Le Metamorphosi. Trad. Niccolo di Agostini*. Venise N. Zoppino di Aristotele, 1537. 4°. Austin, n. 365. 2°. (Prov. Prousteau, XVIIe siècle); J. MAGNUS, *Historia de omnibus gothorum sueborumque regibus*, Rome, de Viottis, 1554. 4°. AUSTIN, n. 319; O. MAGNUS, *Historia de gentibus septentrionalibus*, Rome, de Viottis, 1555. 2°. AUSTIN, n. 320. Voir aussi: C. CUISSARD, *La Bibliothèque d'Orléans*, Orléans, 1894, p. 89.

eux, dus aux frères suédois Magnus, appartenaient au XVIIe siècle à l'hôpital d'Orléans (ancien Hôtel-Dieu), comme l'indique l'ex-libris «Ex Bibliotheca Ptocotrophii Aureliensis, 1685».

Dans les derniers jours de 1567, après l'entrée-surprise de François de La Noue à Orléans, la ville passe de nouveau pour quelques mois aux mains des protestants, hostiles à la paix de Longjumeau. En août de l'année suivante, la cour exige des protestants de France un serment de fidélité au roi Charles IX. A Orléans, la plupart des membres de la noblesse et plusieurs habitants se refusent au serment, mais huit cent quatre vingt quatorze chefs de famille signent le registre.[1] Mahieu que ses fonctions ont en tout cas anobli ne figure pas parmi les signataires. On le voit par ailleurs acquérir un exemplaire des *Poemata* de Théodore de Bèze, imprimés clandestinement vers 1567, et y porter son ex-libris manuscrit sous sa forme latine, «Tho. Maioli et amicorum», celle qu'il fait habituellement porter sur ses reliures, en même temps qu'un bref commentaire de l'une des illustrations ornant la page de titre: «[Mors] sceptra ligonibus aequat». Celle-ci symbolise en effet, par un sceptre, une pioche et un crâne, l'égalité des rois et des humbles devant la mort.[2] Il n'est pas indifférent qu'un fonctionnaire royal souligne, à cette époque, le sens d'un tel emblème.

C'est vraisemblablement au cours de l'été 1571 que Charles IX décide de supprimer les Généralités d'Orléans et de Limoges, créées par son père treize ans auparavant. Celle-ci ne sont pas comprises, en effet, dans l'édit d'octobre 1571 créant pour les autres Généralités de nouveaux offices de «Trésoriers alternatifs», ces derniers devant alterner avec les anciens leurs chevauchées et leurs permanences en ville.[3] Il est donc mis fin aux fonctions de Thomas Mahieu dont la dernière quittance de l'époque a été conservée:

> Je Thomas mahieu Conseiller du Roy Tresorier de France et General de ses finances en la Charge et Generallité de Languedoil naguères establye a orleans a present supprimee Confesse avoir Receu comptant de Mr Raymond de Castaing aussi conseiller dudit Sire et Receveur general de ses finances

---

1. Paris, Bibl. de l'Arsenal, ms 6400 (copie). Publié par F. DE FÉLICE, *Procès-verbaux de la prestation de fidélité au Roy Charles IX par les huguenots, d'Orléans en 1568*. Orléans, 1882.

2. T. DE BÈZE, *Poemata*. S. l., c. 1567. 16°. Paris, Bibl. Nat., Rés. p. Yc. 1765. La reliure a été remplacée au XVIIIe siècle. J. VEYRIN-FORRER, «Autour d'un exemplaire des *Poemata* de Théodore de Bèze portant l'ex-libris 'Tho. Maioli et amicorum', *Parcours et Rencontres*, Paris, sous presse.

3. Edit de Charles IX, octobre 1571, créant dans dix-sept Généralités du Royaume un second trésorier de France. FOURNIVAL, *op. cit.*, p. 287. La suppression du Bureau de recette générale d'Orléans est mentionnée dans l'édit de Charles IX du 23 septembre 1573 et dans celui d' Henri III d'août 1576. Voir *infra*.

en la charge et generallité de Languedoil estably *[sic]* a Bourges la somme de six cens vingt cinq livres tournoys a moy ordonnee pour mes gaiges A cause de mondict estat du quartier de Janvier, Febrier et Mars mil cinq cens soixante et douze a Raison de II^M V C L par an de laquelle somme de VI^C XXV L je me tiens pour content et bien payé et en ay quicté et quicte ledit de Castaing Receveur susdit et tous autres Tesmoing mon seing manuel cy mis le quatriesme Jour dapvril Mil V^c soixante et douze.

Signé: Mahieu

On lit au verso:

Pour servir de Quictance de la somme de six cens Vingt cinq Livres tournoys pour mes gaiges du quartier de Janvier Febvrier et Mars M V C soixante et douze. A cause de mon estat de general des finances en la charge cy devant establye a Orleans.[1]

On peut donc supposer que Thomas Mahieu n'est plus à Orléans au mois d'août 1572, lorsque le massacre de la Saint-Barthélemy y provoque un carnage effroyable dont témoignent les *Memoires de l'Estat de France*, réunis par Simon Goulart,[2] l'*Histoire des martyrs* de Jean Crespin[3] et le récit d'un étudiant allemand, J. W. de Botsheim.[4]

Au mois de septembre 1573, Charles IX rétablit les Généralités d'Orléans et de Limoges, avec chacune leur bureau central de recette et leurs deux offices de Trésorier de France et de Général des finances.[5] Il semblerait donc que Thomas Mahieu ait pu être réintégré dans ses fonctions dès 1574, mais en août 1576, un nouvel édit d'Henri III vient encore modifier la situation: il porte création dans les Généralités d'Orléans, de Limoges et de Lyon, «pour les rendre uniformes avec les autres», d'un deuxième office alternatif de Trésorier de France et d'un deuxième office alternatif de Général des finances, ce qui réduit d'autant leurs prérogatives respectives.[6] L'historien d'Orléans François Le Maire, donne à ce

---

1. Bibl. Nat., Pièces originales 1793, Mahieu (1e numérotation, n. 5).
2. *Memoires de l'Estat de France sous Charles neuviesme. 2e édition.* Meidelbourg, H. Wolf, 1578, vol. 1, pp. 246-253.
3. Voir n. 66.
4. C. READ, «La Saint Barthelemy à Orléans, racontée par Joh. Wilh. de Botzheim, étudiant allemand témoin oculaire, 1572», *Société de l'histoire du protestantisme français, Bulletin*, 1872, pp. 345-392.
5. Edit de Charles IX, septembre 1573, établissant une recette générale à Orléans et créant un Trésorier de France et un Général des finances aux mêmes gages et privilèges que ceux des autres Généralités. FOURNIVAL, *op. cit.*, pp. 289-292; BOURGNEUF, p. 39.
6. Edit d'Henri III, août 1576, créant un office de Trésorier de France et un office de Général des finances alternatifs en chacune des Généralités de Lyon, Limoges et Orléans. Enregistré à Paris, le 23 novembre 1576. FOURNIVAL, *op. cit.*, p. 303; BOURGNEUF, p. 41.

sujet une chronologie légèrement différente. Evoquant le rétablissement de la Généralité d'Orléans par l'édit de 1573, il écrit:

> Neantmoins n'eut lieu qu'en 1575, en laquelle Monsieur Mahieu pourveu de l'office de Tresorier de France, et Monsieur Milon, sieur de Viudeville, exercerent les charges de Tresoriers de France.[1]

Si l'on s'en rapporte à l'édit d'Henri III, ce double exercice de Trésorier à Orléans n'a pu débuter qu'en 1576.

Quoi qu'il en soit, Mahieu s'est défait en 1575 d'un des livres qu'il avait fait relier une quinzaine d'années auparavant à son monogramme, dit complexe, car composé de treize lettres. Il s'agit du *De antiquo statu Burgundiae*, de Guillaume Paradin, imprimé à Lyon en 1542 par Etienne Dolet, natif d'Orléans.[2] Le nouveau possesseur était le chirurgien protestant François Rasse Des Neux, que Mahieu avait dû connaître en 1562, au moment où, chassé de Paris comme tous ses coréligionnaires par une ordonnance du Maréchal de Brissac, Des Neux avait été contraint de chercher refuge à Orléans. Collectionneur très actif depuis plus de trente ans, le chirurgien avait l'habitude de marquer sur ses livres le nom de leur donateur.[3] On peut donc se demander s'il a acheté à Mahieu cet exemplaire ou si quelque autre raison l'a empêché de le nommer.

On connaît trois exemples datés de livres acquis par Thomas Mahieu après sa réintégration à l'office d'Orléans: un commentaire latin de Marco Flaminio sur les Psaumes, édité à Lyon chez Guillaume Rouille en 1576.[4] Le Peucer de 1584, et le *Recueil des Guerres et Traictez d'entre les Roys de France et d'Angleterre*, composé par Jean Du Tillet, greffier civil du Parlement de Paris, et publié à Paris, chez Jacques Du Puys en 1588.[5] Mais approchant probablement de la soixantaine, le trésorier semblait maintenant se contenter d'un style plus sobre pour les reliures dont il passait commande. Le nouveau type de décor, visible sur le premier de ces volumes – le monogramme TDM, inscrit dans une couronne de feuillages – est caractéristique des années soixante et soixante-dix. Il se retrouve sur d'autres volumes frappés du même chiffre, dont l'impression remontait à

---

1. F. LEMAIRE, *op. cit.*, p. 402.
2. G. D. HOBSON, *Maioli*, LXI; M. J. HUSUNG, *op. cit.*, p. 18 et ill. 68, pl. XLII. Sur l'édition, voir C. LONGEON, *Bibliographie des oeuvres d'Etienne Dolet*, Genève, 1980, n. 227.
3. J. VEYRIN-FORRER, «Un collectionneur engagé, François Rasse Des Neux, chirurgien parisien», *La lettre et le texte*, Paris, 1987, pp. 423-477.
4. *In librum Psalmorum*, 1576. G.D. HOBSON, *Bindings in Cambridge libraries*, Cambridge, 1929, p. 85; cité par A.R.A. HOBSON, *French and Italian collectors*, p. 37, n. 17. Sur l'édition, voir BAUDRIER, IX, pp. 358-359.
5. *Recueil* étudié, avec reproduction, par F. ADAMS, «Maioli's Mottoes and Monograms», *Festschrift Otto Schäfer*, Stuttgart, 1987, pp. 457-459.

plus de vingt ans et que Mahieu fit donc relier bien après leur mise sur le marché. Il s'agit là de trois impressions vénitiennes, deux Pétrarque, datés de 1550[1] et de 1553,[2] et un recueil de médailles d'Enea Vico, édité en 1553 également.[3] Sur le Peucer de 1584, plus élaboré, le vélin de la reliure est décoré du même motif, mais le monogramme est répété dans les quatre angles, ainsi qu'au dos, orné lui-même de couronnes de feuillages.[4] Un recueil de chiromancie, publié à Nuremberg en 1560, et dont M. Frederick Adams a la bonté de me signaler la présence à Bruxelles, appartient aussi à la catégorie des reliures plus simples de la période, dont le décor est constitué d'un motif central et d'écoinçons. Seul, le petit monogramme, frappé entre les nerfs du dos, en révèle l'ancien propriétaire.[5]

Cependant, l'ouvrage de Du Tillet, dernier en date des volumes connus portant ce monogramme, fait exception à cette simplicité. Son vélin est orné d'un semé de larmes, de crânes et de croisillons d'os et de flèches, à la manière des reliures exécutées pour les membres de la congrégation des Pénitents, fondée par Henri III en 1583.[6] Si Mahieu n'appartenait pas à la confrérie, du moins le choix de ces emblèmes funèbres sur un livre d'histoire devait-il avoir pour son possesseur une valeur symbolique.

La présence étonnante d'un Thomas Mahieu sur la liste des secrétaires d'Henri III en 1586, puis sur celle des secrétaires d'Henri IV en 1596 suggère qu'il s'agit maintenant d'un fils du trésorier, portant même prénom.[7]

Aux quelque cent-onze reliures connues portant le nom ou l'un des monogrammes de Thomas Mahieu, il est possible d'ajouter celles de deux volumes conservés à la Bibliothèque Nationale de Paris, malheureusement emboîtées et en état précaire. Ces reliures portent toutes deux, au bas du premier plat, l'ex-libris «.THO. MAIOLII ET. AMICORVM.» et, au centre du deuxième, la devise: «INGRATIS / SERVIRE / NEPHAS.». Mais le titre frappé au centre du premier plat a, dans les deux cas, été masqué,

---

1. *Il Petrarcha con expositione d'Alessandro Vellutello*, Venise, G. Giolito e fratelli, 1550. 4°. Rouen, O. 552. G. D. HOBSON, *Cambridge, op. cit.*, p. 85; cité par A. R. A. HOBSON, *ibid*. Je remercie Mlle Neveu, Conservateur à la Bibliothèque municipale de Rouen, qui a bien voulu me donner des précisions sur cet exemplaire auquel est joint une note de G. D. Hobson.
2. *Il Petrarcha*. Comment. G. A. Gesualdo. Venise, G. Giolito, 1553. 2 vol. 4°. Baltimore, Walters Art Gallery. Reliure reproduite par F. ADAMS, *art. cité*, p. 457.
3. *Omnium Caesarum...imagines ex antiquis numismatis desumptae*, Venise, 1553. Bibl. Ste-Geneviève, 4° ZZ 501, Inv. 961. Signalé par A. R. A. HOBSON, *ibid*.
4. Voir n. 72.
5. TRICASSUS MANTUANUS, *Enarratio...principiorum Chyromantiae*, etc. Bruxelles, Bibliothèque Royale, VH 8718A LP.
6. Voir n. 91.
7. Bibl. Nat. ms fr. 7854, pp. 2280 et 2346; ms fr. 7856, pp. 1383 et 1448.

grâce à la superposition de petits fers semblant dater du milieu du XVIIe siècle. On peut néanmoins entrevoir ou deviner sur l'un des volumes (Rés. g. Z. 14), le mot ILLVSTRIVM, et sur l'autre (Rés. g. Z. 15) le nom de l'auteur PLVTARCHI. Ces deux reliures ne paraissent pas cependant avoir recouvert une même édition des *Vitae illustrium virorum*, leurs dimensions ne coïncidant pas.

-Veau brun. Décor d'entrelacs géométriques du type losange-rectangle. Grand cercle central et deux cercles juxtaposés. Rinceaux de filets accompagnés de fers ouverts. Fers plein or dans les angles. Rehauts peints en noir sur les entrelacs, et de couleurs variées sur les fers. Dos long à sept compartiments losangés. Quatre paires de fentes pour les attaches. 350 x 225 x 40 mm. Rés. g. Z. 14.

Les fers ouverts sont ceux du relieur, dit «du Cuspinianus de Grolier».[1]

-Veau brun. Décor asymétrique d'entrelacs courbes du type «cuirs roulés», formé d'un grand cartouche central et de motifs d'écoinçons. Rinceaux de filets accompagnés de quelques fers ouverts à la partie supérieure. Rehauts peints en noir et blanc sur les entrelacs et sur les fers ouverts. Dos long à cinq compartiments losangés et à points d'or. Quatre paires de fentes pour les attaches. 335 x 235 x 40 mm. Rés. g. Z. 15.

Deux des fers ouverts (feuille courbe à extrémité enroulée) ont une forme voisine de ceux que H. M. Nixon attribue au relieur de Pierre Ernest de Mansfeld et qu'on observe sur une reliure recouvrant un recueil de dessins originaux de Jacques Androuet du Cerceau (Paris, Petit Palais, Dutuit 188). Ils s'en distinguent néanmoins. Ils diffèrent également des fers d'aspect similaire qui ornent une reliure exécutée pour Jean Grolier sur une Bible en grec, Venise, 1518 (Paris, Bibl. Sainte-Geneviève, OE 354 Inv. 57).[2] (Pour l'examen et la description de ces deux reliures, j'ai bénéficié du précieux concours de M. Jean Toulet, Directeur de la Réserve des livres rares et précieux de la Bibliothèque Nationale, que je remercie vivement. Mrs Mirjam Foot a bien voulu donner aussi de judicieux avis).

Le premier de ces volumes contient aujourd'hui les *Athenaei Deipnosophistarum libri XV*, édités par Isaac Casaubon sur double colonne, l'une

1. Cf. H. M. NIXON, *Sixteenth-century gold-tooled bookbindings in the Pierpont Morgan Library*, New York, 1971, n. 21; P. NEEDHAM, *Twelve Centuries of bookbindings 400-1600*, New York, 1979, n. 57.
2. E. RAHIR, *La collection Dutuit, livres et manuscrits*, Paris, 1899, n. 188; H. M. NIXON, *Sixteenth-century...*, *op. cit.*, p. 88; H. M. NIXON, «Paris Bindings for Peter Ernst de Mansfeld», in *Les reliures aux armoiries de Pierre Ernest de Mansfeld*, Luxembourg, 1978, p. 48; AUSTIN, *op. cit.*, n. 52.

Fig. 4. Reliure emboîtée portant au premier plat l'ex-libris de Thomas
Mahieu et, au second, la devise INGRATIS SERVIRE NEPHAS.
Bibl. Nat., Impr., Rés. g. Z. 14

Fig. 5. Reliure emboîtée portant au premier plat l'ex-libris de Thomas
Mahieu et, au second, la devise INGRATIS SERVIRE NEPHAS.
Bibl. Nat., Impr., Rés. g. Z. 15

présentant le texte grec, l'autre la version latine de Jacques Dalechamps, Heidelberg, Hieronymus Commelinus, 1598. 2°. Les pages, rognées à la partie supérieure, mesurent 342 x 220 mm.

Dans le second volume se trouvent les *Animadversionum in Athenaei Deipnosophistos libri XV*, d'Isaac Casaubon, Lugduni, apud Antonium de Harsy (excudebat Guichardus Jullerionus), 1600. 2°. Les pages mesurent 330 x 225 mm.

Le papier de garde, inséré lors des emboîtages, est le même pour les deux volumes. Le filigrane présente un écu couronné aux initiales L B, surmonté d'un quatrefeuilles. Sous l'écu, un cartouche renferme le nom de Nicolas Le Bé. Il peut s'agir de Nicolas II, papetier troyen, baptisé en 1622, ou plus vraisemblablement, de Nicolas III, baptisé en 1674 et mort en 1734. Le dessin du filigrane diffère légèrement de ceux de Nicolas Ier Le Bé (mort vers 1604), tels qu'ils sont reproduits dans l'ouvrage de L. Le Clert.[1]

L'*Athenaeus* comporte trois gardes de ce papier. Celle du contreplat est moderne. La couture de ce volume a été refaite à l'époque de l'emboîtage.

Les *Animadversiones* comportent normalement quatre gardes. La couture grecquée du volume est celle qui préexistait à l'emboîtage. Les nerfs ont été passés une fois sous les cartons. Une claie ancienne subsiste.

Le nom du possesseur des deux volumes emboîtés, tracé en rouge sur la page de titre, a été lavé, et son patronyme a été, en outre, recouvert par l'une des nombreuses estampilles apposées par la suite. Grâce à l'obligeance et à la perspicacité de M. Antoine Coron, Conservateur à la Réserve des livres rares et précieux de la Bibliothèque Nationale, il a été possible de lire avec vraisemblance sur les *Animadversiones:* «Guilelmi Ance[l]ij». Seul, le même prénom est visible sur l'*Athenaeus*. Un autre ex-libris «Guilelmi Ancelij», de forme très voisine, apparaît dans un recueil du XVI[e] siècle, dont la première pièce contient le *Dictionarium poeticum* de Hermannus Torrentinus, Paris, R. Estienne, 1535. 8°. (Bibl. Nat., Rés. p. Yc. 182).

Guillaume Ancel, dont la famille était originaire de l'Orléanais, fut diplomate en Allemagne pendant de longues années (1576-1612). En 1610, il se trouvait à Heidelberg en même temps que son ami et correspondant, l'Orléanais Jacques Bongars, chargé comme lui de négociations par Henri IV. Il est possible qu'Ancel ait alors acheté dans cette ville un exemplaire de l'édition de l'*Athenaeus* que Casaubon y avait fait imprimer une douzaine d'années auparavant. Mais c'est à Lyon, dans la maison de Mé-

---

1. L. Le Clert, *Recherches et notes pour servir à l'histoire du papier, principalement à Troyes*, Paris, 1926, vol. I, p. 227; vol. II, p. 375 et pl. XLVI, LXXIV.

ry de Vic – le légataire de la collection Grolier – que Casaubon acheva la rédaction de ses *Animadversiones*, et c'est à Lyon que le livre fut imprimé en 1600. Ancel dut donc se procurer ce dernier livre en France.[1] Toutefois, même s'il a pu posséder des livres provenant de Mahieu, il paraît douteux qu'Ancel ait été homme à faire exécuter les deux emboîtages. Il mourut d'ailleurs en 1615, et cette opération semble avoir été plus tardive. On ignore donc qui en fut l'initiateur.

Le dernier détenteur privé des deux volumes emboîtés fut Jean-Gabriel Petit de Montempuys, ancien recteur de l'Université de Paris, chanoine de Notre-Dame et janséniste ardent, qui les légua, avec toute sa bibliothèque, à son Université le 11 juillet 1762 et mourut l'année suivante.[2] Le catalogue de ses livres, dûment vérifié et paraphé le 18 août 1770, fait mention, à la page 230 de la première partie, des deux ouvrages et de leur reliure en veau.[3] Ceux-ci portent aujourd'hui en commun l'estampille à l'encre rouge BIBLO. / VNIV. / PAR. /, utilisée à partir de 1808, mais seul le premier (l'*Athenaeus*), laisse apparaître également le timbre armorié de Montempuys, frappé en rouge, ainsi qu'une estampille de la «Bibliothèque de l'Université de France». Sur le second (les *Animadversiones*), outre l'estampille citée, se voient celles de la Bibliothèque du Prytanée et de l'Ecole Normale, témoins des migrations des livres de la Sorbonne.

Conformément à une politique d'échanges, instaurée par l'Etat, entre la Bibliothèque Impériale, puis Nationale, et les autres bibliothèques parisiennes, Léopold Delisle, Administrateur de la Bibliothèque Nationale, s'avisa en 1887 de proposer au Conservateur de la Bibliothèque de l'Université à la Sorbonne, Jules de Chantepie, et à l'assentiment du Ministre de l'Instruction Publique, Léopold Faye, un échange des deux volumes «emboîtés dans une reliure exécutée pour Th. Maioli et renfermant primitivement une édition de Plutarque», contre une soixantaine de volumes doubles de la Bibliothèque Nationale.[4] L'expression utilisée par Delisle, «une édition», s'explique difficilement, mais l'échange eut lieu en janvier 1888.

---

1. Les premières pages des deux volumes sont annotées de la même main, peut-être celle d'Ancel.

2. J. ARTIER, «Aux origines de la Sorbonne, la création de la Bibliothèque de l'Université de Paris, 1683-1770», *Mélanges de la Sorbonne*, 11, 1991, pp. 35-58.

3. Bibliothèque de la Sorbonne, ms 113. Je suis reconnaissante à Mme Artier, Conservateur à la Bibliothèque de la Sorbonne, d'avoir favorisé ma recherche à ce sujet.

4. Lettre de Léopold Delisle au Ministre de l'Instruction Publique, 6 décembre 1887. Minute. Archives de la Bibliothèque Nationale.

ANNEXE

Arch. Nat., Minut. Centr., cxxii, 13, 26 novembre 1527. (Minute avec corrections d'une autre main.) J'exprime ma gratitude à Mme Annie Parent-Charon et à Mlle Nathalie Renier qui m'ont aidée à lire ce document.

[1r:] Noble homme maistre Iehan grolier conseiller du Roy nostre sire tresorier de ses guerres et tresorier Receveur general de ses finances tant ordinaires que extraordinaires en ses pays et duché de milan[H] lequel pour lui[H] En son nom fest[H] nomme ordonne constitue et establit[H] et constitue *[sic]* son procureur *general et partant messager especial*[a] Anthoine grolier esleu de lyonnais Auquel seul et pour le tout *ledit constituant*[b] a donné[H] par ces presentes[H] et donne plain povoir puissance et auctorité et mandement especial de poursuivre pourchasser Requerir et demander aux fermiers daciers[c] et gabelliers de ladite duché de milan et autres qui depuis le premier Iour doctobre lan mil V^c et quinze Iusques au dernier iour de decembre Lan mil cinq cens vingt ung Ont tenu et eu charge ou entremise des fermes daces et gabelles dicelle duché pour et ou nom du Roy nostre sire Et pareillement aux commitez plebes vicariatz Et a toutes personnes qui estoient Reddevables audit sire en ladite duché, et sur lesquelz ont esté prins et levez aucuns derniers tant par forme de subventions et annates, que^{Td} pour empruntz faiz et Pour *les affaires du Roy nostre sire*[e] durant le temps dessusdit, de luy monstrer et exhiber les quictances des payemens qui ont esté par eux faiz a feu maistre Iehan mahieu en son vivant commis^{Tf} dudit constituant a lexercice dudit office de tresorier et Receveur general desdites finances de ladite duché Pour et acause des deniers que lesdits fermiers daciers et gabelliers estoient tenuz payer audit tresorier et Receveur general constituant, ou a sondit commis Pour leurs fermes daces et gabelles dudit temps et lesdits commitez plebes et vicariatz et autres personnes a cause des Reddevances par eulx deuses [1v:] audit sire en Icelle duché tant pour[H] taxes de sel Cens Rentes[H] subventions et annattes^{Tg} que pour empruntz faiz pour *les affaires dudit sire* [h]durant ledit temps et prandre et Recouvrer deulx lesdites quictances qui ont esté faictes et baillees par ledit feu maistre Iehan mahieu signees de sa main Pour Iceulx payemens qui sont a present, et se trouveront es mains diceulx fermiers daciers gabelliers et autres Reddevables[H] ou desquels ont esté Receuz prins et levez lesdits deniers[H]comme dit est. Et pour et au lieu dicelles quictances en faire et bailler par ledit Anthoine grolier ou nom et comme procureur dudit maistre Iehan grolier tresorier et Receveur general dessusdit autres quictances servans dacquict et descharge ausdits fermiers daciers gabelliers et autres Reddevables et de qui lesdits deniers ont esté prins et Receuz tout ainsi que si elles estoient faictes et signees de La main dudit tresorier Receveur general constituant – Lesquelles Il a promis et promect par ces presentes avoir pour aggreables Et tenir quictes lesdits fermiers daciers gabelliers et autres personnes Reddevables et de qui Iceulx deniers ont esté prins Receuz des sommes qui y seront contenues et declaress^Ti et generalement dautant faire dire procurer et besongner en ce qui dit est et qui en despend comme ledit constituant feroit et faire poroit si present y estoit en sa personne Iasoit ce que le cas Request mandement plus especial promettant ledit constituant par bonne foy et soubz lobligation de tous ses biens avoir et tenir ferme stable et aggreable tout ce que par sondit procureur sera fait sur ce que dit est et qui en despend et par ce [2r:] le Iuger si mestier est. Ce fut fait et passé Lan Mille^V [cens] vingt sept et le mardi vingt sixiesme Iour de novembre.

Signé: Le Roy

N.B.: Les mots ajoutés au texte sont ici mis entre les deux signes ^H. Les mots substitués au texte primitif sont mis en italique et les mots rayés sont reportés en note. Les mots rayés sans substitution sont signalés par le signe ^T et indiqués en note. Le texte définitif se lit donc sans interruption.

a. *Remplace*: homme noble personne b. *Remplace*: Il. c. *dacier*: collecteur d'impôts.
d. *Mots rayés*: pour amendes comparucions condempnacions et confiscacions et aussi.
e. *Remplace*: le fait de ladite tresorerie et Recepte generale. f. *Mot rayé*: general. g. *Mots rayés*: que pour amendes comparucions condempnacions et confiscacions. h. *Remplace*: le fait dicelle tresorerie et Recepte generale. i. *Mots rayés*: et soubz Lobligation et.

BIBLIOGRAPHY OF A. R. A. HOBSON
The Published Works (up to the end of July, 1993)

1939

1. Archangel Ruined. [A short story]. *The Grasshopper.* An Etonian Magazine, 'Lord's' [July] 1939, pp. 7-8.

1947, 48

2. The Sacred Dance, I and II. *Ballet*, vol. 4, no. 4, October 1947, and vol. 5, no. 5, May 1948. Part I was reprinted in *About the House*, the magazine of the Friends of Covent Garden, Spring 1988, pp. 36-39.

1952

3. Notes on sales. *Book Collector*, vol. I, pp. 116-119, 189-191.

4. Die Versteigerungen 1940 bis 1950 bei Sotheby & Co., London. *Das Antiquariat*, VIII. Jahrgang Nr. 21/22, Wien, 10 Nov. 1952, pp. 417-8.

5. Review of J. Basil Oldham, *English Blind-Stamped Bindings* (The Sandars Lectures 1949), Cambridge, 1952. *The Library*, December 1952, pp. 284-5.

1953

6. Notes on sales. *Book Collector*, vol. 2, pp. 70-1.

7. Query no. 2. Early trade bindings. *Book Collector*, vol. 2, pp. 221-2.

8. *French and Italian Collectors and their Bindings.* Illustrated from examples in the library of J. R. Abbey. pp. XLIII, 190; illus. Roxburghe Club.

9. The Italian Book 1465-1900. Catalogue of an exhibition held at the National Book League, 7 Albemarle Street, London, W. I and the Italian Institute, 39 Belgrave Square, London, S.W.I. January to March 1953. Organizer: J. Irving Davis. 'Mr. A. R. A. Hobson kindly consented to select the book bindings shown, and has contributed an introduction to this section of the exhibition.' Italian book - bindings: pp. 86-7.

1954

10. *The Literature of Bookbinding.*
pp. 15. Cambridge University Press. (*The Book*. no. 2).

11. G. D. HOBSON, *German Renaissance Patrons of Bookbinding*. Edited by A. R. A. Hobson. *Book Collector*, 1954, pp. 171-189, 251-271.

12. Review of Maurice Craig, *Irish Bookbindings, 1600-1800* (London, 1954). *The Library*, September 1954, pp. 210-12.

13. German Bindings. (Review of Ernst Kyriss, *Verzierte gotische Einbände im alten deutschen Sprachgebiet*, vols. I and II, Stuttgart, 1951, 1954). *Times Literary Supplement* (hereafter *T. L. S.*), 14 January 1955, p. 32.

1956

14. A letter. *Book Collector*, vol. 5, pp. 113-4.

15. A binding for Geoffrey Granger. [With one plate]. *Bibliothèque d'humanisme et renaissance*, 18, pp. 280-1.

16. Review of Graham Pollard, *Changes in the style of bookbinding, 1550-1830*, in *The Library*, fifth series, XI, no. 2, June, 1956. *T. L. S.*, 21 September 1956, p. 560. [Anonymous].

17. Review of William Smith Mitchell, *A History of Scottish Bookbinding, 1432-1650* (University of Aberdeen, 1955). *The Library*, September 1956, pp. 215-18.

1957

18. Review of Howard M. Nixon, *Broxbourne Library. Styles and designs of bookbindings from the twelfth to the twentieth century* (Maggs Bros., London, 1956). *Book Collector*, vol. 6, pp. 190, 193-4.

1958

19. The Pillone Library. *Book Collector*, vol. 7, no. 1, Spring 1958, pp. 28-37; pl. 5.

20. Two Renaissance Bindings. 1. A binding presented to René of Anjou, 1459. 2. A binding for Matthias Corvinus, King of Hungary and Bohemia, c. 1480-90. [With two plates]. *Book Collector*, vol. 7, pp. 265-68.

21. Book Collectors. *The Snob Spotter's Guide*, edited and illustrated by Philippe Jullian, London, 1958, p. 30.

1959

22. "The Museum." [A letter, asking for information on a periodical of this name which appeared in 1822-24]. *T. L. S.*, 20 March, 1959, p. 161.

23. Review of Ferdinand Geldner, *Bucheinbände aus elf Jahrhunderten* (Munich, 1958). *Book Collector*, vol. 8, pp. 79-80.

24. Unfamiliar Libraries. v. Waddesdon Manor. *Book Collector*, vol. 8, pp. 131-139: pl. VII.

25. Query 120. Beckfordiana. *Book Collector*, vol. 8, p. 432.

26. The Waddesdon Library. *Gazette des beaux arts*, 54, pp. 87-94.

27. Review of Berthe van Regemorter, *Some early bindings from Egypt in the Chester Beatty Library* (Dublin, 1958). *The Library*, June 1959, pp. 135-37.

1960

28. A new Parisian romanesque binding. *Burlington Magazine*, 102, pp. 263-4.

29. Review of *Grolier 75* (New York, 1959). *The Library*, June 1960, pp. 148-9.

1961

30. Villa Lante, Villa d'Este, Villa Barbaro, Maser, Caprarola, Syon House. In: Sacheverell Sitwell (ed.), *Great Houses of Europe*, London, 1961, pp. 44-48, 76-79, 89-93, 106-110, 258-263.

31. William Beckford's Binders. *Festschrift Ernst Kyriss*, Stuttgart, 1961, pp. 375-381.

32. A.R.A. Hobson and A.N.L. Munby, John Roland Abbey. (Contemporary collectors, XXVI). *Book Collector*, vol. 10, pp. 40-48: pl. XVI.

33. Review of *Festschrift Ernst Kyriss* (Stuttgart, 1961). *Book Collector*, vol. 10, pp. 469, 470, 473.

1962

34. Beautiful and Exotic. (Review of Berthe van Regemorter, *Some Oriental Bindings in the Chester Beatty Library*, Dublin, 1961). *T.L.S.*, 31 August 1962, p. 664.

1963

35. Review of Ilse Schunke, *Die Einbände der Palatina in der Vatikanischen Bibliothek* (Vatican City, 3 vols., 1962). *Book Collector*, vol. 12, pp. 86, 89, 90, 93, 94, 97.

36. Review of Tammaro de Marinis, *La legatura artistica in Italia nei secoli XV e XVI* (Florence, 3 vols., 1960). *Book Collector*, vol. 12, pp. 511, 512, 515, 516, 519.

1964

37. Two Italian Renaissance Bookbindings in the Phillipps Collection.

Studi di bibliografia e storia in onore di Tammaro de Marinis, vol. III, [Verona], pp. 1-4. [With two plates].

38. Aranjuez, The Escorial. In: Sacheverell Sitwell (ed.), *Great Palaces*, London, 1964, pp. 151-55, 157-65.

1965

39. Auden Anatomized. (Review of B. C. Bloomfield, *W. H. Auden. A bibliography*. Charlottesville, Virginia, 1964). *T. L. S.*, 1 July 1965, p. 568.

40. Grolier's Bindings. (Review of [H. M. Nixon] *Bookbindings from the Library of Jean Grolier*. Trustees of the British Museum, 1965). *T. L. S.*, 23 September 1965, p. 836.

1966

41. Major Abbey's Bindings in the Saleroom. *T. L. S.*, 20 January 1966, p. 52. Also reprinted for private distribution as a pamphlet of 9 pp. by the Shenval Press.

1967

42. Note 291. Bindings with the device of a pelican in its piety. *Book Collector*, vol. 16, pp. 509-10.

43. Letter. [On the export control of modern manuscripts, i.e. the Garvin papers. Dated: 30 June 1967]. *The Times*, 7 July 1967, p. 9.

44. Fourth International Congress of Bibliophiles…Transactions. Edited by A. R. A. Hobson. pp. VIII, 94: pl. XII. London: Published by the Organising Committee of the Fourth International Congress of Bibliophiles for the Association Internationale de Bibliophilie.

1969

45. Review of *Fine Bindings 1500-1700 from Oxford Libraries* (Oxford, Bodleian Library, 1968). *The Library*, September 1969, pp. 257-9.

1970

46. Geoffrey Dudley Hobson, *Les reliures à la fanfare*. [Published in 1935]. Additions et corrections. Supplément, etc. By A. R. A. Hobson. pp. 17. Amsterdam, Gérard Th. van Heusden.

47. *Great Libraries*. pp. 320; 40 pp. of coloured plates, and 330 monochrome illustrations. Weidenfeld & Nicolson, 1970. American edition: New York, Putnam. French translation: *Grandes bibliothèques*. [Paris],

Stock, [c. 1971]. German translation: *Grosse Bibliotheken der Alten und der Neuen Welt*. München, Prestel.

1971

48. Query 259. Nancy Cunard's Psalm of the Palms and Sonnets (La Habana 1941). *Book Collector*, vol. 20, p. 250.

49. A Sale by Candle in 1608. [The sale of the library of Giovanni Vincenzo Pinelli at Naples]. Read before the Bibliographical Society on 20 January 1970. *The Library*, September 1971, pp. 215-233.

50. Italian manuscripts. [On the Italian Government's purchases at the Phillipps sales. A letter]. *The Times*, 24 December 1971, p. 11.

1972

51. Art Collections.
In: *Salisbury. A new approach to the City and its neighbourhood*. Edited by Hugh Shortt with photographs by Sir Cecil Beaton. Longman, London, 1972, pp. 114-128.

52. Letter [On the Strachey Trust]. *T.L.S.*, 1 December 1972, p. 1460.

1973

53. Letter [Advocating gilding the sculpture in the pediment of the portico of the British Museum]. *The Times*, 8 January 1973, p. 13.

54. Letter. [On the Visconti Hours]. *T.L.S.*; 9 March 1973, p. 269.

55. 'Absolutely all Auden.' (Review of B.C. Bloomfield and Edward Mendelson, *W. H. Auden. A bibliography 1924-1969*, second edition, Charlottesville, Virginia, 1972). *T.L.S.*, 27 July 1973, p. 883.

1974

56. 'Golden Age of Gilt.' (Review of Howard M. Nixon, *English Restoration Book-bindings*, British Museum, 1974). *T.L.S.*, 23 August 1974, p. 910.

1975

57. Letter. [On the future of the British Library]. *The Times*, 2 January 1975, p. 13.

58. Two Venetian bindings for Diego Hurtado de Mendoza. *Book Collector*, Spring 1975. (To Howard Nixon). pp. 33-36.

59. Auden's Spain. [A letter]. *T.L.S.*, 18 April 1975, p. 428.

60. 'A Palladian elegist'. (Review of Alan G. Thomas, *Great Books and Book Collectors*, London, 1975). *T.L.S.*, 8 August 1975, p. 904.

61. 'Outside appearances'. (Review of Otto Mazal, *Europäische Einbandkunst aus Mittelalter und Neuzeit*, Graz, 1970; *Le siècle d'or de l'imprimerie lyonnaise*, Paris, 1972; Emil van der Vekene, *Bemerkenswerte Einbände in der Nationalbibliothek zu Luxembourg*, Luxembourg, 1972; Bryan D. Maggs, *Bookbinding in Great Britain*. Catalogue 966, London, 1975; Matilde López Serrano, *La encuadernación española*, Madrid, 1972). *T.L.S.*, 19 December 1975, p. 1524.

62. The Treasures of Deene. (Wrongly described as by Handasyde Buchanan. In fact by A. R. A. Hobson). Account of the sale of books from Deene Park at Bonham's on 26 November 1975. *T.L.S.*, 19 December 1975, p. 1525.

63. *Apollo and Pegasus: an enquiry into the formation and dispersal of a Renaissance library.* pp. XVIII, 250: plates. Amsterdam, Gérard Th. van Heusden.

64. The *iter italicum* of Jean Matal. In: *Studies in the book trade in honour of Graham Pollard*, Oxford Bibliographical Society, pp. 33-61.

1976

65. 'Pounds, dollars and Deutschmarks.' By 'Robert Vaughan' [pseudonym of A. R. A. Hobson]. (Review of *American Book Prices Current 1974*, New York, 1974, and Ernst L. Hauswedell, ed., *Jahrbuch der Auktionspreise für Bücher, Handschriften und Autographen*, vol. 24, Hamburg, 1973). *T.L.S.*, 30 January 1976, p. 119.

66. 'On the reserved list'. (Review of Gabriel Austin, ed., Seventh International *Congress of Bibliophiles: Acts*, Paris, 1974). *T.L.S.*, 26 March 1976, p. 356.

67. William Beckford's Library. *The Connoisseur*, vol. 191, no. 770, April 1976, pp. 298-305.

68. 'Bindings in evidence'. (Review of Franz Anselm Schmitt, *Kostbare Einbände, seltene Drucke*, Karlsruhe, 1974, and *The Bibliotheck*, vol. 7, no. 5). *T.L.S.*, 7 May 1976, p. 560.

69. Letter. [In answer to a criticism by Muriel Hutton of the review of G. Austin, *Seventh International Congress of Bibliophiles: Acts*]. *T.L.S.*, 4 June 1976, p. 674.

70. 'Directions for the binder'. (Review of Philip Smith, New Directions in *Bookbinding*, London, 1974). *T.L.S.*, 25 June 1976, p. 805.

71. Manuscripts captured at Vitoria. *Cultural aspects of the Italian Renaissance. Essays in honour of Paul Oskar Kristeller*. Ed. Cecil H. Clough. Manchester University Press; Alfred F. Zambelli, New York, pp. 485-496.

72. The printer of the Greek editions "In Gymnasio Mediceo ad Caballinum Montem". [Vittore Carmelio for Angelo Colocci.]
Studi di biblioteconomia e storia del libro in onore di Francesco Barberi. Roma, Associazione Italiana Biblioteche, pp. 331-335.

1977

73. English Library Buildings of the 17th and 18th Century. *Wolfenbütteler Forschungen*, Bd. 2 (Bremen & Wolfenbüttel), pp. 63-74.

74. The cruise of the biblionauts. (Review of Leona Rostenberg and Madeleine B. Stern, *Old & Rare*, New York, London, 1974). *T. L. S.*, 24 March 1977, p. 340.

75. Obituary of Georges Heilbrun. *Book Collector*, 1977, pp. 569-71.

1978

76. 'Assembly points'. (Review of Colin Steele, *Major Libraries of the World*, London & New York, 1976). *T. L. S.*, 24 February 1978, p. 241.

77. [A letter, correcting an error in an article by Patrick King]. *The Antiquarian Book Monthly Review*, April 1978, p. 164.

78. 'More for the Morgan'. By 'Robert Vaughan' [pseudonym of A. R. A. Hobson]. (Review of Charles Ryskamp, ed., *Seventeenth Report to the Fellows of the Pierpont Morgan Library 1972-1974*, New York, 1976). *T. L. S.*, 5 May 1978, p. 508.

79. Review of Jeremy Cooper, *Under the Hammer. The auctions and auctioneers of London*, Constable, 1977. *Book Auction Records Quarterly*, vol. 75, pt. 2, May 1978, pp. 7-8.

80. 'The Hoard of Haigh Hall'. (Review of Nicolas Barker, *Bibliotheca Lindesiana*, London, for the Roxburghe Club, 1977). *T. L. S.*, 23 June 1978, p. 719.

81. La verità sulle legature cosidette "Canevari" esaminata. *La Bibliofilia*, 80, pp. 85-89.

82. Acquisti di opere a stampa per la biblioteca di Papa Paolo III. *La Bibliofilia*, 80, pp. 177-181.

83. Craftsman into artist. *Designer Bookbinders Review*, 11, 1978, pp. 1-4.

1979

84. Bindings à la grecque. Synopsis. Dixième Congrès International des Bibliophiles. Athens 1979, pp. 59-60.

85. Jacobus Apocellus. *Transactions of the Cambridge Bibliographical Society*. vol. VII, part 3. (To J. C. T. Oates). 1979, pp. 279-283.

1980

86. La biblioteca di Giovanni Battista Grimaldi. (dott. Anthony Hobson, 14 maggio 1980, salone del Banco di Chiavari). *Atti della Società Ligure di Storia Patria*, vol. XX, n.s. (XCIV), 1979 [1980], pp. 108-119.

87. The Stuff of Epics. (Review of H. P. Kraus, *A Rare Book Saga*, London, 1979). *Apollo*, February 1980, p. 166.

88. Housing the Turner bequest. [A letter]. *The Times*, 7 February 1980, p. 17.

89. Obituary of Boyd Alexander. *The Times*, 22 May 1980, p. 18.

90. Neo-classical façades. (Review of J. H. Loudon, *James Scott and William Scott, Bookbinders*, Scolar Press for the National Library of Scotland; another issue, The Moretus Press, New York, 1980). *T. L. S.*, 15 August 1980, p. 922.

91. Review of Mirjam M. Foot, *The Henry Davis Gift. A collection of bookbindings*, vol. i. The British Library, 1978. *Burlington Magazine*, October 1980, pp. 703-4.

92. The Vatican Library. Friends of Lambeth Palace Library. Annual Report 1980, pp. 11-20.

1981

93. 'Trading in Tuscany'. (Review of William A. Pettas, *The Giunti of Florence: Merchant publishers of the sixteenth century*, San Francisco, 1980). *T. L. S.*, 13 February 1981, p. 179.

94. 'Bound for the clerisy'. (Review of F. A. Schmidt-Künsemüller, *Corpus der gotischen Lederschnitteinbände aus dem deutschen Sprachgebiet*, Stuttgart, 1980). *T. L. S.*, 5 June 1981, p. 650.

95. Letter. [Correcting misprints in the review of the book named in the previous entry]. *T. L. S.*, 26 June 1981, p. 729.

96. Pontifical of Hugues de Salins, Besançon mid-eleventh century, and the Phillipps Sales. *Fine Books and Book Collecting. Books and manuscripts acquired from Alan G. Thomas and described by his customers on the occasion of* *his seventieth birthday*. Ed. Christopher de Hamel and Richard A. Linenthal. James Hall, Leamington Spa, pp. 2-4.

97. Suadbar's Letter. [The letter of a ninth-century Irish monk in Bamberg Staatsbibliothek, MS. Class. 6]. 9. Internationaler Bibliophilen-Kongress 1975 in der Schweiz / 9ᵉ Congrès international des Bibliophiles 1975 en Suisse / Akten und Referate / Actes et communications. Zürich, 1981, pp. 37-48.

98. John Roland Abbey (1894-1969). *Dictionary of National Biography 1961-1970*, Oxford 1981, pp. 1-2.

1982

99. Les reliures italiennes de la bibliothèque grecque de François Iᵉʳ. *Revue française de l'histoire du livre*, 51, 1982, pp. 409-426.

100. Who was F.T.? [Suggesting that this book-collector may have been the Spaniard Francisco Torres]. *Philobiblon* 26, 1982, pp. 166-176. (For Otto Schäfer's seventieth birthday).

101. Review of Emile van der Vekene, *Les reliures aux armoiries de Pierre Ernst de Mansfeld* (Luxembourg 1978) and Paul Culot, *Jean-Claude Bozerian* (Brussels 1979). *Burlington Magazine*, October 1982, pp. 636-7.

102. Shades of the Seventeenth Century. Wells Cathedral Library. *Country Life*, 30 December 1982, pp. 2084, 2085.

1983

103. Review of André Masson, *The Pictorial Catalogue. Mural decoration in libraries* (Oxford, 1981). *The Library*, March 1983, pp. 82-83.

104. Review of Lotte Hellinga, *Caxton in focus: the beginning of printing in England* (London, 1982). *Burlington Magazine*, December 1983, p. 755.

105. *Cyril Connolly as a Book Collector*. The Tregara Press, Edinburgh, 1983. pp. 1-24; frontispiece portrait. 150 copies + 50 copies for the author.

1984

106. Letter. [On W. H. Auden's authorship of the pornographic poem 'The Platonic Blow']. *Book Collector*, vol. 33, p. 522.

107. Two early sixteenth-century binders' shops in Rome. *Studia Bibliothecae Wittockianae*. 1. De libris compactis miscellanea, ed. Georges Colin. Bruxelles, 1984, pp. 79-98.

108. Review of Mirjam M. Foot, *The Henry Davis Gift. A collection of bookbindings*. Volume II, 1983; and Howard M. Nixon, *British Bookbindings* *presented by Kenneth H. Oldaker to the Chapter of Westminster Abbey*, London, 1982. *Burlington Magazine*, June 1984, pp. 358-9.

109. 'An inveterate arranger'. (Review of *The Douce Legacy, exhibition catalogue*, Bodleian Library, Oxford, 1984). *T. L. S.*, 21 September 1984, p. 1057.

110. 'Worthy titles only'. (Review of Marianne Tidcombe, T*he bookbindings of T. J. Cobden-Sanderson*, British Library, 1984). *T. L. S.*, 9 November 1984, p. 1282.

1985

111. 'Delectable neatness'. (Review of Howard M. Nixon, *Catalogue of the Pepys Library at Magdalene College, Cambridge: Volume VI. Bindings.* Woodbridge, Suffolk, 1984). *T. L. S.*, 15 February 1985, p. 183.

112. 'For keeping's sake.' (Review of Sophie Malavieille, *Reliures et cartonnages d'éditeur en France au XIXe siècle (1815-1865)*, Paris, 1985). *T. L. S.*, 21 June 1985, p. 707.

113. James Scott of Edinburgh, Bookbinder. Transactions of the Thirteenth Congress [of the Association internationale de Bibliophilie], Edinburgh, 23-29 September 1983, [Edinburgh], 1985, pp. 13-27.

114. Some sixteenth-century buyers of books in Rome and elsewhere. *Humanistica Lovaniensia*, XXXIV A, pp. 65-75: pl. VII. (Roma humanistica. Studia in honorem Rev.[i] adm. Dni Dni Iosaei Ruysschaert).

1986

115. Alan Noel Latimer Munby (1913-1974). *Dictionary of National Biography 1971-1980*, Oxford, 1986, pp. 616-18.

116. 'Impressive in leather.' (Review of Denise Gid, *Catalogue des reliures françaises estampées à froid (XVe-XVIe siècle) de la Bibliothèque Mazarine*, Paris, 1984). *T. L. S.*, 3 January 1986, p. 24.

117. Victoria and Albert Museum. [A letter]. *The Times*, 8 April 1986, p. 17.

118. Biblioteca Apostolica Vaticana. [A letter]. *T. L. S.*, 2 May 1986, p. 473.

119. British Library. [A letter]. *The Times*, 19 September 1986, p. 17.

120. 'For lending and for locals'. (Review of J.C.T. Oates, *Cambridge University Library: a history. Vol. I. From the beginnings to the Copyright Act of Queen Anne*, Cambridge, 1986). *T. L. S.*, 7 November 1986, p. 1244.

1987

121. Review of Hannah D. French, *Bookbinding in Early America: Seven Essays on Masters and Methods* (Worcester, Mass., 1986) and *Early American Bookbinding from the Collection of Michael Papantonio* (Worcester, Mass., 1985). *The Library*, June 1987, pp. 189-192.

122. 'Bibliopegy as trade and art'. (Review of Frank Broomhead, *The Zaehnsdorfs (1842-1947): Craft Bookbinders*, London, 1986; and Elizabeth Greenhill, *Bookbinder: a catalogue raisonné*, Frenich, Foss, 1986). *T.L.S.*, 14 August 1987, p. 878.

123. 'Outside pressures'. (Review of F.A. Schmidt - Künsemüller, *Die abendländischen romanischen Blindstempeleinbände*, Stuttgart, 1985). *T.L.S.*, 6-12 November 1987, p. 1234.

124. A letter from Count MacCarthy - Reagh to J.-B.-B. van Praet. *Festschrift Otto Schäfer zum 75. Geburtstag am 29. Juni 1987*. Herausgegeben von Manfred von Arnim. Stuttgart, Dr. Ernst Hauswedell & Co., 1987, pp. 515-521.

1988

125. 'Decking the leather'. (Review of Joseph McDonnell and Patrick Healy, *Gold-tooled Bookbindings commissioned by Trinity College, Dublin, in the eighteenth century*, Dublin, 1987). *T.L.S.*, 20-26 May 1988, p. 566.

126. 'Mementoes of youth'. (Review of B. H. Breslauer, *Count Heinrich IV zu Castell: a German Renaissance book collector and the bindings made for him during his student years in Orléans, Paris, and Bologna*, Austin, Texas, 1987). *T.L.S.*, 17-23 June 1988, p. 688.

127. Renaissance Bookbinding. [A letter about B. H. Breslauer's *Count Heinrich IV zu Castell*]. *T.L.S.*, 9-15 September 1988, p. 1001.

1989

128. 'Prolifically appreciative'. (Review of Neil Ritchie, *Sacheverell Sitwell: an annotated and descriptive bibliography 1916-1986*, Lucolena in Chianti, 1987). *T.L.S.*, 21-27 April 1989, p. 437.

129. Islamic Influence on Venetian Renaissance Bookbinding. *Venezia e l'Oriente Vicino*. Venezia, Ateneo Veneto, pp. 111-123 (including 15 illustrations).

130. Appropriations from foreign libraries during the French Revolution and Empire. *Bulletin du bibliophile*, 1989, no. 2, pp. 255-272.

131. *Humanists and Bookbinders. The origins and diffusion of the humanistic* *bookbinding 1459-1559.* With a census of historiated plaquette and medallion bindings of the Renaissance. pp. XIX, 296: illus.; 4 colour plates. Cambridge University Press.

132. Plaquettes on Bookbindings. In: *Italian Plaquettes.* Edited by Alison Luchs. National Gallery of Art, Washington. (Studies in the History of Art. vol. 22). pp. 165-173.

133. A Catalogue of the Ahmanson - Murphy Aldine Collection at UCLA. Compiled, or with contributions, by Nicolas Barker, Anthony R. A. Hobson [and six others]. fasc. 1. The Publications of Aldus Manutius the Elder. 1989. fasc. 2. The Publications of Aldus the Elder's Heirs, 1515-1529. 1991. Department of Special Collections, University Research Library, University of California, Los Angeles.

1990

134. Une note sur le fer de reliure d'un dauphin. *Bulletin du bibliophile*, 1990 no. 1, pp. 139-142.

135. Anthony Hobson and Paul Culot, *Italian and French 16th-century Bookbindings. La Reliure en Italie et en France au XVIe siècle.* [Brussels:] Bibliotheca Wittockiana, 1990. pp. 181. Plates in colour and black and white. Edition of 750 copies.

136. Review of F. A. Schmidt - Künsemüller, *Bibliographie zur Geschichte der Einbandkunst von den Anfangen bis 1985* (Wiesbaden, 1987). *The Library*, June 1990, pp. 158-160.

1991

137. Introduction to: *Legatura Romana Barocca, 1565-1700.* Roma: Edizioni Carte Segrete, 1991. pp. 13, 14. (Associazione Amici dei Musei di Roma).

138. Review of Martin Lowry, *Nicholas Jenson and the Rise of Venetian Publishing in Renaissance Europe* (Oxford, Blackwell, 1991). *T. L. S.*, 11 October 1991, p. 31.

139. Decorative book covers. (Review of Staffan Fogelmark, *Flemish and Related Panel-Stamped Bindings*, New York, 1991). *T. L. S.*, 6 December 1991, p. 27.

1992

140. Elgin Marbles. [A letter]. *The Times*, 28 April 1992, p. 11.

141. Wearing the Hammersmith look. (Review of Marianne Tidcombe, *The Doves Bindery*, British Library, 1991). *T. L. S.*, 1 May 1992, p. 27.

142. Frederick A. Bearman, Nati H. Krivatsy and J. Franklin Mowery, *Fine and Historic Bookbindings from the Folger Shakespeare Library*. With an introduction by Anthony Hobson. Washington, D.C., The Folger Shakespeare Library, 1992.

143. Review of J. B. Trapp, *Erasmus, Colet and More: the early Tudor Humanists and their Books* (The Panizzi Lectures, 1990; British Library, 1991). *T. L. S.*, 16 October 1992, p. 32.

1993

144. Review of Howard M. Nixon and Mirjam M. Foot, *The History of Decorated Bookbinding in England* (Oxford, Clarendon Press, 1992). *T. L. S.*, 22 January 1993, p. 23.

145. James ('Julian') Maclaren-Ross. *Dictionary of National Biography. Missing Persons*. Oxford University Press, Oxford and New York, pp. 431-2.

146. *Histoire de la belle Mélusine* and Nicolas Moreau d'Auteuil. *Bulletin du bibliophile*, 1993, no. 1, pp. 95-98.

147. Review of Francesco Malaguzzi, *Legatori e legature del Settecento in Piemonte* (Turin, 1989). *Book Collector*, Spring 1993, pp. 131-133.

TABULA GRATULATORIA

Frederick B. Adams
Peter Amelung
Jean Paul Barbier
Pierre Berès
Maria and Giuseppe Bertola
Alessandro Bettagno
Biblioteca Civica di Verona
Biblioteca Nazionale Centrale di Firenze
Biblioteca Nazionale Marciana
Daniel Bodmer
Heribert Boeder
William H. Bond
Jean A. Bonna
Alice Gertrud and Hans Rudolf Bosch-Gwalter
Leonard E. Boyle O. P.
Michael Brand
Bernard H. Breslauer
Anne Marie de Brignac
Prince Gabriel de Broglie
T. Kimball Brooker
Emmanuel Cappe de Baillon
Centro del bel libro Ascona
Carlo Alberto Chiesa
Bernard L. Clavreuil
The Clothworkers' Company
Emma Coèn-Pirani
John Collins
Antoine Coron
Martin Davies
Rafael Díaz-Casariego
Marianne Diercxsens-Delvaulx
A. I. Doyle

John Dreyfus
Viscount and Viscountess Eccles
Lord Egremont
John Ehrman
Sün Evrard
Bernhard and Ursula Fabian
Conor Fahy
Alberto Falck
Georg and Gisela Floersheim
Folger Shakespeare Library
Fondazione Giorgio Cini
Adrienne Fontainas-Thibaut de Maisières
J. Paul Getty, K. B. E.
Marco Gherzi
Günter Glück
David J. Hall
Robin G. Halwas
Christopher de Hamel
Hartung & Hartung
Henry Heaney
Lotte Hellinga
Hesketh and Ward Ltd
Ingeborg and Adam Heymowski
The Huntington Library
Sue Abbe Kaplan
Roger de Kesel
Koninklijke Bibliotheek Albert I - Bibliotheque Royale Albert I
Mrs. H. P. Kraus
Lambeth Palace Library
D. Courvoisier and E. Lhermitte Librairie Giraud-Badin
Herman Liebaers

TABULA GRATULATORIA

Université de Liege - Centre d'information et de conservation des bibliotheques
Lilly Library, Indiana University
Nenne and Sten G. Lindberg
Richard A. Linenthal
Michele Lombi
Livio Macchi
Maggs Bros. Ltd
Francesco Malaguzzi
Alexandre Mallat
Johan and Ylva Mannerheim
Martino Mardersteig
Felix de Marez Oyens
Stephen C. Massey
William Matheson
André Morel
Paul Morgan
Pierre Mouriau de Meulenacker
The National Library of Wales
The Newberry Library
Conde de Orgaz
Annie Parent - Charon
Henri Paricaud
Diana Parikian
David Pearson
Loredana Pecorini
Earl of Perth
The Pierpont Morgan Library
Eugenio and Sybille Pino
Claudio and Gianna de Polo Saibanti
Arturo G. Pregliasco
Premio Felice Feliciano
Bernard Quaritch Ltd
Francesco Radaeli

Claude Reymond
Per S. and Louise Ridderstad
Neil Ritchie
Renzo Rizzi
Stephen Roe
Carlos Romero de Lecea
Bernard M. Rosenthal
Musée Royal de Mariemont
The Royal Library (National Library of Sweden)
Charles Ryskamp
William H. Scheide
Karl Graf von Schönborn
Alfred von Schulthess
Jaqueline Silvestre de Sacy
Bernard Skalli
Clotilde Spanio
Eric Speeckaert
Kostantinos Sp. Staikos
Stamperia Valdonega
Roger E. Stoddard
J. A. Szirmai
Eleonora Elena Talenti Minghetti
G. Thomas Tanselle
William B. Todd
J. B. Trapp
Norman J. Travis
Conrad Ulrich
Marques de Viesca de La Sierra
James E. Walsh
James M. Wells
David E. Wickham
Marjorie G. Wynne
Giampiero Zazzera

The text was set in Janson (VAL version)
and printed by Stamperia Valdonega
in Verona. The Bodonia acid-free
ivory paper was made by
Cartiere Fedrigoni

OCTOBER

1994